AGRICULTURE IN THE AUSTRALIAN ECONOMY

AGRICULTURE IN THE AUSTRALIAN ECONOMY

Edited by **D. B. Williams**

University of Melbourne

With Contributions by

K. O. Campbell

C. M. Donald

S. F. Harris

F. G. Jarrett

R. M. Parish

G. D'A. Chislett

P. C. Druce

E. S. Hoffman

J. N. Lewis

H. P. Schapper

B. R. Davidson

F. H. Gruen *et al.*

A. W. Hooke

D. H. McKay

A. G. L. Shaw

SYDNEY UNIVERSITY PRESS

1967

SYDNEY UNIVERSITY PRESS
Press Building, University of Sydney, Australia

U.S.A. *Pennsylvania State University Press*
NEW ZEALAND *Price Milburn and Company Limited*
ELSEWHERE *Methuen and Company Limited, London
and their agents*

First published 1967

© 1967 The Australian Group of the International Association
of Agricultural Economists

National Library of Australia registry number AUS67-675

This book is supported by money from
THE ELEANOR SOPHIA WOOD BEQUEST

Printed and bound by Halstead Press, Sydney
Registered in Australia for transmission by post as a book

EDITOR'S FOREWORD

This book contains a series of reviews describing the significance of agricultural industries in the Australian economy. It aims to present an analytical interpretation of the economic forces which have led to the present situation and to describe the significant changes which have occurred in recent years. It does not purport to present research papers which more properly have their place in professional journals now established in Australia. The most important of these for agricultural economists are the *Australian Journal of Agricultural Economics* (Australian Agricultural Economics Society), *Quarterly Review of Agricultural Economics* (Bureau of Agricultural Economics) and the *Review of Marketing and Agricultural Economics* (New South Wales Department of Agriculture).

* * * * *

In recent years, changes in the structure of the Australian economy have insulated it more and more from the effects of fluctuations in world trade. Nevertheless, the interplay between world economic conditions and internal economic policies, from the early years of settlement to the present day, persists as the first of the main themes in the book.

Several authors refer to Australia's historical background of close economic and political ties with the United Kingdom. Nowadays Australian eyes turn more frequently to the United States and to Asia. Our international relations bear increasingly on problems of economic development in these and in other lands.

Within Australia, a federation barely 66 years old, internal economic policies are tuned to the evolving financial relationships between the Commonwealth and the States; and to the growing emphasis on centralized administration and the comparative weakness of local government. Several chapters refer to these important issues.

Other chapters explain unique features of the natural environment, and their influence on the nation's history. The nineteenth century was a time of exploration and settlement of new lands; the twentieth century is proving to be one of scientific exploration and development as Australians come to still closer grips with the environment.

This exploration and development is being influenced increasingly by government policies of different kinds. Agricultural economic analysis is not only concerned with the institutional structure of agriculture and the effects of policy measures specific to the rural sector, but with general economic policies as well. These related aspects of agricultural economics emerge as yet another main theme—not only in this book but also in the work of agricultural economists in Australia.

Indeed, the book reveals much of the scope and character of the profession of agricultural economics which has been established in Australia only in the last 25 years. On the one hand, Australian agricultural economists have been most concerned with economic aspects of land development, irrigation potential, farm incomes and the capital structure of the rural sector, the merits of development of the northern half of the continent, stabilization schemes and international trade, and the strengthening of research and extension services. On the other hand, many of the problems being faced as major issues in other countries such as international aid, rural education, land tenure, rural poverty, transport and the labour situation in farming have so far received relatively little attention.

Editing a book of this kind forces one to steer a course between the individual style and convictions of chapter authors and the cohesiveness of the book as a whole. It has been part of my purpose to preserve the personal tone and contributions of each author, tempting though it has been for me to explain some of the events or local folklore which provide the background to each author's presentation. For such is part of the essence of Australian agricultural economics in 1966 which these pages reflect but do not always reveal.

*   *   *   *   *

Publication of this book marks the first occasion when a conference of the International Association of Agricultural Economists has been held in Australia. In June 1965 the Australian Organizing Committee for the 13th International Conference to be held in Sydney in August 1967 undertook to sponsor a book comprising a series of essays on economic aspects of Australian agriculture. The Organizing Committee subsequently invited K. O. Campbell, S. F. Harris and R. M. Parish, with myself as convenor, to comprise an Editorial Committee for such a book. This Committee planned the scope of the book, proposed a list of chapters, and nominated authors. The remainder of the editorial responsibility has been mine, assisted by informal consultations from time to time with other members of the Editorial Committee.

The book has been produced by the cooperative effort of members of the profession of agricultural economics in Australia. All contributors have agreed to forgo royalties so that the book can be made available at the lowest feasible cost. Final drafts were completed late in 1966. Each chapter has been reviewed by at least two colleagues so that the chapter authors could benefit from the perspective and knowledge of the reviewers: W. T. Allen, A. A. Dawson, J. L. Dillon, P. Duane, G. Edwards, E. N. Fitzpatrick, G. Gutman, N. Honan, A. Johnston, D. Lapidge, A. Lloyd, R. G. Mauldon, A. J. McIntyre, W. Peterson, R. W. Prunster, R. N. Sandiford, E. A. Saxon, D. Tribe and E. J. Waring. In several instances chapter authors also acted as reviewers for other chapters. For all these comments I wish to record my appreciation on behalf of the Editorial Committee, and of the chapter authors; and, also to the Bureau of Agricultural Economics for drawing many of the figures, and to the Bureau of Census and Statistics for permission to reproduce maps and diagrams. I am also grateful to E. A. Saxon, who arranged for the use of these illustrations. My thanks are also recorded to Miss L. Davey for guidance in the preparation of the index and to Mrs H. J. Evans for typing assistance.

Throughout all stages in planning and production of the volume, invaluable guidance and assistance has been provided by the officers of Sydney University Press: Michael Turnbull, Robin Appleton and David New.

Finally, it remains for me to record my personal thanks to the Organizing Committee for the opportunity to accept this task on behalf of the profession here in Australia; to thank the authors of the various chapters for their contributions; and to record my grateful appreciation for the sustained, skilful and patient work of Miss E. Austwick who has prepared the index and assisted me throughout 1966 in fulfilling my responsibility as editor.

University of Melbourne   D. B. WILLIAMS
December 1966

PREFATORY NOTES

Decimal Currency

On 14 February 1966, a dollar and cents decimal currency system was introduced in Australia, under the Currency Act, 1963. One dollar is equal to 100 cents.

The Act prescribes that one pound (old currency) equals two dollars, one shilling equals ten cents and one penny equals five-sixths of one cent.

All monetary amounts in this book have been expressed in the new decimal system. In 1965-66, at the official exchange rates, one Australian dollar was equivalent to 8 shillings sterling, 1·120 U.S. dollars and 403·226 Japanese yen.

Measures

The unit measure for land areas is the acre: 1 acre = ·41 hectares, 1 hectare = 2·47 acres.

The unit measure for quantity measured by weight is the long ton of 2,240 pounds. There are 20 hundredweights (cwt) per ton. A short ton is 2,000 pounds. One pound weight equals 453·9 grams.

One bushel of wheat, at 60 lbs per bushel, weighs 27·22 kilograms.

Official Statistics

In Australia, responsibility for the collection, compilation and publication of official statistics, and for the co-ordination of all governmental statistical activities and services, is vested in a single authority, the Commonwealth Bureau of Census and Statistics. Statutory authority for the Bureau's activities is provided in the Commonwealth Census and Statistics Act, 1905-1966.

The Bureau's Central Office is responsible for overall planning and direction of statistical operations and for the collection, compilation and publication of official statistics relating to Australia and to States as components of Australian totals. State Offices provide statistics for both Commonwealth and State requirements and are responsible for the greater part of the Bureau's data collection activities. State Offices also compile and publish statistics on a State basis and in respect of regions within States and local government areas.

Both the Central and State Offices of the Bureau are organized functionally into divisions which deal with statistics relating to a broad field of social or economic activity, or provide specialist methodological or other services for the Bureau as a whole. The statistics produced by the Bureau cover all important aspects of the economic and social conditions in Australia, including population, employment, primary and secondary industries, public and private finance, retail and wholesale trade, transport and communications, oversea transactions, balance of payments and national accounts. Statistics of agricultural production are the responsibility of the Bureau's Primary Industries Division.

The basic source of agricultural statistics is the Agricultural, Dairying and Pastoral Census which is conducted annually by the Bureau, on 31 March, and covers all 'rural' holdings in Australia. For statistical purposes a 'rural holding' is defined as a piece of land of one acre or more in extent, used for the production of agricultural products, or for the raising of livestock and the production of livestock products. At each census comprehensive physical and technical data are collected, including area of crops, crop production, livestock numbers and production of wool, milk, etc., but at present only limited financial data are obtained.

Current statistics of Australian rural industries are published in a wide range of mimeographed bulletins and a comprehensive summary of official statistics of rural industries is published in the Bureau's annual publication—*Rural Industries Bulletin*.

The Bureau of Census and Statistics also publishes each year the *Official Year Book of the Commonwealth of Australia*. In this book this publication is referred to, for example, as *Year Book*, No 52, 1966, Bureau of Census and Statistics.

Censuses of the Australian population, since Federation, have been conducted by the Bureau in 1911, 1921, 1933, 1947, 1954, 1961 and 1966.

In addition to the statistical series published by the Commonwealth Bureau of Census and Statistics, the Bureau of Agricultural Economics publishes certain statistical data, viz:

(i) Index numbers to measure movements in prices paid and prices received by farmers. These series appear regularly in the *Quarterly Review of Agricultural Economics*.

(ii) Economic surveys of various rural industries, which contain statistical data based on a sample of farms. Reports on these surveys are issued as soon as possible after completion of the relevant surveys.

Farmers and Graziers

Traditionally, in Australia, a 'grazier' is a landholder who does not engage in the cultivation of land, but relies on grazing livestock on unimproved or (more recently) improved pasture for his income. A 'farmer', usually, is a landholder whose income is obtained primarily from the cultivation of land for the production of crops, though returns from grazing this cultivated land and other land not cultivated may also be a substantial part of his income.

Similarly, agriculture in its narrow sense implies the cultivation of land, so that we have 'grazing' industries on the one hand and 'agricultural' industries on the other.

In this book, for purposes of simplicity, agriculture is used in the broader sense including rural industries as a whole, except in those instances where the context makes clear the distinction between grazing and agriculture.

CONTENTS

ILLUSTRATIONS

MAPS

FIGURES

TABLES

B

CHAPTER 1

HISTORY AND DEVELOPMENT OF AUSTRALIAN AGRICULTURE

A. G. L. SHAW

Monash University

BEFORE THE FIRST GOLD RUSHES, 1788-1850

FIRST SETTLEMENTS, 1788-1830

It is our will and pleasure that you do immediately upon your landing after taking measures for securing yourself and the people who accompany you from any attacks or interruptions of the natives . . . proceed to the cultivation of the land . . . and with all convenient speed transmit a report of the actual state and quality of the soil . . . and the most effectual means of improving and cultivating the same.[1]

Such was the instruction given in 1787 by George III, king of England, to Governor Phillip before he set out to establish the new penal settlement at Botany Bay in New South Wales. This was needed because of the over-crowding of the gaols in England which followed the revolt of the British colonies in America in 1775 and the stopping of the transportation of convicts to Virginia and Maryland. At first, hulks had been moored in the Thames to take the prisoners, but they too were soon full and their inmates even appeared as a threat to the law-abiding citizens of London.

A food supply was obviously necessary, even for a penal colony, and as soon as Phillip landed near Sydney in January 1788, he tried to procure one; but he had been supplied with little to help him to carry out his orders to cultivate the land. The ships carried 12 ploughs, but there were neither oxen nor draught horses to draw them.[2] There were no farmers in the expedition, and no free men of any kind to supervise the work of the convicts. Certainly Phillip looked forward to Australia being in the future 'a most valuable acquisition to Great Britain'; nevertheless he warned the British government

1. Instructions to Governor Phillip, 25 April 1787, *Historical Records of Australia*, Sydney 1914, Vol i, pp 11 and 15. (All references to *H.R.A.* are to Series I.)

2. Articles sent by First Fleet, *Historical Records of New South Wales*, Sydney 1893, Vol ii, p 388.

that 'no country can afford less support to the first settlers' than did New South Wales.[3]

Phillip's pessimism about the immediate future was justified. Soil and husbandry were both poor. On the public lands, the convicts toiled unwillingly, and when private farming began on the small grants made to ex-marines or to well-behaved convicts whose sentences had expired ('emancipists'), the grantees had heavy clearing to do and lacked knowledge, capital and livestock. Their tools were poor, their supplies expensive, their labour force unskilled. Of 274 settlers in 1795 only 89 were still on their land in 1800.[4] However as time went on the expanding population provided them with a better market. Supplies became more plentiful and their cost less as trade developed and, with experience, the farmers even began to improve their technique, for all the criticisms directed against them. By 1819 there were 857 emancipist settlers, cultivating on the average 46 acres, while owning 45 sheep and 28 cattle; but when Commissioner J. T. Bigge inquired into the state of the colony that year, he recognized the difficulties which ignorance, lack of capital and the cost of supplies created for these people. It was partly this that led him to lay such stress in his reports on the potentialities of wool growing.

Alongside the small settlers were a more wealthy and prosperous group, drawn largely from the commissioned officers and other officials in the colony, with more skill, knowledge, capital and, in the early days at least, influence. From the first they had been the agricultural leaders in the community. After 1792 they were allowed to receive land grants. By 1794, Capt. John Macarthur could write:

> I have a farm containing 250 acres. Of this year's produce I have sold £400 worth, and I have now in my granaries upwards of 1800 bushels of corn. I have . . . 20 acres of very fine wheat growing, and 80 acres prepared for Indian corn and potatoes . . . My stock consists of a horse, two mares, two cows, 130 goats and upwards of 100 hogs.[5]

Four years later, he had 50 head of cattle, 'about a thousand sheep . . . a good dairy and . . . a plough at work.'[6]

The wealthier settlers did not ignore cultivation, but they soon realized that they could make greater profits from grazing. The demand for meat steadily increased, labour remained scarce and dear, transport was poor and the soil near Sydney favoured the pastoralist more than the farmer. Settle-

---

3. Phillip to Sydney and to Nepean, 9 July 1788, *H.R.A.*, Vol i, pp 47, 56 and 58.

4. B. H. Fletcher, 'Development of Small-scale Farming in New South Wales, 1788-1803', M.A. thesis, University of Sydney 1962, pp 100 ff.

5. Quoted in a letter from Elizabeth Macarthur, 22 August 1794, *H.R.N.S.W.*, Vol ii, p 508.

6. Letter from Elizabeth Macarthur, 1 September 1798, *H.R.N.S.W.*, Vol ii, p 510 (though misdated there).

ment spread to the south-west, along the route to what is now Canberra, where large land grants were made. By 1819, 213 free settlers held, on the average, more than 900 acres each, although of this they cultivated only 60 acres. Such averages, like the 46 acres of the average emancipist farm, conceal wide variations, but they give some clue to the scale of operations of the two groups; while both *cultivated* about the same area on their farms, the free settlers depastured about four times as many cattle and sheep.

The graziers were not yet greatly interested in wool. John Macarthur had won the praise of textile producers for some specimens he took to England in 1802, and both he and the Rileys sent off profitable cargoes between 1814 and 1816; but the fleeces exported from New South Wales averaged only 337,000 lbs a year between 1818 and 1827, and up till 1830 whale and seal oil was a more valuable export than wool. It is too easy to assume that Macarthur's first experiments were followed by instant success, and to forget his complaint that 'my feeble attempt to introduce Merino Sheep still creeps on almost unheeded . . . Few of the settlers can be induced to take the trouble requisite to improve their flocks.'[7] The growing population in New South Wales offered both privately and through the Commissariat a good market for meat. To ship wool to England was slow and expensive. The demand there was uncertain owing to trade fluctuations and competition from Saxony, and the grower was unlikely to receive his money for two years.

So, by as early as 1830, there had appeared a number of features which were to characterize Australia's rural development in the future. First, many assumed that farming was a simple occupation, which required little training and only a modicum of intelligence; hence it was enough to give a man, whether ex-convict, ex-gold digger, ex-soldier or newly arrived immigrant, a few acres of land, and he would magically prosper, without capital, without equipment, and without knowledge. Even by 1830 this had already been proved wrong. Secondly, the Australian climate and environment had shown themselves not to be easy, and certainly different from those of England. They threatened floods and droughts, crop diseases and plagues (of insects if not yet rabbits); there was *not* enough phosphate in the soil—a point whose significance only became apparent late in the nineteenth century. Thirdly markets were unreliable, whether it was a case of gluts succeeding famines in New South Wales, or industrial depressions undermining the purchasing power of English buyers. Fourthly, though explorers had discovered a route across the rugged Blue Mountains in 1813, poor internal communications hampered agricultural development, and even after railways had been built, much of the continent remained handicapped by its isolation. Finally, over-optimistic producers carried each phase of expansion too far, incurring losses

7. John Macarthur to Walter Davidson, 3 September 1818, quoted in C. M. H. Clark (ed), *Select Documents in Australian History, 1788-1850*, Angus and Robertson, Sydney 1950, p 269.

when it became clear that their output could not be absorbed at profitable prices in existing markets.

TWO EARLY PASTORAL BOOMS AND SLUMPS

The first great speculative boom occurred in the 1820s, and in 1831 we find landowners in New South Wales lamenting that:

> Some few Years ago, when the waste Lands of the Colony were first thrown open to the Competition of the Colonists, . . . they naturally were led to associate the idea of existing prices with a more extensive production and many of them, acting under this delusive impulse, pressed forward to purchase Lands at a price, which no present known mode of employing land in the interior will afford . . . The Consequence was inevitable . . . Many purchases of Land so made have been abandoned . . . and many . . . Settlers have been ruined.[8]

Speculation had been rife, stimulated by commissariat purchases for the rapidly increasing number of convicts, by the establishment of the two great chartered companies, the Australian Agricultural Company and the Van Diemen's Land Company, to cultivate their million-acre estates, and by the foundation of new banking enterprises in Australia. As the Presbyterian cleric-cum-historian, the Rev. John Dunmore Lang, put it:

> The *sheep and cattle mania* . . . seized on all ranks and classes of its inhabitants . . . barristers and attorneys; military officers of every rank, and civilians of every department; clergymen and medical men; merchants, settlers, and dealers in general, were there seen promiscuously mingled together . . . and outbidding each other in the most determined manner, either in their own persons or by proxies of certified agricultural character, for the purchase of every scabbed sheep or scarecrow horse or buffalo-cow that was offered for sale in the colony . . .

Then, when this speculative mania was at its height, Lang felt it only proper that 'it pleased Divine Providence . . . to visit the colony . . . with an afflictive drought' which lasted for nearly three years, so that 'the heavens became as brass and the earth as iron'. Coming on top of over speculation its effects were:

> to blast the golden hopes of multitudes, and to bring many respectable families to poverty and ruin . . . Creditors became imperative in their demands for payment . . . Month after month herds of cattle and flocks of sheep were seized and sold, . . . and the price of sheep and cattle consequently fell so rapidly, that . . . the settler's farm was seized and sold also, and himself perhaps ultimately lodged in jail.[9]

8. Memorial of landowners, 1831, *H.R.A.*, Vol xvi, p 343.

9. J. D. Lang, *An Historical Account of New South Wales*, 3rd ed, London 1852, Vol i, pp 213 ff.

The drought was severe, but the fall in English wool prices and the interruption in the flow of British capital which followed the financial crisis there at the end of 1825 was probably a more important cause of the depression.[10] However its lessons were little heeded, and in the 1830s a similar expansion produced a similar result. By 1842, pastoral occupation extended from Adelaide to Brisbane, and wool exports had risen from about one million to nine million lbs. But as the participants in the boom became more reckless, their rosy expectations came to grief. Apart from a fall in the price of wool of about 25 per cent, graziers lost an important source of revenue when new men ceased to come on the scene as buyers for the annual natural increase of stock, and their costs increased as they moved further inland. The slump was due to 'conditions within the wool industry itself',[11] though these in turn caused a reduction of British investment which aggravated the general depression in Australia in the early 1840s.

LAND SALES AND MIGRATION

While this rapid pastoral expansion had been proceeding, agriculture had been somewhat in the doldrums. In 1831, to check the acquisition of land by men who would not cultivate it, and so to prevent 'dispersion' and to preserve a national asset, the British government decided to stop granting colonial land and to sell it instead, at the price of five shillings per acre. This policy was applied in Canada and other British colonies as well as Australia, but here as elsewhere it had a profound effect on rural development. It caused great lamentations from the graziers, but by and large they simply ignored the regulations by 'squatting' on crown land without title. Governor Sir Richard Bourke did not wish 'to seclude settlers from the temporary occupation without payment of . . . tracts of Country in the remote interior', but his fears that the squatters might prefer this 'unauthorised Title to a lawful one acquired even at the slightest expense' proved all too well founded.[12] However the farmer had to buy his land, and this increased his costs just as the cost of transport restricted the areas which he could cultivate. In 1839 the carriage of goods from Goulburn to Sydney, 140 miles by land, was said to cost £14 ($28) per ton; from Sydney to Hobart, 800 miles by sea, £1.10s. ($3) per ton.[13] This meant that Sydney's wheat supply could be more easily brought 600 or so miles by sea from Van Diemen's Land (Tasmania) than from any significant distance inland.

On top of these difficulties was the handicap imposed by the shortage of

10. J. D. Lang, op. cit., p 221; and S. J. Butlin, Foundations of the Australian Monetary System, 1788-1851, Melbourne University Press, Melbourne 1953, pp 208-9.

11. S. J. Butlin, op. cit., p 318.

12. Bourke to Stanley, 26 November 1833, H.R.A., Vol xvii, p 271; Bourke in the Monitor, 21 November 1835, quoted in S. H. Roberts, The Squatting Age in Australia, 1835-1847, Melbourne University Press, Melbourne 1935, p 81.

13. The cost from Sydney to London was £7 ($14) per ton. E. Macarthur, 'Proposal for Steam Navigation', 3 July 1839, H.R.A., Vol xx, pp 219-23.

labour. This had become increasingly severe since the mid-1820s. Convicts, though totalling 50,000 in the 1830s and 100,000 up to 1840, were not enough, and witnesses repeatedly stressed the need of increased free immigration to Select Committees of the New South Wales Legislative Council. In 1840 convict transportation to New South Wales was stopped, and, as was said in 1843, 'men who would have taken a small farm and raised wheat and other agricultural produce found it more profitable to go as a shepherd.'[14] Fortunately this demand for assisted immigration came at a time when, in the United Kingdom, many were becoming worried by periodically heavy unemployment in the English manufacturing districts and by a rapidly growing population, particularly in Ireland, where pressure on the land was acute. Emigration, it was argued, might help to solve these problems, even though it might be described in the phrase of E. G. Wakefield, that ardent propagandist for what he called 'systematic colonisation', as nothing more than 'shovelling out paupers'.[15] But it was cheaper to go to North America, and apart from the migrants' own preferences, neither the poor law authorities nor the Treasury were willing to pay for migration to Australia; so although the Colonial Secretary denied at first that the land revenue was a suitable source of funds for meeting the cost of assisting migrants, its use for this purpose was natural enough when large land sales were bringing in quite substantial sums.[16] Over 100,000 were assisted to Australia between 1830 and 1850. Most were English for the Irish were too poor, and the population of Scotland was relatively small; but groups from both these countries helped to diversify the outlook and experience of the newcomers.

The conjunction of land sales and migration was made explicit in the plans for the foundation of South Australia, where the first settlement was made in December 1836. Land was to be sold at £1 ($2) per acre, and the proceeds of the sales, including large purchases made by the South Australian Company (which was formed for the purpose), were used to bring out

14. R. Windeyer, Legislative Council, 21 December 1843, *Sydney Morning Herald*, 22 December 1843; cf. the evidence given to and reports of Select Committees on Immigration, New South Wales Legislative Council, *Votes and Proceedings*, 1835, 1837, 1838 and 1842.

15. J. L. Morison, 'Emigration and Land Policy, 1815-1873', in *Cambridge History of the British Empire*, Vol II, Cambridge University Press, Cambridge 1940; Select Committee on Emigration, Reports, *Parliamentary Papers*, 1826 (404), iv, and 1826-27 (88, 237 and 550), v; *Parliamentary Debates*, 1826-28, *passim*; Select Committee on State of Ireland, Report, *Parliamentary Papers*, 1825 (129), viii; Select Committee on the Poor in Ireland, *Parliamentary Papers*, 1830 (589, 654 and 665), vii; cf. R. C. Mills, *Colonisation of Australia, 1829-1842*, Sidgwick and Jackson, London 1915, pp 137 ff; and R. B. Madgwick, *Immigration into Eastern Australia, 1788-1857*, London 1937, pp 71 ff. Wakefield's first book was *A Letter from Sydney*, London 1829, republished by J. M. Dent and Sons, London 1929; his final statement of his argument was *A View of the Art of Colonisation*, London 1849. His evidence to the Select Committee on the Disposal of Land in British Colonies, *Parliamentary Papers*, 1836 (512), xi, also illustrates his views.

16. Goderich to Darling, 9 and 23 January and 14 February 1831, *H.R.A.*, Vol xvi, pp 22, 36 and 83. Glenelg in writing to Gipps, 9 August 1838, *H.R.A.*, Vol xix, pp 537-8, evidently did not look up Lord Ripon's (i.e. Goderich's) despatch to which he refers.

migrants.[17] Unfortunately, as in early New South Wales, many land buyers had insufficient capital and knowledge to work their lands properly, the labour force was unskilled, and few were ready to face the hardships of pioneering. However, land near Adelaide, the site chosen for the first settlement, proved more fertile than near Sydney. Transport to the interior was easier, and supplies, tools and livestock were more easily brought from Sydney then than they had been from England in 1788. By the end of 1843 the colony had a wheat surplus for export, though it still yielded pride of place as the 'granary of the continent' to Van Diemen's Land, which had then been settled for 40 years.

The policies followed in South Australia had been partly responsible for the raising of the selling price of crown land to £1 ($2) per acre in the other colonies as well; but intercolonial competition was not the only reason, for the government remained anxious not to waste the nation's land resources, and in passing the Australian Waste Land Sales Act of 1842, as Governor Gipps pointed out, it virtually declared that it would not 'for the present, sell any Land which is not worth 20s. an acre.'[18] None the less the limitation this imposed on purchase was a great grievance to the colonists, who demanded a 'certain facility in obtaining it', though not stating very clearly what this facility should be. At first it was largely the squatters who wanted a cheap and easy access to land, and after a violent agitation they got what they wanted. In 1847, Orders-in-Council made under the Waste Lands Act of 1846 enabled them to take up 14-year leases in 'unsettled' districts and entitled them to be compensated for any improvements they had made. These regulations had the incidental advantage that by maintaining a high price for *purchase*, they made it difficult for small farmers to buy land. Had they been able to do so, they might have interfered with the squatters' occupation; as it was, they were kept off, so it was no wonder that they in their turn began to agitate, more and more vociferously when they became more numerous after the gold rushes of the early 1850s, that the government must 'unlock the land'.

FROM THE FIRST GOLD RUSHES TO THE FIRST WORLD WAR, 1850-1914

RESULTS OF THE GOLD DISCOVERIES

Between 1851 and 1860, attracted by the gold discoveries and the economic development that followed them, 600,000 migrants came to Australia, about

17. The South Australia Act was passed in 1834; cf. E. G. Wakefield, *The New British Province of South Australia*, London 1834; the report of the Select Committee on South Australia, *Parliamentary Papers*, 1841 (394), iv; and D. H. Pike, *Paradise of Dissent*, Longmans, Melbourne 1957.

18. Gipps to Stanley, 17 January 1844, *H.R.A.*, Vol xxiii, p 338, a very important dispatch. The Act is printed in C. M. H. Clark, *Select Documents in Australian History, 1788-1850*, Angus and Robertson, Sydney 1950, p 239.

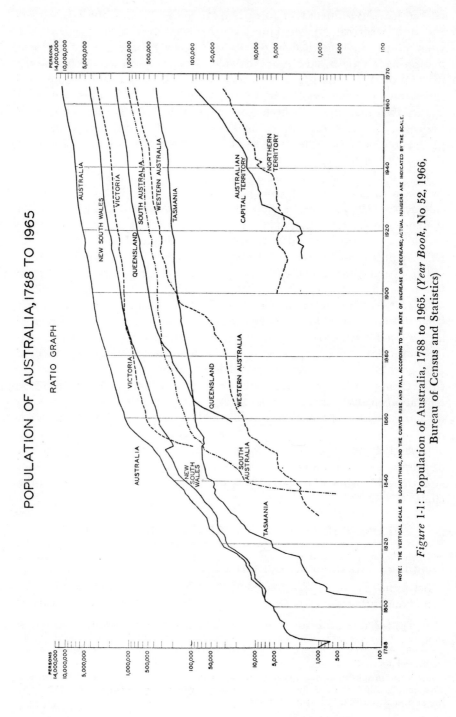

POPULATION OF AUSTRALIA, 1788 TO 1965

RATIO GRAPH

NOTE: THE VERTICAL SCALE IS LOGARITHMIC, AND THE CURVES RISE AND FALL ACCORDING TO THE RATE OF INCREASE OR DECREASE; ACTUAL NUMBERS ARE INDICATED BY THE SCALE.

Figure 1-1: Population of Australia, 1788 to 1965. (*Year Book*, No 52, 1966, Bureau of Census and Statistics)

60 per cent 'unassisted'. Not many came from the European continent, but for the first time, Australia rivalled the United States as a field of migration from the United Kingdom.

Most of the diggers achieved only mediocre success, despite the notoriety of the rare magnificent nugget, and after a couple of years they began to look for a better living elsewhere.[19] The gold rushes temporarily dislocated the Australian economy, its farms and its sheep runs, but in due course these

Table 1-1

Sectoral Shares in Gross Domestic Product, 1861-1900
(percentages based on constant prices)

	1861-65 %	1875-77 %	1886-90 %	1900 %
PRIMARY				
Pastoral	8·5	14·1	12·8	7·7
Agriculture	5·4	5·9	5·8	8·1
Dairying	4·1	3·4	3·5	5·5
Mining	13·8	6·3	4·2	9·7
Total	31·8	29·7	26·3	31·0
SECONDARY				
Manufacturing	5·3	11·0	11·8	12·6
Construction	10·8	14·1	16·5	6·7
Total	16·1	25·1	28·3	19·3
TERTIARY	42·6	36·9	36·7	39·8
HOUSE RENTS	9·5	8·3	8·7	9·7
Total	100·0	100·0	100·0	100·0

SOURCE: N. G. Butlin, *Investment in Australian Economic Development 1861-1900*, Cambridge University Press, Cambridge 1964, p 22.

were enormously stimulated by the immigration and the wealth due to gold, which increased the demand for public services and stimulated the market for food and manufactures. By 1891, after a generation of development by local breweries, brickyards, tanneries, sawmills, potteries, iron foundries, manufacturers of farm implements, boots and clothing, and of candles, pumps and engines for the mines, almost one-third of Australian bread-winners were employed in secondary industry. Manufacturing and construction together then contributed more to the Australian domestic product than did primary industry, though in 1861-65 the value of primary production had been double that of secondary.[20]

19. The best account of mining in Australia is by Geoffrey Blainey, *The Rush that Never Ended*, Melbourne University Press, Melbourne 1963.

20. N. G. Butlin, *Investment in Australian Economic Development, 1861-1900*, Cambridge University Press, Cambridge 1964, ch 1.

Agriculture was immediately stimulated by the increasing population. By 1857 in Victoria there were 8,000 farmers employing 15,000 labourers compared with 3,200 employing 4,300 only four years before. In 1860-61 the cultivated area in all eastern Australia was still about one acre per head—but there were 700,000 more heads. In South Australia, the wheat acreage was almost as much as that of New South Wales and Victoria combined. South Australia had seven times as much land under crop in 1860 as in 1850, and with no gold herself exported more than 2 million bushels to the eastern colonies in the 1860s.

UNLOCKING THE LAND AFTER 1861

In Victoria, as alluvial mining tapered off, many ex-diggers began to seek a farm, and so did many of the migrants who had come to New South Wales. Like so many others in other countries and in other generations they thought that all they had to do was to get on the land. They did not worry about either agricultural knowledge or credit, possibly on the theory that a one-time gold miner would necessarily have both! The debate was similar to that which had been taking place in the United States of America. It finished with somewhat similar results in the U.S. Homestead Act of 1862, the Canadian Dominion Lands Act of 1872, the New South Wales Land Acts of 1861, the Victorian Acts of 1865 and 1869, the Queensland Act of 1868 and the South Australian Act of 1869. Although none of the Australian colonies went as far as the U.S.A. or Canada in providing for 'Homestead' grants free of charge or for ten dollars respectively, all tried to help the farmer acquire his land on 'easy' terms.[21]

Just as in the United States, it was argued that a Homestead Act would free the urban wage earner, so in the Australian colonies it was said that:

> What the industrious man requires is . . . an area . . . of good land, which he himself can select in a suitable locality, of such an extent that he may be able to raise from it the nobler produce of the soil, and by hard work and economy . . . have the reasonable prospect of competence and independence.

Since 'man is a social creature', he should live in communities surrounded 'with all the benign and elevating influences which naturally spring out of

21. R. M. Robertson, *History of the American Economy*, Harcourt Brace, New York 1955, pp 101 ff; cf. the Land Ordinance, 1785; Land Acts of 1796, 1800, 1804, 1820 and 1832; the Pre-emption Act of 1841 and the Homestead Act of 1862. See also S. H. Roberts, *History of Australian Land Settlement*, Macmillan, Melbourne 1924, chs 18-25; R. M. Robertson, *loc. cit.*; W. T. Easterbrook and H. G. J. Aitken, *Canadian Economic History*, Macmillan, Toronto 1961, p 390; and cf. A. S. Morton and C. Martin, *History of Prairie Settlement and 'Dominion Lands' Policy*, Toronto 1938.

settled society'.[22] Such was part of the philosophy behind 'selection' legislation, and closer settlement later on.

Unfortunately, to stimulate such agricultural communities was for many years easier said than done; for it was easier for the wealthy to acquire land on easy terms than for the poor man to acquire it on the same terms. Where social and economic conditions favoured the grazier, as in most of Australia, it was he who was going to get most of the land. No legislation in the 1860s could have brought prosperity to the small farmer, though 'reform' did not hope just to do this. Men wanted to break the squatters' monopoly, and so weaken their political power. By a 'freer' trade in land (in which incidentally transfers could be registered according to the newly instituted Torrens System), they would open it for selection by all; but this would lead to its most economic use, which was not necessarily its use by small cultivators. Between 1860 and 1890 large areas in New South Wales and Victoria were bought by 'squatters', and by 1890 the Riverina in New South Wales and the Western District of Victoria were dominated by huge grazing properties.

THE FARMER

In the second half of the nineteenth century the small men faced great difficulties in both the United States and Australia. The rapidly increasing production of wheat, especially in the United States, reduced its price, which fell by more than a third in the late nineteenth century. In Australia the railways did not reach the best of the country's wheat lands until about 1890 or later; (in the United States, the farmers complained that the railroad corporations were exploiting them). Some of the farmers were stupid, others merely incompetent. If they bought machinery, they increased their output, but also their indebtedness. 'I can give a man accommodation . . . but I cannot give him brains', one money-lender told a Victorian Royal Commission in 1878. 'If he is slated [cheated] that is his business.' Bad farming practices impoverished the soil; but bigger farms, though more efficient, aroused anxiety on social grounds. To make 1,000 acres the normal size of a farm would 'create a laboring class who work on wages on another man's place, instead of a class like the small landowners in France and Germany.' Thus did political prejudice discourage efficient farming.[23]

Bad seasons or debt made it possible for larger cultivators to buy out their impoverished neighbours and so to pave the way for the larger farms which were necessary for the economic use of machinery, for the introduction of

22. P. Papineau, *Homesteads for the People and Manhood Suffrage*, Melbourne 1855; and *Manifesto of the Land League of New South Wales*, 26 April 1859, quoted in C. M. H. Clark, *Select Documents in Australian History, 1851-1900*, Angus and Robertson, Sydney 1955, pp 99 ff.

23. Victoria, Royal Commission on Settlement under the Land Act of 1869, *Votes and Proceedings*, 1879-80, III, No 72, evidence R. W. Bennett, 11 June 1878, and O'Hea, 26 June 1878, quoted in Edgars Dunsdorfs, *The Australian Wheat-Growing Industry, 1788-1948*, Melbourne University Press, Melbourne 1956, pp 125-6 and 129.

mixed farming, for proper fallowing and usually for better general technique. Throughout the nineteenth century manuring was neglected, though machinery was used more, especially the Bull-Ridley stripper, invented in South Australia in 1843, Mullens' scrub-roller and stump-jump plough, invented in 1878, and H. V. McKay's reaper and binder in 1884.[24] But despite these inventions, yield on the Australian wheat fields steadily declined in the latter half of the century from about 13 to about 7 bushels per acre. (See Fig. 3-1.) The railway took the wheat grower further inland where the rainfall was less reliable than nearer the coast; the inventions themselves made it possible to cultivate less fertile lands, especially in the Mallee districts of South Australia and Victoria, where settlement proceeded steadily after 1880.

As the total population had risen from 1 to 3 million, the area under wheat had risen from 650,000 acres in 1860 to 3,400,000 acres in 1892, four-fifths of which was grown in South Australia and Victoria. But owing to the declining yield, output increased only from 10 million to 33 million bushels, and the market remained almost entirely a local one; though New South Wales and Queensland imported from the southern colonies, further expansion had to wait for better transport to Europe and a larger demand there. Highlighting the comparatively slow rate of agricultural development is the fact that when the nineteenth century ended, the United States was producing 87 per cent as much wheat as it would do a generation later, and more than twenty times the Australian production in 1900. By contrast, the average Australian harvests were less than one-quarter of those grown here in the 1920s.[25] (See Table 1-4.)

In the 1880s, Victoria, largely on the prompting of Alfred Deakin, began ambitious irrigation schemes, and in 1887 there were 20,000 acres of irrigated land in the colony, two-thirds under wheat; but it was perhaps fortunate that these early schemes were fairly small for they were nearly all incompetently managed and most were financially unrewarding. Though the local market for agricultural commodities other than wheat also grew with the population, it remained very limited. Dairying expanded in the North Coast and Illawarra districts of New South Wales and in parts of Gippsland and the Western District in Victoria; but the local market in the 1870s was glutted with butter, and even by 1891, production weighed only 42 million lb. Meat found more buyers in Australia, and Australian canned meat was selling in London in the 1860s; but though exports weighed 16 million lb in 1879-80, the expansion of the industry had to wait for successful voyages with re-

---

24. For these inventions, and their inventors, see Edgars Dunsdorfs, *op. cit.*, pp 102, 149, 152 and 156-7.

25. U.S. average output: 1898-1902, 700,000,000 bushels p.a., 1923-27, 800,000,000 p.a., 1933-37, 640,000,000 p.a., U.S. Department of Agriculture, Agricultural Statistics, quoted in S. E. Morison and H. S. Commager, *The Growth of the American Republic*, Oxford University Press, New York 1942, Vol 2, p 756; average Australian production: 1891-1900, 30,000,000 bushels p.a.; 1921-30, 135,000,000 p.a.; 1931-41, 178,000,000 p.a.; *Year Book*, No 48, 1962, p 908, Bureau of Census and Statistics.

frigerated cargoes. These stimulated pioneering in the north in 'out-back' Queensland, and sugar growing was increasing on its eastern coast; but these developments, and fruit growing too, can easily be exaggerated. Certainly between the census taken in 1861 and that in 1891, the numbers engaged in agricultural and pastoral occupations rose from 137,000 to 332,000 though they fell from 29 per cent to 26 per cent of the breadwinners; but this remains very small beer. It is very easy, as is often done, to ante-date the agricultural changes which appeared later, but between 1861-63 and 1876-78 agriculture and dairying grew very little more than the Gross Domestic Product, and during the next ten years they increased less (dairying by much less). The economic expansion of these thirty years was based primarily on railway building, construction and manufacturing, and, up to 1876, on the pastoral industry.[26] In these years it was the wool grower who dominated at least the rural scene.

THE SQUATTER

On the land, the period between 1850 and 1890 marked the hey-day of the 'squattocracy'—as the pastoralists, though no longer squatters, were almost universally called. Their crude bush huts, roofed with bark or shingles, were replaced by luxurious station homesteads, sometimes built on the lines of traditional British architecture, sometimes single-storied with wide verandahs, always surrounded by many outbuildings, to make up what often looked like a little village. However if all had become quite comfortable, and their owners were 'proud gentlemen', as Anthony Trollope said, most of them in his view lacked 'fine tastes in art or literature', though there were exceptions in the Western District of Victoria and the Riverina in New South Wales.[27] It was here that the earliest expansion took place, but gradually the squatters, like some of the farmers, moved into drier areas, the central district of New South Wales and then past the Lachlan river into its arid west, and up to the Maranoa and Warrego rivers in Queensland. (See Map 1-1.) In 1862, New South Wales and Victoria were both grazing about 6 million sheep, with Queensland only a little behind, but by 1891 there were 62 million in New South Wales, 20 million in Queensland and only 13 million in Victoria. Between 1860 and 1894 the whole sheep population had risen from

26. Census figures, N. G. Butlin, *op. cit.*, Table 40, p 194, and cf. his commentary, p 195. Growth rates in different sectors of Gross Domestic Product, *ibid.*, pp 18-19 and see above, p 8.

27. For early squatting conditions: S. H. Roberts, *The Squatting Age in Australia, 1835-47*, Melbourne University Press, Melbourne 1935; E. M. Curr, *Recollections of Squatting in Victoria*, Melbourne 1833, reprinted by Melbourne University Press, Melbourne 1965; Alfred A. Joyce, *A Homestead History* (G. F. James ed), Melbourne University Press, Melbourne 1942; H. W. Haygarth, *Recollections of Bush Life in Australia*, London 1848; and many others. For later, A. Trollope, *Australia and New Zealand*, London 1873; Margaret Kiddle, *Men of Yesterday*, Melbourne University Press, Melbourne 1961; and Alfred A. Joyce, *op. cit.*

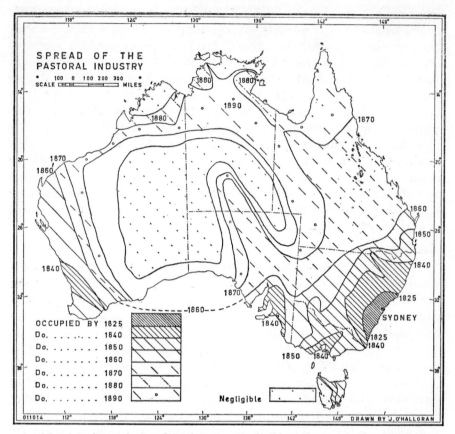

Map 1-1: Stages in Land Settlement. 'Negligible' refers to the late 1930s.
(Reproduced by permission of Methuen and Co. Ltd., and based on
Figure 79 in Griffith Taylor, *Australia*, rev ed 1943)

about 20 million to 100 million, and cattle from 4 million to more than 12
million.[28]

It was in the 1870s that the pastoral industry regained the position it had
held before the gold discoveries in 1851 as the greatest *single* contributor to
Australia's Gross National Product.[29] After 1870 the wool boom reached its
height. Better sheep breeding, more dams, fences, and artesian bores, all
helped to increase output. The average fleece, which weighed about three lbs

28. Statistical Handbook for the Sheep and Wool Industry, Table 1, Bureau of Agricul-
tural Economics, Canberra 1949, Table 1, in C. M. H. Clark, *Select Documents in Australian
History, 1851-1900*, Angus and Robertson, Sydney 1955, pp 177-8. For cattle, *Year Book*,
No 48, 1962, p 962, Bureau of Census and Statistics, and Table in *Australian Encyclopaedia*,
Angus and Robertson, Sydney, 1958, Vol 2, p 295.

29. N. G. Butlin, *op. cit.*, p 22.

14

in 1860, was nearly twice as heavy 30 years later. By 1890 squatters had put up about 2 million miles of fencing in New South Wales alone, and this was only part of the large capital outlay they made for improving and purchasing their properties. They were heavily in debt to banks and pastoral companies, but they had bought their land. Their holdings would impede other rural development in the future; but meantime their social importance and political influence was very great, and the most successful of them founded families who for the time being seemed as if they might form an Australian counterpart to English landed families.

Their investment was made on the assumption that good financial returns would continue; but this proved false. The optimistic expansion itself drove up the cost of properties and stock. As in the 1830s the boom depended, in part, on the continued sale of surplus flocks to newcomers. Transport to western New South Wales was expensive; labour was scarce and therefore dear. Then came the rabbits. They were first 'liberated' on Thomas Austin's property near Geelong, in 1859, but spread steadily throughout the continent to become perhaps Australia's major pest. By 1880 they had entered New South Wales, and their advent was soon followed by droughts, which together with rabbits caused a drastic deterioration of the native pasture. Finally wool receipts began to fall.

Prices, weather, pests and diseases showed that the pastoral expansion after 1884 had been unwarranted and the investment in it misplaced, and that the greater stock carrying capacity which this had produced was a cause of instability not of progress.[30] As 50 years before, excessive expansion led first to instability and then to a collapse, made worse first by the general economic depression and banking smashes of the early 1890s, and then by the great drought from 1895 to 1902. The sheep population was reduced by half and much of the Western District of New South Wales was virtually evacuated.

THE DEPRESSION OF THE 1890s

The depression of the 1890s was not confined to the squatters. Speculative building in the cities ceased and the stoppage of overseas borrowing halted most public works. To the many thus put out of work the multiplier added even more. The failure of some 'land banks' helped to precipitate a 'run' on the ordinary banks: 19 out of 28 had to close permanently or temporarily. Between 1891 and 1900, Gross National Product per head fell by 13 per cent, and would have fallen by more but for opportune gold discoveries in Western Australia.

RECOVERY

After 1900, federation and the removal of interstate tariff barriers put an end to some obstacles to economic progress. All States passed land legislation

30. *Ibid.*, chs 2 and 6.

C

to encourage closer settlement, and by 1914 had purchased 3 million acres of privately owned land for £34 million ($68 million) for the purpose of closer settlement and settled 12,000 families on them. They began to encourage agricultural research. They established rural credit facilities. Unfortunately often the holdings were still uneconomically small, particularly when they were for cereal growing and not dairying. Corruption was not unknown, ministers for political reasons sometimes interfered in the selection of purchases and the staffs of the State agricultural departments and settlement boards were too small to advise and supervise settlers properly, or to subdivide and value estates properly.[31] However the schemes were pressed on enthusiastically.

Irrigation in Victoria was greatly improved by the Water Act of 1905; New South Wales began work on the Murrumbidgee river, with the Burrinjuck dam; in 1914 Victoria, New South Wales and South Australia agreed on a scheme for using the waters of the Murray river. New settlers were encouraged to immigrate, in line with the ideas on Imperial migration and development fervently expressed by Alfred Deakin, Prime Minister 1905-08 and 1909-10. Between 1906 and 1914, 180,000 migrants were assisted to come to Australia, lured by 'turgid panegyrics of farming conditions in Victoria' and by the attractions of 'a land of freedom and opportunity' (New South Wales), 'the state for outdoor life' (South Australia) or the 'state where the future looms larger than ever' (Western Australia).[32]

As a consequence of these governmental activities, and helped by railway extensions (in Gippsland in Victoria, and Illawarra and the North Coast in New South Wales), by milking machines and by refrigeration, dairy cattle increased from 1.25 million in 1900 to 2 million by 1914 and butter production rose from 42 million lbs in 1891 to 212 million lbs in 1911. Butter exports, negligible in 1891, exceeded 100 million lbs in 1911. Now that the railway had penetrated the wheat belt in New South Wales and was doing so in Western Australia, wheat acreage trebled and exports doubled, as world prices rose and shipping improved. By 1911, New South Wales was the largest producer, having almost quintupled her acreage in twenty years, while Victoria and South Australia increased theirs by 80 and 40 per cent respectively. Following the gold rushes of the 1890s, Western Australians too were taking to farming. After first sowing 100,000 acres in wheat in 1903, they had more than a million under wheat ten years later. After more than ten years experimenting by a number of wheat breeders, several of whom achieved some

31. Victoria, Royal Commission on Closer Settlement, Reports, *Parliamentary Papers*, 1915, Vol 2.

32. *Ibid.*, and C. J. King, 'An Outline of Closer Settlement in New South Wales', *Review of Marketing and Agricultural Economics*, Vol 25, Nos 3-4, September-December 1957, p 220. For a very critical account of closer settlement in Victoria see F. W. Eggleston, *State Socialism in Victoria*, P. S. King, London 1932, ch 2; and for a more balanced appraisal of its difficulties, Rural Reconstruction Commission, *Land Utilization and Farm Settlement, Third Report*, Government Printer, Canberra 1944, ch 5.

success, William Farrer (who, like John Macarthur, is commemorated on the new decimal currency notes), produced his variety 'Federation' though by 1930 it had largely been replaced by still better strains. Farmers began to use superphosphate and, though much more slowly, tractors, and government experimental farms and agricultural departments also stimulated the use of better farming techniques. As a result of all these things, between the early 1890s and 1913 yields rose from 8 to nearly 13 bushels to the acre, acreage under crop trebled from about 3·5 to more than 9 million and total output increased from 30 million bushels to more than 100 million bushels.[33]

OTHER DEVELOPMENTS: CATTLE, SUGAR AND FRUIT, 1885-1914

The great drought which culminated in 1902 had affected the cattle industry too. After a marked expansion to nearly 12 million head in 1895, more than half in Queensland, the numbers dropped by one-third, but by 1910 exceeded 11 million again. Meantime tropical agriculture was progressing on fertile patches of the colony's eastern coast with the development of sugar growing. At first this had been done on fairly large estates with indentured 'Kanaka' labour, recruited from Polynesian Pacific islands. During the 1880s small farms and government-financed 'central' mills replaced the larger properties but the Kanaka labour force remained. In the 1890s, about 150,000 tons of sugar were produced from about 80,000 acres, enough to meet about half the Australian demand. After federation in 1901 the Kanakas were repatriated, and the higher wages demanded by white labourers were made possible by a duty on imports and a bounty on local production. With the stimulus, sugar output almost doubled before 1914, though owing to increasing demand even then nearly half the sugar consumed still had to be imported.

Refrigeration also helped to promote the development of fruit growing, particularly in the apple orchards of Tasmania, and in the irrigation districts of Victoria, though here the great expansion was to come after World War I.

FROM THE FIRST WORLD WAR TO THE PRESENT DAY

AFTER WORLD WAR I

After 1918 many Australians, politicians and farming spokesmen alike, seemed to think that the great pre-war advances in agriculture would continue, instead of remembering that in the past over-expansion had been common and periods of advance had been followed by recession. Wartime scarcities and high prices caused exuberant growth to follow the better justified pre-war development. Land settlement schemes for ex-soldiers and

33. During this period Canadian production quadrupled, to 231,000,000 bushels in 1913, but U.S. output was more stable after its earlier growth: 1850, 100 million bushels; 1880, 500 million; 1896-1900, 630 million; 1906-10, 650 million. The world percentage increase was slower in this period than in 1850-1890.

British migrants were pushed ahead without preliminary soil surveys and other investigation and without much use of expert scientific and technical knowledge.[34] Emotional gratitude encouraged a policy of putting ex-servicemen on the land, but it was so meanly implemented that men were settled on small blocks, often on mediocre land, and usually over-capitalized in the

OVERSEA·ARRIVALS AND DEPARTURES·
1925 TO 1965

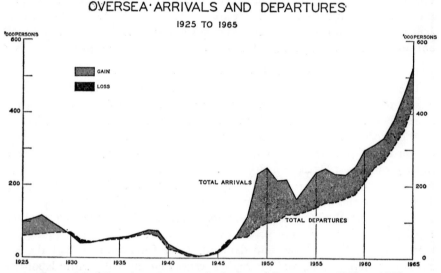

Figure 1-2: Migration: Overseas Arrivals and Departures, 1925 to 1965.
(*Year Book,* No 52, 1966, Bureau of Census and Statistics)

high prices paid for them, in circumstances in which even if the holder had been 'a practical farmer, capable and industrious', it would have been impossible for him to make a living. Still this was only a particular application of what Professor Wadham had in mind when he complained that 'of all the foolish policies of land settlement which have been advocated for general application in many parts of Australia, the endeavour to create a system of small-scale farming is probably the most stupid'. In 1927, the losses of 37,561 soldier settlers amounted to £23·5 million ($47 million) or £630 ($1,260) per head; in 1928 two-thirds of the assets of non-soldier farmers belonged to their creditors, and at the prices then prevailing, they would have needed two or three years' harvests to pay off their debts.[35]

34. W. A. Sinclair, 'Aspects of Economic Growth, 1900-1930', in A. H. Boxer (ed), *Aspects of the Australian Economy,* Melbourne University Press, Melbourne 1965; Commonwealth of Australia, British Economic Mission, Report, *Parliamentary Papers,* 1929; Rural Reconstruction Commission, *Land Utilization and Farm Settlement, Third Report,* Government Printer, Canberra 1944, p 103.

35. S. M. Wadham, 'Difficulties of Small-scale Farming in Australia', in G. L. Wood (ed), *Australia, its Resources and Development,* Macmillan, New York 1947, p 139; Commonwealth of Australia, *Report by Mr. Justice Pike on Losses due to Soldier Settlement.* Government Printer, Canberra 1929; and Edgars Dunsdorfs, *op. cit.,* p 257.

Late in the 1920s wheat prices were not too bad, having fluctuated between 5s. and 6s. (50 and 60 cents) a bushel since 1920. Even so, considering the farmers' costs, this compared unfavourably with 4s. (40 cents) before World War I. Meantime the general average of tariff rates on manufactures had been raised by about 30 per cent in 1921, according to the Prime Minis-

AREA OF CROPS: 1900-1 TO 1964-65

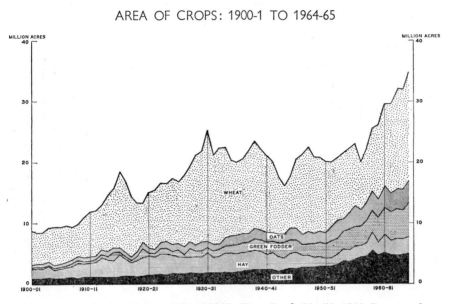

Figure 1-3: Area of Crops, 1901 to 1965. (*Year Book,* No 52, 1966, Bureau of Census and Statistics)

ter, to 'protect industries born during the war, encourage others that are desirable and diversify and extend existing ones'. But though manufacturers could be protected in this way, and their output increased by about 30 per cent in the 1920s, it was more difficult to help the farmer selling so much of his output abroad. However the government could, and did, do something. In 1926 it introduced a scheme for a high home price for butter, maintained by a heavy duty on imports; this made it possible to offset low export prices. After 1925, a similar arrangement was made with sugar growers, who, stimulated by high wartime prices, had so increased their output that Australia became a sugar exporter, though unfortunately only by the time the world market had collapsed. Dried fruit growers, provided with irrigated land, were likewise able to operate only with a high home price and an export subsidy. Altogether, in 1929 a committee inquiring into the effects of the tariff estimated that while the cost of protecting manufacturers was £26 million ($52 million), the cost of protecting primary products was £10 million

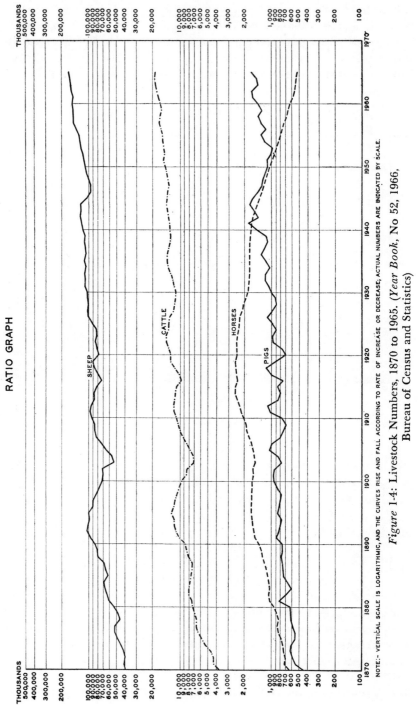

Figure 1·4: **Livestock Numbers, 1870 to 1965.** (*Year Book*, No 52, 1966, Bureau of Census and Statistics)

($20 million) and in addition, primary producers received other help worth a further £12 million ($24 million).[36]

In this assistance, graziers did not share. The beef cattle industry had not taken long to recover from the great droughts of 1892-94 and 1901-02 and had hoped that refrigeration would help its prospects in European markets.

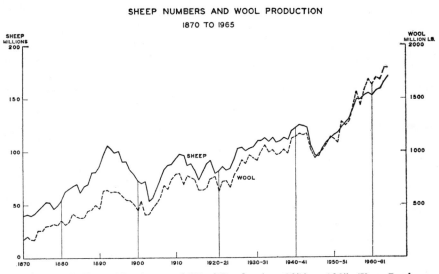

SHEEP NUMBERS AND WOOL PRODUCTION
1870 TO 1965

Figure 1-5: Sheep Numbers and Wool Production, 1870 to 1965. (*Year Book*, No 52, 1966, Bureau of Census and Statistics)

Unfortunately it did more for South America, for not until 1934 was it possible to send 'chilled', as opposed to frozen, meat from Australia to England. Better roads or railways in the north might have helped, but the government did not provide them, and prices in the 1920s were too low for the industry to have been able to make much headway. The wool grower almost alone seemed still able to stand on his own feet. He had long since recovered from the great drought and had not again moved out into regions which were too dry. Prices were quite good and the average weight of fleeces was about nine lbs; from 100 million sheep, total output was more than 900 million lbs, of which three-quarters were exported, 40 per cent to England and 25 per cent to France.

THE GREAT DEPRESSION OF THE 1930s

In this rather uneasy situation, common to most other parts of the world, the Great Depression struck both farmer and grazier hard. With wheat at 2s. (20 cents) a bushel, the lowest price since the days of Queen Elizabeth I, it

36. *The Australian Tariff, an Economic Inquiry*, Melbourne University Press, Melbourne 1929, p 45, and cf. Appendices A, N and O.

was hardly surprising that a record crop in 1930 benefited the grower very little. Already heavily in debt, he too turned to government for help. In 1930 it promised the grower 4s. (40 cents) and next year 3s. (30 cents), but in neither year could it keep its promise because it could not raise the necessary money, even by bank loans. As an exporter, the wheat grower was helped by the 25 per cent devaluation of the Australian pound, but this was not enough. Prices had to be raised further and costs reduced. Farm relief acts granted moratoria and prevented foreclosure for debt. As a result of a fall in the cost of living and the policy of 'sharing the losses' of the Depression, wages and interest rates were reduced by nearly one-quarter. Later a scheme of debt adjustment, adopted to deal with over-capitalization, reduced wheat growers' liabilities by about 10 per cent from about £11 ($22) per acre—though the consequences of World War II and its aftermath brought them down to £3.15s. ($7.50) per acre by 1950. From 1932 to 1936 the government paid bounties to the wheat farmer, and then when the world price fell again in 1938, it introduced a two-price scheme like those already familiar in the dairy and fruit industries. These fixed 'prices high enough to provide bounties on exports'.[37] After 1932 the Ottawa trade agreements granting preferential duties and quotas on the British market had considerably assisted the dairy farmer and meat producer, so that except for the pastoralist (who had of course shared in the general benefits of exchange depreciation and reductions in wages, interest rates and land tax), practically every form of farming activity was receiving direct government help of some kind during the 1930s.

In this Australia's practice was similar to that of other countries, but the payments made were often 'politically troublesome and financially awkward', as the Rural Reconstruction Commission was to put it later. The Commission thought that although government assistance sometimes had 'the psychological effect of discouraging efforts to improve efficiency', on the other hand the 'hard times induced many farmers to think hard', and 'sound scientific experimentation was conducted on a scale never before attempted in Australia'.[38] However these things could not work miracles, for as the Commission reported:

A considerable part of the new farming of 1920-30 had been based on the assumption that farming is easy . . . and that hard work alone will enable a farmer to succeed. Wheat farms had been developed in districts which were too uncertain in their rainfall. Dairy-farms had been established which were too small to enable a man to earn his living . . . Many of these mistakes in planning would have been avoidable if the economics

37. *Ibid.*, p 43; and Edgars Dunsdorfs, *op. cit.*, p 290. It should be noticed that the postwar marketing arrangements in these products have been altered in many respects.

38. Rural Reconstruction Commission, *A General Rural Survey, First Report*, Government Printer, Canberra 1944, paras 61-2.

of agricultural production had been understood when the settlements were inaugurated.[39]

In 1934 the Royal Commission on the Wheat, Flour and Bread Industries had reported that the costs of one-third of the wheat farmers were so high that they could not look forward to making profits at any foreseeable prices. Even so, when war broke out in 1939 the area under crop, 13·3 million acres, was only 12 per cent lower than it had been ten years earlier; in response to low prices the contraction of acreage had been slow.

THE EVE OF WORLD WAR II

In 1939 manufacturing, assisted by the currency devaluation and by cheap coal and steel, had expanded by 40 per cent in ten years. Tertiary industries were growing too, but rural production, which still provided four-fifths of Australia's total exports, appears to have been giving employment to about a quarter of Australia's breadwinners, compared with about one-third before World War I.[40] (See Tables 1-2 and 1-3.) Many rural occupations are 'mixed',

Table 1-2

Value of Production, 1892-1962
($A million)

	1892	1902	1912	1922	1932	1942	1952	1962
		Gross	value			Net	value	
Agricultural	34	48	78	164	99	128	493	733
Pastoral	62	54	105	150	86	171	801	963
Dairying	12	15	32	71	45	68	208	273
Other rural	4	4	8	18	12	14	65	53
Total rural	112	121	223	403	242	381	1,567	2,022
Other primary	33	50	58	62	41	101	295	410
Factories	47	58	95	223	222	633	2,050	4,394
All industries	192	229	376	688	505	1,115	3,912	6,826
	%	%	%	%	%	%	%	%
Total rural as per cent of all industries	58	53	59	59	48	34	40	30

SOURCE: *Year Book*, No 48, 1962 and No 49, 1963. Bureau of Census and Statistics.

but if, bearing this in mind, we accept the Rural Reconstruction Commission's rough division of about a quarter in each of grazing, dairying, wheat growing and 'other rural industries', we can see the cause of a great deal of rural poverty and distress. The value of all primary production between

39. *Ibid.*, para 63; cf. South Australia, Report of Pastoral and Marginal Areas Inquiry, *Parliamentary Proceedings*, 1947, No 52.

40. Rural Reconstruction Commission, *A General Rural Survey, First Report*, Government Printer, Canberra 1944, para 25. These figures, based on the 1933 census, are imperfect, but indicate the general trend.

1928-29 and 1938-39 averaged only one-fifth of the national income, so that the average income of the countryman must have been lower than that of the city dweller; but of this production the pastoralists took nearly half, and this left only about 12 per cent of the national income for 'other' primary producers, who comprised 18 per cent of the total population. So the lot of many farmers was unsatisfactory, and though they could enjoy the frequently praised benefits of country life, they often had to put up with sub-standard housing, and inadequate medical, educational and other community services.[41]

RECENT YEARS, 1940-1964

During World War II the farmer was seriously handicapped by being cut off from world markets, by the shortage of labour, superphosphates and other supplies, and in 1944-45 by a severe drought. Even after 1945 his hopes for better things were disappointed, when labour found employment in the cities more attractive than in the country, and when high taxation and shortage of supplies and equipment continued. But though as late as 1948 many farmers felt misgivings about the future, by that time mechanization had proceeded apace and other difficulties seemed less formidable.[42] During the next few years, despite persistent shortage of materials there was growing prosperity in most rural industries, which culminated in the great wool boom of 1951-52. But within a decade after that, another period of relative difficulty set in. By this time world agricultural production per head of population had returned to its pre-war figure and prices of wool, wheat, butter, meat and sugar tended steadily downward. In real terms, farm incomes tended to fall, and as others were rising it is not surprising that there was a renewed drift from the land. Partly as a result of what were regarded as the hardships of country life and its inadequate returns, by 1961 only 11 per cent of the labour force was working on it, though in this Australia was only following the patterns of Canada and the U.S.A.[43] (See Tables 1-2 and 1-3.)

However, though fewer men stayed on the land, production rose, thanks to technological progress, pasture improvement, better fertilizers, fodder conservation, mechanization, and the destruction of the rabbit by myxomatosis. Between 1949 and 1964 sheep numbers rose by two-thirds to a peak of 170 million, mainly through properties carrying more sheep to the acre; but

41. Rural Reconstruction Commission, *Rural Amenities, Seventh Report*, Government Printer, Canberra 1945; and A. J. and J. J. McIntyre, *Country Towns in Victoria—A Social Survey*, Melbourne University Press, Melbourne 1944; and A. J. Holt, *Wheat Farms in Victoria, A Sociological Survey*, Melbourne University Agriculture School, Melbourne 1946.

42. S. M. Wadham, R. Kent Wilson and Joyce Wood, *Land Utilization in Australia*, 4th ed, Melbourne University Press, Melbourne 1964, pp 265 ff.

43. *Ibid.*, and see W. T. Easterbrook and H. G. J. Aitken, *op. cit.*, p 495; and R. M. Robertson, *op. cit.*, ch 18 and p 461. Between 1920 and 1960 the real income per head of U.S. industrial workers approximately doubled, while that of farmers rose by only 60 per cent, and the numbers on farms in both Canada and the U.S.A. declined absolutely; in the latter from 32·5 million in 1916 to 15 million in 1961.

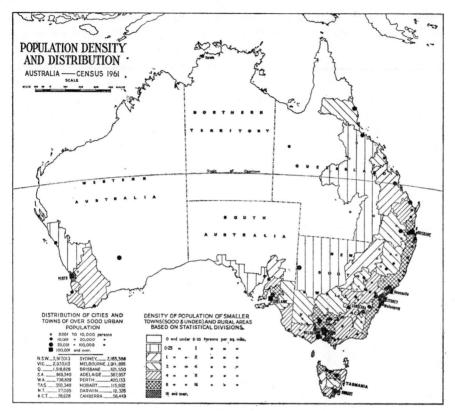

Map 1-2: Population Density and Distribution, 1961. (*Year Book*, No 50, 1964, Bureau of Census and Statistics)

the average weight of each fleece did not change much and remained about 10 lbs per sheep. At the same time beef and veal production rose by about 40 per cent and the area under all crops rose from 20 million acres to more than 33 million; wheat production, at 360 million bushels in 1964-65 was an all time record, double the average of the 1930s and 1950s and treble that of the 1950s. In all, taking the average for 1936-39 as 100, the index for Australian rural production was 109 in 1950-51, 131 in 1955-56 and 153 in 1960-61.[44]

CONCLUSION

All this means, of course, that agriculture is now very much a capital-intensive industry. So much capital assistance needs to be afforded to the farmer in one way or another that rural settlement must be regarded, even

44. S. M. Wadham, R. Kent Wilson and Joyce Wood, *loc. cit.*

25

more than in the past, as a problem involving the investment priorities of the government and other public authorities. This is not new, for throughout Australia's history, the 'state' has played a major role in this development. It has built roads, railways and irrigation works, brought electric power to the farm, carried out research, lent money to primary producers (and sometimes written off their debts), and it has created marketing organizations to help in selling the produce of the land. Large-scale financial institutions like banks and pastoral companies, including State banks, and recently the new Commonwealth Development Bank, have made their contribution. But essentially the pattern of rural investment has been for the government to provide expensive major facilities and for the graziers or farmers then to undertake the less costly work of developing their own estates. Unfortunately, they did not always have the knowledge or the capital needed to do this. Ignorance of the climate and environment caused faulty estimates of costs.

Table 1-3

Rural and Non-Rural Population and Work Force, 1921-1961

| | Census Year | | | | |
	1921 %	1933 %	1947 %	1954 %	1961 %
Population					
Rural	37·3	35·9	31·1	21·0	17·8
Urban	62·7	64·1	68·9	79·0	82·2
Total	100·0	100·0	100·0	100·0	100.0
Work force (males and females)					
Rural industries	20·5	19·1	14·4	12·6	10·3
Other primary	1·7	1·4	1·2	0·7	0·6
Total primary	22·2	20·5	15·6	13·3	10·9
Mining	2·8	2·4	1·7	1·7	1·3
Manufacturing	19·0	17·8	26·0	27·7	27·0
Tertiary and other	56·0	59·3	56·7	57·3	60·8
Total work force	100·0	100·0	100·0	100·0	100·0

SOURCE: Census Reports, Bureau of Census and Statistics.

Likely incomes were often not assessed realistically enough, and the capacity and reliability of overseas markets were exaggerated. Transport was always a difficulty, and when new facilities were provided they helped to encourage successive phases of expansion to be carried too far—as in the pastoral industry in the 1820s, 1830s and 1880s, and as in dairying, sugar and wheat growing in the 1920s; but political pressures and human sympathies then

Table 1-4

Agricultural Development, 1820-1960
(millions)

Year	Human Population	Sheep	Wool Prod.	Wool exports	Cattle	Meat Prod.	Meat exports	Butter Prod.	Butter exports	Crops	Wheat	Wheat Prod.	Wheat exports	Sugar Prod.
	no.	no.	lb.	lb.	no.	cwt.	$A	lb.	lb.	acres	acres	bush.	bush.	tons
1820	0.03	0.3			0.07						0.03			
1842	0.24	6.3			0.17						0.16	2		
1851	0.42	17.0									0.24	4		
1861	1.17	21.0	67	60	3.80					1.2	0.72	10		
1871	1.70	40.0	208	177	4.30		1.2			2.1	1.30	12	1	
1881	2.31	65.0	320	329	8.00		0.8		0.7	4.6	3.00	21	5	0.3
1891	3.24	106.0	634	641	11.10		1.0	47	4.2	5.4	3.30	26	10	0.7
1901	3.82	72.0	539	529	8.50		5.2	103	35.0	8.8	5.10	39	20	1.4
1911	4.57	97.0	798	734	11.80	12	8.6	212	102.0	11.9	7.40	72	55	1.7
1921	5.51	86.0	723	946	14.40	14	11.0	267	127.0	15.0	9.70	129	100	2.4
1931	6.55	111.0	1,007	903	12.30	20	12.8	390	202.0	25.2	14.70	190	127	4.2
1941	7.14	125.0	1,167	938	13.60	19	28.2	376	130.0	21.1	12.00	167	22	5.1
1950	8.31	116.0	1,093	1,184	15.20		60.8	302	125.0	20.1	10.40	184	87	7.0
1960	10.17	155.0	1,689	1,524	16.50	29	177.2	408	176.0	29.6	13.40	274	184	9.1

Sources: Various statistical series for 1820-51; and *Year Books*, Bureau of Census and Statistics, especially No 39, 1953, pp xxviii-xxix, for 1861-1950; and Nos 47-49, 1961-63, for 1960.

resulted in the farmer being protected from paying the full penalty for an over-optimism which was often shared by the majority of the Australian community. Momentarily, the outlook for the new, highly capitalized primary production looks rosy, as an increasing world population demands more food; but while the wool market is threatened by 'synthetics', and so much of Australia's wheat sales remain at the whim of the People's Republic of China, the historian can only remark that over-production has occurred before, without thereby asserting that it is necessarily happening again.

CHAPTER 2

THE ECONOMIC STRUCTURE OF AUSTRALIAN FARMS

B. R. DAVIDSON

University of Sydney

INTRODUCTION

In Australia most farms produce only one or two commodities. This high degree of specialization which is one of the most distinctive features of the nation's agriculture, arose mainly because of the importance of the export market. From the early days of settlement the major rural industries, which produced wool, wheat, beef and dairy products could only expand if a large proportion of these commodities were exported. Even in 1965, when Australia had a population of over 11 million, between 50 and 60 per cent of the nation's agricultural production was exported. In the past, the proportion exported was even higher and local consumption played a minor part in deciding what to produce.

As distinctive as the degree of specialization is the relative proportion of land and labour used. Over 90 per cent of Australia's 253,000 rural holdings are operated by their owners who, with their families, form more than 60 per cent of the total farm labour force of 280,000 people. They operate 1,184 million acres of land, an average of one person working in agriculture for each 4,228 acres, in rural holdings.[1]

The high proportion of land to labour used, has reacted on, and been influenced by, the other main characteristic mentioned—specialization. During the nineteenth century the restrictions on production imposed by the export market and by the amount of labour available led to distinct and highly specialized types of farming in different zones of Australia. These differences persist to the present day.

DETERMINANTS OF LAND USE

The distribution of the various types of farming is determined by the following environmental factors, listed in descending order of importance:

1. *Year Book*, No 51, 1965, Bureau of Census and Statistics.

(i) The availability of soil moisture and its distribution throughout the year

(ii) Topography

(iii) The nature of the original vegetation

(iv) Soil fertility

Each of the environmental factors is dealt with in turn in the discussion which follows.[2]

SOIL MOISTURE AND TOPOGRAPHY

Rainfall in Australia depends on two distinct weather patterns. The southern half of the continent receives its rain in the winter from the Antarctic cyclones and anticyclones which move across the continent from west to east. The northern half receives its rainfall in the summer from the northwest monsoon and the south-east trade winds. In southern Queensland and northern New South Wales the two systems overlap and rainfall is distributed throughout the year. The amount of rainfall and its reliability both decrease as the distance from the coast increases. (See Map 2-1 and Map 2-2.) The winter rainfall of southern Australia is as reliable as the same amounts of rainfall in other parts of the world, but the summer rainfall is at least 10 per cent less reliable than the same amounts of rainfall in other continents.[3]

Because temperatures and evaporation are higher in northern than in southern Australia, more rain is needed to obtain the same level of soil moisture in the north. Soil moisture is insufficient to initiate plant growth in any month in which $\left(\dfrac{\text{precipitation}}{\text{saturation deficit}^{\,0.75}}\right)$ or $\left(\dfrac{P}{\text{S.D.}^{\,0.75}}\right)$ is less than 4 and a period during which $\dfrac{P}{\text{S.D.}^{\,0.75}}$ exceeds 8 is required if reasonably high crop yields are to be obtained.[4] (For example, at Alice Springs $\dfrac{P}{\text{S.D.}^{0.75}}$ does not exceed 4 in any month and cropping is impossible. Around Adelaide cropping is feasible as $\dfrac{P}{\text{S.D.}^{\,0.75}}$ exceeds 4 for six months of the year and is greater than 8 for five of these months.) The continent can be divided into a series of moisture regions depending on the number of months in which $\dfrac{P}{\text{S.D.}^{\,0.75}}$ exceeds the values of 4 and 8. (See Map

2. In this chapter, 'regions' are areas defined in terms of natural features, such as climate, vegetation and soil; 'zones' are areas defined in terms of land use, and sub-zones are subdivisions within the zones.

3. G. W. Leeper, 'The Reliability of Rainfall in Australia as Compared with the Rest of the World', *Journal of the Australian Institute of Agricultural Science*, Vol 11, No 4, December 1945.

4. J. A. Prescott and J. A. Thomas, 'The Length of Growing Season in Australia as Determined by the Effectiveness of Rainfall', South Australian Branch *Proceedings* for the 1948-49 Session of the Royal Geographical Society of Australasia, Vol 50, December 1949.

2-5.) The probability of obtaining high yields from crops and pastures increases as the number of months in which $\dfrac{P}{S.D.^{0.75}}$ exceeds 8 increases.

A large amount of Australian research work has been aimed at developing crops and pasture species which will flourish in the short Australian growing season. Even so, practically all of the species developed so far require a season

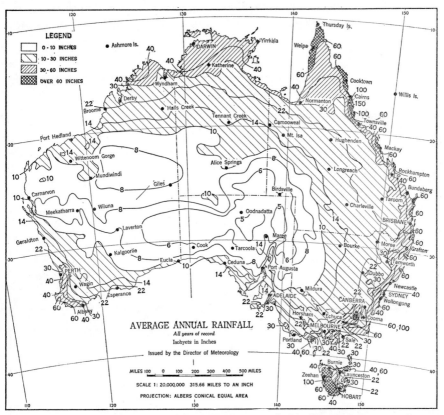

Map 2-1: Average Annual Rainfall. (*Year Book*, No 52, 1966, Bureau of Census and Statistics)

with enough soil moisture to sustain plant growth for at least five months— but four-fifths of Australia's 1,904 million acres have a growing season of less than five months. Part of this area has no vegetative cover and the remainder supports hardy native shrubs, herbs and grasses which are only capable of supporting livestock at extremely low stocking rates.[5] Approximately half cannot even be used for sparse grazing.[6]

5. S. M. Wadham, R. Kent Wilson and Joyce Wood, *Land Utilization in Australia*, 4th ed, Melbourne University Press, Melbourne 1964, p 56.
6. *Ibid.*, p 5.

D

In the tropics, small areas on the Queensland coast are used for intensive sugar production and isolated areas are used for dairying and cash cropping. Apart from these areas, all of that part of the wet tropical region with a growing season of more than five months is used for sparse cattle grazing. This wet tropical area, together with the usable portion of the continent with a growing season of less than five months, is referred to as the Pastoral Zone. In the Pastoral Zone, cattle grazing is the dominant form of land use in the northern tropical part, while sheep grazing predominates in the southern non-tropical section.

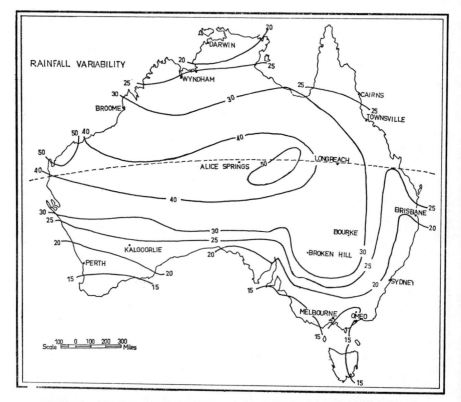

Map 2-2: Rainfall Variability. The annual rainfalls were tabulated, and their departures from the mean obtained in each year. These departures (ignoring sign) were then averaged, and the result expressed as a percentage of the total rainfall. Thus at Sydney the average rainfall for 75 years is 48·5 inches. The average departure is 9·5 inches, or 20 per cent. This last figure is plotted on the chart. All values have been calculated over at least 40 years. This map, first printed in *The Australian Environment*, is revised from an early version by Griffith Taylor. (Reproduced by permission of Melbourne University Press, from S. M. Wadham, R. Kent Wilson and Joyce Wood, *Land Utilization in Australia*, 1964)

The land with a growing season of more than five months south of the tropic is limited to the eastern coast of the continent and to its south-eastern and south-western corners. It can be subdivided into two regions. One is capable of sustaining exotic perennial plants which require sufficient moisture for growth for at least nine months. The other region, with a growing season of from five to nine months, will only support annual exotic pastures and crops. Together, these two regions comprise 460 million acres of land, but only 390 million acres can be regarded as potentially arable land. Either topography or the skeletal soils of the remaining 70 million acres prevent cultivation.[7]

The distribution of potential arable land with growing seasons of different length is shown in Table 2-1. Of the area which is used for any purpose other than sparse grazing, 98 per cent is south of the tropic. Most of the agricultural production in this southern area depends on the soil having adequate moisture during the winter months. Cereals, particularly wheat, can only be grown where there is adequate moisture during the winter months. Pasture species capable of intensive grazing are limited to perennial grasses and clovers such as rye grass, paspalum, kikuyu grass, phalaris and white clover, or to annual grasses and clovers such as Wimmera rye grass, subterranean clover and medics which depend on winter rainfall. In recent years, more research has been directed at finding species of grasses and legumes which will provide adequate pasture in summer rainfall areas, but as yet these species are not widely used.

VEGETATION

The region of Australia with a growing season of more than nine months was originally covered with dense eucalypt forest, with a heavy undergrowth of other species. These forests are extremely expensive to clear either with hand labour or with mechanical devices.

The region with a growing season of from five to nine months was mainly a savannah woodland of sparse medium-sized eucalypt species or dense stands of small eucalypts (Mallee scrub) or acacia species (Brigalow). These types of vegetation can be cleared cheaply, although regrowth continues to be a major problem in the Brigalow country.

SOILS

Almost all Australian soils are deficient in phosphorus and nitrogen; the deficiency is greatest where rainfall is heaviest (i.e. in regions with the longest growing season). The main exceptions are isolated areas of recently formed alluvial, volcanic and forest soils.

In the early days of land settlement in Australia, little was known of the mineral deficiencies of Australian soils, and only isolated areas of fertile soils

7. B. R. Davidson, 'The Distribution of Agricultural Land in Australia', *Journal of the Australian Institute of Agricultural Science*, Vol 27, No 4, December 1961.

Table 2-1
Potential Arable Land, Areas
(million acres)

Length of growing season	More than nine months				Five to nine months			Total area in all moisture zones	Per cent of total area in each State
Number of months within the specified growing season with $P/SD^{0.75} > 8$	8 or more	4-8	4	4[a]	4-8	4	4[a]		
TROPICAL									
Northern Territory	—	—	—	—	17·9	—	—	17·9	25
Queensland	—	2·1	—	—	19·0	2·6	29·5	53·2	75
Western Australia	—	—	—	—	—	—	—	—	—
Total	—	2·1	—	—	36·9	2·6	29·5	71·1	100
Per cent of total tropical	—	3·0	—	—	52·0	4·0	41·0	100·0	—
TEMPERATE									
Queensland	2·8	14·7	5·4	8·5	—	2·8	46·4	80·6	26
Western Australia	—	4·0	—	—	36·0	12·0	—	52·0	16
New South Wales	28·3	30·7	7·8	—	14·0	28·1	—	108·9	35
Victoria	8·5	10·2	—	—	16·9	7·0	—	42·6	13
South Australia	—	0·3	—	—	10·8	12·1	—	23·2	7
Tasmania	6·6	1·8	—	—	—	—	—	8·4	3
Total	46·2	61·7	13·2	8·5	77·7	62·0	46·4	315·7	100
Per cent of total temperate	14·0	19·0	4·0	3·0	25·0	20·0	15·0	100	
Total Australia	46·2	63·8	13·2	8·5	114·6	64·6	75·9	386·8	
Per cent of total Australia	12·0	16·0	3·0	2·0	30·0	17·0	20·0	100	

a. Regions with a broken growing season of the length specified.

SOURCE: B. R. Davidson, 'The Distribution of Agricultural Land in Australia', *Journal of the Australian Institute of Agricultural Science*, Vol 27, No 4, December 1961.

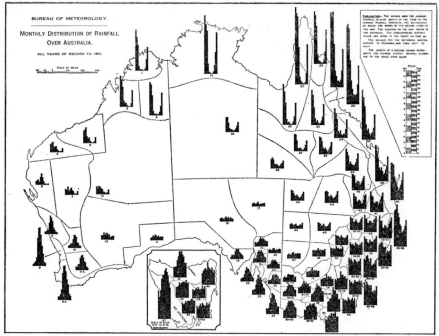

Map 2-3: Monthly Distribution of Rainfall. (*Year Book*, No 52, 1966, Bureau of Census and Statistics)

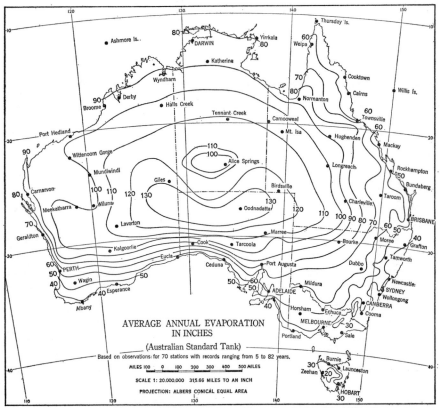

Map 2-4: Average Annual Evaporation. (*Year Book*, No 52, 1966, Bureau of Census and Statistics)

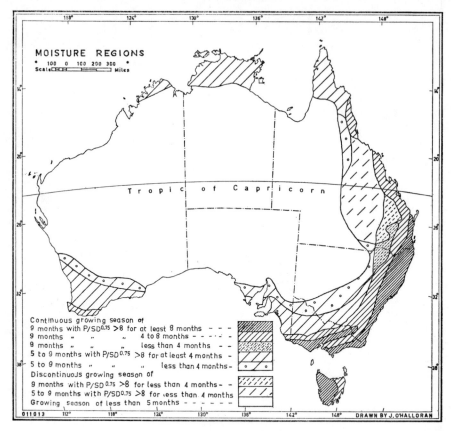

MOISTURE REGIONS
100   0   100 200 300
Scale ⊏⊐⊏⊐ ⊏⊐⊏⊐ Miles

T r o p i c   o f   C a p r i c o r n

Continuous growing season of
9 months with P/SD⁰·⁷⁵ >8 for at least 8 months – – –
9 months   „   „   „   4 to 8 months – – · – ·
9 months   „   „   „   less than 4 months – – –
5 to 9 months with P/SD⁰·⁷⁵ >8 for at least 4 months –
5 to 9 months   „   „   „   less than 4 months –
Discontinuous growing season of
9 months with P/SD⁰·⁷⁵ >8 for less than 4 months – –
5 to 9 months with P/SD⁰·⁷⁵ >8 for less than 4 months
Growing season of less than 5 months – – – – – –

DRAWN BY J. O'HALLORAN

Map 2-5: Moisture Regions

were cleared in the region with a growing season of more than nine months. This region originally produced most of Australia's food crops, but is now used almost exclusively for dairying on perennial pastures in southern Australia and for sugar cane in northern Australia.

Most of Australia's sheep were originally pastured in the savannah woodland areas towards the inland, because these areas were much cheaper to clear; and the wetter part, where the soils are poorer, is still used for wool or mutton production and for beef raising. The drier parts contained large areas of red brown earths where wheat could be produced once the problems of mechanical harvesting and suitable varieties were solved. The discovery of phosphate deficiency in these soils and the application of superphosphate to wheat in the 1890s, established them as part of Australia's wheat belt. The wheat belt was extended in the 1920s when the Mallee lands on their drier inland margin were cleared and brought into production.

The widespread use of annual legumes, subterranean clover and several

36

species of medic, in the 1930s and 1940s intensified rather than altered the existing pattern of farming. Legumes and superphosphate increased the carrying capacity of pastures in the high rainfall region and enabled sheep to be grazed in the wheat belt. The use of legumes in rotation with wheat solved the problem of declining soil nitrogen levels. In the 1940s and 1950s, some undeveloped parts of the wheat belt and of the high rainfall region were brought into production when it was discovered that they required trace elements such as molybdenum, zinc and copper, as well as phosphate.

FARMING AND GRAZING ZONES

The specialized farming zones, producing sugar, dairy products, sheep and beef, and wheat and sheep, together with the Pastoral Zone are shown in Map 2-6. The relation between land use and the length of growing season can be seen by comparing Map 2-5 with Map 2-6. The irrigation of 2 million acres of land has enabled dairying, fruit, rice, cotton and sugar production to be carried out in areas with a growing season of less than nine months. Most of this area is adjacent to the Murray and Murrumbidgee rivers in south-eastern Australia, but smaller irrigation schemes exist elsewhere. (See Map 2-6 and Map 12-2.)

Because Australian agriculture is so highly specialized, there is a greater uniformity in the type of farming or grazing practised within any one farming zone than in most European 'type of farming' areas. The farm unit may vary in area, size of output, and level of development, but the agricultural techniques used are remarkably uniform in any one zone. Even in irrigated regions, where a greater range of production possibilities exists, not many different commodities are produced because of the limited local markets.

The capital invested in farms, the costs incurred and the returns obtained by farmers in most farming zones have been estimated in economic surveys carried out by the Bureau of Agricultural Economics (BAE). The physical and financial results of these surveys in each Australian State are shown in Tables 2-4 to 2-8 and in Table 2-10. The detailed financial structure of farming in each farming zone based on the BAE surveys is shown in Table 2-3.

Although the surveys were carried out over different periods of time (from 1957 to 1964) in different farming zones, they are the only studies which give any indication of the physical and financial structure of the different types of farming on an Australia-wide basis.

The same surveys can also be used in conjunction with the BAE's index of farm costs and prices and the crop and livestock statistics of the Bureau of Census and Statistics to estimate the total agricultural output from each zone.[8] The exact method of calculation varies with the zone and the product concerned.

8. *Personal communication,* Bureau of Agricultural Economics.

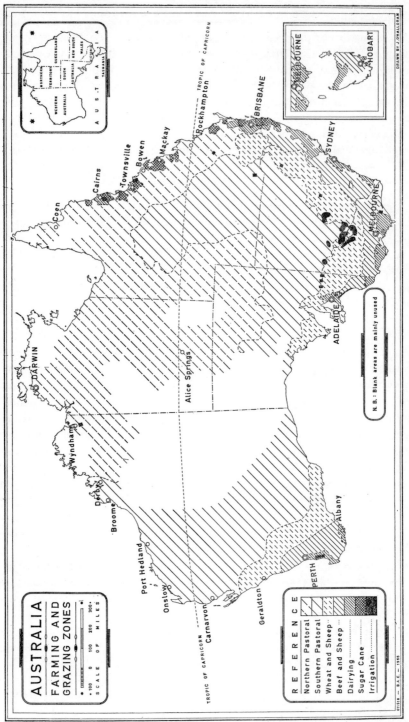

Map 2-6: Farming and Grazing Zones

The Southern Pastoral, and Wheat and Sheep Zones shown in Map 2-6 are synonymous with the BAE Pastoral Zone and Wheat-Sheep Zones.[9] The Beef and Sheep Zone is slightly smaller than the High Rainfall Zone of the BAE survey, as it excludes those shires where the revenue from dairy cattle exceeded the combined revenue from sheep and beef.[10] A comparison of the physical and economic structure of farming in the different zones reveals that any zone with a shorter growing season has larger holdings, a higher production per holding, and a higher net average farm income than a zone with a longer growing season. The converse is true of production per acre which increases as the growing season increases. Thus average farm income is highest in zones with a low and unreliable rainfall where yields are lowest. Somewhat ironically, a higher proportion of the nation's low-income farmers are in zones with a long growing season, where the highest crop and animal yields are obtained. (See Tables 2-3 to 2-8.)

THE PASTORAL ZONE

Large-scale sheep and cattle grazing is Australia's oldest form of land use. The Pastoral Zone can be looked upon as the area of Australia where the European settler has so far failed to find a more lucrative form of land use than that with which he first succeeded in early days of settlement. In this Zone, little attempt has been made to alter the original vegetation, apart from ecological changes which have occurred through the introduction of grazing animals and the partial clearing of forests, where they existed. Livestock exist by grazing native grasses, herbs or shrubs. In much of the Zone livestock rely on artesian bores as a source of water, but in other parts, earth tanks have been constructed to store water.

The Pastoral Zone is also unique in Australian agriculture because it depends on employed rather than on family labour. Many of the properties, particularly those in remote areas, are operated by a manager employed by large pastoral companies which supply the necessary capital for plant and livestock. On cattle stations in the Northern Territory and Western Australia, aborigines form more than half of the labour force.[11]

The southern non-tropical section of the Pastoral Zone is predominantly grazed by sheep and the northern tropical section is grazed entirely by cattle. Those two areas form two distinct sub-zones with different physical and economic characteristics.

The Northern Pastoral Sub-zone. This sub-zone, with a usable area of 287 million acres, contains practically all of the land north of the Tropic of

9. *The Australian Sheep Industry Survey, 1960-61 to 1962-63,* Bureau of Agricultural Economics, 1965.

10. Surveys published by the Bureau of Agricultural Economics have formed the basis of many of the tables and calculations in the following discussion, but the author is entirely responsible for the conclusions drawn.

11. *Year Book,* No 51, 1965, p 981, Bureau of Census and Statistics.

Capricorn. Only the isolated areas of fertile soil used for dairying and sugar production on the Queensland coast are excluded. It also contains the areas of Mulga scrub south of the tropic in the Northern Territory. (See Map 2-6.)

Table 2-2
Pastoral and Farming Zones, Areas

	Total area m. acres	Area used m. acres	Per cent used
Pastoral			
Northern (beef only)	{ 1,500·0	654·3	55·2
Southern (sheep and beef)		287·4	24·3
Wheat and sheep	175·3	132·0	11·2
Beef and sheep	126·2	75·0	6·3
Dairy	98·5	32·2	2·7
Sugar	1·0	1·0	0·1
Irrigation	2·6	2·6	0·2
TOTAL	1,903·6	1,184·5	100·0

SOURCES: *The Australian Sheep Industry Survey*, 1960-61 to 1962-63, Bureau of Agricultural Economics, 1965; and *Year Book*, No 51, 1965, Bureau of Census and Statistics.

The 287 million acres of land used for grazing cattle in the northern pastoral sub-zone comprise one-quarter of the total land used for rural production in Australia and supports one-third of the nation's beef cattle. Yet these lands only produce 15 per cent of the nation's beef and less than 2 per cent of the nation's total rural output.[12] The harsh environment and the isolation of the sub-zone limit its productivity. In the postwar years a great deal of scientific research has been devoted to finding methods of developing this area, and in more recent years favourable beef prices and new methods of pasture development have encouraged higher rates of development.

In the spear grass (*Heteropogon contortus*) country on the Queensland coast where the rainfall ranges between 80 and 100 inches, cattle are carried at the rate of 20 to 30 beasts per square mile. In north-central Queensland in the Mitchell grass (*Astrebla squarrosa*) and Flinders grass (*Iseilema* spp) country, the rainfall is between 20 and 50 inches per annum, and the carrying capacity is between 10 and 20 beasts per square mile. On the other hand, Cape York Peninsula and the northern part of the Northern Territory have carrying capacities of 3 beasts per square mile, although the annual rainfall exceeds 40 inches. Even the Mulga scrub (*Acacia aneura*) in the Alice Springs area with an annual rainfall of 10 inches carries 6 beasts per square mile.[13]

12. B. R. Davidson, *The Northern Myth*, Melbourne University Press, Melbourne 1965, p 88; and also B. R. Davidson: Unpublished data.

13. C. S. Christian in *The Australian Environment*, Melbourne University Press, Melbourne 1960; and W. A. Beattie, *The Beef Cattle Industry in Australia*, Commonwealth Scientific and Industrial Research Organization, Bulletin No 278, Melbourne 1956, p 26.

Properties increase in size as carrying capacity decreases, and range from 10,000 acres in the spear grass country on the Queensland coast to approximately 1·5 to 2 million acres in the Northern Territory and Western Australia. Some large companies operate groups of stations with a total area of more than 10 million acres. In the Northern Territory and Western Australia, most of the holdings are unfenced and much of the land is leased from the government at a low rental. Despite some improvement in recent years, husbandry is largely limited to mustering, branding and drafting-off the finished cattle for market.

The quality of the grazing is extremely low and deteriorates progressively during the dry season; cattle lose weight during this period and do not regain it until the following wet season.[14] Because of this alternate gain and loss in weight, cattle in the remote areas are not ready for market or strong enough to survive the long walk to the abattoirs or the railhead until they are five or six years of age, and the quality of the meat produced is poor. Abattoirs exist along the Queensland coast, at Katherine and Darwin in the Northern Territory, and at Wyndham, Derby and Broome in Western Australia. Some cattle stations in the Northern Territory also send large numbers of store cattle for fattening in Queensland.[15] Cattle from the Alice Springs area are marketed in Adelaide. The total number of cattle in different parts of the sub-zone and their movement is shown in Map 2-7.

The Southern Pastoral Sub-zone. The southern part of the Pastoral Zone comprises 654 million acres of land with a growing season of less than five months. Most of the sub-zone is south of the Tropic of Capricorn. (See Map 2-6.)

The southern pastoral sub-zone supports 48 million sheep and 3 million cattle, or approximately 30 per cent of the sheep and 20 per cent of the total beef cattle in Australia. Although the sub-zone occupies some 25 per cent of the land used for agriculture in Australia, it only produces about 10 per cent of the nation's total rural production, mainly because the number of livestock which can be carried per acre is extremely low.[16]

The rates of stocking and the average size of holding in various parts of the southern pastoral sub-zone are shown in Table 2-3. Holdings range in size from 5,000 acres in areas where 1 sheep can be carried on every 5 acres, to over a million acres where cattle are grazed at a rate of 3 beasts per square mile and sheep at the rate of 1 per 100 acres. Generally, holdings are larger and stocking rates lower in the drier areas.

14. M. J. T. Norman and W. Arndt, *Performance of Beef Cattle on Native and Sown Pastures at Katherine, N.T.*, Commonwealth Scientific and Industrial Research Organization, Land Research and Regional Survey Technical Paper No 4, Melbourne 1959.

15. *Northern Territory Report for 1964-65*, Department of Territories, Canberra, pp 30-3.

16. *The Australian Sheep Industry Survey 1960-61 to 1962-63*, Bureau of Agricultural Economics, 1965, p 10; and also B. R. Davidson: Unpublished data.

Table 2-3

Economic Structure of Farms in Each Zone, Various Periods

	Southern Pastoral 1960-63 %	Wheat and sheep 1960-63 %	Sheep and beef 1960-63 %	Dairying Whole milk 1961-64 %	Dairying Butterfat 1961-64 %	Irrigation Rice farms 1957-59 %	Irrigation Sheep farms 1957-59 %
CAPITAL							
Land	39·9	54·9	58·9	55·3	49·4	61·5	64·2
Improvements	27·5	17·2	15·2	15·5	17·0	12·1	11·3
Plant	7·1	13·5	9·1	10·8	10·8	11·0	6·9
Sheep	21·2	10·9	12·0	—	—	} 15·4	} 17·6
Beef cattle	4·1	3·3	4·7	—	—		
Dairy cattle[a]	—	—	—	18·4	22·8	—	—
Other	0·2	0·2	0·1	—	—	—	—
Total	100·0	100·0	100·0	100·0	100·0	100·0	100·0
RETURNS							
Wool	79·9	38·0	59·8	} 2·2	} 3·1	17·5	41·6
Sheep	10·8	13·3	14·2			13·5	29·0
Cattle	8·1	7·3	14·4	4·3	10·6	8·0	19·9
Wheat	—	30·7	—	—	—	2·3	4·2
Rice	—	—	—	—	—	52·2	—
Other crops[b]	—	6·3	5·7	7·1	4·3	6·2	4·5
Dairy products	—	—	—	79·8	64·9	—	—
Pigs	—	—	—	0·8	12·4	—	—
Other	1·2	4·4	5·9	5·8	4·7	0·3	0·8
Total	100·0	100·0	100·0	100·0	100·0	100·0	100·0

Costs							
Labour	40·9	36·6	40·8	39·0	51·7	27·4	28·6
Machinery and fuel	9·2	14·6	10·0	12·1	10·5	16·2	18·2
Water	—	—	—	—	—	13·8	10·3
Fertilizer	0·1	5·7	9·5	3·7	3·1	5·1	6·1
Seed	0·3	1·5	1·3	1·2	1·1	3·5	2·4
Other crops	—	0·9	—	1·2	1·1	3·4	1·2
Fodder	1·6	1·8	1·3	14·0	7·6	0·2	0·6
Other livestock	13·7	8·0	9·8	2·5	2·1	4·6	2·4
Fixed	34·2	30·9	27·3	26·3	22·8	25·8	30·2
Total	100·0	100·0	100·0	100·0	100·0	100·0	100·0

a. Includes other livestock on dairy farms.

b. Includes all crops, except wheat on wheat and sheep farms, and rice on rice farms.

Sources: Adapted from the following publications of the Bureau of Agricultural Economics:

The Australian Sheep Industry Survey, 1960-61 to 1962-63; 'Some Initial Results of the Australian Dairy Industry Survey 1961-62 to 1963-64', *Quarterly Review of Agricultural Economics*, Vol 18, No 4, October 1965; 'Some Further Initial Results of the Australian Dairy Industry Survey', *Quarterly Review of Agricultural Economics*, Vol 19, No 1, January 1966; *Riverina Continuous Farm Study*, 1957-58 and 1958-59.

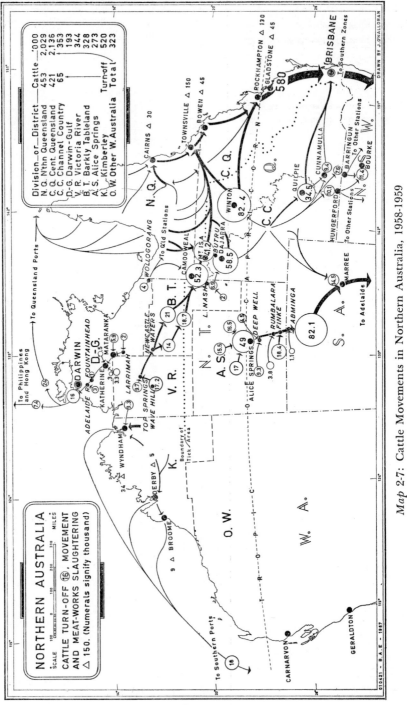

Map 2:7: Cattle Movements in Northern Australia, 1958-1959

Capital equipment is limited to fences, bores, yards and motor vehicles. As stock are not hand fed, machinery other than motor vehicles is not required. Buildings are limited to housing and shearing sheds. The distribution of capital on properties in the zone is shown in Table 2-3.

Animal husbandry is limited to mustering, dipping for pest control, shearing and marking sheep. Consequently, a small labour force can handle large numbers of sheep grazing over a vast acreage. Shearing is carried out by contractors who also employ the additional labour required at shearing time. Because average lambing percentages are low, and livestock mortality is high during droughts, sheep are retained in the flock for a longer period than in other zones. These two factors result in a low turn-off of sheep. As hand feeding is often uneconomical during droughts, losses of over 30 per cent of both sheep and cattle have occurred in severe droughts, which in the past have occurred every 20 or 30 years.

In spite of the low output per acre in the southern pastoral sub-zone, net return per unit of capital is as high as in other zones. The financial and physical structure of sheep properties in different parts of the southern pastoral sub-zone are shown in Tables 2-3 and 2-4.

In Western and South Australia where sheep are grazed in semi-desert regions, stocking rates are lower than in other States. Variations in the profitability of grazing between the different States are determined by the output per sheep, the size of flock and the value of land.[17] The average flock size is smaller in New South Wales than in Western Australia, but the higher output per sheep offsets this. As most pastoral land in Western Australia is leased, the amount of farmer capital invested in land is low compared with the other States, where a larger proportion of properties is privately owned. A better comparison of the relative efficiency of resource use in each State can be obtained by comparing the returns to capital, excluding investment in land and land clearing. When this adjustment is made, New South Wales and South Australia, the States with the highest output per sheep, emerge with the highest return to capital. (See Table 2-4.)

One of the puzzling features of the Pastoral Zone is its inability to attract more capital for permanent improvements in fencing and water supplies for stock. Some research work suggests that the marginal returns for investment in these assets is extremely high.[18] It is possible that the high risks of the Pastoral Zone coupled with the insecurity of land tenure have discouraged investment. There is also a lack of research results indicating the exact increase in returns which might be expected from particular improvements.

The southern pastoral sub-zone illustrates how appropriate forms of land

17. F. H. Gruen, 'The Profitability of Wool Growing: A Comparison of Different Zones', *Farm Policy*, Vol 4, No 2, September 1964.

18. J. H. Duloy, 'The Allocation of Resources in the Woolgrowing Industry', *Australian Journal of Agricultural Economics*, Vol 5, No 2, December 1961.

use can be developed to establish an efficient form of agriculture in a harsh environment. It is efficient because although output per unit of land is low, it uses few resources other than land and livestock, and output per man is high.

Table 2-4

Southern Pastoral Zone: Physical and Financial Characteristics of Properties, 1960-61 to 1962-63

	Qld.	N.S.W.	S.A.	W.A.
Area of holding (acres)	35,465	29,524	58,723	443,212
Sheep per farm (no.)	6,636	5,123	3,206	9,096
Cattle per farm (no.)	159	114	86	140
Sheep Units per 100 acres[a]	22·3	20·5	6·6	2·3
Wool per sheep (lbs)	8·7	10·0	11·0	8·6
	$	$	$	$
Capital	151,879	167,099	104,782	124,235
Gross returns	32,942	34,334	21,838	45,528
Costs[b]	25,704	21,092	14,744	32,460
Net return	7,238	13,242	7,094	13,068
	%	%	%	%
Net return on capital including land	4·8	7·9	6·8	10·5
Net return as a per cent of total capital excluding land	7·2	14·5	11·2	10·8

a. Sheep Units = number of sheep + (number of cattle × 8).
b. Including an allowance for the operator at the ruling wage rate, but excluding interest.

Source: Adapted from *The Australian Sheep Industry Survey*, 1960-61 to 1962-63, Bureau of Agricultural Economics, 1965.

THE WHEAT AND SHEEP ZONE

Although the Wheat and Sheep Zone is entirely within the region with a five to nine months' growing season and only occupies 11 per cent of the land in Australia used for crop and livestock production, it produces one-third of the nation's agricultural output. In addition to producing most of the nation's wheat, the Zone supported 61 million sheep or approximately 40 per cent of the nation's sheep and 2·8 million or 20 per cent of the nation's beef cattle in 1964.[19] In the south of the continent, wheat can be produced with a growing season as short as five months; but in the north where summer rainfall predominates, summer fallowing to conserve moisture is neces-

19. *The Australian Sheep Industry Survey 1960-61 to 1962-63*, Bureau of Agricultural Economics, 1965, p 36; and also B. R. Davidson: Unpublished data.

sary. With the introduction of subterranean clover in the 1930s, rotations of clover and wheat were developed over large parts of the southern section of the wheat belt. More recently other pasture legumes have also been used and mixed sheep and wheat farming has become the normal practice. Soils vary widely in this region, but self-mulching chernozems, red brown earths and Mallee sands are the dominant types. With the exception of some chernozems, all are deficient in phosphate and many of the sands require trace elements.

The area of most commercial wheat and sheep farms varies between 500 and 5,000 acres. Farms are smaller in the wetter areas and larger in the drier parts of the Zone. Both wheat yields and sheep carrying capacity decline as rainfall decreases, and it is necessary to operate on a larger scale in the drier areas to maintain the same return to capital as in the areas with higher rainfall. Furthermore the variability of rainfall increases as rainfall decreases and the risk of crop failure as well as the loss of sheep through drought is highest in the driest parts of the wheat belt.

The physical and financial structure of farms in the Wheat and Sheep Zone of the different States is shown in Tables 2-3 and 2-5. By European standards the yield of wheat is low, but Australian farmers are able to sell wheat competitively in world markets because they operate on a large scale. Output per man and per unit of machinery is far higher than on most European farms, and slightly higher than on North American farms.[20]

In the wetter parts of the wheat belt, prime lambs are produced. This form of sheep farming, in conjunction with wheat growing, predominates in Victoria and New South Wales where large local markets exist for meat. Approximately half of the properties in these two States run prime lamb producing flocks. In the less populated States, sheep are mainly kept for wool production.[21]

The Wheat and Sheep Zone produces one-third of Australia's agricultural output.[22] Sheep provide approximately half the total revenue of farms in all parts of the Zone, but they are more important in Queensland and New South Wales. Cattle are of minor importance in all States except Queensland. The cost structure is relatively uniform in all States.

A small proportion of wheat is grown on a share basis. The share farmer usually provides all the machinery and an agreed proportion of the fuel, seed

20. *The Farm as a Business*, Part 6, Ministry of Agriculture, Fisheries and Food, London 1963, pp 5-9; J. C. MacKenzie, 'Farm Mechanization and Labour in the South Central Red River Valley of Manitoba', *Economic Annalist*, Vol 23, No 6, December 1953; I. H. Ellis and N. L. Ulsaker, *Crop Input Output Relationships*, Department of Agricultural Economics, North Dakota Agricultural College, Bulletin No 409, June 1957; and G. J. Tyler, 'Labour Requirements on Wheat Farms in the North Western Slopes of N.S.W.', *Review of Marketing and Agricultural Economics*, Vol 31, No 2, June 1963.

21. *The Australian Sheep Industry Survey 1960-61 to 1962-63*, Bureau of Agricultural Economics, 1965, p 44.

22. B. R. Davidson: Unpublished data.

and fertilizer. The owner provides the remaining proportion of the variable inputs and the land. Returns are divided between share farmers and land-owners on various bases. Share farming is usually restricted to the wheat enterprise and is not used in the sheep enterprise.

Table 2-5

Wheat and Sheep Zone: Physical and Financial Characteristics of Farms, 1960-61 to 1962-63

	Qld.	N.S.W.	Vic.	S.A.	W.A.
Area of farm (acres)	4,018	2,153	2,170	2,151	3,566
Land use	%	%	%	%	%
Wheat	4·7	11·7	13·1	9·8	13·6
Other crops	3·7	4·8	5·1	8·1	7·8
Improved pasture	2·0	28·2	34·6	19·5	29·0
Native pasture	89·6	55·3	47·2	62·6	49·6
Total	100·0	100·0	100·0	100·0	100·0
Sheep per farm (no.)	1,666	1,710	808	802	1,486
Cattle per farm (no.)	72	51	36	35	35
Wheat yield per acre (bush.)[a]	20·5	18·9	21·3	17·4	14·4
Sheep Units per acre of pasture[b]	0·6	1·2	0·6	0·6	0·6
Wool per sheep (lbs)	8·4	8·8	8·8	10·3	8·0
	$	$	$	$	$
Capital	94,351	95,115	61,704	49,860	67,637
Gross returns	14,778	18,290	11,384	11,026	18,120
Costs[c]	11,200	12,862	8,332	8,342	11,810
Net return	3,578	5,428	3,052	2,684	6,310
	%	%	%	%	%
Net return on capital	3·8	5·7	4·9	5·4	9·3

a. Average State yields 1955-56 to 1965-66.
b. Sheep Units = number of sheep + (number of cattle × 8).
c. Including an allowance for the operator at the ruling wage rate, but excluding interest.
SOURCES: Adapted from *The Australian Sheep Industry Survey*, 1957-58 to 1959-60 and 1960-61 to 1962-63, Bureau of Agricultural Economics.

The Australian Wheat and Sheep Zone could be expanded into both drier and wetter regions. Approximately 6 million acres of undeveloped land are suitable for wheat production in Western Australia and could be cleared and brought into production.[23] Large areas of uncleared land in the Brigalow belt in Queensland are suitable for wheat production.[24] Wheat varieties with a

23. J. S. Nalson and A. W. Hogstrum, 'Farm Population and Land Development in Western Australia', *Farm Policy*, Vol 4, No 4, March 1965.
24. *The Economics of Brigalow Development in the Fitzroy Basin*, Bureau of Agricultural Economics, 1963.

shorter growing reason and legumes adapted to drier conditions would allow a further expansion of the dry margin of this Zone, particularly in Western Australia where rainfall is less variable than in the eastern States.

THE SHEEP AND BEEF ZONE

The wetter portion of the savannah woodlands, with a growing season of more than six months has always supported a large proportion of Australia's sheep flocks. In 1964, 50 million sheep or approximately 30 per cent of Australia's flocks and 3·6 million or 25 per cent of the nation's beef cattle grazed in this Zone. It is only in recent years that the introduction of improved pastures into the Wheat and Sheep Zone has reduced this Zone from the position of maintaining most of Australia's sheep population.

In some respects, the Sheep and Beef Zone is the least developed of all Australia's agricultural zones. Some areas have not been cleared completely or have reverted to eucalypt forest. Many of the soils are leached podsols naturally deficient in phosphorus, nitrogen and sometimes trace elements. Most of the Zone could be sown to perennial grasses and either annual or perennial clovers once these soil deficiencies are remedied. At present, less than two-thirds of the Zone is sown to improved pasture, which could be more heavily stocked. The attitude of many farmers, lack of capital and a shortage of livestock have prevented farmers from taking immediate advantage of recent research work which suggests that improved pastures can be stocked more heavily.[25]

Farm size varies from 10,000 acres to 100 or 200 acres. The latter are no longer economic units and incomes are so low that it is difficult to find capital for improvements. On large holdings the economic incentive is often lacking as a satisfactory income can be earned by grazing a large number of sheep at a low stocking rate.

Beef cattle have always been run in conjunction with sheep in this Zone. The proportion of cattle to sheep has normally varied with the relative prices of wool and meat which, until recently, have favoured sheep production.

Where pastures have been improved, prime lamb production is often more important than wool production. Ewe flocks on prime lamb farms may consist of dual purpose breeds such as the Corriedale or Polwarth. These breeds were developed by fixing crosses between the Merino and the English longwool breeds of sheep. Approximately 40 per cent of ewe flocks in the Zone produce prime lambs. Only 10 per cent of prime lambs are exported, the remainder are consumed locally.

The physical and financial characteristics of farms in the Beef and Sheep Zone in each State are shown in Tables 2-3 and 2-6.

Capital equipment in the Sheep and Beef Zone is mainly in the form of

25. *Rural Research in CSIRO*, Commonwealth Scientific and Industrial Research Organization, No 52, 1965, pp 2-9.

fencing and water supplies. Buildings are limited to shearing, hay, and machinery sheds. Both sheep and cattle can graze throughout the year and hand feeding is normally limited to drought feeding using purchased grain or hay made on the property. A high proportion of the total capital is invested in livestock. As the Zone is relatively moist, sheep must be protected against internal parasites, foot rot and blow flies. The major cost items are family labour and superphosphate for pastures. Because livestock rely almost entirely on grazing very little cropping is necessary, so that machinery and feed costs are low.

Although many farms produce prime lambs, wool is the source of over 50 per cent of the revenue of farms. Sales of beef, prime lambs and surplus sheep are of secondary importance to wool in all parts of the Zone. (See Table 2-3.) Land values are high, and returns to capital including land are lower than in other zones. There is little doubt that farm incomes could be increased by

Table 2-6

Sheep and Beef Zone: Physical and Financial Characteristics of Farms, 1960-61 to 1962-63

	N.S.W.	Vic.	Tas.	S.A.	W.A.
Area of farm (acres)	1,584	824	1,835	980	1,449
Land use	%	%	%	%	%
Crops	3·2	4·3	2·6	9·1	14·2
Improved pasture	46·8	73·8	22·3	72·4	63·7
Native pasture	48·7	19·8	59·8	16·6	17·4
Not used	1·3	2·1	15·3	1·9	4·7
Total	100·0	100·0	100·0	100·0	100·0
Sheep per farm (no.)	1,682	1,218	1,167	1,176	1,323
Cattle per farm (no.)	83	59	53	52	44
Sheep Units per acre of pasture[a]	1·5	2·2	1·0	1·8	1·4
Wool per sheep (lbs)	8·9	7·9	7·5	9·3	9·1
	$	$	$	$	$
Capital	85,875	69,889	57,026	59,836	51,099
Gross returns	13,294	10,330	10,066	10,340	11,254
Costs[b]	10,478	8,116	9,296	8,102	8,348
Net return	2,816	2,214	778	2,238	2,904
	%	%	%	%	%
Net return on capital	3·3	3·2	1·4	3·7	5·7

a. Sheep Units = number of sheep + (number of cattle × 8).
b. Including an allowance for the operator at the ruling wage rate, but excluding interest.

SOURCE: Adapted from *The Australian Sheep Industry Survey*, 1960-61 to 1962-63, Bureau of Agricultural Economics, 1965.

increasing stocking rates in this Zone, even at lower prices for wool and meat than those now prevailing.

THE DAIRY ZONE

Most of Australia's 3·0 million milking cows and 1·6 million young dairy cattle are restricted to irrigation areas and to those regions where the soil moisture is sufficient to sustain plant growth for at least nine months of the year. The location of these dairying areas is shown in Map 2-6. The non-irrigated dairy areas were originally covered with heavy eucalypt forest. As little was known of soil deficiencies, only the fertile alluvial flats, recent volcanic soil and forest soils were cleared. Consequently, most of these dairy-ing areas are clearings within a forest. In some areas, as in the Strzelecki ranges in Victoria, the whole forest was cleared as all of the soil was fertile.

Herds may contain as many as 200 cows, but the average herd size is approximately 50 cows, milked mechanically by family labour.

In the southern dairying areas, cows obtain most of their fodder by grazing improved pastures consisting of white clover and perennial rye grass. Most of the pasture is top dressed with superphosphate. Grazing is supplemented with hay or silage during the winter, but by European standards the amount of hand feeding is small. One ton of hay per cow is the average amount of fodder conserved in most southern dairy areas.

In the northern dairying areas in Queensland and northern New South Wales dairy pastures are paspalum and kikuyu grass dominant, but much more reliance is placed on fodder crops in this area. Less hay is conserved and greater amounts of concentrates are fed.

From an economic point of view the dairying industry is divided into two distinct sectors, based on the marketing arrangements as described in Chap-ter 14, depending on whether the milk is used for whole milk consumption as such, or is used to manufacture butter or milk products.

Fresh milk for local consumption is produced in definite areas which are close to the capital cities in most States. The amount of whole milk farmers in these areas can sell at the domestic price is limited by a quota, and the excess must be sold at the lower manufacturing price.

The physical and financial structure of farms producing whole milk in the various States is shown in Tables 2-3 and 2-7. Variations in farm income are caused by the different prices paid for whole milk by the various milk boards in the different States, the proportion of total milk produced which farmers are able to sell at whole milk prices, and by environmental factors. Gross returns are low in Queensland because of the low output per cow, but high in Victoria and Tasmania where yields per cow are high. South Australia and Tasmania are unique as whole milk production is coupled with fruit and vegetable production. The unsuitable environment reduces the profitability of dairy farming in Queensland. The smaller herds in South Australia and

Tasmania are less profitable than the larger herds in Victoria and New South Wales. (See Table 2-7.)

Except in Queensland, whole milk producers earn a satisfactory income because they are protected from competition from other farmers outside the whole milk area by milk marketing regulations, and from the more efficient farmers within the area by the individual quota system.

Table 2-7

Dairy Zone: Whole Milk Area: Physical and Financial Characteristics of Farms, 1961-62 to 1963-64

	Qld.	N.S.W.	Vic.	Tas.	S.A.	W.A.
Area of holding (acres)	433	325	202	263	273	470
Land use	%	%	%	%	%	%
Natural pasture	52	52	3	6	13	9
Sown pasture	11	25	89	49	59	76
Crops	7	6	6	10	11	3
Fruit	—	—	—	1	7	—
Other	30	17	2	34	10	12
Total	100	100	100	100	100	100
Dairy cows (no.)	55	59	63	39	35	82
Total cattle (no.)	87	90	84	62	52	124
Milk per dairy cow (gals)	342	495	606	623	563	476
Area of crops and pastures per dairy cow (acres)	5·5	4·6	3·1	4·4	6·5	5·1
	$	$	$	$	$	$
Capital	27,179	35,696	44,646	48,394	42,656	79,157
Gross returns	7,648	10,285	11,339	11,790	9,420	14,070
Costs[a]	7,589	8,456	8,542	9,726	7,596	9,929
Net return	59	1,829	2,797	2,064	1,824	4,141
	%	%	%	%	%	%
Net return on capital	0·2	5·1	6·3	4·3	4·3	5·2

a. Including an allowance for the operator at the ruling wage rate and adjusted for the hours worked, but excluding interest.

Sources: Adapted from 'Some Further Initial Results of the Australian Dairy Industry Survey, 1961-62 to 1963-64', *Quarterly Review of Agricultural Economics*, Vol 19, No 1, January 1966; and *Personal communication*, Bureau of Agricultural Economics.

In the butterfat areas, by contrast, incomes are normally low in spite of the extremely heavy direct subsidy and a home support price. (See Table 2-8.) Even in the southern States, where farms have a high proportion of improved perennial pastures, farm incomes are low by Australian standards. This situation might seem surprising as New Zealand farmers have managed to sell butterfat competitively on the European market without any form of subsidy. Most of Australia's dairying areas have a climatic environment which is less favourable to pasture production than New Zealand. This is particularly true of the northern dairying areas in the Zone. Australian dairy herds are smaller than New Zealand herds and in many areas, farms would have to be amalgamated before larger herds could be milked.

Table 2-8

Dairy Zone: Butterfat Area: Physical and Financial Characteristics of Farms, 1961-62 to 1963-64

	Qld.	N.S.W.	Vic.	Tas.	S.A.	W.A.
Area of holding (acres)	577	296	241	439	363	467
Land use	%	%	%	%	%	%
Natural pasture	65	61	26	6	18	10
Sown pasture	10	14	52	34	64	48
Crops	12	3	5	8	9	3
Other	13	22	17	52	9	39
Total	100	100	100	100	100	100
Dairy cows (no.)	55	53	49	44	38	41
Total cattle (no.)	84	78	74	69	62	79
Milk per dairy cow (gals)	364	341	625	520	536	444
Area of crops and pastures per dairy cow	8·4	4·7	4·0	4·6	7·0	7·7
	$	$	$	$	$	$
Capital	31,030	22,940	34,950	38,724	40,248	29,166
Gross returns	6,836	5,356	7,488	7,236	7,046	5,240
Costs[a]	6,134	5,480	6,387	6,464	6,668	5,064
Net return[a]	702	−124	1,101	772	378	176
	%	%	%	%	%	%
Net return on capital	2·3	—	3·2	2·0	0·9	0·6

a. Including an allowance for the operator at the ruling wage rate adjusted for the hours worked, but excluding interest.

SOURCES: Adapted from 'Some Initial Results of the Australian Dairy Survey 1961-62 to 1963-64', *Quarterly Review of Agricultural Economics*, Vol 18, No 4, October 1965; and *Personal communication*, Bureau of Agricultural Economics.

The incomes of farmers producing milk for butterfat are supplemented by revenue from pigs reared on skimmed milk, but the actual contribution of this enterprise to total revenue is small. It is highest in Queensland where cheap grain sorghum is available as a source of feed. Other supplementary enterprises, particularly prime lambs in Tasmania and South Australia and beef production in other States, are just as important as pigs as a source of revenue. These sideline enterprises have been developed in an attempt to solve the problem of low incomes which characterize much of that part of the Australian dairying industry which only produces milk for manufacturing purposes.

THE SUGAR ZONE

Since its establishment south of the tropic in the 1860s, the sugar industry has expanded north of the tropic where higher yields are obtained. Research in the fields of disease control, fertilizer use and the selection of better varieties has led to an increase in the yield of sugar cane per acre and of sugar per ton of sugar cane. Sugar cane is grown on most of the fertile soils along the Queensland coast in the frost-free areas within 50 miles of the east coast. (See Map 2-6.) The crop is mechanically planted and generally ratooned at least once. Most of it is cut by hand, but the proportion harvested mechanically is increasing rapidly.

Published surveys of the costs and returns of sugar farms do not exist, but marketing arrangements and the restriction of acreage have ensured satisfactory profits except in periods of extremely low world prices such as in 1966. Whenever a world sugar shortage has occurred and prices have risen as in the early 1960s, the sugar industry has been allowed to expand but has failed to contract when the world sugar price has fallen.

At first sight the sugar industry appears to be the ideal primary industry for the Australian tropics. Over the years, the area grown and the yield per acre has increased until yields are among the highest in the world. The gross value of the crop is half the total gross value of all rural industry in tropical Queensland and approximately half of the 300,000 people in North Queensland are supported by this industry. However, the sugar industry receives a subsidy in the form of a home support price of approximately $26 million per annum which is equal to 26 per cent of the value of the crop.[26]

IRRIGATION ZONES

Small-scale irrigation schemes have been in operation in south-eastern Australia since 1870 and large-scale water storages were constructed on the Murray and Murrumbidgee rivers between 1910 and 1920.

The location of the various irrigation schemes is shown in Maps 2-6, 12-3. As the Murray-Goulburn-Murrumbidgee-Darling river system is the only large river system in the drier regions of southern Australia, it is not surprising that 2·3 million of Australia's 2·6 million acres of irrigated land are located on these rivers. Utilization of irrigated land in Australia is shown in Table 2-9. Over half of the total area is sown to pastures or fodder crops which are used for dairying and prime lamb production. Rice is the only major cereal crop produced under irrigation and although yields are among the highest

---

26. S. F. Harris, 'Some Measures of Levels of Protection in Australia's Rural Industries', *Australian Journal of Agricultural Economics*, Vol 8, No 2, December 1964.

in the world, rice acreages are restricted and the crop is protected by means of a home support price. Fruits, vines and vegetables occupy the remainder of the irrigated acreage. In recent years, cotton has been produced on irrigation schemes on the Ord and Namoi rivers and tobacco has been grown on the Barwon river. Satisfactory crops have been grown and Australia is now supplying half of its own tobacco and cotton requirements, but both crops require protection.

Table 2-9

Area of Land Irrigated, 1963-1964

	Acres	%
Cotton	4,715	0·2
Hops	1,463	0·1
Orchards	120,902	4·5
Rice	59,331	2·2
Sugar cane	98,204	3·7
Tobacco	14,366	0·5
Vegetables	89,861	3·4
Vineyards	86,987	3·3
Other crops (including fodder and fallow land)	426,669	16·1
Total crops	902,498	34·0
Pastures	1,521,538	57·0
Other	233,761	9·0
TOTAL	2,657,797	100·0

SOURCE: *Year Book,* No 51, 1965, Bureau of Census and Statistics.

Irrigation settlements were designed for intensive farming of Australia's drier areas and farm size was determined by the minimum area considered necessary to maintain the farmer and his family. This was normally 40 acres for fruit and vegetable farms, 600 acres for larger-scale farming such as prime lamb production, and approximately 100 acres for dairying.

In most irrigation schemes water is delivered to the farm by a State government authority. The farm has a specific amount of water allotted to it and additional water can only be purchased after the basic rights of all farmers have been met. Flood and furrow irrigation are the most common methods of applying water in any scheme where water is supplied by the State. Where farmers irrigate by pumping directly from rivers spray irrigation is far more common.

State support has ensured that most irrigation farming is now profitable although many farmers failed to succeed as irrigation farmers, and although in some areas, whole schemes failed because of bad irrigation practice. The physical and financial characteristics of two of the main types of irrigated farms on the Murrumbidgee Irrigation Area are shown in Table 2-10.

Table 2-10

Irrigation Zone: Murrumbidgee Irrigation Area, N.S.W.: Physical and Financial Characteristics of Farms, 1957-58 to 1958-59

	Rice farms	Sheep farms
Area of holding (acres)	1,005	1,794
Area irrigated (acres)	519	400·5
Utilization of irrigated area	%	%
Rice	12·9	—
Other cereals	19·9	12·4
Sown pasture	66·2	84·9
Fodder crop	1·0	2·7
Total	100·0	100·0
	$	$
Capital	83,974	96,600
Returns	19,295	12,700
Costs*a*	11,269	8,217
Net return	8,026	4,483
	%	%
Net return on capital	9·6	4·6

a. Including an allowance for the operator at the award wage rate.

SOURCE: *Riverina Continuous Farm Study, First Annual Report 1957-58. Riverina Continuous Farm Study, Second Annual Report 1958-59.* Bureau of Agricultural Economics.

Even though no large-scale irrigation scheme has been able to recover the initial costs of its headworks, and many farm products produced under irrigation require subsidies, there is continual pressure in Australia for the expansion of this type of farming.

CONCLUSION

The first successful form of land use in Australia was wool production on a large scale. The systems of extensive land use which have evolved are an adaption of European farming to the Australian physical and economic environment. Although more intensive systems of farming are now profitable, the high cost of labour still imposes limits on the price which can be paid for bringing land into production and on the intensity of land use which is profitable. Generally, it is still only extensive large-scale farming which yields satisfactory returns on the capital invested. Intensive farming is only likely to be profitable if techniques are developed which enable large areas of land to be operated with little labour. Land use in Australia is still primarily determined by rainfall and by the markets and transport facilities available.

Chapter 3

INNOVATION IN AGRICULTURE

C. M. Donald

University of Adelaide

When the first grain was sown in Sydney in 1788, Australia's agricultural resources could scarcely have been more meagre—an unknown climate, the miserably poor soil of the Sydney area, convict labour and inexperienced husbandmen. It is not surprising that the first wheat crop was a failure or that the second gave but four bushels of wheat per acre.

Since that time our agricultural resources have vastly increased. We have better plants and animals, more power and machines, and above all we have learnt to raise the fertility of our soils. Though the climate carries serious drought hazards, we have made some progress in adapting our agriculture to its vagaries.

In looking back to 1788, we realize that for well over a century our agriculture was exploitive. Little was done to conserve or build resources. Our settlers were making extensive environmental changes, but of necessity these changes were directed to exploitation rather than to conservation—to clearing, fencing and cultivation. Animals and plants were introduced, and total production increased as livestock and cropping penetrated more deeply into the continent. There was little thought of improving crop or animal yields, in the sense of yield per acre or per animal, but only of embracing more and more land or of making better use of the scant work force. Ring-barking, burning and the log roller for clearing, stump-jump implements and the stripper harvester, fencing and watering points, road and rail transport—these physical innovations were the substance of agricultural expansion. The development of the Australian Merino sheep stood almost alone in the first century of settlement as a major advance at the biological level.

By 1900 wheat yields had seriously declined; many pastures especially in drier areas had been overgrazed and damaged. It can perhaps be said that 1901, the year of federation of the Commonwealth of Australia, was the very nadir of our agriculture. Wheat yields were desperately low, pastures were deteriorating and both sheep and cattle numbers were declining.

THE NATURE OF INNOVATIONS

But from this time onwards, intensification of production, as distinct from simple expansion, began through the application of science to the growth of plants and animals. Innovations by the farmer and pastoralist, valuable as they continued to be, were supplemented and progressively superseded by contributions from the departments of agriculture and the agricultural colleges, which were founded towards the close of last century. The first faculty of agriculture was established in Sydney in 1910, the Waite Agricultural Research Institute in 1925 and the Council for Scientific and Industrial Research (now the Commonwealth Scientific and Industrial Research Organization) in 1926.

The steps that lifted our agriculture from its plight at the turn of the century, and which have continued to give us increasing production, are few in number. The most important ones were plants and animals better adapted to Australian conditions, chemical fertilizers (notably superphosphate), the control of diseases and pests, new types of machines, more power, and improved transport.

In particular since World War II, the progress of our agriculture and indeed of the whole Australian economy has depended in considerable measure on the practice known as 'pasture improvement', based on the use of exotic leguminous plants. These pastures, with nutrients from the fertilizers and nitrogen contributed by the legumes, have raised the fertility and productivity of our soils to a remarkable degree. They have been sown to replace native grassland, on lands newly cleared from forest and scrub, or as short-term 'ley pastures' in rotation with cereals. They carry more animals and better fed animals; furthermore when grown in cereal rotations they have given significant lifts in crop yields. Basically the practice of pasture improvement is one of raising the low soil fertility, which has kept Australian yields at depressed levels for so long. In a study of a typical district in which inferior native pasture was replaced by sown fertilized legumes, the soil organic matter, a prime index of fertility, was raised three-fold within 15 years.[1]

Though only one-third of Australia has sufficient rainfall for the establishment of improved pastures, estimates of the ultimate potential consequent on pasture development in these areas are as high as 450 million sheep (160 million at present) and 85 million cattle (19 million at present).[2] Several studies have suggested that pasture improvement is not only economically

1. C. M. Donald and C. H. Williams, 'Fertility and Productivity of a Podzolic Soil as Influenced by Subterranean Clover (*Trifolium subterraneum L.*) and Superphosphate', *Australian Journal of Agricultural Research*, Vol 5, No 4, October 1954.

2. J. Griffiths Davies and A. G. Eyles, 'Expansion of Australian Pastoral Production', *Journal of the Australian Institute of Agricultural Science*, Vol 31, No 2, June 1965.

sound,[3] but is superior to other forms of rural investment.[4] The surge in animal production, especially of sheep, which has occurred across southern Australia as a result of pasture improvement will be repeated with cattle numbers in tropical and subtropical areas of good rainfall, where knowledge of suitable techniques is now becoming available.

In the past quarter century there has been a marked increase not only in the yields of cereals but also of the more intensive crops. This has been due mainly to three factors—the much heavier use of fertilizers, the use of new varieties and the more effective control of pests and diseases. These practices have raised the yield of raw sugar in the past 30 years from 2·6 to 4·0 tons per acre, of potatoes from 2·5 to 5·0 tons per acre and of apples from 95 to nearly 200 bushels per acre.

Over most of Australia, limited or erratic rainfall is a major factor restricting yields. There is much political and public advocacy of irrigation as a key method of modifying the environment and of increasing production. We now have 2·5 million acres of irrigation (80 per cent of it on the Murray-Murrumbidgee river system in New South Wales and Victoria), in a total of 60 million acres of crops and sown pastures. These irrigated lands are the backbone of several industries (fruit canning, dried vine fruits, rice) and of the economy of many regions. Yet it is idle to envisage any extension of irrigation in Australia to a degree comparable to that of India or the United States. Because Australia is a dry country, our production would be increased by more irrigation; but for the very same reason there are few rivers of significant size as sources of irrigation water. Though irrigation will be extended, prospective schemes are progressively less attractive and less significant; further, they are now subject to more stringent economic analysis than has applied to earlier schemes.

On the other hand the potential for the development of lands under natural rainfall is huge, so that the percentage of our total production drawn from irrigated agriculture will decline in the coming decades. The effective use of water in Australian agriculture will depend more on practices relating to natural-rainfall agriculture than on any extension of irrigated lands.

Though Australia has only 8 tractors per 1,000 arable acres compared with 20 in the United Kingdom, mechanization is well advanced; our relatively low figure for tractors is associated with large farm size and the large area worked per tractor. Mechanization has been adopted in clearing operations, in dairying, horticulture, cereal production and indeed in all branches of agriculture. It has contributed both by saving manpower and by permitting greater speed and efficiency of operation—the simple but important races

3. F. H. Gruen, 'The Economics of Pasture Improvement', in Alan Barnard (ed), *The Simple Fleece*, Melbourne University Press, Melbourne 1962, ch 24.

4. J. H. Duloy, 'The Productivity of Investment in the Pastoral Industry', in *Sheep and Wool Extension Course Handbook*, Bureau of Agricultural Economics, Canberra 1962.

against time, such as the harvest to beat predicted wind or rain, or the critical soil cultivation. Mechanization is enabling development which hitherto has been difficult or even impossible, notably through the clearing of low value land, and the aerial application of seed and fertilizers to terrain inaccessible by land machines. No less than 16·6 million acres were fertilized, sprayed or dusted from the air in 1964-65 and this figure continues to rise steeply.

There have been great differences in the rapidity with which innovations have been adopted in Australian agriculture. The rate depends not only on the capital outlay involved or the potential profit, but also on the simplicity of the change and even its appeal in aesthetic terms. (The adoption of the surgical 'Mules operation' to reduce the susceptibility of sheep to fly strike was checked by the bloodiness of the operation, but the practice is now being undertaken by contractors.) The most rapid adoption has been of those innovations which are cheap, simple and clearly profitable. A notable example is the use of trace elements on pastures; a farmer accustomed to using superphosphate as a fertilizer can substitute the words 'molybdenum super' for 'super' on his fertilizer order, pay an additional 10 per cent or so and, without modification of farm procedure, look forward to a substantial increase in production. Much the same simplicity has applied to the substitution of new fungicides, pesticides and weedicides for the old. Indeed the farmer now accepts, and expects, progress and changes in the agricultural chemicals at his disposal.

On the other hand, some of the most valuable innovations, in particular those influencing land use, have been accepted all too slowly. Many wheat growers have been slow to adopt proven methods of ley farming, even though neighbours may have shown spectacular increases in production.

Admittedly a factor operating against some changes in land use is that output may be temporarily reduced. For example when a wheat-sheep farmer moves from an intensive cropping system to one with a greater proportion of ley, his total grain production will be less until the improved fertility and yield compensate for the decreased area of crop. Furthermore land use changes have implications for the whole management system of the farm, and this too causes hesitancy. In many instances too, there has been an unwillingness to accept heavier taxation rates. Yet it is progress in land use which can and will contribute so much to increased production and to the stability of our agriculture.

In the following pages, innovation in several sectors of Australian agriculture is reviewed.

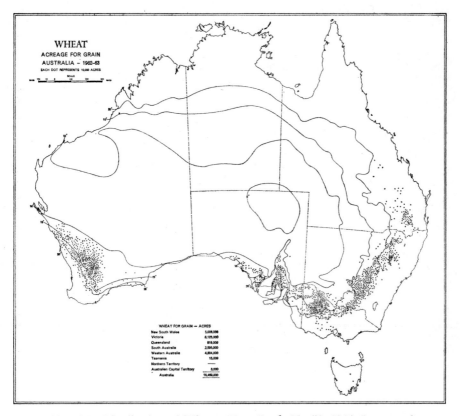

Map 3-1: Distribution of Wheat. (*Year Book*, No 50, 1964, Bureau of Census and Statistics)

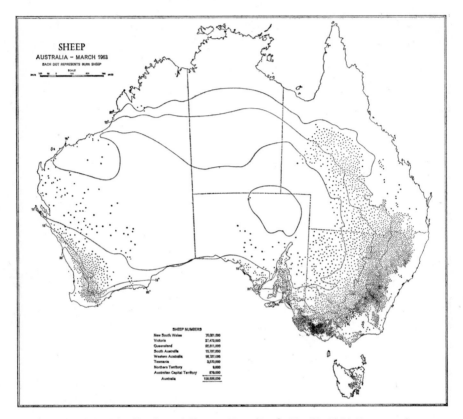

Map 3-2: Distribution of Sheep. (*Year Book*, No 50, 1964, Bureau of Census and Statistics)

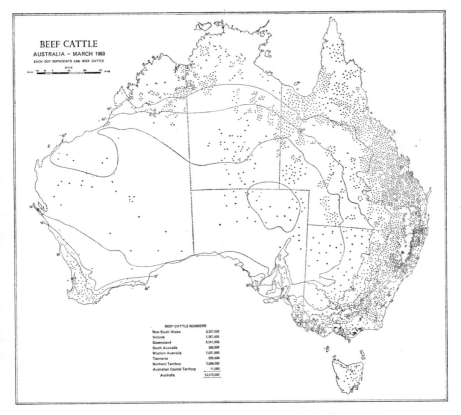

Map 3-3: Distribution of Beef Cattle. (*Year Book*, No 50, 1964, Bureau
of Census and Statistics)

F

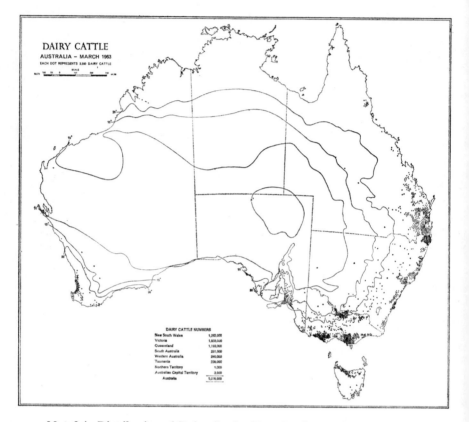

Map 3-4: Distribution of Dairy Cattle. (*Year Book*, No 50, 1964, Bureau of Census and Statistics)

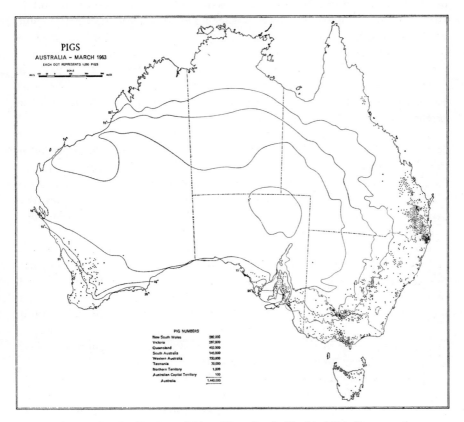

Map 3-5: Distribution of Pigs. (*Year Book*, No 54, 1964, Bureau of Census and Statistics)

THE PHYSICAL CONQUEST OF THE ENVIRONMENT

LAND CLEARING

Most of the better watered parts of Australia carry forest or woodland. For a century or more the task of clearing with the axe and the firestick, simple tackle or crude poisons, limited the areas of land devoted to cropping and, in large measure, to dairying. On the other hand, sheep and beef cattle could be pastured in savannah woodland, on shrub steppe and various other native plant communities; in consequence sheep and beef raising developed at a far greater speed than could crop production. By 1890 the sheep flocks of Australia had attained well over half the present-day numbers; on the other hand, the area of wheat in 1890 was less than one-quarter of the present acreage.

Clearing continues to be an important factor in the progress of Australian agriculture. Since World War II the nature of the operation has changed in dramatic fashion, from a labour-intensive to a capital-intensive operation, based on the bulldozer, the tractor-drawn chain and the massive scrub plough, while the cost per acre has progressively declined. The enormous capacity of this equipment is illustrated by the current rate of clearing new land in Western Australia—nearly a million acres a year.

Most of the postwar clearing has been stimulated by our new knowledge of how to gain immediate economic production from the cleared land, particularly through sown pastures. Prior to World War II the clearing of much of the scrub and heath in South Australia and Western Australia could lead only to inferior pasture, without hope of economic return. The definition of suitable pasture plants and fertilizers, including trace elements, now permits satisfactory pasture in these areas. But the contribution through new clearing techniques has itself been no less a factor.

Clearing is undertaken less and less by the individual landholder. If he seeks to extend the cleared area on his own property, he will usually engage a contractor with heavy machinery. But, as explained in Chapter 12, in the development of new farms it is now common for government agencies or industrial or private firms to undertake the whole series of operations from clearing to land preparation, seeding and fertilization, using heavy machinery under contract and usually tackling an area of land intended for subdivision into several properties.

The economics of clearing rests on many factors. Yet the broad picture in Australia is that a knowledge of improved techniques of production has eventually made clearing a worthwhile operation—however unattractive it has at first seemed. We can, for example, list on a time scale the clearing of great areas of Mallee (dwarf eucalypt scrub) in South Australia and Victoria in the period 1910-1930 following the recognition of their potential for cereals; the clearing of areas such as the Ninety Mile Plain in South

Australia in the 1950s following the demonstration of efficient livestock production from pastures fertilized with trace elements; the acceleration in the 1960s of the clearing of the Brigalow scrub in Queensland with the keener understanding of the capacity of these lands for beef production; and finally a clearing operation which is as yet uneconomic—the clearing of the woodland of the 'Top End' of the Northern Territory. Progress in this region will probably be based on the development of beef production through pasture establishment among the trees, and then, in later decades, on clearing.

Over Australia as a whole, clearing will continue to contribute to agricultural expansion for the remainder of this century. For example an estimated 20 million acres remain to be cleared in the south-west region of Western Australia, and this may take anything up to 40 years to complete. But the relative importance of 'new land' has decreased in recent years, not because the clearing is slower (indeed the reverse is the case), but because our knowledge of how to gain greater production from the lands already cleared has also advanced so much.

FENCES AND WATER SUPPLIES

The other components of the physical attack on the environment have been the erection of fences and the construction of watering points for livestock. Shepherding was introduced from the United Kingdom but the practice ceased during the gold rushes of the 1850s, when shepherds, along with able bodied men from all other tasks and professions, headed for the gold fields. But the sheep and cattle subsisted well enough without the shepherd who was now replaced by fences and, on larger properties, boundary riders to keep the fences in order.

Fencing currently involves heavy capital input in Australian grazing practice. There are few cropping enterprises in Australia without livestock (horticulture and sugar production mainly) and no open grazing domain. Nor are there the great areas of unfenced crop lands or grazing lands such as are found in most other countries. Indeed, at least in terms of boundary fences, Australia is one of the most fully fenced countries in the world.

Will more fencing pay? It is clear that the control of livestock movements, of mating and of weaning by fencing is economically sound, though this is at present barely true of extensive cattle properties in parts of northern Australia. Subdivision beyond these minimal needs for stock management is based principally on the management of pastures rather than of the animals, and here there is an altogether inadequate knowledge of the degree to which further subdivision should be practised. While subdivision is certainly inadequate in many regions, the paddock size in some districts may already have moved below the economic optimum.

The provision of stock water is a problem of varying intensity in particular parts of Australia. In most low rainfall pastoral areas, attention to water supply is the first call on management; it may be the limiting factor to subdivision or it may prevent the use of distant parts of the property; on many larger pastoral properties, artificial waters provide a form of grazing control in lieu of fencing. Obviously in such situations improved water supply can increase carrying capacity.

In other regions there is varying dependence on surface dams, shallow or deep bores, artesian water or, more rarely, streams. There are many areas in which supplies are critically low almost every summer. Improved machinery for the construction of dams and the sinking of bores has assisted greatly in the provision of stock water. Apart from this, attempts have been made to use anti-evaporants, notably cetyl alcohol, which forms a thin film on the surface of the water and greatly reduces water loss. Unfortunately this technique has proved disappointing because the film of alcohol is readily broken by wind movement. This problem is of major importance, since evaporation from open dams ranges from 40 to 80 inches p.a., and up to 130 inches in some inland areas. (Map 2-4.) Oddly enough the progress made with pasture improvement has aggravated the problem of stock water supply on many properties. Whereas formerly there was a considerable surface or sub-surface run-off from native pasture, the greatly increased water use by sown, fertilized pasture has seriously decreased the amount of water entering storage dams.

As the development of the Australian environment proceeds, so the limitations due to low rainfall over much of the continent become more and more sharply defined.

DEVELOPING BIOLOGICAL RESOURCES

The Australian aborigines were collectors and hunters. Yet none of the hundreds of plants or animals on which they depended has entered the Australian agricultural or pastoral industries as a domesticated species. Native pasture species still occupy most of the continent, wholly so in drier areas, and they support great numbers of livestock. Yet all attempts to use them as artificially sown species indicate their unsuitability for this purpose.

This unsuitability has probably resulted from two factors. The first was the lack of any indigenous agriculture which, over many centuries, could have selected more productive genotypes. The second factor was the adaptation of our native flora to the low fertility of most of our soils and its consequent inability to respond to improved soil conditions. The lack of any commercial use of our native animals, notably the kangaroo, has been in part due to prejudice, but more particularly to the prior domestication, known productivity and availability of European species and breeds. Some wildlife workers are advocating a re-examination of the kangaroo for commercial meat and hide production.

Thus all our crops, sown pasture species and domesticated animals have been introduced from overseas.

BREEDS OF LIVESTOCK

There has been a notable contrast in our approach to the choice of breeds of sheep and cattle respectively. Early in the history of settlement, John Macarthur recognized that the Merino, a breed of Spanish origin, would form a better basis for an Australian wool industry than would breeds from the United Kingdom or India. The Merino is more tolerant of high temperatures, it can walk farther for feed or water and it is incomparably superior as a producer of high quality wool. Today purebred Merinos constitute 75 per cent of the Australian flock while Merino crossbreds contribute a further 13 per cent; the British breeds are dominant only in more favoured areas, or those devoted to prime lamb production.

Though there has been marked progress by Australian landholders in breeding Merinos for heavier and better fleeces, the breed suffers the disability of low reproductive rates compared with most of the northern European breeds. This is a particular disadvantage at the present time when a substantial increase in the national flock is urgently needed to keep pace with pasture development, and a positive programme towards better reproductive rates is being given high priority in research programmes.

In the dairying and beef industries, in contrast to the sheep industry, there has been almost exclusive dependence on northern European breeds. Even within the tropics the Shorthorn, a British beef breed, predominates. It is perhaps unfortunate that there was no Macarthur in earlier years to recognize that while northern European cattle are well adapted to our temperate regions, Zebu or part-Zebu animals might well form a better basis for beef production in the tropics. Although there has been some use of Zebus in cattle breeding programmes from 1912 onwards in north Queensland, it was not till 1933 and again in the 1950s that significant imports of Zebu animals were made.[5] Now such Zebu-cross breeds as the Santa Gertrudis (developed in the U.S.), the Brangus (Brahman x mainly Aberdeen Angus), Braford (Brahman x mainly Hereford) and Droughtmaster (Brahman x mainly Shorthorn) are making rapid progress in tropical and subtropical Queensland because of their better adaptation to the climate, their more efficient use of low grade fodder and their greater resistance to tick infestation—and hence more rapid liveweight gains. Much prejudice remains against these unshapely animals (witness the adjective!) but performance in the tropics will be the decisive factor.

NEW PLANT VARIETIES

The pattern of development of our plant resources has been very different from that of the animals. Few crop varieties are now common to Australia and the United Kingdom. Our earliest wheats, English varieties, were ill-suited to our environment, yet apart from some farmers' selections they

5. J. Francis, 'Role of Exotic Cattle in Northern Australia', *Australian Veterinary Journal*, Vol 40, No 3, March 1964.

continued in use for over a century. In 1901 William Farrer, a highly successful and imaginative wheat breeder, released the most notable of his new varieties, 'Federation'. Within a few years almost the entire Australian crop was of locally bred strains. Since that time there has been successive replacement by newer Australian varieties, combining improved disease resistance and better yield. Yet our progress since the days of Farrer though very real, has hardly been notable. In the past 30 years our increase in yields due to varietal improvement (this is apart from environmental change) has been about 0·6 per cent per annum compared with figures of up to 1 per cent in some countries. We now need varieties with greater capacity to respond to the improved soil fertility engendered by ley farming or by the heavier use of fertilizers. Our present varieties have been bred for performance at a low or moderate level of fertility and they respond but weakly to a more liberal nutritional regime.

The contribution by plant breeders to other crops has been patchy. Nearly 90 per cent of our sugar crop is grown from locally bred varieties, and all our oats are Australian-bred. On the other hand the principal barley variety is a farmer's selection, made 50 years ago. Barley varieties are now being bred with a 30 per cent greater yield—but the long delay is a reflection of the inadequacy of plant breeding programmes in Australia.

Our array of sown pasture plants is of considerable interest. We began with those of the United Kingdom, such species as perennial ryegrass (*Lolium perenne L.*), cocksfoot (*Dactylis glomerata L.*), white clover (*Trifolium repens L.*) and red clover (*Trifolium pratense L.*). But they were adapted only to the climatically favoured parts of southern Australia. One of the greatest advances in Australian agriculture, perhaps *the* greatest so far, came with the development as sown pasture plants of a number of annual legumes, from the Mediterranean region in Europe, notably subterranean clover (*Trifolium subterraneum L.*). These plants are adapted to the dry summer and the winter growing season of the Mediterranean type climate of so much of southern Australia. They have enabled sweeping extension of the climatic zone in which improved pastures could be sown—from about 60,000 to over 250,000 square miles. None of these plants had been used in the Mediterranean region itself or elsewhere as sown species. They have transformed the animal production levels of the pastures to which they contribute and the yield of the crops grown in rotation with them. It is a salutary thought that some 30 years—spanning the period from the 1890s to the third decade of this century—elapsed between the recognition by a farmer, Amos Howard, of the value of subterranean clover and its general advocacy by departments of agriculture.

The success across southern Australia in developing subterranean clover and various other 'unknown plants' into important sown species is now influencing the approach being adopted in the summer rainfall zones of

Queensland and the Northern Territory. For many years both producers and research workers affirmed that 'the sub-clover ideas in the south won't work here in the north', but now the same principles and even many of the same practices are proving applicable. Here again there are no 'traditional' pasture plants offering from other parts of the globe. But a whole range of species under study in Queensland shows promise of transforming beef production levels; and among these the most notable is Townsville lucerne (*Stylosanthes humilis*) which seems to be as well adapted to the short summer rainfall season of northern areas as are the Mediterranean annuals to the winter rainfall season of the south. Within the past few years it has become un-equivocally clear that great areas of Queensland and the Northern Territory will be transformed by the use of Townsville lucerne, given time and the capital required for land development.

Though our native flora has contributed nothing to our crops or sown pastures, the Australian record is one of considerable success in developing many exotic species, previously of unrecognized worth, as valuable pasture plants. They have been used both within Australia and in other parts of the world.

SOIL FERTILITY AND CROP PRODUCTION

The site of the first farm in Australia was thus described: 'the bulk of the soil is shallow and sandy with outcrops of rock at too frequent intervals.'[6] This infertility was to foreshadow the limitation to production over much of Australia. Though rainfall is clearly the prime limitation to agriculture over the continent as a whole, the poor soils of the regions of favourable rainfall seriously restrict their production. The widespread podzolic, lateritic and solonized soils are low in nitrogen and phosphorus and commonly in other major and minor nutrients. In one district for example, the Wallum of south-east Queensland, the soil is deficient in phosphorus, nitrogen, potassium, calcium, copper, zinc and molybdenum. Though a few areas, such as the black earths of New South Wales and Queensland, are relatively fertile and are still commonly cropped without fertilizer, most Australian soils are infertile—often acutely so.

SOIL DEPLETION

At the time of European settlement the systems used for the maintenance or improvement of soil fertility in the United Kingdom had no application in Australia. Because of our mild winters, stock were unhoused and there was no farmyard manure or compost heap. Where sheep were grazed for wool production there was little pressure on soil fertility, but where crops were grown or milk was produced, the depletion of the meagre fertility soon led to declining production.

6. Robert D. Watt, *The Romance of the Australian Land Industries*, Angus & Robertson, Sydney 1955.

Our wheat yields fell from 12·8 bushels per acre in the 1870s to a disastrous 7·3 bushels in the last decade of the century. Undoubtedly the depletion of the phosphorus and nitrogen of the soil was the paramount factor. At the turn of the century, two major innovations partially remedied these two deficiencies. The first was the use of superphosphate. In 45 field trials in South Australia, Victoria and New South Wales the average yield was 8·1 bushels without fertilizer and 13·4 bushels with 60 lbs of superphosphate per acre.[7] Almost concurrently, the bare cultivated fallow was introduced into

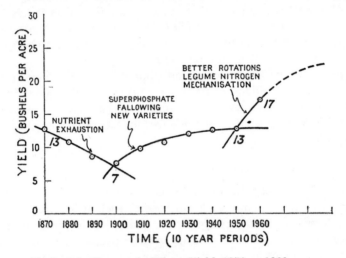

Figure 3-1: Changes in Wheat Yield, 1870 to 1960

the wheat rotation, primarily (so it was then thought) to permit water storage in the soil before the crop was sown. In fact however, a major effect of the cultivated fallow was the more rapid breakdown of the soil organic matter; this process released nitrogen for the ensuing crop. Thus the phosphorus deficiency was remedied by superphosphate, and the nitrogen deficiency through accelerated exploitation of the soil by bare fallowing.

The new wheat varieties bred by Farrer were also released at this time; the total effect of improved soil fertility and better varieties was an abrupt reversal in the trend in wheat yields. (Figure 3-1.) They increased until 1930 when they levelled off at about 12·5 bushels continuing with little change to 1950. In fact, however, yields in many districts were already declining by 1950.[8] The bare fallow, though giving an immediate improvement in crop

7. C. M. Donald, 'The Progress of Australian Agriculture and the Role of Pastures in Environmental Change', Farrer Memorial Oration, *Australian Journal of Science*, Vol 27, No 7, January 1965.

8. E. A. Cornish, 'Yield Trends in the Wheat Belt of South Australia during 1896-1941', *Australian Journal of Scientific Research, Series B Biological Science*, Vol 2, No 2, May 1949.

yields, led to such serious loss of soil structure that altogether new problems arose. In lower rainfall areas and on lighter soils, whole landscapes began to drift as the wind swept across exposed, powdery soils. In better watered districts, wheat paddocks were washed and gullied by rainfall unable to penetrate the over-cultivated and structureless soil.

SOIL CONSERVATION

It was at this stage that 'soil conservation' became a major component, almost a dogma, of Australian agriculture, as in a number of other countries. The first Australian soil conservation service was formed in New South Wales in 1938 and all States soon established these agencies. Incredible as it may seem, the tendency was to regard soil conservation as an activity distinct from crop or animal production. In several instances a soil conservation service was established as an independent agency from the department of agriculture, and this absurd situation still persists in some States.

In the early years there was great emphasis on mechanical means of soil conservation, on banks, furrows, concrete spillways and so on, sometimes with a Canute-like approach to wind or water. While these devices still have a valuable role, the emphasis has moved towards the protection of soil surfaces by plants and their residues, and towards sound crop rotation systems. Yet the adoption of suitable rotations for wheat production in Australia has been depressingly slow. Though departments of agriculture had long recognized the steps that were needed, it was not until the 1950s that soil conservation and increased production were effectively integrated through the inclusion of temporary pastures in cereal rotations. Better returns from wool production stimulated this change in land use.

It is here necessary to emphasize again the point that the Australian wheat grower is always also a sheep farmer. This is a contrasting situation from most parts of the world, where the cereal grower is commonly devoted exclusively to his crop production. To the maize grower of the mid-west United States, a year of sweet clover in the rotation may assist to maintain fertility, but it is a year lost from cropping. To the Australian wheat grower, a clover pasture in the rotation not only serves to maintain fertility and crop yields, but also permits increased flock numbers and profits. He develops a new flexibility towards changing price levels or economic circumstances, moving the emphasis towards wool, mutton, or prime lambs, on the one hand, or towards increased grain production on the other.

The influence of legume leys in cereal rotations has often been dramatic. Wheat yields rise markedly and the number of sheep may be doubled or trebled. A study on 14 properties in the Wagga Wagga district in southern New South Wales showed an increase in average wheat yields from 21 to 35 bushels per acre due to the inclusion of clover leys in the rotation;[9] in County

9. *Personal communication.* A. C. Taylor, Wagga Agricultural Research Institute.

Gawler, north of Adelaide, South Australia, the decennial wheat yield of 16 bushels in 1931-40 was raised to 24 bushels in 1951-60, principally due to legume leys;[10] a property in 18-inch rainfall country showed an increase in wheat yields from 25 to 44 bushels per acre, and in wool production from 2,300 to 7,400 lbs per annum when ley farming was adopted.[11] At the national level wheat yields rose from 13 bushels in 1940-50 to 17 bushels in 1950-60. Continued increases due to these factors will occur for at least a further two decades; but before then cereal yields may move on to yet a third of the upward curves since 1900.

FUTURE POTENTIAL

At least two new contributory factors lie in prospect. The first is the breeding of wheat varieties of altogether new potential. Work in Mexico and in the north-west United States, based in part on Japanese varieties, has led to the production of wheats capable of 30 per cent or more greater yield than the varieties formerly in use. There is every indication that Australian breeding programmes can make good use of these new types of wheat. The second factor is the potential contribution by cheaper fertilizer nitrogen, used as a supplement to the nitrogen contributed by legumes grown in rotation with the crop; this trend may well be accelerated by the subsidy introduced in 1966 of about 25 per cent on nitrogenous fertilizers. Our decennial yield to 1960 was 17 bushels; my forecast in 1964 was for an average yield of 22 bushels in the decade 1970-1980, but already there are signs that this may prove to be conservative.[12]

Our next largest crop after the winter-growing cereals (wheat, barley and oats) is sugar cane. With one of the highest yields in the world, it provides a notable contrast from our wheat yields, which are only about 40 per cent of those of northern Europe. We may ask why this should be so. Several factors contribute. The first is that our sugar cane is grown in areas of high rainfall (some 15 per cent also receives supplemental irrigation) so that it is a crop produced in an 'un-Australian environment' of relative freedom from water stress. Within this favourable environment our technical innovation has proved highly successful. The same is true of our small irrigated rice industry on the Murrumbidgee Irrigation Area where yields are the highest in the world. A second feature, both in sugar cane and rice, has been the stimulation of innovation towards high yields by the restriction of acreage in these industries. Heavy fertilizer use, effective pest control and strong plant breeding programmes are parts of a progressive attitude towards increased yield per unit area. The sugar industry has also been notable for its closely

10. G. D. Webber, 'Clovers will lift soil fertility and production: the story of the Lower North', *Journal of the South Australian Department of Agriculture*, Vol 67, No 11, June 1964.

11. J. R. Goode, 'Clover leys lift wheat and wool output', *Journal of the South Australian Department of Agriculture*, Vol 66, No 10, May 1963.

12. C. M. Donald, *op. cit.*

knit structure, demonstrated both by the strength of its industry organizations (see Chapter 5) and by its effective research on production and processing.

New fertility levels and new varieties provide the key to increased crop yields in Australia.

PROGRESS IN ANIMAL PRODUCTION

THE EARLY YEARS

At the beginning of last century, John Macarthur recognized that wool production had great potential in Australia because of the suitability of the environment for sheep, the compactness and high value per unit of weight of the product for both internal and overseas transport, the low labour needs and the strong demand for wool in Europe. The crossing of the Blue Mountains in New South Wales and the penetration inland from other points of settlement revealed seemingly limitless areas of rolling savannah woodland or level plain, suitable for sheep raising. There followed a period in which the rate of growth of our flocks was governed not by limitations of the environment but rather by the rate of natural increase of the sheep. The environment was continually extending as settlement flowed inland.

In contrast, the dairy industry, centred mainly around the capital cities on the coast, and the beef industry, grew only at a rate commensurate with local demand or, in some States, with the rate of felling of forest. It was not till the development of refrigerated shipping, to which Mort of Sydney was a notable contributor, that the market for both milk products and meat was sharply expanded by new export prospects.

At the production level there was little innovation, apart from the development of the Australian Merino, already discussed. The native pastures of the drier areas were seriously overstocked during the latter part of last century and this brittle relationship led to the catastrophic decline in sheep numbers from 100 million to 54 million when drought years were experienced in the decade 1893 to 1902.

ANIMAL HEALTH AND PRODUCTION

Since that time, and especially since 1930, there has been particular progress in the control of stock diseases and pests. Indeed almost all diseases have been partially or fully controlled and Australia is a country relatively free from major contagious livestock diseases. 'Black disease', liver fluke and pulpy kidney are no longer serious. The current campaign against pleuropneumonia of cattle holds promise also that this disease will soon be eradicated from Australia. On the other hand, the sheep blowfly, internal parasites and the cattle tick still rank as extremely costly pests.

There have similarly been notable contributions to production through research on mineral deficiencies of sheep and cattle, especially deficiencies of copper and cobalt, through the understanding of nutrition, fertility, reproduction, neonatal mortality and growth, and by progress on nutritional disorders of grazing animals, such as infertility on subterranean clover and staggers on *Phalaris*.

These impressive advances have related especially to health and reproduction. On the other hand the dominant factor governing the growth in the *number* of animals in Australia has been the provision of more and better fodder, and this in turn has been strongly dependent on better pastures. Almost half (48 per cent) of the increase in stock numbers in the period 1948 to 1963 was due to this single factor—pasture improvement.[13] The balance can be attributed to a great array of factors—to the control of rabbits by myxomatosis, disease control, flock management, fodder conservation, fencing, watering, irrigation, improved transport and so on.

In this same period, 1948 to 1963, each additional acre of sown pasture led to an increase of 1·6 sheep (or its equivalent in cattle) in the national flock.[14] We now realize that this increase is far below the capacity of the sown pasture. A landholder might increase his flock from 400 to 1,000, when he replaced 400 acres of native grassland with sown, fertilized pasture. In fact the potential number of animals he can now carry is likely to be 1,500 to 2,000.

In 1966 we are faced with the situation that numbers have lagged so far behind the new potential that we need many millions of additional sheep—now. No Australian agriculturist predicted this acute shortage of animals. It may seem surprising that this problem was not foreseen, but all our thinking had been in terms of improving the environment as the controlling factor in the system. But so great has been the area of newly cleared lands, and so marked the trend to increase the stock numbers on 'older land', that at least 30 million more sheep are needed today to exploit our pastures to best profit. For the first time in our history we must ask in some regions, especially in Western Australia—'Should we cease to clear new land until our stock numbers catch up? Is it a good investment to clear more land if our existing pastures can carry all our additional animals for the next ten years?' Landholders will supply the answer and provide the compromise between these alternative paths of development as the prices of land, livestock and materials for production respond to this situation.

The contribution to increased animal production by pasture development must now be joined by research aimed at increasing the net rate of natural increase. We do not know what the maximum rate may be. The rate for the sheep flock since 1945 (3·3 per cent per annum until the 1966 drought) has been appreciably below that of the period 1870 to 1895 (3·9 per cent per annum) when, for quite different reasons, there was virtually no environ-

13. C. M. Donald, *op. cit.*
14. *Ibid.*

mental limitation to numbers. But the withdrawal of animals for meat production is now far greater than in earlier years.

Various techniques for an increased rate of flock growth, as well as genetic
selection, are now being explored, including more frequent lambing, hor-
mone therapy, and the retention of breeding ewes to a greater age.

Particularly in the sheep industry, the present demand for more animals
tends to negate the emphasis on improvement by selection and breeding.
Selection pressure is minimal when numbers are short. Further, the progress
which can be made in production per animal and especially per unit area
by animal selection, for example by selection for fleece weight in Merinos,
is trivial compared to that attainable in Australia by environmental change,
notably by pasture improvement. Selection may lead to increases of 10 per
cent, pasture improvement to increases of 200 per cent. Meanwhile the huge
prices paid for champion stud animals, based on their appearance, have no
sound economic basis, and similar sums spent on fertilizer or other resources
would give much greater increases in production. In the context of the
present shortage of sheep, blue ribands could well be awarded not to the
most shapely ram, but to the sire most potent in giving a high lambing percentage by his daughters.

THE CONTROL OF PESTS

Australia has both advantages and disadvantages from its long period of biological isolation from other continents. At the time of European settlement,
Australia was free from most of the contagious diseases of man, and from all
diseases of domestic livestock and commercial crop plants. There were few
insects or plants in the Australian fauna or flora with serious pest potential.
This happy state of affairs could scarcely be expected to persist as animals
and crops were introduced from Europe and other continents. Of our many
pests and diseases, some, such as the sheep blowfly, are endemic to the country, but most of them were unknowingly introduced with animals, seeds,
plants, packing and bedding from overseas.

QUARANTINE

Nevertheless, mainly by good luck, we found ourselves a few decades ago
still free from many serious pests—from rabies, foot-and-mouth disease, rin-
derpest, blue tongue, fireblight of apples, maize smut, sirex wasp of pines,
many weeds, nearly all diseases of rice—and so on. Quarantine measures to
exclude these pests have become progressively tighter over the years. At times
these restrictions have detrimental or embarrassing aspects; the prohibition
of the introduction of new breeds of cattle and sheep is a serious restriction
to our livestock industries; the equine events were excluded from the 1956
Olympic Games in Melbourne. Nevertheless there is general acceptance of
the great value of our quarantine system. It is of course far from infallible—

every packing case, the mud on boots, the piece of untanned leather or smoked sausage is a possible source of disease, weed or insect pest. In 1952, the sirex wasp of pines became established in Tasmania and in 1962, despite most strenuous quarantine efforts, it became established on the mainland.

While our isolation assists quarantine to a notable degree, it also carries complementary hazards in pest and disease incidence. When a weed is accidentally introduced from overseas, it may flourish as it has never done in its native land. Insect pests and diseases suffered by the weed may be left behind, and in these circumstances the weed may prosper fantastically.

THE CLASSIC CASES : PRICKLY PEAR AND RABBITS

Such was the case with prickly pear (*Opuntia inermis*). This cactus, introduced last century, found a 'perfect environment' in the Brigalow and Belah areas of Queensland, climatically favourable and devoid of all predators or disease. It increased to form well nigh continuous thickets, impenetrable to man or beast, over hundreds of square miles. By 1925 it occupied some 60 million acres of land in the 20-30-inch rainfall zone of Queensland and New South Wales, and was estimated to be spreading at a million acres per annum.[15] The Prickly Pear Board, established for the sole purpose of controlling this pest, made many attacks, finally to achieve spectacular success with the introduction from Argentina of a parasitic insect, *Cactoblastis cactorum*, which in a few incredible months reduced the vast community of prickly pear to a mass of rotting pulp.

The rabbit too found Australia's environment eminently suitable, though even today ecologists might be hard pressed to say why. But suitable it was to an extraordinary degree. On Christmas Day, 1859, the clipper *Lightning* brought 24 wild rabbits to a Geelong landholder named Austin. He was interested in them as game and in this regard his venture was a notable success, for he is said to have destroyed 20,000 rabbits on his own property during the next six years. By the close of the century rabbits infested two-thirds of the continent, all but the desert and tropical areas. Their numbers attained hundreds of millions, consuming and harming pastures and crops. But the cost was far greater than the loss of fodder. Landholders were involved in heavy outlay for rabbit-proof fencing and for sustained programmes of partial control through trapping, poisoning and digging. Australia never learned 'to live with the rabbit'. To most affected landholders, rabbits were the hated enemy, detested as no other pest has ever been.

Then came myxomatosis, a virus disease of rabbits from South America. After long years of testing and disappointment (even the animal ecologists were saying: 'It can't work'), myxomatosis swept through southern and eastern Australia in 1950 and 1951, wiping out an estimated 100 to 1,000 million

15. A. P. Dodd, *The Biological Campaign Against Prickly Pear*, Government Printer, Brisbane 1940.

rabbits.[16] The Bureau of Agricultural Economics estimated that the increase in the income of wool growers due to myxomatosis in 1952-53 (a year of high wool prices) was $60 million.[17]

Rabbits are still a pest, at times seriously so in particular localities. Poisoning campaigns, now based on far more effective poisons and a fuller understanding of the behaviour of the rabbit, are sponsored in several States. But the rabbit is no longer public enemy No. 1 of the rural areas, though the increasing resistance of the rabbit population to myxomatosis and the widespread occurrence of attenuated strains of the virus are maintaining a lively awareness of possible resurgence of the rabbit plague.

MODERN CHEMICALS

The pattern of pest and disease incidence and control is usually less dramatic than that of the prickly pear or the rabbit. In the livestock industries, notable success has been achieved in the control of infectious diseases and parasites, so that emphasis has tended to move from disease control to more positive aspects of animal production. Australian research on plant pests has led to the control of bunt, flagsmut and rust of wheat, bunchy top of bananas and various other diseases, and to the control of various weeds and insect pests by management practice. In recent years much of our control of pests has depended on overseas advances—on the application to Australian situations and to Australian pests of insecticides, weedicides and fungicides developed at great cost by major overseas firms.

These new substances have led to a complete revision of our attitude to weed control. Until 20 years ago, the use of chemicals (such as arsenates and chlorates) in weed control was regarded only as a palliative which could do no more than check the weed, or facilitate more permanent control by the modification of cultural methods. But today the modern organic weedicides are of such potency and specificity that in some instances full and quasi-permanent control by chemical means can be readily attained. In other instances (skeleton weed is an example) the control of weeds by chemical means though technically quite feasible, is too expensive for general use; here management must for the time being be the basis of control.

Despite the great advances already made, pests involve us in enormous annual loss of income. Few estimates are available, but in 1962-63 the losses to the sheep industry alone due to parasites and their control (blowfly and external and internal parasites) was reckoned at $55 million.[18]

16. F. Fenner and F. N. Ratcliffe, *Myxomatosis*, Cambridge University Press, Cambridge 1965.
17. Quoted in 'Value of Myxomatosis', *Rural Research in CSIRO*, No 8, June 1954, p 11.
18. J. N. Cumming, 'An Estimate of Costs to the Sheep Industry due to Blowflies and Parasites', *Quarterly Review of Agricultural Economics*, Vol 17, No 4, October 1964.

G

ERRORS OF INNOVATION

It is hardly surprising that mistakes have been made in this new environment; in retrospect some are understandable, others less easy to forgive.

LAND USE

As in all 'younger' wheat producing countries of the world, the arid limit of cultivation has necessarily been defined by experience, involving great personal hardship and loss. It has always seemed that if wheat could be grown on one property, it could be grown on the next. And so in the 1930s wheat was progressively pushed into areas of low and erratic rainfall notably in South Australia and New South Wales, only to recede as the normal succession of seasons, then regarded as calamitous drought years, followed. Abandoned farm homes and the destruction of much valuable perennial vegetation stand as the record of these hapless farming ventures; the recent boundaries seem to represent a stable limit in current technical circumstances, but they are in danger of transgression, especially in New South Wales, under the influence of the current price outlook for wheat.

Our experience in overgrazing low rainfall pastoral country is also part of a common world pattern. The first settler based his rates of stocking on the total quantity of forage present rather than on the annual growth increment of the delicately adapted native flora. The outcome was inevitable. It is illustrated by sheep numbers in the arid western division of New South Wales, which attained 13·6 million in 1891, only to collapse to 5·4 million in the drought years to 1900 and subsequently never to exceed 9 million. Catastrophic as this experience may have been, there was perhaps no other way of learning the stock carrying capacity of these arid environments. But having learnt, we have failed utterly to take effective corrective action. Gross overgrazing and deterioration continues over much of our dry pastoral zone. Whereas the United States, with experience similar to our own, has enacted legislation to avoid further abuse or devastation of these arid lands, Australia has done next to nothing to protect its low-rainfall pastoral areas. Nominal control of stock numbers exists in some regions (e.g. by the Pastoral Board in South Australia), but it is almost wholly ineffective in conserving the vegetation, and should be succeeded by more effective measures. The deterioration in much of our dry country is appalling.

There have been other mistakes in land use. Reference has already been made to the excessive use of bare fallowing in much of our cereal land. Though the bare fallow still has a role in some districts, we have been able in most areas largely to discontinue its use, and to adopt more rational and productive systems with surprisingly little permanent damage to the soil or landscape.

There have also been misjudgements or mistakes in the location or design of some of our irrigation projects, so that productivity has been less than expected, usually because of unsuitable soil type, leading to poor water penetration, poor aeration or salinity. Some of these difficulties can be overcome, usually at considerable expense. Others remain. It is proper then, that we now err towards conservatism in assessing the remaining irrigation proposals of any magnitude, perhaps even exaggerating both the technical and economic problems involved.

These errors in land use are for the most part understandable, since we lacked the experience to forecast the outcome. But in at least some instances there have been disastrous plunges which need not have occurred. Such was the Humpty Doo Scheme for rice production in the Northern Territory in the 1950s, financed largely by private overseas capital, and referred to in Chapter 12. Here there was a heavy input of men and machinery, of power and transport facilities. Indeed the major deficiency was of knowledge—knowledge of the environment, especially the water resources, and knowledge of how rice should be grown in this region. The parallel with the Groundnut Scheme of Africa is inescapable. And the outcome was the same—total failure.

Since our most important innovation in land use has been the sowing of leguminous pastures, we may well ask whether there has been undue tardiness in the adoption of this practice. Though the farm use of subterranean clover began in the 1920s, it was not until the postwar years that the area of improved pastures showed spectacular increase.

There were several factors which held back pasture improvement in the depressed years of the 1930s. In some districts the techniques in terms of suitable fertilizers, plants and establishment methods were not understood. But in some regions the procedures were well resolved, and were clearly of economic value. The factors checking their adoption were the lack of knowledge of the practice among landholders, the unavailability of capital in a period of low prices, and sociological barriers. It is perhaps not easy to segregate these factors.

Certainly on many sheep and cattle properties, well suited to sown pastures, landholders were reluctant to adopt this profitable practice, not primarily because of capital costs, but because it was a different and more complex form of land use than the traditional grazing of untreated native grassland. Education towards such changes was inadequate. In many instances landholders felt that they were 'well enough off' without making changes, but even this attitude was probably a misgiving about the unknown. There was also a potential loss of social status for the grazier who 'went farming' by establishing sown pastures. In retrospect we must conclude that the delayed adoption of pasture improvement was due to the inadequacy of our extension services—and we must recognize the heavy cost of such inadequacy.

THE DAIRY INDUSTRY

The dairy industry has long been a weaker, heavily protected sector of our rural economy. To what extent has this been due to a failure to develop or adopt innovation? It is of interest to look at the report of the Commonwealth Committee set up in 1959 to enquire into the 'conditions, structure and problems' of the dairy industry, and the steps needed to give it 'an efficient, economic and stable basis'.[19]

It was recommended that more research, extension, artificial breeding and herd recording be undertaken throughout the industry. Further, the committee stated that there was need for finance on a quarter of all farms to raise production to an estimated potential of at least 8,000 lbs butterfat; this was to be achieved by more clearing, pasture development, fodder conservation, structural and plant improvement, irrigation, stock improvement, increased farm area and diversification to complementary (non-dairying) activities. In brief, all possible areas of technical progress were listed and it is clear that problems of marginal producers were not specific in character but constituted a general technical and economic malaise.

The question arises as to the suitability of the various environments of Australia for dairy production. The committee reported that because of the paucity of the information available it was unable to make a proper comparison of production per cow with that of other countries, though such data are a critical part of the evaluation of the industry. FAO production figures, while subject to many qualifications, show that the Australian dairying environments are, on average, among the less favourable in the major dairying countries. While our most favoured areas are well suited to dairy farming, it is clear that our least productive areas are, in world context, low grade environments for dairy production. Other chapters discuss the issue of subsidization in the dairy industry, but it is evident that partly because of this subsidization Australia sustains dairying in some regions grossly ill-suited to this industry.

The marginal sectors of the industry need to be examined not in terms of the buildings or equipment they have, nor whether their farms are fully cleared or whether herd recording is practised or even whether they have good cows, but above all in terms of the basic factors governing the productivity of the environment for dairy farming. These are the suitability of the climate, the availability of good fodder plants and the agronomic knowledge of how to grow and store them. Dairy farming is an industry for processing plant products into milk and the basis of its prosperity will always be successful plant production or low cost purchased feeds. In the Australian context nearly all else follows.

The lack of innovation on marginal dairy farms in Australia is an economic

19. *Report of the Dairy Industry Committee of Enquiry*, Government Printer, Canberra 1960.

consequence of the environment and not the prime cause of their marginal status. Future measures should be directed almost exclusively towards concentrating the industry into the favourable sectors of the environment.

INNOVATIONS FROM OVERSEAS

It is of interest to look overseas, and to ask whether agricultural practices of potential value to Australia have been effectively adopted in this country. Has there been a failure on our part to introduce valuable innovations? The instance most frequently cited by overseas visitors is our low consumption of nitrogenous fertilizers. Here, they say, is obvious backwardness in our agriculture. But the situation is more complex than appears on the surface; though our use of nitrogen will undoubtedly increase, our pattern of fertilizer consumption is unlikely, for valid technical reasons, to move closely towards that of Europe or the U.S.A.[20] A second example is the virtual absence in Australia of the feedlot system for beef production. Here the answer is simple—it does not pay at our current grain and beef prices. Perhaps our failure to adopt useful overseas innovation lies in more complex areas, notably in extension training and farm management. Certainly it is in these fields that we lack the effectiveness of contact with overseas workers that we have already developed in the research area. In the technical fields our opportunity for 'picking up' overseas development is reasonably good.

THE PATTERN OF PROGRESS

To the early settler, Australia had several notable advantages as an environment for agriculture. First it was of vast size, so that low production per acre could be compensated in varying degree by large holdings. Secondly the winters were mild, and animals could subsist without shelter. And thirdly, large areas of land were suited to immediate exploitation for grazing or, following the clearing of woodland, for cultivation. Our agriculture entered a phase of ready occupation and exploitation, but with low levels of production. This phase has continued in most regions until well into this century and is still operative over great tracts of land in all parts of the continent and especially in the north.

As the environment became known, the two major disabilities for agriculture were apparent—the infertility of our soils and the limitations of rainfall; though many other issues have faced us, these were and these remain our great problems in agriculture. By innovation we are solving one of these problems and making some progress with the other.

So far as fertility is concerned, it is now the view of Australian agronomists that if the rainfall is adequate, then the use of fertilizers and legumes will permit amelioration even of the poorest soils and thereby enable greatly

20. C. M. Donald, 'The Impact of Cheap Nitrogen', *Journal of the Australian Institute of Agricultural Science*, Vol 26, No 4, December 1960.

increased production. In many regions cultural problems remain unresolved: What pasture or crop species are to be used? What establishment techniques? What soil deficiencies must be met? And so on. But we believe we can see clearly the principles involved, and we are confident that we can fill in the jig-saw of technical needs.

As our agronomic knowledge extends, the criterion of 'adequacy of rainfall' becomes progressively less stringent both in terms of the total incidence of the rainfall and of the length of the growing season. Our crops or sown pastures reach to the 10-inch isohyet in the winter rainfall zone of Western Australia; at the other extreme they are extending to the acutely short monsoon season (40 inches in three and a half months) of the 'Top End' of the Northern Territory. But in the semi-arid grazing lands of low, non-seasonal rainfall neither crops nor sown pastures are practicable, or likely to be so in the foreseeable future.

The progressive extension of our crops and sown pastures has involved innovation of many kinds to meet our rainfall deficiencies. The measures have included irrigation, the development of fodder plants suited to low or strongly seasonal rainfall, the breeding of cereals of appropriate maturity and response to water stress, diverse means of water storage for livestock, soil management systems for water conservation and fodder conservation for stress periods. Perhaps we can fairly say that in many regions we can now successfully handle the 'normal' seasonal droughts, whether regularly in winter or in summer, and no matter how intense. But the great droughts, the 'old man droughts', when seasonal rains fail—and fail yet again—are cataclysmic in their effects on animal numbers and crop production. Here our progress is but slight. Perhaps the most significant mitigation of drought losses has been attained through better transport (especially road transport) and greater freedom of movement through reduction of disease control restrictions. But alleviation of losses may well call for co-ordination of farming or grazing operations in different areas, such as agistment facilities, related stock movements, the establishment of fodder reserves and perhaps the investment of public funds in the storage of fodder or transport of stock.

We have some acquired skill in husbanding limited water or fodder resources, but sometimes it is sound economics to let animals die when conditions are extreme. Australia's deep susceptibility to drought losses is due not only to climate but to topography; whereas a drought stricken area in the western United States is rarely more than a hundred or two miles from high mountains or irrigated lands which can provide agistment for affected animals, droughts in Australia may extend over half the continent because of the generally low and uniform topography. Rain-making, of which we have such high hopes and to which Australia's scientists have made notable contributions, stands unproven as a practical undertaking, with great expectations by some authorities, marked conservatism by others. Much more study of the incidence and of the economic and technical implications of droughts, and of the possible means of meeting them is needed.

Australia is a land in which first settlement though not too difficult, gave but low productivity. The task of raising production towards higher and more profitable levels has involved the development of techniques new in world agriculture, either in principle or mode of application—innovation on a grand scale.

Illustrations of this two-stage progress abound. It was not technically difficult for settlers on the Tablelands of New South Wales (here one pays tribute to their fortitude in isolated regions) to establish and graze flocks of Merino sheep for wool production on the native pastures of the region. Much of it was woodland, so that fencing and water points were the main needs. This simple land use continued for 100 years or more, with wool production in 1945 at 5 to 10 lbs per acre. The lift towards new production levels has involved many innovations—the realization of the gross defects of the native pastures, even of the esteemed wallaby grass, the use as sown pastures of Mediterranean plants such as subterranean clover and various grasses, the adoption of cheap techniques of establishment, and the definition and correction of deficiencies of major and trace elements. These advances were made in various parts of Australia, but were aggregated, tested and applied to great effect on these tablelands. And *in toto* they permit an increase in production to 40, 50 and even 100 or more pounds of wool per acre.

A second example of ready exploitation at a low production level may be cited from the cereal and sheep farming lands of Yorke Peninsula, South Australia. Relatively light 'Mallee' eucalypts were rolled and burned. Shallow cultivation permitted cereal production with wheat yields of 5 bushels per acre in the latter part of last century; sheep could be grazed on volunteer pasture and on crop stubble. With the aid of phosphatic fertilizers, and of rotations involving a leguminous pasture plant called 'barrel medic', previously unknown to agriculture, and again by the correction of trace element deficiencies, yields now exceed 20 bushels per acre, while stock numbers are commonly doubled.

A third instance is provided by the Brigalow regions of Queensland. Despite moderate soil fertility, these areas have lain in the first low-level stage of beef production until the present decade, when new techniques of clearing and fodder production have attracted heavy capital input and entry into the second phase of greatly increased production.

This is often the pattern—land easily occupied and made productive at a low level; land of difficult climate and infertile soils on which output cannot be raised without new techniques and heavy capital input. Only in the past quarter century have we made notable progress in this second phase.

There were no environments elsewhere from which we could borrow an effective pattern of land use. Certainly there are climatic analogues, such as the Mediterranean Basin with much of southern Australia, or northern Nigeria with parts of the Northern Territory, but climate is only a part (though the most important part) of the agricultural environment. The problems of developing an agriculture in southern Australia involved not only the arid summer, but also the seemingly impossible task of making good use of vast areas of infertile soils with limited labour and capital. This we are now doing in dimension unknown in land development elsewhere. It is 'land reclamation' on a grand scale. And now the process begins in the north, where progress in the next quarter century may well match that of the postwar period in the south.

The economic climate of Australia has been sufficiently favourable since World War II to provide heavy capital inflow to attractive enterprises; in turn the attractiveness of investment in agriculture has rested heavily on scientific advances. The development of the Ninety Mile Plain in South Australia, the Esperance country of Western Australia or the Tablelands of New South Wales has been a direct response to new knowledge of how to grow crops, pastures and animals in each of those areas. Queensland has long lain in the agricultural doldrums, not because it was 'too far away' or 'too undeveloped' or 'too hot' or 'short of capital', but simply because of the lack of knowledge of what could be done to increase the productivity of the pastures. Now that these problems are being resolved, a rapid inflow of resources is occurring.

Despite the indispensability of capital, transport, machinery and power as resource inputs, the condition precedent to agricultural progress in Australia will continue to be an expanding knowledge in each region of how to grow better plants and produce better animals.

CHAPTER 4

ORGANIZATION AND ADMINISTRATION

P. C. DRUCE

New South Wales Department of Agriculture

GOVERNMENT SERVICES FOR AGRICULTURE

This chapter provides an outline of the administrative services which have been established in Australia, relating to agriculture, with special reference to research, extension and education.

The administrative structure of Australian agriculture has been profoundly influenced by the tradition that services to agriculture are a responsibility of government and by the fact that Australia is a federation of six States and Commonwealth territories.

Before federation in 1901, the self-governing colonies—now states—did not (and still do not) have written constitutions. They followed British parliamentary and governmental practice and procedures. The Commonwealth of Australia on the other hand has a formal constitution which prescribes certain powers specific to the Commonwealth. The States have retained all those powers which they possessed prior to federation, except those that were withdrawn from them or which, under the constitution, were specifically allotted to the Commonwealth.

The present administrative structure of agriculture in Australia is a result of the division of responsibilities between States and Commonwealth as provided for by the Federal constitution. Except in relation to a few particular topics where the legal position has been widely disputed State and Commonwealth responsibilities are clearly defined.

Constitutionally, the responsibility for agriculture and pastoral production rests with the States. The position with the marketing of agricultural products is more complex; here responsibilities are shared—the Commonwealth is responsible for all matters pertaining to export while the States are responsible for intra-state trade. Neither the States nor the Commonwealth can control interstate trade by individual action, except for quarantine purposes. However, by acting together they can exercise some degree of control, even though limited by the complexity of the constitution and by uncertainties in its legal interpretation.

Before federation each colony had an established department of agriculture or its equivalent, and a department of lands concerned with land settlement. For the most part, these departments retained the powers and functions they enjoyed prior to 1901, except in respect of foreign trade. The main concern of the colonial land and agricultural administrations had been with land settlement and regulatory matters, although limited agricultural advisory services had been introduced and small research programmes were in operation. Little research and no extension was carried out other than by colonial administrations.

In the nineteenth century and in the early years of this century, land settlement policies were of immense importance. As has been explained in Chapters 1 and 8, they influenced the rate and nature of development in the rural industries. While no longer a dominating factor in rural development, land policy is still important. Much farm land is leased from the Crown and, to a limited extent, the promotion of closer settlement and land development continues in various parts of the Commonwealth.

Control over the movement of plants and animals is an important aspect of agricultural administration. Australia is entirely free of a number of the most economically serious diseases of livestock and plants. Hence the importation from most overseas countries of many types of livestock is prohibited, and there are stringent regulations governing the conditions under which seeds, plants and plant products can be introduced. The Commonwealth Department of Health is responsible for quarantine policy in respect to entry of livestock and plants from overseas, but most of the detailed administration is carried out by State departments of agriculture on behalf of the Commonwealth. Some States are free or relatively free of certain pests and diseases which cause severe losses in other parts of the Commonwealth. Consequently some local restrictions, administered by State authorities, have been placed on the movement of plants and animals.

In the early years of the twentieth century both research and extension in agriculture remained predominantly functions of State administrations. In extension, it is only very recently that there has been any change in organizational pattern, with commercial and private extension services assuming positions of some importance. The States still dominate the extension field but they are no longer the only extension authorities.

In research, change began with the establishment of the Institute of Science and Industry by the Commonwealth government in 1920. Since then the situation has altered markedly and the Commonwealth, through the Commonwealth Scientific and Industrial Research Organization (CSIRO), now carries out more research in agriculture than all State government instrumentalities combined. Rural research in the universities developed even more recently. With a few isolated exceptions, it was only in the post-World War II period that agricultural research in the universities became significant.

Furthermore, administration in Australia is highly centralized. Unlike that of many other countries, local government is relatively undeveloped and administration is centred on State capitals and on Canberra, the national capital. There has been some limited decentralization of administration in some States but this has not involved the transfer of any responsibilities to local government authorities. Thus rural people do not generally have any direct voice in the formulation of policies for agricultural research, extension or education.

AGRICULTURAL ADMINISTRATION

The six States, primarily, are responsible for land settlement and agricultural production and hence for the provision of services to agriculture. Nevertheless, the Commonwealth government has taken an increasingly active interest in agricultural affairs in the past quarter century.

Commonwealth and State instrumentalities concerned with the administration of agriculture are described briefly in the following sections.

COMMONWEALTH

There are seven Commonwealth departments concerned directly with various aspects of agricultural administration. These are the Departments of Primary Industry, Trade and Industry, Territories, National Development, Interior, Health and the Treasury. Also important is the CSIRO, which is established by legislation and is governed by an executive, the members of which are appointed by the Commonwealth government. The Reserve Bank of Australia and the Commonwealth Banking Corporation are other statutory Commonwealth instrumentalities concerned with agriculture. There is also the Australian National University which, while independent of government, was established and is largely financed by the Commonwealth. The University undertakes postgraduate research relating to the rural industries, trade and rural population but it does not yet provide undergraduate training in agricultural subjects, though courses are available in agricultural economics.

The Department of Primary Industry is the only Commonwealth department concerned exclusively with the primary industries. Its main functions relate to the co-ordination of marketing and price stabilization schemes involving Commonwealth-State collaboration, the marketing of primary products overseas, War Service Land Settlement and agricultural economics research, through its Bureau of Agricultural Economics.

The Department of Territories is concerned with all phases of administration, including agricultural production, in the Northern Territory and in Australia's overseas territories, particularly the Territory of Papua and New Guinea. The Department of Interior is responsible for administration, including agriculture, in the Australian Capital Territory. In these Territories

89

these departments have similar responsibilities to State departments of agriculture, as well as other responsibilities. The Department of Trade and Industry is concerned with trade policy and promotion on overseas markets. The Department of Health is responsible for the administration of animal and plant quarantine where introductions of plant material and livestock from overseas is concerned. The Department of National Development, through its Northern Division, is concerned, in particular, with the development of the less populated areas in the northern part of the Australian continent.

STATE

The functions and administrative structure of State agricultural services do not vary greatly, although there are some differences of detail. In most States there are three or four departments concerned with aspects of agricultural administration, research and extension. There are departments of agriculture (in all States except Queensland, where the equivalent department is known as Primary Industries); departments of lands; and the Treasury. In most States there is also a water conservation and irrigation authority and in New South Wales and Victoria, there are separate authorities responsible for soil conservation.

Departments of education provide limited educational facilities in agriculture at the secondary school level. Universities, agricultural colleges and technical colleges are responsible for tertiary education. The universities are largely State financed but independent educational institutions; agricultural colleges are administered in most States by the departments of agriculture.

There are also State government owned agricultural banks operating in all States. These banks administer various forms of special credit facilities for farmers and some also provide normal commercial banking services. (See Chapter 11.)

State Departments of Agriculture   The functions of the State departments of agriculture are similar although there is some variation in internal organization. These departments are responsible for almost all aspects of agricultural administration except land settlement and in some States, soil and water conservation. Forestry administration and research are the concern of separate instrumentalities.

The activities of departments of agriculture can be classified as: regulatory (quarantine, disease and pest control; however, in some States some of these activities are carried out by separately constituted bodies); research (mainly applied); extension; and, as already noted, education. The departments are, without exception, organized on a divisional basis. The divisional structure of the largest of the State departments—New South Wales—is fairly typical of most others except that in some States there are fewer divisions and in Western Australia some divisions are organized on a regional basis. The New

South Wales department comprises the Divisions of Animal Industry, Dairying, Horticulture, Plant Industry, Information Services, Marketing and Agricultural Economics and Science Services (comprised of the Biology, Botany, Chemistry and Entomology Branches). There is also a central administrative unit which includes Accounts and Records branches, branches administering research stations and regional extension services, a pastures protection section, a legal and registrations branch, a biometrical branch and an architect's branch.

CO-ORDINATION OF STATE AND COMMONWEALTH ACTIVITIES

Because responsibilities for the regulation and promotion of trade in agricultural products are divided between the Commonwealth and the States there is a need for some co-ordination of administrative activities and, some would claim, of research and extension activities also.

In 1934 the Australian Agricultural Council was formed with a view to ensuring continuing collaboration between States and the Commonwealth at ministerial level. The Council normally meets twice each year. It consists of the Commonwealth ministers for Primary Industry and Territories (the latter permanently co-opted) and the State ministers for agriculture, with power to co-opt the services of other Commonwealth and State ministers as required. The functions of the Council have been officially described[1] as:

(i) generally to promote the welfare and development of agricultural industries;

(ii) to arrange the mutual exchange of information regarding agricultural production and marketing;

(iii) to co-operate for the purpose of ensuring the improvement of the quality of agricultural products and the maintenance of high grade standards;

(iv) to ensure, as far as possible, a balance between production and available markets;

(v) to consider the requirements of agricultural industries in regard to organized marketing;

(vi) to promote the adoption of a uniform policy on external marketing problems, . . .;

(vii) to consult in regard to proposals for the granting of financial assistance to agricultural industries; and

(viii) to consider matters submitted to the council by the Standing Committee on Agriculture.

The Standing Committee on Agriculture is a permanent technical committee whose main function is to advise the Australian Agricultural Council.

1. Rural Reconstruction Commission, *Farming Efficiency and Costs, and Factors Relating Thereto, Sixth Report*, Government Printer, Canberra 1945, p 86.

It invariably meets for two or three days immediately before Agricultural Council meetings and occasionally at other times. It is comprised of the permanent heads of the State departments of agriculture, the Secretary of the Commonwealth Department of Primary Industry, and representatives of the Commonwealth departments of Health, Territories, Treasury and Trade and Industry, and CSIRO.

The Australian Agricultural Council has no powers vested in it but it provides a forum for the States and the Commonwealth on all matters pertaining to agriculture. It may and does make recommendations to governments on policy issues. Usually, but not invariably, such recommendations are accepted. Despite its lack of formal authority, the Australian Agricultural Council serves a useful purpose in co-ordinating State and Commonwealth activities in agriculture, particularly in administrative matters such as plant quarantine, and in securing agreement on marketing schemes that require Commonwealth and State collaboration.

RURAL RESEARCH

The Commonwealth Scientific and Industrial Research Organization (CSIRO), the State departments of agriculture and the universities are the main bodies conducting rural research in Australia. A limited amount of research is undertaken by public companies and private organizations, mainly in the fields of veterinary medicine and agricultural chemicals.

GOVERNMENT RESEARCH ORGANIZATIONS

Commonwealth An estimate of total expenditure by public and semi-public bodies on agricultural research in Australia in 1960-61 showed that at that time CSIRO spent $12 million or 54 per cent of the total research expenditure. Government departments spent $7 million or 32 per cent; and universities $3 million or 14 per cent.[2] Although absolute expenditure has increased, the relative position is unlikely to have changed greatly; any change which may have occurred would probably be in the direction of increasing the relative proportion of expenditure by CSIRO and the universities.

In terms of resources available to it, CSIRO is now by far the most important single research organization. This organization, which is financed primarily by the Commonwealth government, was established in 1926 as the Council for Scientific and Industrial Research (CSIR), replacing the Institute of Science and Industry which had been founded six years previously. In 1949 some legislative changes were made to the constitution and the name of the organization was changed to the present title.

For about the first 12 years of its existence, CSIR was concerned almost exclusively with research on problems of the rural industries. In 1937 its

2. G. F. Donaldson, 'The Financing of Agricultural Research by Levies on Farm Produce', *Review of Marketing and Agricultural Economics*, Vol 32, No 4, December 1964, p 192.

functions were extended to embrace research on problems of secondary industry; but substantially more resources are still devoted to rural than to industrial research, as is indicated by expenditure on investigations in 1964-65.[3] In that year gross expenditure on investigations was almost $31 million. The distribution of this expenditure to various categories of research is shown in Table 4-1.

Table 4-1

CSIRO: Categories of Expenditure, 1964-1965

		%
Rural research		
Agricultural research	39·0	
Research into processing of agricultural products	8·7	
Wool textile research	4·9	
Total		52·6
Other research		
Industrial and mining research	26·7	
General physical research	6·2	
Fisheries research	2·3	
Total		35·2
Other categories		
Research services and administration	12·2	12·2
TOTAL		100·0

SOURCE: *CSIRO Annual Report*, 1964-65, Melbourne 1965.

CSIRO is administered by an executive appointed by the Commonwealth government, but in the choice of its research programmes it has a large measure of independence from government. It is organized on a divisional basis (there being 32 divisions) together with a number of research sections (research groups which are usually smaller in size than a division or in an earlier stage of development). The organization is highly decentralized. Headquarters of the various divisions are distributed between all the mainland capital cities other than Perth, and at Geelong, Victoria. Laboratories and other research centres are distributed widely throughout Australia.

CSIRO research covers a wide range of subjects and is both fundamental and applied. An example of the breadth and scope of its work may be seen in its cattle research programme. This:

is aimed at improvement in production through attack on several broad fronts. These include work basic to the development of cattle breeds for both beef and dairy purposes suited to the hot environment of the north; investigation and development of methods of control of diseases and pests; the development of new pasture species for the tropical and

3. *CSIRO Annual Report*, 1964-65, Melbourne 1965, p 8.

sub-tropical areas of Australia; and an investigation of the relation between poor nutrition and reproductive performance.[4]

In addition to research covering virtually all technical aspects in rural
production, CSIRO is concerned with research in food processing. It is also
particularly active in wool textile research and has been responsible for
several important advances in wool processing which have world-wide commercial significance. CSIRO does not usually undertake economic research.

The only other Commonwealth research organization of any significance
is the Bureau of Agricultural Economics (BAE), which is a division of the
Department of Primary Industry and as such is subject to the control of the
Minister for Primary Industry. Its functions have been described officially as
fact finding and economic analysis. It is required: to maintain a continuous
review of the economic outlook for each major rural industry; to assess the
effects of general economic trends and policies on the rural sector of the
economy and, in turn, examine the implications of alternative rural policies
for the economy as a whole; to undertake economic research into all phases
of the wool industry; to analyse and assess the earnings and costs of farm
production with special reference to the various factors affecting economic
efficiency; and to investigate and report on the suitability of rural develop-
men projects . . . and provide a technical assessment of the agricultural and
economic potentialities of such projects.[5]

The BAE is primarily concerned with commodity and policy research, and
with broad industry surveys of an economic character designed to assess the
general economic position of producers within an industry. Some surveys in
addition provide data for use in government-industry negotiations for stabilization arrangements and other policy purposes. Some of its industry surveys
are sufficiently detailed to provide data of value for management purposes.
Applied research within the BAE has tended to concentrate on the major
industries, specifically the sheep and beef industries, particularly in those
States in which departments of agriculture and universities have not developed specialized agricultural economics research units.

State   Research at State government level is carried out mainly by State departments of agriculture and by conservation services in those States where
these are separate from agriculture departments.

Most research by State departments and other State instrumentalities is of
an applied character. The emphasis in the past has been on technical research, but some States are now developing economic research units. The first
of these, which was also the first agricultural economics research unit estab-

4. *Ibid.,* p 28.

5. 'Historical Background and Evolution of Functions of the Department of Primary
Industry', Department of Primary Industry, Canberra 1960, pp 18 and 19.

lished in Australia, was set up in New South Wales in 1941. All State departments of agriculture now have agricultural economists on their staff.

In general, the technical research activities of State departments of agriculture are organized on a regional basis, much of the work being conducted at strategically located research stations and experiment farms. For instance, in 1966, the New South Wales Department of Agriculture had 20 research institutes and stations. The scope of the research conducted at these stations varies greatly. At some a wide range of applied research is undertaken and workers at one station may cover such diverse fields as animal nutrition and breeding, plant introduction, crop breeding, fertilizer response rates, biological and entomological research. Others are highly specialized. For instance, at the Tropical Fruit Research Station at Alstonville, research is restricted to technical aspects of tropical fruit production including the introduction and breeding of new varieties. Even more specialized is the Cattle Tick Research Station at Lismore.

For the most part, State department research stations are relatively small organizations which, on the whole, confine themselves to the immediate problems of the area in which they are located. Recently, however, there has been an effort to develop major regional research centres. A notable example is the New South Wales Department of Agriculture's Agricultural Research Institute at Wagga Wagga in southern New South Wales, where in addition to the applied research typical of State research work, some more fundamental work is being undertaken.

In addition to the research facilities provided by State departments of agriculture, the soil conservation services in New South Wales and Victoria have regional research stations. In some States, also, there are other research institutions which are State- or industry-financed but are independent of agriculture departments. The most notable example is the Bureau of Sugar Experiment Stations in Queensland. The Bureau was originally part of the Queensland Department of Agriculture and Stock (now Department of Primary Industries) but in 1950, control was vested in a board with substantial industry representation. The board's activities are financed largely by the sugar industry with a contribution by the Queensland government, which is represented on the board. The Bureau of Sugar Experiment Stations maintains research laboratories in Brisbane and at four regional centres. Virtually all technical research for the Australian sugar industry is undertaken by the Bureau; it also provides advisory services to the industry. Its activities range over the fields of soil technology, agronomy, pathology, entomology, cane breeding, and sugar milling.

RESEARCH IN THE UNIVERSITIES

Australian universities did not establish schools or faculties of agriculture until at least two or three decades after State governments had set up departments of agriculture.

In the early stages of their development, university schools of agriculture were concerned almost exclusively with teaching at the undergraduate level. Before World War II, postgraduate students were rare and, with a few exceptions, research activities at universities were severely restricted. Since then, with increasing emphasis on postgraduate training for higher degrees and the provision of more funds, much more research is being conducted in universities. Nevertheless, they are still primarily teaching institutions.

All the older universities and some of the newer ones, including the universities of New England, New South Wales and Monash, are engaged in research associated with the rural industries. An exception to the general pre-war situation was the Waite Agricultural Research Institute which was founded in 1925 by the University of Adelaide. This institute has occupied and continues to occupy an important position in Australian rural research.

In the field of agricultural economics, research at the university level has developed rapidly in the past decade; eight universities have facilities for training and research in agricultural economics. The largest groups are at the University of New England (Faculty of Agricultural Economics) and at the John Thompson Agricultural Economics Centre at the University of Western Australia's Institute of Agriculture.

FINANCING RURAL RESEARCH

In the nineteenth century virtually all rural research in Australia was financed directly by State governments. Although Commonwealth contributions began after federation, they were not substantial until after the establishment of the Institute of Science and Industry (later CSIR and then CSIRO) in 1920. From time to time, industry organizations contributed funds to research but until recently, such contributions were relatively unimportant. Private research endowments have been uncommon. With the increasing importance of universities in research in the post-World War II period there has been some widening in the sources of research funds, although all universities are becoming increasingly dependent on government finance.

Important developments in the provision of finance for research have occurred since 1955, when the Commonwealth government adopted a policy designed to encourage primary producers to contribute funds for research purposes. These funds are supplemented by grants from the Commonwealth government according to specified conditions.

At the present time five industries provide funds for research through compulsory levies on produce marketed. The industries concerned are tobacco (1955), wool (1957), wheat (1957), dairying (1958), beef (1960, repealed 1965), meat (1965). The funds raised are paid into industry trust accounts administered by the Minister for Primary Industry. Research committees have been established by legislation to make recommendations to the Minister on the allocation of the funds:

Following the recommendation of the respective committees, the funds are allocated to separate research projects submitted by research units in State and Commonwealth departments, C.S.I.R.O., the universities and other organisations. Funds are also used to provide scholarships and finance the dissemination of research findings, although these activities receive only a minor proportion of the monies allocated. The type of research supported varies from industry to industry, but all industries support primarily biological research relating to farm production.[6]

In addition to the industries for which research levy schemes are operating, others (such as the rice, banana and poultry industries), provide finance to assist governmental research institutions and universities on specific research assignments. The contribution to research made by industry levies is now quite substantial. Of over $16 million spent by CSIRO in 1964-65 directly on agricultural research, the processing of agricultural products and wool textile work, almost $5·7 million or about 36 per cent was contributed by joint Commonwealth-industry trust funds. Contributions by these trust funds to State government research institutions are of importance, though much smaller, both absolutely and proportionally to total research expenditure by these organizations.

The increasing importance of industry levies in financing research has tended to alter further the relative importance of the various research organizations. A high proportion of the funds are now being devoted to research projects in CSIRO and the universities. For instance, of a total allocation in 1962-63 of approximately $5·979 million by the Wool Research Trust Fund, CSIRO was allocated $4·816 million or 80·5 per cent; universities $265,957 or 4·4 per cent; State departments of agriculture $119,975 or 2·0 per cent; the remaining 13·1 per cent was allocated to various other organizations.

AGRICULTURAL EXTENSION

Agricultural extension in Australia is primarily the responsibility of State governments. However, in the past decade, there has been some change in the extension structure. Although the States retain their dominant position in extension they are no longer the only authorities offering extension and advisory services to farmers. Recently, universities, the Commonwealth government and private organizations of various kinds have been increasing their interest and active participation in extension.

An important new development has been the advent of the cooperative farm advisory club and the private agricultural consultant which, for a fee, provide professional advice to individual farmers. At the same time, a basic

6. G. F. Donaldson, *op. cit.*, p 186.

change in extension outlook is occurring. A purely technical orientation is gradually giving way to an approach founded on farm management.

So far only two State departments of agriculture, New South Wales and Queensland, have made any real progress in providing limited extension services in farm economics. However, the need for such services has been recognized by the other States. In New South Wales and Queensland and, to a lesser extent in some other States, in-service training in farm management economics is being undertaken. Most extension personnel in New South Wales and Queensland have now received some training in farm management theory and techniques. At the same time, decentralized economic research programmes are being developed, but progress has been slow because of the inability of State departments of agriculture to retain well qualified and experienced research staff.

Group extension programmes in farm economics centred on schools and courses, usually of from three to five days duration, have also been developed and have proved popular with farmers. Generally, these courses aim to introduce the farmer to the use of economic theory in farm management and to demonstrate proven farm management techniques, particularly budgeting.

Because of the limited number of departmental extension workers in the field, individual advice on specific farming problems is restricted and must inevitably remain limited. Nevertheless, some extension officers devote a large proportion of their time to individual contacts with farmers. On the other hand most extension services make wide use of group methods, including field days and farm walks, schools and conventions, as well as mass media.

In the different States, there is considerable variation in the initial training of extension staff. For this and other reasons, data purporting to show the ratio of extension officers (full-time equivalent) to farming and grazing properties must be treated with some reserve. According to official statements prepared for the Australian Extension Conference in 1962,[7] the ratio of extension officers to rural holdings was low in Victoria, where extension officers are for the most part university graduates; and high in Queensland, where many of the people used in extension have had no formal training. For Australia as a whole, the ratio is one official extension officer per 200 to 300 holdings. In Victoria in 1962 the ratio was estimated to be one adviser to 400 holdings and in Queensland one to 124 holdings; in other States the ratio lies between these two figures.

In two States, New South Wales and South Australia, there are extension organizations known as the Agricultural Bureaux. These are farmers' groups sponsored and supported by departments of agriculture. They supplement official group extension activities. The Agricultural Bureaux are active in organizing conferences, schools, field days and conventions designed to pro-

7. 'Agricultural Extension Services in Western Australia', *Reviews, Papers and Reports,* Australian Agricultural Extension Conference 1962, CSIRO, Melbourne 1963, p 51.

vide landholders with up-to-date information on research findings and new techniques. They also aim to educate farmers in leadership activities.

In some States there are limited women's extension services providing advisory services to farm women on home-making and associated matters.

All State departments of agriculture, and also the soil conservation authorities in New South Wales and Victoria, publish extension journals of various kinds, some monthly and some quarterly. These are available either free or at a nominal charge to farmers within the State of publication.[8]

NEW DEVELOPMENTS IN EXTENSION

By far the most important of the new developments has been the growth of the cooperative farm management club and the establishment of agricultural scientists in private practice, as agricultural consultants. There can be little doubt that the club advisory and private consultant services will continue to expand, although expansion will be inhibited, as it already has been, by lack of suitable personnel.

The first farm management club in Australia was established in 1956, at Bombala in New South Wales. Since 1959 the movement has developed rapidly but recently there has been a tendency for the clubs to be replaced or supplemented by private consultants who operate independently of any organization or group. The Australian farm management club is modelled directly on similar clubs in New Zealand which commenced operations a decade earlier. Normally a group of from 30 to 50 farmers incorporate a club which is governed by an executive elected from the farmer members of the group. The group appoints a qualified agriculturist as an adviser, on a contract for a specified period (usually three years). The farmer-members of the club also enter into contracts which usually bind them to club membership. Annual fees are generally between $150 and $400 depending on the size of the property. In return for these fees the farmer is, as a rule, entitled to a specified minimum number of visits and associated advice from the adviser each year. The farmer is able to consult the adviser on all technical and production problems, other than veterinary aspects, concerning his farm.

There has been a tendency for club advisers not to renew their contract and to establish themselves as private consultants. When this happens the consultant usually works with a group of farmers each of whom retain him on a contract basis. However, unlike the club adviser, he is able to accept other clients and assignments as they arise.

In early 1966, there were over 80 club advisers and about 40 private consultants operating throughout Australia compared with an estimated 1,300 extension and advisory workers (full-time equivalent). Thus the club advisers and private consultants represented almost 10 per cent of all extension

8. See also Commonwealth of Australia, *Report of the Committee of Economic Enquiry*, Canberra 1965, Vol I, p 181.

workers, even though their advisory efforts were confined to about $2 \cdot 5$ per cent of the farm population.

THE UNIVERSITIES IN EXTENSION

Until a decade ago, Australian universities generally did not actively participate in rural extension. Their extension activities, although expanding, are still quite restricted with the notable exception of the University of New England at Armidale, N.S.W. This university has an extension department which is concerned with adult education generally and has specific interests in rural extension. It participates actively in extension programmes for farm people, particularly in the northern part of New South Wales.

Over and above the increasing university participation in extension, there has been a marked expansion of extension and advisory activity on the part of some firms selling farm machinery and farm requisites particularly agricultural chemicals and fertilizers. Such services are usually provided in association with sales programmes and for this reason their impartiality must sometimes be suspect. Nevertheless commercial services are providing a useful, if limited, supplement to official and private professional extension services.

FINANCING THE EXTENSION SERVICES

In most countries, extension and advisory activities provided by the governmental extension services are free, although some make nominal charges for extension publications. In Australia until 1948, the cost of providing advisory services to Australian farmers was borne entirely by State governments. Since 1948, the Commonwealth has contributed about $500,000 per annum to enable the States to expand their extension services for dairy farmers. In 1952 this grant was supplemented by a further annual grant of $500,000 for extension activities in areas other than dairying. In later years the amount provided has fluctuated but has gradually increased. By 1965-66, when the original grant scheme terminated, the total amount granted by the Commonwealth to States for extension purposes was $1 \cdot 4$ million per year. In 1966-67 a new expanded scheme of Commonwealth financial assistance was introduced. It provides for an expenditure of $2 \cdot 9$ million in the first year, rising to $4 million within five years. Not all of this money will be used for extension; some will be devoted to applied regional research, which is considered to be essential to the improvement of extension services especially in the initial years of the scheme.

No estimate of total expenditure on rural extension services is available, but the Commonwealth grant of $2 \cdot 9$ million for extension may be placed in some perspective by considering expenditure in New South Wales. In 1963-64, the State Department of Agriculture spent $11 \cdot 753$ million, provided directly by the State government. About one-quarter of this was spent on extension. A further $2 \cdot 690$ million was provided from various sources including Commonwealth extension grants, which in that year amounted to $336,000 or 2·3 per cent of total expenditure by the Department of Agriculture on all services, and about 10 per cent of expenditure on extension.

The newly developing farm management club and private consultant services are not subsidized, but are financed entirely by the farmers using the service. In most States, an informal, but firm liaison exists between the government extension services and the private advisory services. University extension services are financed from university funds, but fees to cover major expenses are usually charged to farmers attending schools and conferences.

AGRICULTURAL EDUCATION

SECONDARY EDUCATION

Secondary education in Australia is the responsibility of State departments of education and about 75 per cent of children attend schools conducted by these departments. The remainder attend private schools, most of them conducted by churches. Agricultural subjects are taught in some schools, mainly in country areas. With a few exceptions, however, comprehensive vocational training in agriculture at the secondary school level is not provided. The emphasis is rather on general education, with minor specialization in agriculture in many country secondary schools. Exceptions of some note are a few agricultural high schools in New South Wales, Tasmania, South Australia and Western Australia and several private agricultural high schools conducted by churches. In 1963 about 4 per cent of boys in Australian secondary schools were studying an 'agricultural' subject, but probably less than 1 per cent were receiving comprehensive vocational training in agriculture.[9]

Supplementary to formal secondary education in agriculture, there is a junior farmer or rural youth movement in each State. In most States this is sponsored and administered by the department of education; in some the department of agriculture is the administrative authority. Older secondary school children are encouraged to participate in rural youth activities as are young people who have left school.

TERTIARY EDUCATION

Tertiary education in agriculture is available at different levels and is presented by three distinct types of educational establishments:

(i) Technical colleges (or other technical education authority);
(ii) Agricultural colleges; and
(iii) Universities.

9. For a more detailed discussion of agricultural education, see R. N. Farquhar, *Agricultural Education in Australia*, Australian Council for Educational Research, Melbourne 1966.

Technical Education   In each State, except Tasmania, there is a technical education authority providing a variety of forms of technical education in agriculture, much of it on a part-time basis and some of it by correspondence.

Courses in sheep and wool, usually with emphasis on wool classing, are provided on either a full- or part-time basis in most States. In Tasmania only limited correspondence courses are available. Technical courses have a strong vocational component and include the manual arts, farm mechanics, landscape gardening, and the like. However, in some States, such as New South Wales, the technical educational authorities provide quite a wide range of courses in general agriculture, horticulture, fruit growing, poultry farming, elementary veterinary science and many others. Most of these courses are part-time and many are available in a number of country centres.

Agricultural Colleges   There are eight State and two private agricultural colleges in Australia. Four of these are in New South Wales, three in Victoria and one in each of the other mainland states. The State colleges, other than Yanco, now enrol almost 1,500 students, while the two private colleges provide for an additional 130 students.

Agricultural colleges established in the latter decades of the nineteenth century, were the first educational institutions in Australia concerned with training for rural occupations. They have played a major part in the education of farmers, extension workers and agricultural administrators over a period of more than 80 years. Their relative importance and status have tended to decline as universities have developed schools of agriculture.

The first Australian agricultural college—Roseworthy in South Australia—was established in 1884, 26 years before the first chair of agriculture was established, at the University of Sydney in 1910. By the end of the nineteenth century there was a college in each of the eastern mainland States with two in Victoria. In Western Australia, Muresk College was established in 1925.

Until recently the only agricultural colleges were those financed by State governments and administered in most States by departments of agriculture. In recent years two privately sponsored colleges have opened in Victoria and New South Wales and it appears likely that more such colleges will be established.

The colleges are all fully residential. In general three-year diploma courses are offered at the State colleges with two-year courses at the private colleges. However, some two-year courses in special fields are offered at State colleges and all courses at the Muresk Agricultural College, Western Australia, are of two-years duration.

When the older colleges were established in the latter part of the nineteenth century their defined function was to train potential farmers in the art and technology of farming. However, in the absence of any teaching facilities in agriculture at the universities, the colleges were soon providing a training for extension and experimental workers, as well as agricultural administrators and others engaged in commercial aspects of agriculture. In recent years probably less than 50 per cent of college diplomates have taken up farming as a career, but because training of farmers has remained a function, albeit a less important one, of the colleges, entrance standards, curricula and the level of instruction have continued until very recently to be geared basically to the original purpose for which the colleges were established. As a consequence the standard of the diploma awarded by colleges has suffered as a professional qualification. However, in recent years, the colleges seem to have recognized the need to re-examine their objectives and raise their standards.

In New South Wales the need for specific shorter-term training for farmers' sons and others who intend making a career of farming, and whose basic secondary education is not necessarily of particularly high standard, has been recognized. A one-year course has been established at a newly created Agricultural College at Yanco. This college is in an entirely different category to the other agricultural colleges and is intended purely as a training ground for prospective farmers.

The Universities   By 1967 there will be 14 universities in Australia providing undergraduate courses; this compares with 7 in 1945 (the expansion has been predominantly in New South Wales). Eight of these provide courses in agriculture or closely associated subjects; three are in New South Wales and one in each of the other States. In addition, Monash, at Melbourne, provides courses and carries out some research in agricultural economics, although it has no school or faculty of agriculture.

The University of Sydney was the first Australian university to establish a Chair in Agriculture. However, it was not until 1910, 60 years after the university's foundation, that this Chair was established. Degree courses in agriculture are now available in at least one university in each State but this is quite a recent development. Until the 1920s an agricultural education at university level was available only at Sydney and Melbourne. Degree courses in Veterinary Science are offered at Sydney, Melbourne and Queensland.

Only in the past 30 years have the universities exerted any great influence on agricultural administration or on extension and, with few exceptions, it is only in the past 20 years that they have participated actively and to any significant extent in rural research.

Several universities, notably the Universities of Sydney and Western Australia, offer specialized undergraduate training in agricultural economics within their Faculties of Agriculture; only the University of New England offers courses leading to a degree in Agricultural Economics; it also offers a degree in Rural Science. The University of New South Wales provides a course in Wool Technology leading to a degree of Bachelor of Science and also has courses in Wool Commerce and Food Technology. All these universities provide postgraduate facilities leading to the Master's degree and to the degree of Doctor of Philosophy or Doctor of Science.

Some universities also offer a variety of postgraduate diploma courses. For instance, the University of Sydney offers such courses as agricultural chemistry, agricultural economics, entomology, genetics, micro-biology, science, plant pathology, animal husbandry, poultry husbandry and dairy husbandry.

An important recent development is the provision of postgraduate diploma courses in agricultural extension at the Universities of Queensland and Melbourne.

Although the number of universities in Australia has doubled since 1949, when the first of the 'new' universities was established, expansion in the facilities provided for training agricultural scientists has been limited. As a consequence of this and other factors, there is a continuing shortage of trained agriculturists and agricultural economists in Australia; trained veterinarians are also in short supply. The situation in respect of agricultural scientists can be illustrated by a recent report by a sub-committee of the Victorian Branch of the Australian Institute of Agricultural Science,[10] in which it was estimated that the output of graduates in Agriculture at the University of Melbourne would fall short of requirements in each year to 1969 by 54 under 'average conditions' and by 111 under 'optimum conditions'. These figures suggest that university enrolments in Victoria need to slightly more than double to enable 'normal' needs to be met in the next five years and more than treble to allow 'optimum' needs to be met. In this context 'average conditions' were defined to represent 'estimated recruitment based on financial and other limiting factors', whereas 'optimum conditions' represent 'estimated full establishment needs assuming no limiting factors'.

It is clear that universities such as Melbourne and Sydney, both of which impose entrance quotas in agricultural science, as well as other faculties, need to expand their facilities for undergraduate training in agricultural science. At the same time there is a need for some of the new universities which do not yet provide schools or faculties of agriculture to expand their activities to encompass agriculture. Until this is done there will certainly be a continuing and possibly a growing shortage of trained agriculturists for research, extension and teaching in Australia.

10. For further details see 'The Demand for Graduates in Agricultural Science from Victoria', *Report of a Sub-Committee of the Victorian Branch of the Australian Institute of Agricultural Science*, A.I.A.S., Melbourne 1965.

CHAPTER 5

PRIMARY PRODUCER ORGANIZATIONS

G. D'A. CHISLETT

INTRODUCTION

The main purpose of this chapter is to show how Australian primary producers have organized themselves for the purpose of protecting and advancing their economic welfare.

Particular features or characteristics of various organizations have been selected to illustrate some of the principal pressures which have caused producers to organize in a variety of ways, and which have subsequently caused organizations to develop in differing directions. Finally some of the present pressures bearing on the future form and activities of the organizations are discussed.[1]

In Australia, there are eight major national primary producer organizations. Six of these are based primarily on a commodity structure, i.e. they represent the wool, meat, wheat (and other grains), dairy and sugar industries. The State organizations affiliated with these six national commodity based organizations are shown in Table 5-1. The relative importance of each commodity is described in Chapter 6, especially Table 6-13.

The two other bodies which function at the national level are: the National Farmers' Union of Australia, a confederation of organizations to which most of the commodity organizations belong; and the Australian Primary Producers' Union which provides for any primary producer to become a member regardless of his principal farming activity.

A variety of local or regional commodity organizations exists amongst the producers of minor commodities, such as eggs, apples and pears, potatoes, tobacco leaf, dried vine fruits; but apart from the Australian Apple and Pear Growers' Association, they are not actively organized at the national level.

1. This approach and orientation differs from that of Campbell, who in his 1966 paper 'Australian Farm Organizations and Farm Policy' defined his purpose as being 'to survey the structure and operation of the Australian farm organizations and to discuss their role in the formation of public policy in this country.' See K. O. Campbell, 'Australian Farm Organizations and Agricultural Policy', *Australian Journal of Agricultural Economics,* Vol 10, No 2, December 1966.

G. D'A. CHISLETT

ORIGINS OF GRAZIERS' ORGANIZATIONS

The graziers' organizations have their origin in the industrial unrest associated with the depression of the 1890s, almost a decade before federation. During this period, the Amalgamated Shearers' Union, formed in 1886, and the Queensland Shearers' Union practically demanded that only unionist shearers should be employed by Queensland pastoralists,[2] and in May 1890, the Australian Labour Federation declared the intention of the waterside unions to block the shipment of wool shorn by non-unionists.

Unorganized pastoralists were not able to resist the Union demands and some agreed that only union shearers would be employed. Alarmed by this decision, groups of pastoralists in Queensland and in the 'southern colonies' which, for some years, had been dealing with local problems, saw the need for State-wide bodies and a federal council to protect their interests.

The pastoralists quickly established their own (employers') unions in New South Wales, Victoria and South Australia. In December 1890, the United Pastoralists' Association of Queensland was formed. At an 'Intercolonial Conference' held in Sydney in December 1890, the Pastoralists' Federal Council of Australia was established:

> so that the influence and sphere of operations of the combination now extended from the Gulf of Carpentaria to Bass Strait, from the Seaboard of Queensland and New South Wales to the western boundary of South Australia.[3]

Meanwhile in July 1890, a Shearers' Manifesto had been issued by the Amalgamated Shearers' Union (A.S.U.) appealing to every unionist 'to draw such a cordon of Unionism around the Australian Continent as will effectually prevent a bale of wool leaving unless shorn by Union Shearers.'[4]

The pastoralists were mainly concerned with the 'freedom of contract', that is, the right to employ whom they wished. In January 1891, shearers were asked to sign on under an agreement form prepared by the Pastoralists' Federal Council which contemplated the right of non-unionists to work in the shed, alongside unionists. Many shearers refused to sign on. A great struggle ensued in Queensland and New South Wales: pastoralists tried to continue shearing without union labour, and members of the A.S.U. attempted to disrupt operations.

This culminated in a conference in Sydney in August 1891 between the

2. Official statement by the Pastoralists' Federal Council of Australia to the Royal Commission on Labour, London 1891.

3. *Secretary's Report*, First Annual Meeting, Pastoralists' Union of Victoria.

4. Official Statement by the Pastoralists' Federal Council of Australia to the Royal Commission on Labour, London 1891.

Pastoralists' Federal Council and the Amalgamated Shearers' Union at which it was ceded 'that employers shall be free to employ and shearers shall be free to accept employment, whether belonging to shearers' or other unions or not, without favour, molestation or intimidation on either side.'[5] Following this preliminary, an agreement for the conduct of shearing was made and subsequently it was universally adopted throughout the colonies. In these early years the industrial and political structure of employer and employee organizations found their beginnings.

Later, it was problems in marketing, and differences in interests of various groups of producers which led to the formation of new producer organizations.

THE WOOL AND MEAT INDUSTRIES

AUSTRALIAN WOOLGROWERS' AND GRAZIERS' COUNCIL

The A.W.G.C. is essentially the same body as the Pastoralists' Federal Council of Australia, formed in 1890.

In 1920, the Graziers' Federal Council (as it had become) formed the Australian Woolgrowers' Council especially to deal with wool marketing problems arising from World War I. This body was re-absorbed into the Graziers' Federal Council in 1960, whereupon the amalgamated bodies adopted the title of Australian Woolgrowers' and Graziers' Council. The State affiliates of the A.W.G.C. are shown in Table 5-1.

In 1966 work relating to conditions of employment in the grazing industry, to which it owes its origin, is still one of the main functions of the Australian Woolgrowers' and Graziers' Council. It is one of the four principal members of the national employers' committee which determines policy for, and conducts, national wages cases before the Commonwealth Arbitration Commission. The A.W.G.C. employs an industrial officer who represents eight of the ten employer organizations which are parties to the Federal Pastoral Industry Award. This award prescribes the conditions and wages for employees on grazing properties, except Queensland properties which are covered by a State award.

The A.W.G.C. carries its general commercial interest to the international level, through the national committee of the International Chamber of Commerce; and has long been active in tariffs; it is one of three major organizations represented on the executive committee of the Australian Tariff Council, which represents the low tariff advocates within the Australian economy. As the two commodities, wool and meat, which the Council represents are sold at world market prices, it is concerned that local cost levels should be kept as closely as possible to parity with overseas prices.

5. *Ibid.*

AUSTRALIAN WOOL AND MEAT PRODUCERS' FEDERATION

The other industry organization representing wool and meat producers is the Australian Wool and Meat Producers' Federation (A.W.M.P.F.). It consists basically of associations which broke away from the Australian Woolgrowers' Council in 1939. The break away arose from differences in attitudes towards wool marketing, an issue which still divides wool producers. The State organizations affiliated with the A.W.M.P.F. are shown in Table 5-1.

There is a great imbalance in the wool industry between the number of producers and the source of wool production. About one-quarter of the holdings in the industry produce about two-thirds of the wool clip. Most wool growers are relatively small producers who, in the main are producing combinations of wool, wheat and prime lambs, and membership by one producer of several commodity based producer organizations is common.

The A.W.M.P.F. is founded on members from the mixed farming field, whereas the A.W.G.C. membership is based largely on the sheep and cattle industries,[6] especially in the pastoral sector. Differences in backgrounds and attitudes between the two organizations place great difficulties in the way of achieving and maintaining an industry consensus.

Despite these differences in ideals and interest, the A.W.G.C. and the A.W.M.P.F. are represented on several agencies which influence conditions of production in, or government decisions relating to, the wool industry.

In 1962, as part of the reorganization proposed by the Philp Enquiry[7] the Australian Wool Industry Conference was formed by the Council and the Federation as a forum to which the government could look for an industry policy, particularly on matters relating to wool promotion and research. Subsequently certain statutory functions were conferred on the Conference by the Wool Industry Act of 1962 and the Wool Tax Acts (1964). These functions had formerly been exercised by the Council and the Federation independently. They include the nomination of persons to represent growers on the Australian Wool Board, and recommendation to the government of the rate of levy to be placed on growers to finance wool promotion and research. Originally the Wool Industry Conference comprised 25 representatives each from the Council and the Federation. In 1965, 5 representatives of the Wool Section of the Australian Primary Producers' Union were admitted.

The Council and the Federation also share the grower representation on the Australian Wool Industry Tripartite Council. This is a consultative body of wool growers, selling brokers and buyers which meets mainly to discuss the mechanics and problems of selling wool through the auction system.

6. 'Wool and Politics', *Current Affairs Bulletin*, Department of Adult Education, University of Sydney, Vol 36, No 12, October 1965.

7. *Report of the Wool Marketing Committee of Enquiry*, Government Printer, Canberra 1962.

Shipping is of vital importance to wool and meat producers and the wool and meat industry has been active, over the years, in representing the views of producers who sell so much of their produce to overseas markets.

There is established an official machinery for determining freight rates and regulating shipping services for commodities carried on conference lines. These 'conference lines' are groups of shipowners formed for the purpose of rationalizing services between groups of ports e.g. the U.K.–Australia conference. They are recognized by Commonwealth legislation which permits certain restrictive trade practices amongst shipowners in return for guaranteed services.

A grazier has always occupied the chair of the Australian Oversea Transport Association which formally ratifies shipping contracts between conference line shipowners and shippers. Wool and meat producers are jointly represented by the Council and the Federation on the Federal Exporters' Oversea Transport Committee which represents the shippers of export products.

THE WHEAT INDUSTRY

AUSTRALIAN WHEAT GROWERS' FEDERATION

The Australian Wheat Growers' Federation (A.W.G.F.) was founded in 1930. State affiliates are shown in Table 5-1. The Secretary of the South Australian Association has been re-elected annually to act as Secretary to the Federation, ever since its foundation.

In 1963 when it was decided that a full-time economic research officer should be appointed by the A.W.G.F., the salary was provided from wheat research funds, made available by the State Wheat Industry Research Committees which are raised by statutory levy on all wheat production, whether or not growers are affiliated with the Federation.

With two exceptions the affiliated organizations comprising the A.W.G.F. are also affiliated with the Australian Wool and Meat Producers' Federation, so that basically the same State associations meet and function separately on the national level in respect of wheat on the one hand and wool and meat on the other. The exceptions are the Queensland Graingrowers' Association which is not affiliated with any federal livestock organization and the Graziers' Association of New South Wales which is affiliated with the Australian Woolgrowers' and Graziers' Council.

During the 1950s, the Graziers' Association of New South Wales was forced, by the decline in relative returns from wool growing, to cater for the wheat interests of its members. This involved finding means to represent them at the national level, as the A.W.G.C. does not deal with cereals.

The Australian Wheat Growers' Federation did not view favourably the original application for affiliation from the Graziers' Association in 1962. Finally, it agreed to allow the Association to send an observer to its meetings. Continued pressure for full membership over a period of four years finally resulted in the admission of the Graziers' Association in 1966. This preserved the A.W.G.F. as the sole spokesman for wheat at the national level and forestalled possible development of interest and influence in that commodity by the Australian Woolgrowers' and Graziers' Council.

The constitution of the A.W.G.F. is particularly concerned with legislation. This reflects the preoccupation of wheat growers with wheat marketing. The Federation has representation on the Wheat Index Committee which assesses year to year movements in the cost of wheat production under the wheat stabilization scheme.

THE DAIRY INDUSTRY

AUSTRALIAN DAIRY FARMERS' FEDERATION

The Australian Dairy Farmers' Federation (A.D.F.F.) was formed in 1942. Its State affiliates are shown in Table 5-1.

Secretarial services for this Federation are provided from the office of the Queensland Dairymen's Organization. In 1916, New South Wales dairy farmers were unable to secure adequate returns for butter, because this commodity was price controlled under the wartime Necessary Commodities Act. They decided that their interests were not strongly enough represented through the Farmers' and Settlers' Association (now the United Farmers' and Woolgrowers' Association) which had accommodated them until then. Consequently, another specialist commodity organization, the Primary Producers' Union of New South Wales, was formed. (This body is not connected with the A.P.P.U.) The P.P.U. was soon involved in wartime schemes for controlling the supply and shipping of butter to the United Kingdom, which marked the beginning of close association and participation in dairy marketing arrangements which has been a feature of these organizations over the years.

In 1924 the Australian Dairy Produce Board was established to regulate the export of dairy products. Ten years later the Commonwealth Dairy Produce Equalization Committee Ltd, a non-profit company, was established for the purpose of equalizing local and export returns from butter and cheese on a voluntary basis i.e. by agreement within the industry.

In order to sustain local prices for butter and cheese and to equalize returns to each manufacturer irrespective of his domestic and export sales, it was found necessary to allot quotas to manufacturers. This could only be achieved through complementary Commonwealth-State legislation: various States and the Commonwealth government passed the necessary Acts in 1933, under which the State Dairy Products Boards were set up.

The Commonwealth Dairy Produce Act was rendered invalid in 1936 when the Privy Council in the *James* case decided that the Commonwealth government lacked the power to regulate interstate trade. Since then the equalization arrangements have continued by voluntary agreement between the butter and cheese factories and the Equalization Committee.

In 1955 the Australian Dairy Produce Board was made the sole exporter of butter and cheese to Britain and was given power in other export markets to trade in competition with private exporters.

The complex mixture of control, voluntary agreement and price manipulation raises some very difficult policy and administrative issues for the industry as well as for governments, which have the responsibility of balancing the political pressures exerted by this troubled industry with the public interest.

To facilitate the consultation and liaison necessary to make the whole complex system function, the Australian Dairy Industry Council was formed in May 1956. It consists of representatives of the A.D.F.F., the Australian Dairy Produce Board and the Commonwealth Dairy Produce Equalization Committee. It represents the industry as a whole, as distinct from the producers only and it has been described by the Minister for Primary Industry as the 'Parliament of the Dairy Industry'. One of its important functions is to determine the wholesale price structure for butter and cheese sold on the domestic market, which it does on the basis of a report from the Dairy Cost Index Committee: this Committee in turn consists of one representative of each of the Federation, the Board and the Equalization Committee.

The domestic wholesale prices for butter and cheese are thus determined by the industry and returns to producers are supplemented from an annual bounty of $27 million paid by the Federal government for distribution to producers supplying milk and cream to factories.

At the State level, the various dairy organizations are represented on yet another list of committees associated with the distribution and marketing of this politically sensitive commodity. For example, the Victorian Dairyfarmers' Association has representatives on the Victorian Dairy Products Board, Filled Milk Advisory Committee, Milk Pasteurisation Committee, Dairy Industry Cold Storage Committee and the Cream Industry Association. Throughout Australia 14 State boards are concerned with the regulation of milk, butter and cheese on all of which dairy producer organizations are represented. This representation makes quite heavy demands on the time and finances of the limited number of men who are able and prepared to be involved in industry activities of this kind.

Producers generally aim to ensure that their representatives are in a majority on commodity boards set up by the Federal government in order to retain industry control of the commodity. In the case of dairy products, the A.D.F.F. has three representatives out of thirteen on the Australian

I

Dairy Produce Board, and the six representatives of the cooperative butter factories lean towards the producers' views.

Today, the main constitutional objectives of the Australian Dairy Farmers' Federation are:

(i) to co-ordinate the efforts of dairy farmers' organizations;
(ii) to protect and promote the interests of dairy farmers;
(iii) to ensure adequate representation of dairy farmers' views on all bodies directly affecting the industry;
(iv) to ensure for dairy farmers 'a fair return for their capital and labour.'

THE SUGAR INDUSTRY

Sugar growing is the most highly organized, or controlled, of Australia's rural industries. As described in Chapters 14 and 15 a complex system has been evolved for marketing sugar both locally and overseas. Under the terms of the Commonwealth-State agreement relating to sugar marketing, the Queensland Sugar Board acquires or purchases all sugar produced, sells it through agents and hands the proceeds to the millowners for distribution amongst themselves and growers according to the determinations of the Cane Prices Board. However, as the production of sugar cane is mainly confined to Queensland, with only a small tonnage grown in northern New South Wales, there is no federal commodity organization comparable with those which have been described for other commodities.

The Australian Cane Growers' Council consists of the Queensland Cane Growers' Council and the New South Wales Cane Growers' Council, but is dominated by the Queensland organization.

QUEENSLAND CANE GROWERS' COUNCIL

In sharp contrast to the producer organizations in other States, in which membership is voluntary, the Queensland Cane Growers' Council is a statutory body established under the Primary Producers' Organization and Marketing Act (1926-65) which empowers the government to 'declare' a commodity, the producers of which are then obliged to join the industry organization nominated in the declaration and pay membership levies to it. The Council is the successor to the United Cane Growers' Association, a voluntary body formed in 1913 by the amalgamation of cane growers' local groups which were then pressing for cane prices to be fixed by the government.

The particular concern of the Queensland Cane Growers' Council is with the growers' interests in the complicated system governing the detailed control of production, distribution and marketing; its functions include 'the stabilization of the price of sugar for the purpose of ensuring to the grower a fair return for his labour and capital invested . . .' and 'securing additional markets for the distribution of products and improved means of distribution.'[8]

The line of communication from the Council to the farm is through district cane growers' executives of which there are 12, and beyond them there are 31 mill suppliers' committees, which are charged *inter alia* with the duties of establishing branches, controlling and directing their operations; formulating schemes for meeting the requirements of the locality and securing cooperation amongst cane growers supplying the respective mill. They are also required to encourage the development and use of mechanical harvesting and cane-loading machines.[9] They are responsible to the district executives, whose duties are similar to those of the mill committees, except that they cover a wider area. Both are bound to comply with the instructions and directions of the Queensland Cane Growers' Council and to supply and provide to that Council all such information, whether statistical or otherwise, as it may from time to time require.

AUSTRALIAN SUGAR PRODUCERS' ASSOCIATION

Despite the fact that every grower must pay an annual levy to the Queensland Cane Growers' Council and that the Council has functioned efficiently, the Australian Sugar Producers' Association, a voluntary organization formed in 1907, has continued to function. The founders of the Association, who were predominantly growers, stated that their first objective was 'To promote combined action on the part of the Australian Sugar Growers and Manufacturers, and others interested in the sugar industry, for the protection and advancement of the industry.'

The Association has been represented on the delegations conducting negotiations under the Commonwealth Sugar Agreement (annually) and the International Sugar Agreements, alongside delegates from the Australian Cane Growers' Council. Although the A.S.P.A. is regarded as mainly a millers' organization its standing amongst growers is indicated by the fact that in respect of the 1965 season, growers of 75 per cent of the Queensland cane and 40 per cent of the New South Wales crop were financial members of the Association.

ORGANIZATION AND ACTIVITIES

Most of the organizations, particularly the commodity associations, function along fairly similar lines. Representatives interview producers for the purpose of getting them into membership, local branches are formed and in some associations these are grouped into district councils. In most cases membership fees are low. Subscription rates for the graziers' associations,

8. *Constitution of the Queensland Cane Growers' Council*, Queensland Government Printer, Brisbane.

9. *Ibid.*

which are related to the number of sheep and cattle depastured, produce relatively higher fees.

Wool and meat producers in New South Wales, for example, are served by nearly 400 local branches of the United Farmers' and Woolgrowers' Association and about 150 local branches of the Graziers' Association of New South Wales, though many branches are not active.

As a general practice the initiative in decision making still comes from local branches, and local branch resolutions may go to council meetings or the annual general meeting, which is the supreme policy-making body. Policies are established by putting local resolutions to the scrutiny of larger, more representative groupings. This is necessarily a slow process.

Major proposals, particularly those involving the industry in accepting a responsibility to finance a scheme of marketing, promotion or research for which producers must find finance, tend to originate at the state or national executive level. Industry leaders, working in association with governments and their departments, provide a channel for the testing of new proposals. In the case of the major proposal to have a reserve price scheme for wool marketing, issues were referred down to producers at branch level and a government referendum of wool growers was held in 1965.

Arrangements for secretarial services vary. The A.P.P.U. Federal office is located in Canberra, while the N.F.U. office in Sydney will move to Canberra in 1967. The A.W.G.C. is equipped with its own secretariat in Sydney, whereas the A.W.M.P.F. draws its requirements from its New South Wales affiliate.

Most of the representations by organizations arise from resolutions passed at meetings. They are mostly directed to governments or other public authorities such as departments and industry boards, usually by correspondence. These formal representations are supplemented by personal contacts from day to day.

The main stream of policy on the major matters of concern to the individual organizations normally develops through the medium of discussion between organizational executives and ministers and their departmental heads. Very contentious issues usually call for a formal deputation to the appropriate minister. Professional lobbyists are not used.

Most of the major organizations have an affiliation with a rural weekly newspaper or publish their own; but their communication with the metropolitan and urban community so far has been very slight.

THE TWO 'UNIONS'

NATIONAL FARMERS' UNION OF AUSTRALIA

Formation of the National Farmers' Union of Australia, (N.F.U.) in 1943, was a result of the Empire Producers' conference held in Australia in 1936. Its principal objects as stated in its constitution are 'to unite organizations of primary producers in Australia and its mandated territories and to preserve the identity of such organizations and their rights of self determination . . .' and 'to secure uniformity of policy among and unity of action by or on behalf of its affiliated organizations . . .'

Some of the main matters in which it has power to take action relate to taxation, tariffs, transport and communications, animal health, education and scientific and economic research.

The member organizations of the N.F.U. are shown in Table 5-2. The Australian Woolgrowers' and Graziers' Council withdrew in 1965. The secretariat for the N.F.U. was established in 1959.

The N.F.U. has been recognized by the Federal government as a convenient medium for some purposes, but in terms of influence on government policies it has not yet proved itself so influential as some of its constituent members.

During the 1950s, the N.F.U. was active in the field of international trade and tariffs. In the early 1960s, the Union and the A.W.G.C. combined to resist the use of higher tariffs as a partial substitute for the import controls, which were being abandoned after having been introduced in 1952.

These activities generated considerable friction between the two organizations and the Minister for Trade and Industry, who eventually expressed surprise at the protests of the Union and pointed out that 'some of the greatest of Australia's primary industries (represented by N.F.U.) are or may be dependent upon quantitative restrictions for protection . . .'[10] The Minister went on to mention various commodities, including sugar and dairy products. This statement exposed the weakness of the N.F.U. as a vehicle for criticizing the extent of protection.

In 1965, the A.W.G.C. which had been one of the foundation members and mainstays of the N.F.U. resigned, partly because the interests of the unprotected wool and meat producers had proved to be not sufficiently in harmony with those of the other members to warrant the expense of maintaining membership.[11]

As well as conflicts of interest such as these, the N.F.U. suffers acutely from

10. Commonwealth of Australia, *Parliamentary Debates*, Hansard, 21 February 1962, Government Printer, Canberra.

11. One of the reviewers, A. A. Dawson, commented as follows on this point: 'Probably the biggest financial problem of an organization such as the N.F.U. arises from the ease with which a member organization can withdraw. The A.W.G.C. withdrawal from the N.F.U. has shown primary producers how easy it is for a group of producers to withdraw from a loosely federated organization. So far as conflict of interest is concerned, it does not arise in the case of the A.P.P.U., where each commodity section operates by itself and determines its own policy. There is therefore no question of a majority producing one commodity overruling a minority producing another. The Federal Council, which deals with general purpose matters, consists of Federal and State Presidents, plus two representatives from each State, with no reference to commodities, because Federal Council does not deal with commodities. Federal Conference consists of Federal Councillors, plus 10 delegates from each State and Chairman of Federal Produce Committees. Again, produce matters are not discussed.'

the problem faced by all national organizations—the weight of representation to be accorded each member and each commodity. The necessity to restrict the maximum number of delegates, in order that meetings shall not be unwieldy, usually results in the larger organizations being under-represented. Similarly, there is such a disproportion between the value of production of the major and minor commodities that the achievement of an equitable balance in general assemblies of producers poses practical difficulties, which cannot always be satisfactorily resolved.

Although the concept of a union of commodity organizations still enjoys wide support, the organizational and financial hurdles which have handicapped the progress of the N.F.U. have to be overcome before a sound basis for development will exist.[12]

For some years discussions have been taking place between representatives of the N.F.U. and the Australian Primary Producers' Union about a possible basis for uniting the two organizations.

AUSTRALIAN PRIMARY PRODUCERS' UNION

The A.P.P.U. has State divisions in Victoria, New South Wales and Queensland and affiliated organizations functioning as divisions in South Australia and Tasmania.

It was formed at Warrnambool, Victoria, in September 1943 with the principal aim of uniting 'into one Commonwealth-wide Union all sections of Primary Production.'[13]

It was launched in the spirit of idealism which characterized plans for postwar reconstruction and which persists even to the present day in the form of continuing efforts to achieve 'unity' among primary producers. In 1943 the sponsors of the Union were influenced by the Department of War Organization of Industry, the views of which, in relation to rural industry, are reflected in the report of the Rural Reconstruction Commission.

The Commission recommended—with one of its four members dissenting—the establishment of a National Council of Farmers and subsidiaries through which 'the sectional interests of individual industries would become subservient to the common good, and the development of . . . "group individualism" . . . in any particular farming industry would be discouraged.'[14]

The report envisaged that within the structure of the Council, not only all farmers but local governing bodies, State and Federal governments, consumers and farm employees would be represented. The plan was designed to secure conformity with a notional 'national interest'.

12. Campbell records the view that the possibility of the establishment of a new Australian Farmers' Federation 'was one of the reasons motivating the A.W.G.C. to withdraw from the N.F.U.', *op. cit.*, p 116.

13. *A.P.P.U. Constitution.*

14. Rural Reconstruction Commission, *Commercial Policy in Relation to Agriculture, Tenth Report*, Government Printer, Canberra 1946.

In 1950 the Federal Secretary of the Union said, 'In establishing the A.P.P.U., now in four States as the largest single producer organization in Australia, we have tried to follow the principles set out in the tenth Report of the Rural Reconstruction Commission.'[15]

The newly formed Union naturally met resistance from the established commodity organizations most of which were already associated with the Primary Producers' Council of Australia (later renamed the National Farmers' Union).

In 1951 the A.P.P.U. applied for registration as an organization of employers under the Commonwealth Conciliation and Arbitration Act. Registration was opposed by other primary producer organizations registered with the court and was refused by the court on the grounds that the Union failed to specify the industry in connection with which it was formed and because of deficiencies in its rules, which, at that time, permitted *inter alia* the enrolment of persons who were not usually employers. In 1952, the Union sought to nominate employers' representatives on a number of Conciliation Committees under the N.S.W. Industrial Arbitration Act and its application was refused on objections by other employers' organizations.

For many years, the extent to which producers of particular commodities were formally subservient to the general assembly of A.P.P.U. members was a controversial and crucial question. Originally the A.P.P.U. constitution provided for State produce sections to send representatives to Federal produce committees which would in turn report to the Federal council and make recommendations with regard to matters especially affecting growers of the respective products. The Federal council was subject to any directions given, or regulations made, by the annual Federal conference of the A.P.P.U. In effect producers of particular products had limited rights of self-determination in policy matters. But in 1963 an important new development altered this provision.

In 1963 the A.P.P.U. applied for admission to the Australian Wool Industry Conference. This application was rejected by the Conference principally for the reason that the wool produce section was subject to the Union's Federal council for its policy.[16]

The functions and charter of Federal produce sections at that time were:

Subject to any regulations made or directions given by Federal Council, the duty of a Federal Produce Committee is to deal with all Federal matters especially affecting the members of its Produce Section, and to

15. Letter dated 17 October 1950, from the Federal Secretary of the A.P.P.U., addressed to the Prime Minister, the Leader of the Country Party and the Leader of the Opposition in Federal Parliament.

16. Some of the main points raised during consideration of A.P.P.U. membership of the A.W.I.C. were autonomy of produce sections, the number of wool grower members and the extent of cross membership between the A.P.P.U. and other wool industry organizations.

investigate, report, and make recommendations to Federal Council on those matters.[17]

In order to gain admission of the Wool Section of the A.P.P.U. to the Conference in 1965 some substantial amendments were made to the Union's constitution. Produce sections were made autonomous in the conduct of their respective commodity business so that their policy decisions automatically became Union policy.[18]

Through this constitutional amendment the monolithic mould in which the Union was originally cast was replaced by a structure more resembling the N.F.U. concept. The autonomous produce sections, in matters of commodity policy, correspond to the independent commodity organizations which belong to the N.F.U., and the functions of the N.F.U. (which are confined to non-commodity matters) are similar to the general purpose part of the A.P.P.U. namely the Federal council and Federal conference.

In 1966 years of unity talks between representatives of the A.P.P.U. and the N.F.U. culminated in agreement on the constitution for a proposed Australian Farmers' Federation which would absorb the N.F.U. and the general purpose (but not the commodity) functions of the A.P.P.U. However, inability to agree on the financing of the new body caused postponement of the merger. For the time being it was decided to hold joint meetings of the executive committee of the N.F.U. and the Federal Council of the A.P.P.U.

Negotiations at State level resulted, in September 1966, in the South Australian division of the A.P.P.U. merging with the South Australian Wheat and Woolgrowers' Association to form the 'United Farmers and Graziers of South Australia Incorporated'. The constitution of the new organization does not formally identify it with the A.P.P.U. or either of the national organizations with which the South Australian Wheat and Woolgrowers' Association was affiliated. Apart from an agreement to maintain existing affiliations in the interim the commodity sections are free eventually to determine their respective relationships with Federal organizations.

In Victoria, negotiations which had been proceeding for years finally came to fruition late in 1966 when it was agreed that the Victorian Division of the A.P.P.U. will also merge with the Victorian Wheat and Woolgrowers' Association to form the Victorian Farmers' Union. But some problems arising from the effects of the proposed merger on relationships of each State body with its Federal affiliates remained to be resolved.

17. *A.P.P.U. Annual Report 1965*, p 6.

18. On this point, A. A. Dawson comments: 'The A.W.I.C. may take credit for the redrafting of a clause in the A.P.P.U. Constitution, but this only meant that the Constitution was brought into line with the practice which has been in operation for many years.'

The Constitution of the A.W.I.C., as it stood in 1966 with provision for A.P.P.U. membership is reproduced in the *Pastoral Review and Graziers Record*, Vol 77, No 12, December 1966.

It is envisaged that the merged State bodies would refer their general purpose (non-commodity) business to the proposed Australian Farmers' Federation. The medium for dealing with commodity business at Federal level, under this scheme, remains to be clarified.

At the Federal level commodity matters have predominated the activities of the A.P.P.U. Activities and policies of a general nature, the development of which were originally expected as a logical extension of the basic structure of the Union, have not been generated to the extent anticipated.

The N.F.U., not being concerned directly in commodity questions, has a better opportunity to formulate constructive proposals relating generally to production, marketing and economic affairs. The A.P.P.U. has an advantage in being better able to cater for the minor commodities which find it impractical to establish their own self-contained organizations.

Both Unions have received expressions of encouragement, from time to time from Federal ministers. They both participate in the six-monthly consultations between the prime minister and other cabinet ministers and industry representatives at which rural industry is also represented by the A.W.G.C. and the A.W.M.P.F.

With the admission of the A.P.P.U. to the International Federation of Agricultural Producers in 1964, both Unions now represent Australian producers on that Federation.

UNITY AND DIVERSITY

Unity, or diversity, amongst organizations representing primary producers has been a subject of debate ever since the origin of the various commodity associations.

During the last 20 years the controversy has revolved around the relative merits of 'union' or 'unity' (represented by the A.P.P.U.) and confederation in the form of the N.F.U.

The 'unionists' have claimed that the multiplicity of organizations was responsible for:

> absence of any long-range policy based on sound principles and economics, [a] purely sectional outlook, [the] dividing influence of party politics, public quarrelling, no effective co-ordination by any central authority [and] no method of enforcing decisions of conferences.[19]

These faults were seen as the cause of:

> growers being played off politically against each other, [or] playing into the hands of well organized consumer interests, middlemen, processors; very few producer elected boards and very little grower control of marketing; marketing boards loaded against producers with nonproducers and overseas and local prices fixed under costs of production because costs were not officially known.[20]

19. A.P.P.U., *Victorian Division Handbook*, June 1953.
20. *Ibid.*

Table 5-1

Organizations Representing the Five Major Commodities

Commodity	National organization		State affiliates
WOOL AND MEAT	Australian Woolgrowers' and Graziers' Council (A.W.G.C.)	N.S.W.	Graziers' Association of New South Wales; Graziers' Association of Riverina; Pastoralists' Association of West Darling
		Vic.	Graziers' Association of Victoria
		Qld.	United Graziers' Association of Queensland
		S.A.	Stockowners' Association of South Australia
		W.A.	Pastoralists and Graziers Association of Western Australia Inc.
		Tas.	Tasmanian Farmers', Stockowners' and Orchardists' Association
		N.T.	Northern Territory Pastoral Lessees' Association; Centralian Pastoralists' Association
	Australian Wool and Meat Producers' Federation (A.W.M.P.F.)	N.S.W.	United Farmers' and Woolgrowers' Association of New South Wales
		Vic.	Victorian Wheat and Woolgrowers' Association
		Qld.	Selectors' Association of Queensland
		S.A.	South Australian Wheat and Woolgrowers' Association[a]
		W.A.	Farmers' Union of Western Australia Inc.
WHEAT	Australian Wheat Growers' Federation (A.W.G.F.)	N.S.W.	United Farmers' and Woolgrowers' Association of New South Wales
		Vic.	Victorian Wheat and Woolgrowers' Association
		Qld.	Queensland Grain Growers' Association
		S.A.	South Australian Wheat and Woolgrowers' Association[a]
		W.A.	Farmers' Union of Western Australia Inc.

DAIRY PRODUCE	Australian Dairy Farmers' Federation (A.D.F.F.)	N.S.W. Vic. Qld. S.A. W.A. Tas.	Primary Producers' Union of New South Wales Victorian Dairy Farmers' Association Queensland Dairymen's State Council South Australian Dairymen's Association Inc.; South East Dairymen's Association of South Australia Farmers' Union of Western Australia Inc. Tasmanian Farmers' Federation
SUGAR	Australian Cane Growers' Council	N.S.W.	New South Wales Cane Growers' Council
	Australian Sugar Producers' Association Ltd	Qld.	Queensland Cane Growers' Council

a. Now the United Farmers and Graziers of South Australia Inc. after merging with the South Australian division of the A.P.P.U. in September 1966.

SOURCE: *Australian Primary Industry Organizations*, Department of Primary Industry, Canberra, December 1965.

However, this catalogue of traditional farmer complaints is not necessarily a result of the lack of one organization representing all producers.

Lack of finance to appoint adequate staff at the executive level in producer organizations, rather than the structural form of the organizations, is responsible for some of the shortcomings attributed to more fundamental causes, though obviously lack of finance reflects lack of support by members.

Table 5-2
The National Farmers' Union of Australia and the Australian Primary Producers' Union

Member Organizations of the National Farmers' Union of Australia

Australian Wheat Growers' Federation
Australian Wool and Meat Producers' Federation
Australian Association of Stud Merino Breeders
Australian Dairy Farmers' Federation
Australian Cane Growers' Council
Australian Apple and Pear Growers' Association
Australian Citrus Growers' Federation
Australian Canning Fruitgrowers' Association
Australian Vegetable Growers' Federation
Australian Banana Growers' Council
Ricegrowers' Association of Australia

Council of Agriculture (Queensland)
New South Wales Chamber of the National Farmers' Union
Tasmanian Farmers' Council
National Farmers' Union of South Australia Inc.
Farmers' Union of Western Australia Inc.
Highland Farmers' and Settlers' Association (Territory of Papua and New Guinea)

Through these different members, a total of 77 organizations are associated in the National Farmers' Union group.

Structure of the Australian Primary Producers' Union

Victoria	— Victorian Division (affiliation with Victorian Wheat and Woolgrowers' Association proposed for 1967)
South Australia	— United Farmers and Graziers of South Australia Inc. (affiliated division as from 1966)
Tasmania	— Tasmanian Farmers' Federation (affiliated division)
New South Wales	— New South Wales Division
Queensland	— Queensland Division
Federal Office	— Canberra

Federal Produce Committees for Barley, Dairying, Fruit and Vegetables. Meat, Oats (and Hay, Maize and Coarse Grains), Pigs, Potatoes, Poultry, Vine Fruits, Wheat and Wool, co-ordinate Divisional Produce Section policies. A Federal Council deals with general purpose matters between annual meetings of the Federal Conference.

The real question is, having achieved a united front, what are the united producers able to do which they could not do before? It is implicit that the united body will work for the welfare of all producers but this can only be done through specific actions: at this stage conflicting interests are exposed. Conflicts of interest arise in the field of assistance to industry, in particular. Action which is to the advantage of one group of producers may be to the disadvantage of the remainder, if there are limited resources available for such assistance at any particular time: for example if the introduction of a subsidy on nitrogenous fertilizers is in any sense at the expense of the restoration of the real value of the superphosphate subsidy; or research and extension resources may be concentrated in certain industries or areas. This applies also to sub groups within the recipient group: for example, subsidies on output, which are usually introduced in response to the plight of the low-income farmer, actually benefit the larger and more efficient farmers to a far greater extent.

The basic limitation to unity of action by all primary producers, is the relatively small number of specific matters on which interests are really common and deep enough to secure the solid support of the whole over a sustained period of time.[21]

Moreover as the 'non-unionists' have remonstrated, union and unity are not synonymous in practice. If the ability to speak consistently 'with one voice' is a necessary condition for unity, this could only be achieved within a union by binding minorities to accept the decisions of the majority. In a multi-commodity, multi-regional union this requirement limits activities to those on which a high degree of unanimity or apathy exists. Extension of united action beyond the perimeter will result in discord or the formation of splinter groups.[22]

21. Again, A. A. Dawson's comment implies a contrary view: 'The N.F.U. Constitution lists no fewer than 25 items of common interest, which may vary in depth, but undoubtedly secure the solid support of many producers.' Yet if one notes the activities of the different organizations, rather than their Constitutions, my argument in the text is sustained.

22. A. R. Johnston, General Secretary of the United Farmers' and Woolgrowers' Association of N.S.W., in letters published in *The Land* newspaper issues of 17 November 1966 and 15 December 1966 states: 'If independent commodity sections and their chairmen are permitted to announce their independent decisions without some attempt to first gain universal backing, we may not achieve a great deal towards the objective of building a united force to protect the primary producers' position in the future development of Australia . . .

'The commodities represented in separate specialist Federations have the right, not only to process the commodity matters, but also to take a stand on general issues which they feel have a direct and substantial impact upon the producers of that commodity. The Federations appoint representatives to a general purpose body known as a National Farmers' Union, in which an endeavour is made to make common agreement on non-commodity matters such as tariffs, trade, economic growth, taxation, education, defence, and a whole range of social issues. . . . Where common ground is not achieved, the Federations are completely free to take independent action . . . the right of independent action must necessarily be fully preserved at all times.'

The very existence of numerous organizations, by facilitating the expression of different points of view, encourages the belief among some advocates of particular systems of organization that theirs has achieved the ability to speak with a united voice and that it should therefore be adopted universally.

Analogies with other countries or with regions within Australia where a large degree of unity apparently exists, cannot be generalized to Australian rural industry as a whole because, in its total geographic and economic dimensions, it is relatively diverse.

Cleavages will always persist between the producers who want 'orderly marketing' schemes and those who do not, and between producers who have secured a privileged market for their output and those who have not, and between producers of protected and unprotected commodities on questions such as tariffs and subsidies. These potential splits are part of the defensive armoury of governments which, backed by their control of the Treasury, ensure that the government will be the senior partner in any liaison which might grow out of the achievement of greater unity amongst producers.[23]

The apparent contradiction between claims that greater unity would enable producers to approach governments with strength and the expressed desire of ministers for the creation of such a formidable pressure group, prompts some producers to fear that instead of 'speaking with one voice' to the government, they may find themselves 'listening with one ear'.

POLITICS

It seems to be fairly widely assumed that there is a direct association between the producer organizations and political parties, particularly the Australian Country Party. This belief had some validity in the early years of the Party, but it no longer applies. Originally, farm organizations acted as the electorate basis for Country Party members who began to appear in State parliaments during the period of the World War I.[24] The principal bodies included the Farmers' and Settlers' Association of N.S.W. which then had counterparts by name in Western Australia and South Australia. The latter, together with some of the other founding organizations, have disappeared, either through attrition or through merging into the Australian Country Party framework. The last of the major associations to terminate its affiliation with the Country Party was the Farmers' and Settlers' Association of

23. Campbell, commenting on this same point, writes of the 'rather futile compulsion to achieve a unified voice in an industry . . . the interests of the community are best protected under a pluralistic set-up where practising politicians and administrators receive advice (perhaps widely divergent advice at times) from several farm organizations', *op. cit.*, pp 125-6.

24. Ulrich Ellis, *A History of the Australian Country Party*, Melbourne University Press, Melbourne 1963.

N.S.W. (now the United Farmers' and Woolgrowers' Association), which decided in 1944, that the connection could be prejudicial to membership or to the success of its representations.[25]

None of the primary producers' organizations with which this chapter is concerned has any formal link with a political party. The constitutions of many of the associations explicitly require the organization to be non-party political. Even wider restrictions apply in the case of the Australian Primary Producers' Union, the constitution of which provides that, 'No question of a party political nature shall be entertained or discussed at a meeting of a Branch, a District Council, a Sectional Committee or the Central Executive.'

As is the case for many other producers' organizations, a prominent clause in the A.W.G.F.'s Constitution declares that 'The Federation shall be and remain strictly non-party political . . .' and a subsequent clause provides that the Federation shall consist (only) of 'organizations of bona-fide wheatgrowers which are non-party political . . .' As a further precaution it is provided that:

> No Member of Parliament shall act as an officer of the Federation. Any officer of the Federation on being elected to Parliament shall *ipso facto* vacate his office, with the exception of the original members of the Council of the Federation and the secretary. No affiliated organization shall have a Member of Parliament acting as a delegate on its behalf at any meeting of the Federation.

Naturally, there is a discernible cross membership between those who are active in the administration of industry organizations and the Country Party organization in the electorate. Both are based on country residents of which only a very small proportion is prepared to be active in organizations; and some producers work their way up through industry politics and step across into parliamentary politics. But this is not the easy or normal route. It is becoming increasingly difficult to combine the three roles of producer, industry politician and party politician. The growing complexity of the problems demands more time than most producers can afford to spare.

Party politicians are not popular within the activities of producer organizations. As long ago as 1925 producers were warned: 'Watch out for the man who tries to grind his axe on the P.P.U. grindstone.'[26] The party politician cannot bind himself to the policy of a producer organization, because his role is that of negotiating a workable compromise between conflicting interests. He is constantly trying to stabilize a situation by balancing countervailing pressures against each other. Therefore he cannot be identified with

25. W. A. Bayley, *History of the Farmers' and Settlers' Association of New South Wales*, Farmers' and Settlers' Association, 1957.

26. M. P. Dunlop, *'Looking Backward—What the P.P.U. has done'*, Primary Producers' Union, 1925.

a particular producer organization. It is basically for this reason that those organizations which were instrumental in the formation of the Country Party subsequently severed their formal associations.[27]

A direct line of responsibility from a producer organization or even a political organization in the electorate, through to a parliamentary party is not a viable relationship, especially if the party is in office. Parliamentary parties have shown the virtues of being free of responsibility to non-parliamentary bodies.

This detachment between the party organization at parliamentary and electorate levels has been strongly preserved by the Liberal Party of Australia, despite repeated moves within the electorate to bring the parliamentary members under control. The Australian Labor Party has been seriously damaged, to put it mildly, because the parliamentary party is answerable to an electorate body.

Quite apart from the fact that direct links between outside bodies and a parliamentary party have not proved satisfactory to either side, the Country Party is subject to the same limitations as the rural organizations when it comes to speaking with one voice for rural industry.

In contrast with the primary producer organizations, none of the three major political parties has a really active electorate organization capable of formulating the wishes of producers into policies. Consequently the political parties are not significant as policy-making groups: this is the role of the industry organizations which, when they have defined a policy, convey it to the appropriate government department or board, not to a political party. In the public spheres the industry organizations virtually serve as extensions of the structure required in a democratic system of government for the formulation of policy and its administration.

This applies particularly in relation to the Federal government which operates under a constitution which gives it very limited powers over primary industry.

Without this informal and flexible means of consulting and negotiating with rural industry, governments, especially the Commonwealth, would find the administration of their responsibilities most difficult. The leader of the Australian Country Party in Federal parliament has acknowledged this role in the following words:

> Those of us who are in government are drawn from many activities of life; we have different experiences and we're preoccupied with many things that are not close to industry, and I say, as one who's been a long time in government, we do need to be kept closely informed, closely

---

27. Campbell quite validly has pointed out that 'such close liaison [between the administrator and the administrated] in agricultural administration since the Liberal-Country Party coalition came to power in 1949 owes something to traditional Country Party philosophy', *op. cit.*, p 118.

advised—may I add, sanely, responsibly advised—by those who are occupying their whole lives in their own industrial activities.[28]

CONCLUSION

Australia is now a highly industrialized and urbanized community within which rural industry is of declining relative importance. Primary commodities are also increasingly subject to competition from substitutes made in factories. Rural industry is less the cause of changes in the level and direction of economic activity and less able to influence the changing economy. Rural industry has to accommodate itself to these new situations.

Primary producer organizations are very slowly responding to the changing circumstances by revitalizing their administration and improving their staffing. There is a growing realization of the necessity for the gathering and analysis of intelligence information as a basis for policy making; for high calibre staff to advise and act for the organizations; and for representations to be soundly based on fact. Weight of numbers is giving way to weight of argument.

As a consequence of these improvements it is to be expected that the present pre-occupation with current problems and concentration of attention on governments will be enlightened by more forward planning of policies and greater interest in broader issues. Then, when the strategy of positively adapting to change becomes more widely accepted, the organizations will not only be striving to ensure that change suits their members, but they will increasingly be involved in assisting their members to adjust to change.

28. Address by J. McEwen, Acting Prime Minister, Minister for Trade and Industry and Leader of the Australian Country Party, to the United Farmers' and Graziers' Association of South Australia, Adelaide, 9 September 1966.

K

CHAPTER 6

AGRICULTURE IN THE ECONOMY

D. H. McKay

Bureau of Agricultural Economics

THE AUSTRALIAN ECONOMY

Most of Australia's Gross National Product is contributed by secondary and tertiary industries, and most of Australia's work force is employed in these sectors.

In the 1961 census, 27·0 per cent of the work force was engaged in manufacturing industry, 58·8 per cent in tertiary industry, and 1·3 per cent in mining. Only 10·9 per cent was engaged in primary production, including 0·6 per cent in forestry and fishing industries, so that 10·3 per cent could be said to be employed in rural industries.

A comparison of the percentage of the work force in rural industries with some other countries shows that in the early 1960s the United States had 6·8 per cent of its work force engaged in agriculture, the United Kingdom 3·8 per cent, France 19 per cent, Germany 11·6 per cent and Japan 25·6 per cent.

Another measure of the significance of the rural sector of the economy is the proportion of Gross National Product provided by rural industries. Only 13 per cent of Gross Domestic Product in Australia is derived from primary production. Despite the low proportion of our rural work force in rural industries, and the high proportion in secondary industries, Australia is an important trading nation, exporting principally agricultural products and minerals. Imports are for the most part secondary products, capital and labour (by immigration). Whilst Australia ranks forty-first in order of world population (11·5 million), she ranks about thirteenth in order of value of trade, and about tenth in exports per head. In 1963, imports were 15 per cent and exports 13·7 per cent of G.D.P. but exports were a much higher proportion of the gross value of primary, mining and secondary production. Australia's exports in 1964-65 were 74 per cent of rural origin, 10 per cent minerals (excluding gold) and 13 per cent manufactures. Imports, on the other hand, comprised about 7 per cent of agricultural products, while the remaining 93 per cent were capital goods and manufactured products in various stages of processing.

Australia continues to be a substantial importer of capital. Annual private overseas investment in companies in Australia has grown rapidly from about $U.S. 95 million in 1948-49 to almost $U.S. 600 million in 1964-65. There is also some non-private investment in Australia (averaging about $U.S. 20 million over five recent years) and some outflow of Australian capital, averaging $U.S. 15 million over the ten years ended 1964-65.

Australia is 6,000 miles to 12,000 miles distant from her major trading partners. In 1964-65, freight and insurance payable on imports amounted to $333 million or 12 per cent of the f.o.b. value of imports. Freight and other 'invisible' items represent a very substantial element in Australia's balance of payments; for instance, gross 'invisible' debits in 1964-65 totalled $1,319 million, although this was reduced to a debit of $614 million after 'invisible' overseas earnings had been credited. In addition, internal freights are a substantial element of costs within Australia.

In international negotiations, for a number of reasons, countries are nowadays being increasingly classified into two categories—developed and developing. Australia has consistently maintained that there are some countries which do not easily fit into either category, and has gained recognition as being one of these. Australia has much in common with the developed (industrialized) countries when national income, education, health services and other measures of development are considered. However, in terms of industrial development, the potential of untapped resources and reliance upon a narrow range of agricultural and mineral exports, Australia has much in common with the developing countries.[1]

When comparing the Australian economy in 1937 and in 1965, Reddaway observed that it had become much less a 'dependent economy', that is, it was less dependent for its cycles on external forces, principally prices for pastoral products:

> Australia's future progress will be influenced much more by the actions of the Australian people and governments than by world forces. In this important sense she is not, to my mind, a dependent economy, except to the extent that any country is affected in its progress by the success or otherwise of the whole world in securing a good advance.[2]

AGRICULTURE IN THE ECONOMY

The farm sector in Australia now contributes a relatively small and declining proportion of Gross Domestic Product.

Furthermore, it employs a relatively small and declining proportion of the

1. For a full discussion of the Australian attitude on this matter see H. W. Arndt, 'Australia—Developed, Developing or Midway?', *Economic Record*, Vol 41, No 95, September 1965.

2. W. B. Reddaway, 'The Australian Economy, 1937 and 1965', *Economic Record*, Vol 41, No 96, December 1965.

work force, even though it provides the bulk of export income. In recent years both farm production and exports have been expanding, and yet, as is explained in other chapters, the farm sector still has considerable capacity for growth, provided markets can be found at prices which induce this growth. In recent years, prices received by farmers have moved downwards while prices paid for materials and services have moved upwards.

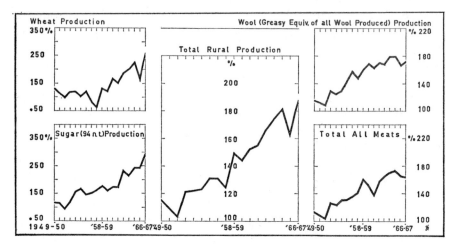

Figure 6-1: Index of Volume of Rural Production: Total and Major Commodities, 1949-50 to 1966-67. Base: Average 1936-37 to 1938-39 = 100. (Bureau of Agricultural Economics)

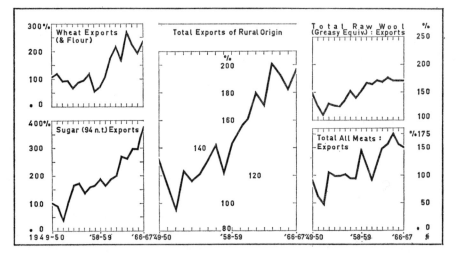

Figure 6-2: Index of Volume of Exports of Rural Origin: Total and Major Commodities, 1949-50 to 1966-67 (financial years). Base: Average 1936-37 to 1938-39 = 100. (Bureau of Agricultural Economics)

Table 6-1

Selected Countries: Composition of Gross Domestic Product,[a] 1963

Country	Primary[b]	Mining	Manu-facturing	Tertiary and other	Total
	%	%	%	%	%
Australia[c]	13	2	28	57	100
Belgium	7	3	30	60	100
Canada	8	4	26	62	100
Denmark	12	—	30	58	100
France	9	2	36	53	100
West Germany	5	5	40	50	100
Italy	16	1	33	50	100
Japan	13	1	31	55	100
Norway	9	1	26	64	100
United Kingdom	4	3	35	58	100
United States	4	1	29	66	100

a. Gross Domestic Product as used in United Nations publications is equivalent to Gross National Product in Australian national accounts.
b. Including forestry and fisheries.
c. 1962-63.

SOURCE: *Yearbook of National Accounts Statistics*, U.N., 1964.

Table 6-2

Primary Industries as a Proportion of Gross National Product, 1948-49 to 1965-66

Period		G.N.P. at Factor Cost	
	Total	Primary industries[a]	Primary industries as per cent of total
Average of 3 years ended	$Am.	$Am.	%
1950-51	5,151	1,315	25·5
1953-54	7,502	1,463	19·5
1956-57	9,487	1,545	16·3
1959-60	11,223	1,532	13·7
1962-63	13,644	1,734	12·7
Year			
1963-64	16,167	2,234	13·8
1964-65	17,641	2,156	12·2
1965-66	18,367		

a. Includes fishing and forestry, which accounts for about 6 to 7 per cent of the total.
SOURCE: *Australian National Accounts*, Bureau of Census and Statistics.

Despite the pressures of higher costs and lower returns, farm incomes have been maintained by the expansion of production, and the primary industries now contribute about 13 per cent of Gross National Product at factor cost. This proportion is higher than in most of the industrialized countries (Table 6-1) and has been relatively stable in recent years after falling from the very high level of some 25 per cent in the early 1950s—a period of boom prices for most commodities, notably wool. (Table 6-2.) The Australian experience—of a declining proportion of G.N.P. provided by the rural sector—is broadly similar to that of most other countries. (Table 6-3.)

Table 6-3

Selected Countries: Primary Industries[a] as a Proportion of
Gross Domestic Product, 1950-1960

Country	1950	1960	Change	Ratio
	1	2	2−1	2÷1
Australia	29·0	13·0	−16·0	0·45
Brazil	28·6	28·2	−0·4	0·99
Canada	13·2	6·9	−6·3	0·52
Denmark	21·0	14·4	−6·6	0·69
France	14·7	9·7	−5·0	0·66
India	51·3	48·7	−2·6	0·95
Japan	26·0	15·4	−10·6	0·59
New Zealand	41·7	25·2	−16·5	0·60
United Kingdom	6·0	4·1	−1·9	0·68
United States	7·3	4·1	−3·2	0·56

a. Including fishing and forestry.

Sources: New Zealand: *Monthly Abstract of Statistics*, Department of Statistics, Wellington, N. Z.

All Others: *Yearbook of National Accounts Statistics*, U.N., 1964.

In Australia the decline in the proportion of G.D.P. contributed by agriculture was not due to relative price movements alone. The prices received for all rural products fell by about 10 per cent from 1950-51 to the end of 1964. Over the same period, the volume of factory production more than doubled, while the volume of rural output increased by about 70 per cent. But, when farm income is considered, these same influences, together with an increase in prices paid by farmers of the order of 72 per cent have contributed to reduce the share of farm income in the Net National Product. (Table 6-4.)

Table 6-4

Farm Income as a Proportion of Net National Product,[a]
1936-37 to 1965-66

Period	Farm Income	
	$Am.	Per cent of net national product
Average of 3 years ended		
1938-39	n.a.	—[b]
1947-48	480[c]	16·6
1950-51	1,047	21·7
1953-54	1,047	14·7
1956-57	979	11·1
1959-60	894	8·7
1962-63	1,041	8·4
Year		
1963-64	1,455	9·9
1964-65	1,307	8·1
1965-66[d]	1,025	6·1

n.a. Not available.
a. Net National Product is equivalent to G.N.P. at factor cost less allowance for depreciation.
b. Probably rather less than 10 per cent.
c. Adjusted from official figures to provide comparability with later years.
d. Preliminary estimate by the Bureau of Agricultural Economics.

SOURCES: *Australian National Accounts*, Bureau of Census and Statistics; and Bureau of Agricultural Economics.

AGRICULTURE AND EXPORT INCOME

The agricultural sector fulfils an important role in the total economy as an earner of export income. On the criteria of shares of Gross National Product, and proportions of the work force employed in the different sectors, the Australian economy is a highly industrialized one. But in terms of export earnings and the balance of payments, the Australian economy is heavily dependent on rural exports as the major source of overseas funds. (Table 6-5.)

In any discussions or negotiations on international trade Australia is immediately identified, and identifies herself, as an 'agricultural exporter'. Agricultural products accounted for 74 per cent of all exports in 1964-65. This compares with figures of 88 per cent in the 1920s and 85 per cent in the 1930s and in the early 1950s. (Table 6-5.) Although there has been some growth in the export of manufactured products, the most striking increase in recent years has been in mineral exports. Exploitation of large iron ore

Table 6-5

Composition of Exports, 1923-24 to 1964-65

Item	1923-24 to 1927-28	1934-35 to 1938-39	1950-51 to 1954-55	1955-56 to 1959-60	1962-63	1963-64	1964-65
	%	%	%	%	%	%	%
Wool[a]	45·3	38·3	52·0	43·9	35·8	35·1	31·1
Wheat and flour	19·2	15·6	10·1	7·4	11·7	14·8	12·9
Dairy products[b]	6·2	9·3	3·9	4·6	3·8	3·3	4·1
Meats[c]	4·1	8·2	6·2	8·2	10·7	8·9	11·0
Sugar	2·0	2·7	2·6	3·4	4·3	5·7	4·4
Fruits[d]	2·3	4·2	3·1	3·7	3·3	3·2	3·2
Other agricultural products	8·8	7·1	7·5	8·1	8·2	7·4	7·0
Total rural exports	87·9	85·4	85·4	79·3	77·8	78·4	73·7
Minerals[e]	2·1	1·8	2·2	3·1	3·3	3·4	5·3
Other	10·0	12·8	12·4	17·6	18·9	18·2	21·0
Total exports[f]	100·0	100·0	100·0	100·0	100·0	100·0	100·0
Value of total exports $Am. f.o.b.	272·7	254·9	1,631·7	1,717·5	2,118·0	2,736·7	2,591·7

a. For wool, the total includes greasy, scoured, washed and tops.
b. Butter, butter substitutes, cheese and total milk and cream.
c. All meats, including canned and frozen meats.
d. Dried, fresh and preserved fruits.
e. Rocks, minerals (including ores and concentrates) and hydrocarbons in solid or semi-solid form.
f. Total exports comprise total merchandise exports of Australian produce, including ships' and aircraft stores, but excluding bullion and specie.

SOURCE: *Oversea Trade*, Bureau of Census and Statistics.

deposits and other mineral developments will continue to increase both the relative and absolute contribution of mining to export earnings.

In recent years, the aggregate volume of rural exports has been increasing steadily and a little faster than the increases in aggregate rural output. (Table 6-14.) Increasing domestic consumption of some products has been more than offset by increases in exports of some major export products, such as wool and wheat. The proportion of production exported varies widely among agricultural products. For wool it is about 96 per cent, wheat 80 per cent and beef 41 per cent. It is estimated that some 60 per cent of total agricultural production is exported. (Table 6-7.)

Few developed countries have greater dependence on agricultural exports than Australia. Among Western European countries, only Denmark and Ireland approach the Australian situation, while both Canada and the United States have less than half the Australian figure. The less developed countries exhibit the characteristic tendency of such economies of almost complete dependence on the export of primary products.

Table 6-6

Volume of Exports and Terms of Trade, 1948-49 to 1965-66
(Index Numbers: Base 1959-1960 = 100)

Period	Exports of rural origin	Value of all exports at constant prices	Export prices	Import prices	Terms of trade
Average of 3 years ended					
1950-51	81	68	122	76	160
1953-54	72	70	127	95	134
1956-57	86	83	113	95	119
Year					
1957-58	79	83	102	99	103
1958-59	93	94	89	99	90
1959-60	100	100	100	100	100
1960-61	105	105	94	101	93
1961-62	118	120	96	101	95
1962-63	112	117	101	101	100
1963-64	131	137	114	103	111
1964-65	126	135	105	104	101
1965-66	119	137	107	107	100

SOURCES: *Balance of Payments*, 1963-64 to 1964-65, Bureau of Census and Statistics; and Index of Exports of Rural Origin, Bureau of Agricultural Economics.

Table 6-7

Major Rural Products: Proportion of Production Exported,
Selected Periods

Products	Average of 3 years ending 30 June 1955 %	Average of 3 years ending 30 June 1965 %
Wool[a]	95·3	96·1
Beef and veal	18·4	40·6
Mutton	10·4	30·4
Lamb	23·4	10·3
Butter	29·5	44·1
Cheese	49·0	45·6
Wheat[b]	65·7	79·5
Sugar	53·4	63·9
Dried vine fruits	82·9	70·5
Fresh apples	42·4	40·8

a. Includes wool on skins, tops, noils and waste, etc. An adjustment for the net increase in stocks for export has been made.
b. Includes flour as wheat. An adjustment for the net increase in stocks for export has been made.

SOURCE: Derived from statistics published by the Bureau of Census and Statistics and the Australian Meat Board.

Table 6-8

Australian Exports as a Proportion of World Exports,
Selected Years 1948-1964

Year	All exports %	Wool %	Wheat %	Meat %	Sugar %	Dried vine fruits[a] %	Fresh apples %
Av. 1948-52	2·5	43·4	10·4	16·3	3·1	13·8	10·3
1953	2·4	41·0	7·7	22·5	4·8	18·4	9·7
1958	1·5	44·9	4·3	12·8	4·7	23·9	13·0
1959	1·7	42·1	5·0	14·8	5·5	23·6	6·3
1960	1·5	45·7	7·4	12·2	4·1	14·0	6·6
1961	1·7	42·4	10·6	9·8	3·9	16·4	7·0
1962	1·7	44·7	14·6	10·6	4·6	16·5	8·0
1963	1·8	44·2	9·7	11·7	6·6	15·5	9·0
1964	1·8	48·5	13·4	12·6	6·5	18·6	9·2

a. Raisins and currants from 1948 to 1958. Raisins from 1959 to 1964.

See also Table 16-3.

SOURCES: *Trade Yearbook*, FAO, 1965; *Monthly Bulletins of Statistics*, U.N., and *Statistical Yearbook*, 1963, U.N.

Australia is by far the major exporter of wool and among the top half-dozen countries for a number of other products such as wheat, meat, sugar and dairy products. (Table 6-8.)

International trading prices for most commodities are subject to wide variation. Consequently, the dependence on agricultural exports (and other raw materials) is a potential source of instability in the Australian balance of payments. This instability caused by price fluctuations may be increased by fluctuations in production.

The Australian environment is such that wide fluctuations in production can and do occur, and domestic consumption for most products is relatively more stable, so that exports are in some sense a residual. Hence the volume of exports tends to fluctuate more widely than production. It sometimes happens (without suggesting any causal relationship) that production and price move in the same direction so that the amplitude of the fluctuations can be magnified.

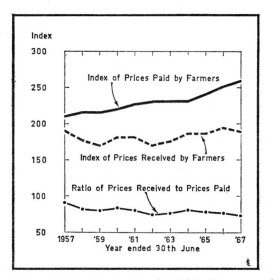

Figure 6-3: Index of Prices Received and Paid by Farmers and Ratio of Prices Received to Prices Paid, 1956-57 to 1966-67. Base: Average of 5 years ended June 1950 = 100. (Bureau of Agricultural Economics)

Wool contributes some 35 per cent of total export earnings so that any fluctuations in wool prices can have a significant influence on the balance of payments position. In the short run, the supply of Australian wool is very inelastic so that small shifts in demand can cause substantial price fluctuations. A measure of the influence of these price fluctuations on export earnings is given by the fact that each one cent variation in the annual average price of wool means a variation of $17 million in export income.

137

By contrast, wheat prices have been relatively stable. Prices for Australian wheat have varied little more than 15 per cent from highest to lowest (taking the U.K. market as a barometer) in the last 10 years. The major features of the wheat situation are the chronic tendency for world supply to exceed world demand, the relatively slow growth in the 'old' commercial markets, and, for Australia, the primacy of China as a destination for exports. In recent years China has taken some 38 per cent of all Australian wheat exports.

Because of the importance of rural products as a source of Australia's export income, the relatively slow rate of growth in world trade in food and raw materials has been of particular importance. Between 1948 and 1962, the volume of world trade in manufactures expanded at a rate of about 7 per cent annually, while that in food and raw materials increased by about 5·3 per cent annually. The food component in 'food and raw materials' probably expanded at a rate less than 5 per cent each year, especially *commercial* trade as distinct from aid programmes. The slow rate of growth in commercial trade in food products reflects a number of factors, including the policies of agricultural protection followed by many of the major industrialized countries, the low income elasticity of demand for foodstuffs, and the replacement of a number of agricultural raw materials by synthetics.

AGRICULTURAL IMPORTS

The agricultural sector is a relatively small user of imports in its production processes. Haig[3] has estimated that imports of materials used by the agricultural sector represent about 5 per cent of agricultural output. The proportions are 7 per cent for the food, drink and tobacco industries; 16 per cent for metals and engineering, and up to 39 per cent for the chemical and oil industries.

On the debit side of the balance of payments, Australia is a minor importer of agricultural commodities, which comprise less than 7 per cent of the import bill. Principal among this type of imports are the tropical beverages, coffee, cocoa and tea. Tobacco, and fish products are other moderately important imports. For the rest there is a large number of specialty items—cheeses, jams and canned foodstuffs of infinite variety. Among the fibres, Australia imports carpet wool, jute and cotton. Australia is rapidly reducing cotton imports through increased domestic production.

AGRICULTURE AND INTERNATIONAL CAPITAL MOVEMENTS

In the early period of Australia's history there were substantial inflows of foreign capital into the pastoral industries. Much of this became domiciled in Australia, so that today there is relatively little dividend outflow on this account.

3. B. D. Haig, 'Input-Output Relationships, 1958-59', *Economic Record*, Vol 41, No 93, March 1965, p 123.

The great inflow of foreign capital in recent times has been directed almost entirely to the secondary or tertiary sectors of the economy. A very small proportion indeed has been invested in the agricultural sector, though there has been some for food processing.

The significance of this investment sometimes goes beyond the immediate capital sum involved. It may have an important bearing on the development of a particular industry or region, or both. It was largely United States capital and 'know-how' which stimulated the development of a cotton industry in northern New South Wales. The Esperance area of Western Australia has had a large injection of United States capital, as also has the beef industry on the previously undeveloped Cape York Peninsula. Similarly, some of the coastal country of Queensland is being developed with foreign capital. Such investment often acts as a stimulant for further Australian investment.

FARM AND NON-FARM INCOMES

Farm income as a percentage of national income has been relatively stable over the past few years, after sharp falls from the wool boom years of the early 1950s. Several studies of the relationship of farm incomes to non-farm incomes indicate that the average farm income compares favourably with the average non-farm income. (Table 6-9.)

Farm incomes in Australia differ from non-farm incomes in three important respects. First, year to year fluctuations in farm income are much greater—whether these fluctuations be downwards or upwards. Second, farm incomes show a very wide dispersion about the mean—a characteristic of self-employed incomes, but not of wage and salary incomes.[4] Third, farm incomes have fluctuated widely without showing a clear trend in one direction or the other. Non-farm self-employed incomes have shown a steady upward growth—in only one out of the last 15 years was there a (very small) fall in self-employed incomes.

The first of these characteristics of farm income, the large year to year fluctuations in farm income, is a reflection of the price and production instability characteristics of farming operations in Australia. They further reflect the dominance of wool, the commodity most subject to price instability, and grains, commodities which are most subject to production instability. Annual fluctuations in farm income in Australia tend to be wider than in other major agricultural countries. An examination of Table 6-9 shows that year to year movements in farm income of plus or minus 40 per cent are common. Gruen[5] has shown that over the period 1938 to 1956 the

4. E. S. Hoffman and J. R. Hume, 'Farm and Non-Farm Incomes in Australia', *Quarterly Review of Agricultural Economics*, Vol 18, No 3, July 1965.

5. F. H. Gruen, 'Capital Formation in Australian Agriculture', *International Journal of Agrarian Affairs*, Vol 2, No 4, January 1958.

Table 6-9

Farm and Non-Farm Incomes, 1948-49 to 1965-66

Period	Gross value of rural production $Am.	Farm income[a] $Am.	Farm income as per cent of national income %	Primary producers $A	Average Actual Income Non-farm self-employed $A	Male wage & salary earners $A
Average of 3 years ended						
1950-51	1,719	1,047	22·1	n.a.	n.a.	n.a.
1953-54	2,182	1,047	15·0	3,044[b]	2,374[b]	1,585[b]
1956-57	2,358	980	11·4	2,803	2,702	1,835
Year						
1957-58	2,258	713	7·8	2,462	2,720	1,972
1958-59	2,523	963	9·7	2,538	2,782	2,036
1959-60	2,656	1,006	9·2	2,824	2,956	2,200
1960-61	2,745	1,022	8·8	2,855	2,996	2,300
1961-62	2,734	951	7·9	2,786	3,028	2,324
1962-63	3,013	1,150	8·9	3,147	3,121	2,387
1963-64	3,425	1,455	10·1	3,909	3,411	2,574
1964-65	3,455	1,307	8·3	3,650[c]	3,600[c]	2,770[c]
1965-66[c]	3,296	1,025	6·2			

a. Farm income = income accruing to farm sector minus wages and salaries.
b. Average of two years only.
c. Preliminary estimates by the Bureau of Agricultural Economics.

SOURCES: *Australian National Accounts*, Bureau of Census and Statistics; and *Annual Reports and Statistics*, Commissioner of Taxation, Canberra.

average percentage variation from the preceding year was 35·8 for Australian farm income, 18·5 for Canadian farm income and 13·8 for realized income of United States farmers.

This erratic behaviour of farm incomes poses a number of problems. Farm operators find difficulty in forward planning; there are national problems of instability in the balance of payments; and when a region depends on one product for much of its income, regional income deficiencies may emerge, of greater or lesser degree. (See Chapter 2.)

The second characteristic of Australian farm incomes—wide dispersion about the mean—reflects both the wide range in scale of farm enterprise and the differing incomes earned in particular industries. While it is true that Australia has no major 'small farm problem', each industry has a 'tail' of small farms with low income earning potential—a 'tail' which is much longer in some industries than others.

So far as the third characteristic is concerned, over the last 10 years or so, farm incomes have fallen in real terms. While prices received by farmers have tended to fall, the prices paid by farmers have risen steadily (Table 6-10) and incomes have been maintained only by increasing the volume of production.

Australian experience of the farm income trend in recent years is rather different from that in most other countries at a similar stage of development.

Table 6-10

Indexes of Prices Paid and Received by Farmers
(Average of 5 years ended June 1950 = 100)

Period	Index of prices paid[a]	Index of prices received all products
Average of 3 years ended		
1950-51	121	153
1953-54	185	186
1956-57	200	182
Year		
1957-58	215	177
1958-59	215	169
1959-60	219	181
1960-61	227	182
1961-62	230	171
1962-63	231	177
1963-64	232	187
1964-65	241	187
1965-66	252	193

a. Includes farm production and marketing expenses and farm family living expenses.
SOURCE: Bureau of Agricultural Economics.

Slattery[6] has shown that, with the exception of Australia and New Zealand, farm incomes are mostly below, and often substantially below, comparable incomes in other sectors. For example, in 1963, in the United States the average incomes of farmers and farm managers were less than 40 per cent of the average incomes of comparable non-farm people; in Germany about 75 per cent; in Sweden about 55 per cent; in Denmark about 55 per cent; and in Canada about 80 per cent.

RURAL POPULATION AND WORK FORCE

The farm population is declining both in absolute terms and as a proportion of the total population.

On-farm employment opportunities in the rural sector have also declined. The most significant decline occurred during the 1939-45 war, indicating that there had been substantial under-employment of labour on farms during the 1930s. The war acted as a stimulus for many of these people to leave rural employment. Increased employment opportunities in the secondary and tertiary sectors since the war have led to a continued net migration from farms. Thus, there has been a small decline in the absolute numbers, and a relatively large decline in the proportion of the total work force employed in rural industries.

Table 6-12 refers to males only as there are few females working full time in rural industries. If females are included the proportion of the work force in agriculture in 1961 was 10·3 per cent. There is evidence of a continuing decline since 1961, but this has been offset by the increasing use of contract services by farmers. Some important contract services are for fencing, timber clearing, farm water supplies (earth tanks, dams and bores) and the use of aircraft for spreading fertilizers and weedicides.

Even though the farm work force is decreasing, the volume of farm output is constantly increasing. The volume of rural output increased by some 75 per cent between 1947 and 1965, while the male work force fell by about 13 per cent. Clearly there has been a marked increase in labour productivity, probably of the order of 4 per cent (compound) per labour unit per annum. However, to the extent that contract services have been increasingly used on farms, such crude estimates of increases in labour productivity per farm worker are overstated.

At the same time there has been a substantially increased use of capital on farms. Allowing for difficulties of weighting between major capital items and other errors of estimation, the increase in total capital used on farms from 1947 to the mid-1960s probably lies between 100 per cent and 150 per cent. Either figure is above the comparable increase in rural production. There is

6. M. M. Slattery, 'Relative Income of Farmers—Some International Comparisons', *Quarterly Review of Agricultural Economics*, Vol 19, No 3, July 1966.

clear evidence that the volume of current inputs (other than labour) has increased in relation to output. This is particularly so of fertilizers, fuels and agricultural chemicals. Because of these changes in the volume and the proportion of major categories of resources needed for production, it is of considerable significance to measure, as best we can, their effects on the productivity of rural industries.

Any meaningful measure of changes in productivity must attempt to relate labour, capital and current inputs to one another, and to output. Saxon[7] has made one of the few attempts to measure increases in rural productivity, by adding the volume of all rural inputs. He then calculated the change in rural productivity from 1947 to 1963 at about 20 per cent. In any case, the increase in labour productivity has been largely possible because of increased use of capital and current inputs. Future increases in labour productivity will no doubt be accompanied by the use of more capital as well as current inputs.

Table 6-11

Persons Living Permanently on Rural Holdings, 1950-1966

	Total population	Persons[a] living permanently on rural holdings	
	000	000	Per cent of total
As at 31 March			
1950	8,120	974[b]	12·0
1954	8,947	1,009[b]	11·2
1958	9,798	1,035	10·6
1961	10,455	1,015	9·7
1965	11,288	1,003	9·0
1966	11,506	995	8·6

a. Includes females and children.
b. Includes an allowance for holdings in New South Wales not counted before 1956.

Source: Bureau of Census and Statistics.

IMPORTANCE OF DIFFERENT RURAL INDUSTRIES

From the point of view of land use and the structure of the rural sector, any attempts to identify 'industries' based on commodities produced in different regions may be somewhat unrealistic. (See Chapter 2.) Despite this limitation, however, the importance of the major commodities may be assessed in a number of ways, some of which are capable of being quantified (see Table 6-13), while some are not. The more readily quantifiable criteria are:

7. E. A. Saxon, 'Productivity in Australian Rural Industries', *Quarterly Review of Agricultural Economics*, Vol 16, No 4, October 1963.

L

(i) contribution to the gross value of rural production;
(ii) contribution to export earnings;
(iii) utilization of the farm labour force; and
(iv) utilization of the land resource.

The other criteria which are either less capable or incapable of quantification are:

(i) capacity for, and rate of growth in terms of the four preceding criteria;
(ii) regional importance, including new land development;
(iii) ancillary employment opportunities;
(iv) social structure and political importance.

So far as quantifiable criteria are concerned, it is possible to measure the areas of land used for different purposes, but such measurement has doubtful meaning (in a 'comparability' sense) for the grazing industries. More than three-quarters of Australia is arid or semi-arid and has no other use than extensive grazing by sheep (principally in the south) or cattle (principally in the north). Some difficulties of measurement occur in attempting to allocate the labour force over a commodity grouping, since a large number of farmers describe themselves (correctly) as carrying out 'mixed farming' or simply 'grazing'. Some adjustments have, therefore, been made to the work force figures as presented in official statistics to permit them to fit the classification by commodities used in Table 6-13.

Table 6-12

Males Employed in Rural Industries,[a] 1939-1961

	Males employed in rural industries			Total male work force	Rural as per cent of total
	Employers and self-employed	Employees etc.	Total rural		
	000	000	000	000	%
National Register[b]					
July 1939	300·0	202·0	502·0	2,107	23·8
Census June 1947	256·6	178·6	435·2	2,479	17·6
Census June 1954	262·2	173·7	435·9	2,857	15·3
Census June 1961	247·0	160·3	396·5	3,166	12·5

a. This category includes those engaged in Agriculture, Grazing and Dairying in the Census return. See also Tables 1-3 and 9-1.

b. Includes only occupied males. Subdivision of self-employed and employees not comparable with that in later census years.

SOURCES: *Labour Report*, 1944, and *Census Reports*, Bureau of Census and Statistics.

Table 6-13

Comparative Importance of Rural Industries According
to Selected Criteria

Industry	Value of production 1962-63 to 1964-65 %	Value of exports 1962-63 to 1964-65 %	Criterion Employment of male labour 1961 —a %	—b %	Crop acreages average 1962-63 to 1964-65 %
Wool	27·1	47·5		23·0	
Mutton and lamb	4·9	1·9		4·0	
Total sheep industry	32·0	49·4 ⎫	27·8	27·0	
Beef	13·3	9·4 ⎭		11·0	
Dairying and pig farming	13·0	5·2	22·2	20·0c	
Wheat	14·6	17·3	9·5d	12·0	51·5
Other cereals	3·9	1·9	—e	3·0	18·8
Sugar	4·3	6·3	4·6	5·0	1·7
Fruit and vines	5·2	3·9	7·1	7·0	1·4
Vegetables	3·3	—	3·7	4·0	0·8
Poultry	4·1	0·3	1·8	3·0	
Other	6·3	6·3	23·3f	8·0	25·8g
TOTAL	100·0	100·0	100·0	100·0	100·0

a. As derived from census reports.
b. Figures in preceding column after approximate allocation of those engaged in mixed farming and after approximate adjustment for overlap.
c. Portion of dairy labour has been allocated to beef production.
d. Incorporates wheat-sheep, 7·2 per cent; and wheat, 2·3 per cent.
e. Included in 'other'.
f. Of this 23·3 per cent, 17·6 per cent was attributable to 'mixed farming'.
g. Other crops, including hay and green fodder.

SOURCES: *Rural Land Use and Crop Statistics; Value of Production Bulletin; Oversea Trade Bulletin*; and *Census Reports*, Bureau of Census and Statistics.

The obvious points which emerge are the overwhelming importance of the sheep industry. It ranks first by all measures. The table also shows the great importance of wheat which is Australia's major crop, and is second among all rural industries in two important measures—value of production and export earnings. The importance of the dairy industry can be seen in the number of people it employs, and that of the beef industry by the measures of value of production, which are greater than those for dairying. The sugar industry and the horticultural industries are about equal. Sugar is more important in terms of export earnings, and horticulture in terms of value of production and employment.

The four qualitative criteria (relating to capacity for growth, regional importance, ancillary employment opportunities, and social structure and political importance) are no less important for being just that. In relation to the future development and direction of the economy, the first, growth capabilities, is of great importance. A measure of past performance which gives a much limited and greatly qualified view of the future is the annual rate of growth in volume and value, both total and export, for major commodities in recent years. (See Table 6-14.)

Table 6-14

Exports of Rural Origin and Rural Production, 1949-50 to 1965-66
(Annual rates of growth: per cent per annum[a])

Product	Exports of rural origin		Rural production	
	Quantum	Value f.o.b.	Quantum	Value
Wool: raw greasy equivalent	2·9	0·7	3·1	0·2
Wheat and flour	6·3	4·8	3·9	4·1
Beef and veal	10·1	19·9	2·7	8·1
Mutton	15·2	24·3	5·2 ⎱	6·8
Lamb	−2·6	0·6	4·3 ⎰	
Canned meats	−5·9	−5·0	−3·7	n.a.
All meats	5·6	10·6	3·1	7·5
Butter	5·4	4·3	1·9	4·6
All dairy products	3·5	3·6	2·8	4·9
Sugar	8·9	9·7	5·2	8·3
Apples fresh	6·0	8·3	5·1	5·4
Dried vine fruits	2·9	7·1	2·1	5·1
Canned fruits	4·7	5·4	n.a.	n.a.
All rural products	4·2	2·8	3·1	3·6

a. Calculated by least-squares method.

SOURCES: Bureau of Census and Statistics and Bureau of Agricultural Economics.

In considerations of future economic policy, assumptions made about the market outlook, relative price movements and other things, such as the scope for innovation, are crucial. It is for this reason that assessment of capacity for growth and development potential for each of our major rural commodities is so important.

Seasonal influences will always intrude themselves into such reckonings. For example, the 1965-66 drought in Eastern Australia reduced output in many industries, notably wheat, wool, beef and dairying. For wool and beef its effect on the rate of growth will be felt for some years to come.

A brief review of the current market outlook for major commodities in 1966 suggests that wool production can go on expanding, and that market outlets will be found at prices within the range of the last five years. Competition from synthetic fibres will place a limit on upward movement of wool prices.

Wheat acreage may expand more slowly from current levels (if at all) and there will continue to be long-term improvements in yield. An increase in production is feasible only if markets remain open, including especially the Chinese market. The successful negotiation of an international grains agreement within the GATT-Kennedy Round framework would help sustain disposal possibilities and price.

The outlook for beef is good. Beef has the capacity for further expansion of production, and markets for increased supplies at near present prices are available. The prospects for expansion of the dairy industry are not so good. The domestic market is growing very slowly, and export opportunities for the short and medium term are limited. In the long term, markets of substantial size may open in Asia but competition for those markets will be strong.

Sugar has expanded very rapidly in the last few years. This industry could also expand further very rapidly if markets were available. The international sugar situation is always highly volatile. In 1966 the open market sugar price is at a record low, yet three or four years ago it was at a record high. Attempts are now being made to negotiate a new international sugar agreement, which will have an important bearing on the future of the Australian sugar in-dustry.

The second non-quantifiable criterion of importance for rural industries relates to the importance of the commodity in particular regions. Some industries have an importance beyond that revealed in quantitative measures, in the sense that particular regions or communities are almost wholly dependent on them. The Queensland coast has been developed and settled by means of the sugar industry. The irrigation areas and districts of southern New South Wales have as the core of their economy rice and fruit. Settlements along the Murray valley are heavily dependent on dried vine fruits. In the recent development of the Ord river region in Western Australia and the Namoi region in New South Wales, cotton has been the key commodity, even though its role in the total economy is small.

The social and political importance of an industry is the sum of the other criteria and introduces one or two others not discussed. Regional concentration, employment intensity, and income status are probably the key criteria in this context.

The third non-quantifiable factor determining the importance of rural industries is the ancillary employment opportunities. These ancillary employment opportunities created by an industry, and more particularly by growth in an industry, are largely determined by the degree of processing undertaken before export of the relevant product. A large number of people are already engaged in the transport, marketing and handling of wool for export, so that further growth of the industry will not require much more labour in these fields. Sugar and dairy products on the other hand are processed here in Australia and ancillary employment opportunities offered by growth in these industries are relatively high.

ECONOMIC POLICY AND RURAL INDUSTRIES

The basic aims of Australia's economic policy may be summarized as:

    (i) a high rate of economic growth;

    (ii) a high rate of population growth;

    (iii) full employment.

Subsidiary to these major policy goals and contributing to them are such aims as increasing productivity, increasing real incomes per head, stable costs and prices, and external viability.

These goals, with the notable exception of population growth, are common to most countries. They pose problems of emphasis on some occasions, and at other times they may have the appearance of mutual inconsistency, when efforts to achieve the three major objectives tend to put pressure on domestic costs and prices, and strengthen the demand for imports. Policy measures employed to restrain these pressures may have as a consequence a reduction in the level of economic activity and consequent unemployment. Again, these are not uncommon problems.

So far as the agricultural sector of the economy is concerned, the national policy goals and the measures employed to pursue them have made great demands on the rural industries and have put the agricultural sector under considerable pressure. The pressure has been that of the 'cost price squeeze',[8] yet rural industries have been required to expand production at a rate sufficient to meet the increasing consumption needs of a growing population and the increasing export income requirement of an expanding economy.

Policy measures have been taken by governments over a long period to foster the growth of the secondary industry sector of the economy. Secondary industries have been encouraged so as to meet the full employment and population growth goals, and to some extent to achieve the stability derived from a more diversely based economy. These policy measures, notably the tariff, were intended to have, and have had, the effect of influencing the allocation of resources away from agriculture by raising the returns to resources engaged in secondary industry. In this way they also have the effect

8. F. H. Gruen, 'Australian Agriculture and the Cost Price Squeeze', *Australian Journal of Agricultural Economics*, Vol 6, No 1, September 1962.

of increasing farmers' costs. The maintenance of full employment and the operations of the Arbitration Commission[9] within the context of tariff protection for industry have also helped to raise labour costs in the economy as a whole. Such measures affect the costs of agricultural producers, and in the event farmers have been faced with continuing increases in costs.

At the same time, however, the postwar period has been one in which the rate of growth of the economy has been largely dependent upon exports of agricultural commodities. As will be explained in more detail in later chapters, some categories of rural industries in Australia are not protected at all, (e.g. wool and beef) some are relatively unprotected, (e.g. the grains) while some are heavily protected, (e.g. cotton and tobacco). Successive governments have therefore found it necessary to take specific action which has the effect of diverting resources back to the rural sector. Most of these measures will be dealt with in greater detail in other chapters; they will simply be stated at this point.

(i) Some industries have stabilization schemes, which have tended to become price supporting. These schemes become difficult to sustain if domestic costs and world prices diverge widely.

(ii) Marketing boards have been established—sometimes, but not exclusively, in association with stabilization schemes.

(iii) There are some subsidies on resources used, such as the subsidies on superphosphate and nitrogenous fertilizers.

(iv) There are some internal freight concessions which become widely operative in times of drought.

(v) There are a number of taxation concessions available to primary producers which act largely as investment incentives.

(vi) Some special credit arrangements apply to primary producers.

(vii) Governments, and producers, contribute heavily to rural research and extension activities.

(viii) There is some public investment, e.g. beef roads, which is both cost reducing and a production incentive.

(ix) Trade-treaty arrangements and international commodity agreements have been established.

This seems a formidable list which, in a simple enumeration, tends to exaggerate the degree of government intervention in agriculture. Quite long lists could be similarly constructed for virtually all sectors of the economy and, of course, the number of items in a list does not indicate their relative importance. In a country which exports such a high proportion of its agricul-

9. For a review of the operation of the Australian arbitration system see *Report of the Committee of Economic Enquiry*, Commonwealth of Australia, Canberra 1965, Vol I, pp 132-149.

tural products, it is simply not possible for governments to undertake the massive support of agriculture that is undertaken in industrialized food importing countries—nor would this necessarily be the right course of action.

Devaluation of the currency is sometimes put forward as an alternative to the situation where the Governments appear to be compensating the agricultural sector for the effects of the protection granted under the tariff to Australian industry. To some writers, the economic benefits from devaluation do not appear substantial. Gruen[10] has noted 'any income gains to exporters from devaluation could be eroded fairly quickly by a continuation of cost increases at our present long term average of $2\frac{1}{2}$-3% per annum.'[11] Irrespective of the validity of this argument, it would seem, however, that political rather than economic objections to devaluation will be the important elements ruling out devaluation as a practical policy at least in the near future.

What action, then, can be taken to maintain a viable agriculture?

In the agricultural sector there is still tremendous scope for increased productivity, even within the limits of present technology. Research programmes at all levels must be maintained, and the practical application of successful research results must be capable of quick transmission to farmers. Farmers in turn must have the management capacity to adapt their farm programmes to new technology. There is room for structural adjustment in a number of rural industries. This is a polite euphemism for the elimination of small and/or high cost farms which do not have the potential to become economically viable—within any reasonable expectation of advances in technology, and of cost and price levels likely to prevail.

Finally, in the rural sector, there is room for greater efficiency in the handling and processing of rural products, from the farm gate to the wharfside and beyond. Further public investment in transport and roads may be required.

Technological advances may bring increased productivity and will certainly bring increased production. This suggests that there must be increasing attention to market development and market diversification. Undue dependence on a fairly narrow range of export commodities carries its own dangers and overdependence on a narrow range of market outlets multiplies these dangers. Negotiations in the area of international commodity arrangements may help to maintain access to markets and put a floor under international prices at a level which could encourage investment and efficient production in Australia. Such a level for the commodities currently under discussion would be much lower than the levels of support currently operating in all importing and some exporting countries. Again, the success of

10. F. H. Gruen, 'Australian Agriculture and the Cost Price Squeeze', loc. cit., p 15.

11. For a further view on devaluation in the Australian context see Report of the Committee of Economic Enquiry, Commonwealth of Australia, 1965, Vol I, pp 356-360.

these efforts may be related to the effects on imports of measures taken to protect domestic industries.

No doubt the policy of 'compensatory action' to offset price increases will be continued, but the limitations and marginal effects of such policies indicate clearly that they are not a panacea to cost increases. With its heavy dependence on exports, the well being of the agricultural sector itself is at stake.

Apart from measures specific to the rural industries, there is the obvious exhortation (and it can be no more than that) to those responsible for the management of the general economy to increase efficiency or reduce inefficiency of the non-farm sector so as to minimize the inflationary content inherent in our national policy goals.

A combination of all these courses of action, with possible variations in emphasis from time to time and between industries, will provide the agricultural sector with a base for growth of an order sufficient to meet the growing needs of the economy.

CHAPTER 7

CHANGES IN SUPPLY OF AGRICULTURAL PRODUCTS

F. H. GRUEN, L. E. WARD AND A. POWELL

Monash University

FACTORS AFFECTING CHANGES IN OUTPUT

The annual production of most agricultural commodities is strongly influenced by decisions farmers have made at different times in the past—just how far in the past will depend on the particular product. For instance, in the case of peaches an interval of nine years normally elapses between planting and the time when trees reach their full bearing potential. On the other hand, in the case of annual crops, acreage can be changed significantly between one season and the next. Even in the case of annual crops however, it may take more than one year for farmers to change from one cropping programme to another, to purchase equipment necessary for a substantial enlargement of acreage or to clear additional areas. For meat production the time lags between decisions to change the level of output and the actual attainment of these new levels are likely to be even more complex. Since output of meat can be changed at short notice at the *expense of future production*, the level of production at any one time will depend not only on the present effects of past decisions about the most desirable size of the breeding herd but also on farmers' estimates of the profitability of sending animals to slaughter now rather than in the future.

Economists often classify the various conditions which influence the level and pattern of output into a number of categories. The first of these is technological. Over time changes take place in the degree and form of man's control over nature and these give rise to trends in productivity which are in large part autonomous; that is, the innovations do not require substantial capital investment, though they may often demand increased managerial skills. The long-term increases in wool, milk and crop yields are usually regarded as good examples of such innovations, though sometimes some part of these long-term increases in yields are produced by economic factors. Some of these will be discussed later.

Secondly, changes in *relative* prices for different products will encourage producers to shift their resources between the various forms of production possible on their farms. Thus there have been substantial movements in the relative levels of production of wool, wheat, coarse grains, sheep meats, beef and dairy products in Australia in the postwar period in response to changes in the relative prices of these various commodities.

③ Thirdly, buoyant overall levels of farm prices—or alternatively the creation of new investment opportunities as a result of technical advances—may inspire an entirely new level of confidence in the future. The result may be a spurt of developmental expenditure and machinery purchases which in turn lifts the *aggregate* level of farm output.

④ Finally, farm output at any one point of time will also be affected by factors over which farmers have little or no control in the short run. These are the effects of variations in weather, either directly such as by rainfall and temperature, or indirectly such as by some diseases and predators. They are often referred to as seasonal effects in Australian parlance.

No systematic treatment of methods of estimation of these various factors is possible here. Instead we will concentrate on describing the changes in output which have occurred in Australia, including where possible, a discussion of the reasons for such movements. Some results of a more detailed study of short-term supply responses for six of the most important Australian farm products will also be included.

THE HISTORICAL RECORD

Table 7-1 gives two measures of the postwar movements in farm output. The first of these is the Commonwealth Statistician's index of the volume of Australian farm production. The second is a seasonally adjusted output series which attempts to estimate—admittedly crudely—what the level of output would have been if seasonal conditions had been 'normal'. The basic method used to derive this second series from the first, was to assume that any short-term deviations of 'yield' from the 'norm' are due to the influence of varying seasonal conditions. (This will not be strictly true, but most of the year to year variations in yields are caused by weather effects.)

Normal yields at any point of time were obtained by deriving regressions of wheat, coarse grain, wool and milk yields on time. The actual deviations from the expected value were then calculated for each year. Variations in sheep and cattle losses each year about the median were also estimated and ascribed to weather conditions. The assumption was then made that such variations in sheep and cattle losses would have affected sheep and cattle available for slaughter in the current year. This approach could obviously not provide a completely accurate picture of the influence of changing weather conditions. For instance, livestock losses in severe drought years such as 1944-46 and 1965-66 will affect output in later years. Fortunately our discussion deals with a 20-year period (from 1945-46 to 1964-65) which happens to exclude such major droughts and we have not attempted to cope with this particular problem.

An examination of the two series of Australian farm output since 1945 leads to the following observations:

(i) As might be expected, the seasonally adjusted series rises more consistently over time than the Statistician's series. In particular, the sudden dips in production in 1950-51, 1951-52 and 1957-58 are eliminated in the seasonally adjusted series.

(ii) At the end of World War II, Australian farm output was about 10 per cent below pre-war levels; however this was largely the result of poor seasonal conditions. The adjusted index shows output in 1945-46 and 1946-47 to be almost equal to the pre-war level.

(iii) In the three years 1946-47 to 1948-49 there was a gradual upward move-

Table 7-1
Farm Production: Indexes of Quantity
(1936-37 to 1938-39 = 100)

Financial year	Statistician's index	'Seasonally adjusted' index[a]
1945-46	92	98
1946-47	91	101
1947-48	109	105
1948-49	109	109
1949-50	115	109
1950-51	109	110
1951-52	103	110
1952-53	121	113
1953-54	122	120
1954-55	123	119
1955-56	131	123
1956-57	131	129
1957-58	124	142
1958-59	149	140
1959-60	144	147
1960-61	152	145
1961-62	155	155
1962-63	166	164
1963-64	174	163
1964-65[b]	187	167
1965-66[b]	160	n.a.

a.   The method of seasonal adjustment is outlined in the text.
b.   Estimated by the Bureau of Agricultural Economics.
n.a. Not available.

SOURCES: *Primary Industries Part 1—Rural Industries Bulletin,* Bureau of Census and Statistics, Nos 40-56, 1945-46 to 1961-62. *Trends in Australian Rural Production and Exports,* Bureau of Agricultural Economics, No 35, September 1965, Table 1.

ment in both indices. This was followed by a sharp decline in the non-adjusted series between 1949-50 and 1951-52. This decline in farm output was partly responsible for the serious balance of payments crisis in 1952. As a result of this crisis the Federal government adopted a long-term policy designed to encourage a more vigorous growth of farm production. To this end the government extended taxation concessions designed to stimulate developmental expenditure; made efforts to secure a high priority for agriculture in obtaining those materials still in short supply; refunded some $150 million to wheat growers at the end of the first stabilization scheme; raised the home consumption price of wheat above the official 'cost of production' and boosted the price received for commercial butter by almost 50 per cent between 1950-51 and 1952-53. In addition the Federal government laid down a series of production aims calling for an increase of 24 per cent in total farm production by 1957-58.

(iv) After the introduction of these measures the Statistician's index of farm output did indeed turn upwards; and reached 23 per cent above the pre-war base by 1954-55. In succeeding years it increased even further, but in 1957-58 largely because of bad seasonal conditions, it actually stood at 124.

(v) The seasonally adjusted output index, which includes changes in livestock inventories, shows a slow increase in farm output of about 2 per cent per annum between 1945-46 and 1952-53. From about 1952-53 on, until the onset of the 1965-66 drought, the rate of increase of farm production stepped up to an average of about 3 to 3·5 per cent per annum. This break in the series in the early 1950s is probably attributable mainly to three factors: firstly, the pervasive influence of high wool prices in the early 1950s which encouraged large-scale developmental expenditure; secondly, the elimination of shortages of fertilizers, machinery and production materials in the early 1950s as a result of both government measures to give agriculture greater priority and of the return to less inflationary conditions in the economy as a whole; thirdly, the virtual elimination of rabbits in the early 1950s following the introduction of the myxoma virus. This influence was important both directly, by increasing the amount of pasture available for sheep and cattle—and also indirectly by reducing the costs of rabbit control measures and thus making pasture improvement expenditure more profitable.

(vi) Part of the very rapid rise in farm output between 1962-63 and 1964-65 was the result of exceptionally favourable seasonal conditions. Thus over the five-year period 1960-61 to 1964-65 the Statistician's index rose by 35 points, compared to 22 points for the seasonally adjusted series.

GROWTH IN PRODUCTION

Compared with earlier periods in the twentieth century the expansion in farm output in the postwar period has been particularly rapid. This expansion has been achieved without any major changes in either the land base, the number of farms or the total farm labour force. Because of changes in data collection methods, no long-term series describing these changes are available. Since 1948-49 there has probably been an increase of 10 per cent in the total area in rural holdings; more significantly, substantial areas of land have been cleared, but figures are only available for some States. The number of rural holdings has also risen slightly. The total farm labour force has probably declined by 5 to 10 per cent, most of this decline having taken place since the 1954 census.

Reasons for Postwar expansion of farm output

The expansion in farm output in the postwar years has been made possible by (i) a high rate of developmental expenditure and capital formation since 1950, (ii) the use of increasing quantities of purchased inputs such as fertilizers and other chemicals, fuel, fencing materials, and (iii) the technical advances made by agricultural scientists and others. Our attempts to obtain statistical estimates of the relative contribution made to changes in total output by these various factors have not been very successful. This is partly because of the difficulties of measurement of the various factors used and partly because the separate effects of the variables have been overshadowed by the general tendency of capital services, other inputs and technical knowledge to increase together. This effectively prevents us from estimating statistically the separate effects of the individual factors.

WOOL AND SHEEP MEATS

The Bureau of Agricultural Economics in its continuous Sheep Industry Survey classifies farms into three broad zones, the Pastoral, Wheat-Sheep and High Rainfall Zones. The Pastoral Zone, the most arid area towards the centre of the continent, sometimes verging on desert, accounts for a declining proportion of the Australian sheep population; its proportion having dropped from 37 per cent of the total, 20 years ago, to 29 per cent in 1962-63. In the southern parts of the Pastoral Zone the possibilities for the substitution of products other than wool are small. Low rainfall precludes cropping and the production of prime lambs apart from the occasional, unpredictable, exceptional season.

In the other two Zones, there are far greater possibilities for substitution. In the Wheat-Sheep Zone, wheat and coarse grains, prime lambs or cattle are possible alternatives. In the High Rainfall Zone, prime lambs, coarse grains and beef can be substituted for wool.

There is evidence of considerable substitution between wool and the other products in the postwar period. High wool prices in the postwar decade encouraged farmers to increase wool production as quickly as possible, to some extent at the expense of other possible avenues of expansion.

Growth in *wool production* can be the result of an expansion of sheep numbers or of an increase in wool cut per sheep. The steady, long-term increase in *fleece weights per sheep* has been responsible for only a small part

Table 7-2

Changes in Sheep Numbers, 1949-1963

(as per cent of sheep and lambs at beginning of each year)

Period	Number of sheep and lambs at beginning of each year[a]	Average annual gain	Crude rate of natural increase	Crude death rate	Crude adult sheep slaughter rate	Crude lamb slaughter rate
	I	II	III	IV	V	VI
1949 to 1957	100·0	4·1	26·7	6·2	11·3	4·9
1957 to 1963	100·0	1·0	27·2	6·2	14·6	5·5

a. As at 1 April each year. Livestock statistics are recorded as at 31 March each year.

Explanation: Columns III − IV − V − VI = Column II (discrepancies due to rounding).

SOURCE: *Statistical Bulletin, Livestock Numbers Australia*, No 23, 31 March 1965 (and earlier issues), Bureau of Census and Statistics.

of the postwar expansion of wool production. Donald allocates 17 per cent of the increase in wool production for the period 1947-1963 to the increase in the average fleece weight per sheep and 83 per cent to the increase in sheep numbers.[1]

Growth in sheep numbers has not been uniform during the postwar period. After 1957 there was a distinct slowing down in the annual rate of increase in sheep numbers. (See Table 7-2.) The table provides a dissection of the components of changes in the Australian sheep population for two periods, before and after 1957. The first of these was a period of relatively high wool prices. From 1949 to 1957 the ratio of the price received by farmers for their wool to the price farmers paid for their production requisites fell only once to 80 (average of five years to June 1950 = 100). The second period of six years from 1957 to 1963 was one in which this ratio never rose as high as 80.

During the period 1949 to 1957, sheep numbers rose by an average of 4·1 per cent per annum, compared with an average increase of slightly less than 1 per cent per annum during the second period. This contrast was not due to the differences in seasonal conditions during the two periods: deaths as a percentage of the number of sheep and lambs at the beginning of each year averaged 6·2 per cent per annum in each of the two periods. Nor was it due to any reduction in lambing percentages: in fact the crude rate of natural increase averaged 26·7 per cent in period one and rose to 27·2 per cent in the later period.

The much smaller rise in sheep numbers during the second period was entirely the result of an increase in slaughterings, particularly of adult sheep. Adult sheep slaughtered as a proportion of stock numbers at the beginning of the respective periods rose by 29 per cent. Total mutton production fluctuated between 220 and 250 thousand tons between 1952-53 and 1956-57; in the next three years it rose to 370 thousand tons and remained near this level until 1965. This was not the result of any improvement in mutton prices relative to wool, as they both tended to decline at the same rate. Under price regimes so far experienced, mutton appears to be essentially a by-product whose production responds in the main to changes in wool prices, rather than to changes in its own price.[2]

For lambs, the increase from 1949-51 to 1957-63 in slaughterings compared to opening stock numbers, was less than for mutton. Total lamb production rose from around 145 thousand tons in the mid-1950s to about 200 thousand tons at the end of the decade. Because producers respond to lamb prices

1. C. M. Donald, 'The Progress of Australian Agriculture and the Role of Pastures in Environmental Change', Farrer Memorial Oration delivered at the University of Sydney, September 1964, *Australian Journal of Science*, Vol 27, No 7, p 191.

2. As pointed out by one of our reviewers, E. J. Waring, a demographic explanation of changes in mutton production is also plausible. According to figures prepared by Waring, there is a close relation between mutton production and the number of lambs marked five years earlier.

more readily than they do to mutton prices, the decline in lamb prices resulting from the original shift from wool to lamb may have been somewhat more effective in dampening the increase in output.

CEREALS

Of the three cereals wheat, oats and barley considered here, wheat is by far the most important, normally accounting for more than two-thirds of the total acreage sown to cereals.

Changes in *wheat* production can be broken down into changes in yields per acre and changes in the area sown to wheat. While wheat yields have fluctuated significantly from year to year, the national average yield has increased by upwards of 60 per cent over the last 30 years. Each year brought an average increase of nearly a quarter of a bushel per acre. This long-term trend reflects mainly the steady adoption of 'best practice' techniques of cropping and advances in plant breeding. A simple linear regression of wheat yield per acre as a function of time gave the following results:

$$Y = 3 \cdot 150 + 0 \cdot 242\ T \qquad\qquad (R^2 = 0 \cdot 419),$$
$$ (\cdot 495) \quad (0 \cdot 054)$$

where Y = national average wheat yield in bushels per acre,

T = time in calendar years (T = 31 for 1930-31.)

This regression was based on data for 1930-31 to 1963-64 and no significant departure from linearity could be detected in the yield series.

In contrast to the steady, long-term increase in wheat yields, the area sown to wheat has shown pronounced long-term swings. Schematically these movements can be shown by giving the wheat acreages at the troughs and peaks of each swing.

Australian wheat acreages in selected years

Pre-war average: (1936-37 to 1938-39)—13·5 million acres
Wartime trough: (1943-44)   — 7·9 „   „
First postwar peak: (1947-48)   —13·9 „   „
Postwar trough: (1956-57)   — 7·9 „   „
1966-67 (forecast)   —20·5 „   „

While there is probably room for some disagreement about the relative importance of the various factors operating, the main reasons for the fluctuations in acreage are clear. Thus the decline during the early war years can be attributed to the acreage restrictions operating and the general scarcities which favoured the less intensive pastoral industry. Initially price conditions also favoured wool production. From about 1942, price conditions turned in favour of wheat; by 1945-46 the wool-wheat price ratio was more favourable to wheat than it had been since the mid-1920s. As soon as acreage restrictions were lifted there was a marked increase in plantings. This also reflected the desire of returned servicemen for quick cash crops.

M

Four main factors were responsible for the decline in wheat plantings after 1947-48:

(i) The relative rise in wool prices for 1949-50 and subsequent years. Thus from 1950-51 until 1956-57 the wool-wheat price ratio remained more favourable to wool than it had been in any of the preceding thirty years.

(ii) The low level of the first advance paid on wheat delivered to the Wheat Board. (The first advance payment is made to growers soon after the crop is delivered to the wheat silos in country areas. Subsequent payments are made by the Wheat Board as the wheat is sold. On some occasions it has taken three or four years before the final payments have been made.) Prior to 1952 the first advance ranged from 30 to 55 per cent of the final price realized as compared with first advances of 78-85 per cent after 1952.

(iii) The increase in pasture improvement which, at least initially, increased the relative profitability of running sheep. McLennan has shown that the decline of wheat acreages between 1949-50 and 1954-55 was particularly marked in those safer, high rainfall sections of the wheat belt where pasture improvement has expanded most rapidly.[3] This was closely connected with the need to get away from the narrow exploitative rotations practised in many parts of the wheat belt in earlier years, the argument being that it was only the prosperity of the early 1950s which allowed farmers to switch to less exploitative forms of land use.

(iv) In some parts of the wheat belt there was a switch from wheat to other grains such as barley and oats because relative prices favoured such changes.

The expansion of the wheat acreage from the low of 1956-57 to more than 18 million acres in 1964-65 is probably again largely due to changing price relationships between wool and wheat. Wool prices have fallen significantly from the levels of the early 1950s, whilst wheat prices received by growers have risen slowly (from $1·25 per bushel in 1956-57 to $1·44 in 1961-62; since then there has been a small decline). Other factors which may have contributed to the expansion are (i) the rise in yields, which has raised the profitability of wheat growing and (ii) the extension of the wheat belt, partly outside traditional climatic zones and partly in newly cleared areas within recognized wheat-growing districts (such as in Western Australia).

Of the other cereals, *oats and barley* are the most important. Peak postwar barley production amounted to 68 million bushels in 1960-61, almost four times the 1948-49 figure of 17·8 million bushels. Oat production reached a peak of 87 million bushels in 1958-59, again almost four times the 1948-49 production of 23·6 million bushels. Most of the considerable annual fluctuations in production are the result of variation in yields. These in turn are largely due to changing seasonal conditions though there has been a long run tendency for both barley and oat yields to rise over time. On average, annual

3. L. McLennan, 'Movements in Wheat Acreage in Australia', *Quarterly Review of Agricultural Economics*, Vol 9, No 1, January 1956.

oat yields have risen by $0 \cdot 19$ ($\pm 0 \cdot 06$) bushels per acre; whilst on average annual barley yields have risen by $0 \cdot 13$ ($\pm 0 \cdot 07$) bushels. These increases are somewhat less than those recorded for wheat for the same period (namely 1930-31 to 1962-63). This may reflect the relatively greater investment in the breeding of new wheat varieties and more effective weed and pest control.

Areas sown to oats and barley have also tended to rise substantially in the postwar period, reaching their respective peaks in 1958-59 and in 1960-61. Since then they have tended to decline, partly because of the upward trend in wheat sowings. The major factor responsible for changing acreages of these two grains are the relative prices which farmers expect to receive for wheat, barley and oats. Thus in the early 1950s, when coarse grains were fetching high prices in Europe, some farmers on the heavier wheat soils turned their attention to oats. By 1956 the overseas price had fallen to a level which made the grain unattractive compared with wheat which had the benefit of a guaranteed price for part of its production.[4]

BEEF AND DAIRY CATTLE

Australian production of *beef and veal* increased about 100 per cent between the immediate postwar period (1945-46 to 1947-48) and the most recent three year average (1963-64 to 1965-66). In an unpublished paper, Dillon has attempted to estimate the factors responsible for this increase in production. Dillon's analysis is restricted to the period 1945-1962, a period when total beef and veal production (estimated from time trends) rose by 360 thousand tons, or 75 per cent. Of this increase $16 \cdot 1$ thousand tons, or about 5 per cent, is attributed to increased production from dairy herds; $192 \cdot 8$ thousand tons, or 53 per cent of the total, to increased beef cattle numbers and $151 \cdot 5$ thousand tons, or 42 per cent of the total to increased production per beef animal.

While dairy farmers have contributed relatively little to the total long run expansion of beef production, the evidence suggests that a large proportion of the short run, annual, changes in beef production comes from the national dairy herd. (This point is discussed in more detail below.)

Beef cattle numbers have risen in both northern and southern areas of the continent because of (i) the generally satisfactory prices for beef and (ii) the enhanced economic security resulting from the Australia-U.K. Fifteen Year Meat Agreement (1952-1967). For northern areas, these factors have stimulated private investment in watering facilities, fencing and various other improvements which have raised the carrying capacity of properties running beef cattle. In southern areas beef production is mostly carried on jointly with wool and sheep-wheat production. The complementary relationship between sheep and cattle has allowed farmers to increase numbers of both types of livestock as investment in pasture improvement proceeded. In addition, the rise in the beef-wool price ratio since 1956-57 has probably en-

4. S. M. Wadham, R. Kent Wilson and Joyce Wood, *Land Utilization in Australia*, 3rd ed, Melbourne University Press, Melbourne 1956, p 242.

couraged some substitution of cattle for sheep, though the time lags involved are such that it is difficult to obtain a statistical estimate of this relationship.

Increased production per animal in the beef herd probably resulted mainly from the following factors: (i) improved rates of growth in beef cattle due to genetic improvement and better animal husbandry; (ii) a lowering in the average turn-off of beef cattle. As a result of these factors, the turn-off rate rose from 22 per cent in 1945 to 28 per cent in 1962, whilst the proportion of breeders in the national beef herd rose from 44 per cent to 49 per cent during the same period.

Total Australian *milk production* (including milk used for butter manufacture) has risen by about 40 per cent since the end of World War II. Most of this increase is attributable to the rise in milk yields per cow rather than to an increase in dairy cow numbers. Since the early 1950s, yields per cow have increased at an average annual compound rate of 1·7 per cent per annum. This is faster than in earlier years (for the whole period from 1946-47 to 1963-64 the average growth rate was 1·4 per cent; whilst during the 1930s average national yields per cow were declining) but it is not particularly impressive by international standards.

The main factor responsible for this increase in yields was probably the better feeding of dairy cattle on improved pastures. It is significant that milk yields per cow have remained static in Queensland during the last 30 years, whilst Victorian average yields have risen by about one-quarter over this period. Until recently there has been practically no pasture improvement in Queensland.

Other factors which have played a part in lifting the national average yield per cow are: (i) the gradual concentration of cow numbers in those areas where higher milk yields have been obtained. Thus the increase in cow numbers in Victoria and Tasmania (and the relative reduction in Queensland and New South Wales) has accounted for about one-quarter of the rise in average Australian milk yields over the period 1953-56 to 1962-64. In addition, cow numbers may have increased more in those areas (or on those farms) which obtain the higher price payable for supplying the whole milk trade as opposed to butter, cheese and condensed products. In New South Wales milk yields from Milk Board supplying areas have been estimated to be 15 to 20 per cent above those from other areas. This difference results from the use of high-yielding low-butterfat producing cows and from an economic reaction of farmers in these areas to the higher product/input price ratio prevailing in the 'milk-zones'. (ii) Better breeding and better management generally have probably made some contribution to the increase in average yields per cow.

Changes in dairy cow numbers have not been very marked in the postwar period. Between 1946 and 1950 dairy cow numbers increased from 3 to 3·2 million; in the next two years numbers declined again to the 1946 levels. After 1952 they increased gradually to a peak of 3·45 million in 1957; since then they have fluctuated between the relatively narrow limits of 3·16 and 3·36 million head.

The major economic factors likely to influence cow numbers are: (i) the price received for dairy products and (ii) the price received for dairy cows slaughtered. The expected long-term dairy product price is relevant to the decision whether to keep or slaughter cows; hence, in attempting to estimate a supply relation for dairy products, we used a distributed lag with declining weights for prices in earlier years.[5] On the other hand, the relevant price series for beef may be a short or long run series. If dairymen are considering shifting into beef as a major enterprise they will be interested in the long run expected price for beef cattle; however, dairy farmers may also exploit abnormally high or low prices for beef ruling in the short run by accelerating or postponing their culling programmes. From this point of view the short run beef price is relevant.

Hence one equation was derived explaining movements in dairy cow numbers in terms of the long run dairy product price and the short run beef price (lagged by six months). This equation, given below, explained over 80 per cent of the annual variation in dairy cow numbers, with both regression coefficients being statistically significant and having the expected sign.

$$\text{Log } C_t = 3\cdot373 + 0\cdot243 \log P^*{}_D - 0\cdot171 \log P_{B,t-\frac{1}{2}}$$
$$\quad\quad\quad (0\cdot034) \quad\quad\quad (0\cdot028)$$
$$S_{1\cdot23} = 0\cdot00667, R^2 = 0\cdot813,$$

where C_t is the number of dairy cows in year t,

    $P^*{}_D$ the long-term expected price for dairy products,[6]

    $P_{B,t-\frac{1}{2}}$ the price for beef, lagged by six months for the period 1946-47 to 1964-65.

A further equation giving the number of dairy cows as a function of long-term prices for both beef and dairy products was also fitted; this gave very similar elasticity coefficients but a somewhat lower coefficient of determination.

5. Nerlove's 'adaptive expectations' model was used. This assumed that

$p^*{}_t = \beta p_{t-1} + \beta(1-\beta) p_{t-2} + \ldots + (1-\beta)^{n-1} p_{t-n}$
where $p^*{}_t$ is the price expected to prevail in period t,
      p_{t-1} the price actually received in period t−1 (and similarly for other subscripts),
and β is a constant labelled 'the coefficient of expectation' which is either arbitrarily chosen or obtained from the data as that β which gives the best statistical fit. We initially used β equals 0·45, since a regression of dairy cow numbers on prices of dairy products (lagged one year) and dairy cow numbers (lagged one year) gave a regression coefficient of 0·55 for the lagged dairy cow numbers ($\beta = 1-0\cdot55$). Cf. M. Nerlove, *The Dynamics of Supply*, The Johns Hopkins Press, Baltimore 1958.

6. Using 'coefficients of expectation' of 0·4 or 0·6 in deriving $P^*{}_D$ gave similar results with slightly lower coefficients of determination.

$$\text{Log } C_t = 3 \cdot 352 + 0 \cdot 233 \log P^*{}_D - 0 \cdot 152 \log P^*{}_B$$
$$(0 \cdot 046) \qquad (0 \cdot 037)$$
$$S_{1 \cdot 23} = 0 \cdot 00848, \ R^2 = 0 \cdot 701,$$

in which the 'coefficient of expectation' for both dairy and beef prices equals $0 \cdot 6$.

It would be very difficult to disentangle the long and short run responses of dairy production to changes in beef prices, and it cannot be adequately attempted within the framework of our study.[7]

While changes in beef and dairy prices explain most of the change in the national dairy herd, there have been significant differential movements in cow numbers in the different States. These have already been referred to briefly above; within the framework of our aggregate analysis we do not propose to examine the reasons for the differential supply response in the different States.

The quantity of milk channelled into different end uses has varied over time. As pointed out earlier, the whole milk market is relatively more profitable than other markets; the consumption of whole milk has grown slightly less rapidly than population growth, but there is little evidence of factors other than population growth influencing the size of the whole milk market. Butter manufacture appears to be a 'residual' use of milk available for processing; it accounts for about 80 per cent of the total milk used for processing (i.e. for manufacture into butter, cheese and condensed products) but for 92 per cent of all *changes* in milk available for processing.

OTHER PRODUCTS

Table 7-3 gives the movements in production and acreage for some of the more important products not mentioned so far.

Of these products *sugar* is by far the most important. The production of sugar has almost trebled in the postwar period, whilst sugar acreage has increased about 100 per cent. Sugar cane output has been rigidly controlled for many years by a complicated system of controls on acreage and peak tonnages of cane. Changes in output therefore reflect, in the main, conscious administrative decisions, taken in the light of prospective export market de-

---

7. Using a weighted index of all meat prices (P_M) instead of beef prices alone, and a β value of $0 \cdot 6$ the above equation was recomputed for the period 1946-47 to 1964-65:

$$\text{Log } C_t = 3 \cdot 4351 + 0 \cdot 292 \log P^*{}_D - 0 \cdot 248 \log P^*{}_M,$$
$$(0 \cdot 047) \qquad (0 \cdot 048)$$
$$S_{1 \cdot 23} = 0 \cdot 00728, \qquad R^2 = 0 \cdot 780.$$

The 'all meat' price index exhibits less year-to-year fluctuation than the beef index, which partly explains its higher elasticity coefficient. Further, it accounts for response by dairy farmers to changes in mutton and lamb prices (log $P^*{}_M$ has a student's t value of $5 \cdot 166$ compared to $4 \cdot 108$ for log $P^*{}_B$).

Table 7-3

Selected Products: Movements in Production and Acreage, 1936-37 to 1965-66[a]

(1957-58 to 1959-60 = 100)

		1936-37 to 1938-39	1945-46 to 1947-48	1948-49 to 1950-51	1951-52 to 1953-54	1954-55 to 1956-57	1957-58 to 1959-60	1960-61 to 1962-63	1963-64 to 1965-66
Sugar cane	Production	60	46	70	74	93	100	116	142
	acreage	73	65	74	85	105	100	107	135
Potatoes	Production	62	98	78	86	80	100	95	90
	acreage	104	141	115	115	92	100	91	88
Apples	Production	79	95	65	78	87	100	122	139
	bearing acreage	124	116	110	103	101	100	102	105
Citrus	Production	65	73	88	83	96	100	121	145
	bearing acreage	87	91	93	96	102	100	103	110
Peaches	Production	86	89	82	104	93	100	125	168
	bearing acreage	119	140	140	129	119	100	123	153
Rice (paddy)	Production	38	44	56	59	75	100	106	127
	acreage	49	61	75	76	91	100	106	130
All grapes	Production	86	91	80	102	87	100	106	129
	bearing acreage	93	99	100	102	102	100	98	101
Dried vinefruits	Production	98	90	76	105	88	100	100	122

a. Averages for triennial periods shown.

SOURCES: *Primary Industries Part 1—Rural Industries Bulletin*, Bureau of Census and Statistics. *Trends in Rural Production and Exports*, Bureau of Agricultural Economics, No 36, December 1965.

velopments. Similarly production of *rice* is determined, though less completely, by the administrative control of irrigation water and acreages.

For fruits, annual changes in production result, in the main, from variations in yields. Bearing acreages normally change only slowly and with considerable lags in response to expected changes in economic returns. There is evidence that the proportion of fruit channelled into various end uses (such as canning, drying and to supply the fresh fruit market), responds fairly readily to changes in the prices offered in the various markets.

SIX-SECTOR SUPPLY ANALYSIS

We have made an attempt to measure the short run effect of price changes on output for six of the most important rural products. They are: wheat, wool, dairy products, lamb, beef and veal, and coarse grains. These products account for the major part of the crop-livestock complex of Australian rural industry and they are highly interdependent in that they compete in a very real way for the same resources.

The supply model applied specified that planned output of each product depended on (i) certain shift variables (which were not immediately affected by changes in expected prices and which included, in certain cases, climatic indexes), (ii) the relative expected prices of the various products produced, and (iii) a random shock.[8] The shift component was free to move through time as investment and technology moved the supply curves outwards; however, the parameters determining the movement of the supply schedules in response to changes in relative prices remained fixed.

In order to apply this model, suitable indicators of planned output and expected price were required. Planned output was expressed in units such as crop acreages, number of sheep shorn, or dairy cows kept.[9] This had two purposes: first to remove some of the influence of weather fluctuations on output; and second to remove some of the effect of 'autonomous' trends in productivity (e.g., of innovations such as the secular upward trend in wheat yields per acre or wool cuts per sheep shorn). Expected prices were generated by means of the Koyck-Nerlove 'adaptive expectations' model which was mentioned earlier (cf. footnote 5). Because of the limited number of observations and the large number of parameters already in the system, there was

8. For a detailed explanation of the analytical tools used, see Alan A. Powell and F. H. Gruen, 'The Constant Elasticity of Transformation Production Frontier and Linear Supply Systems', *International Economic Review* (forthcoming) and F. H. Gruen and others, *Long Term Projections of Agricultural Supply and Demand: Australia, 1965 to 1980*, Department of Economics, Monash University, Melbourne 1967, ch 6.

9. The adjusted time series are given in Alan A. Powell and F. H. Gruen, 'Problems in Aggregate Agricultural Supply Analysis, I: The Construction of Time Series for Analysis', *Review of Marketing and Agricultural Economics,* Vol 34, No 3, September 1966, pp 112-35.

little scope for experimenting with different models of price expectations.[10]

Table 7-4 gives one set of estimates of the short run (i.e., one-year) supply elasticities of the various products with respect to changes in the own price of each of these products and with respect to changes in the prices of other important competing products. Thus an own price elasticity of 0·181 for wheat indicates that for every 10 per cent increase in the expected price of wheat, production will increase by 1·81 per cent within one year. This increased production 'comes from' a movement of resources out of wool and coarse grain production; the coefficients for the expected prices of these products showing that about 60 per cent comes from a reduction in wool production and the remainder from a switch from coarse grain to wheat acreage. Similar movements for other products can be read from the table.

One conclusion emerging from Table 7-4 which is rather surprising relates to the supply equation for lamb. One would normally expect that most of the change in lamb production results from a change in the price of lamb relative to that of wool. However, as shown in the table, movements between wool and lamb accounted for less than one-fifth of the total supply reaction for lamb—the remainder 'came from' dairying.[11] However, a more thorough examination of the lamb production data suggests that our conclusion may not be as erroneous as it appears at first sight. As one observer has put it:

> Since 1958, lamb production has again entered an expansion era, but this time expansion is not taking place in the traditional lamb-producing areas. In those districts which normally produce export lambs, farmers do not appear to be expanding production. In northern Victoria, for instance, there are now fewer ewes joined to British breed rams than there were five years ago. The same trend is obvious in the Wimmera. The greatest expansion is taking place *in districts where out-of-season lamb can be produced* . . . (italics in the original).[12]

Out-of-season lambs are produced in irrigation areas and in high rainfall districts where, in many cases, dairying is an important, alternative form of land use.

---

10. It was decided, therefore, to treat distributed lags parametrically, generating expected price-series from the raw price data for various arbitrary assumptions about Nerlove's coefficient of expectation (cf. footnote 5). In order to limit the range of possibilities, fixed ratios between the coefficients of expectations for the various products were adopted—the ratios depending on the relative variabilities of the price series for the different products. For pragmatic reasons, the infinite lag series was truncated after seven years, lag coefficients being adjusted upwards to sum to unity.

11. The estimated partial transformation elasticity between lamb and dairying was −0·27 and statistically different from zero at the 5 per cent level; the estimated partial transformation elasticity between wool and lamb was only −0·05, and statistically non-significant.

12. G. J. R. Coles, 'Lamb Producers' Aims . . .', *Papers of the Australian Beef and Lamb Symposium*, Melbourne, 15th September 1965, Australian Meat Board and the Royal Agricultural Society of Victoria, p 71.

Table 7-4

Price Elasticities[a] of Supply: Short Run[b] Estimates[c]

Product	Elasticity with respect to the expected price of						
	Wool	Lamb	Wheat	Coarse grains	Beef and veal[d]	Dairy	Sum
Wool[e]	+0·051	−0·006	−0·045	0	0	0	0
Lamb[f]	−0·047	+0·253	0	0	0	−0·206	0
Wheat[g]	−0·109	0	+0·181	−0·072	0	0	0
Coarse grains[g]	0	0	−0·212	+0·212	0	0	0
Beef and veal[f]	0	0	0	0	+0·162	−0·162	0
Dairy products[h]	0	−0·063	0	0	−0·133	+0·196	0

a. Elasticities evaluated at sample mean outputs and expected prices. Results based on time series data from 1947-48 to 1964-65.

b. 'Short run' indicates an adjustment period of one year.

c. All results conditional on an assumed coefficient of expectations (β) of 0·6 for wool. With the exception of wheat, and beef and veal, other β-values are in inverse proportion to the coefficients of variation of their price series, with wool providing the numeraire. Wheat price series were specially derived from institutional considerations (see Powell and Gruen, 'Problems in Aggregate Supply Analysis: I.' op. cit.). Beef price is 'short price', as measured by spot price, lagged six months.

d. Elasticities with respect to 'short run' price of beef with its 'long run' expected price held constant.

e. Wool output measured by numbers of adult sheep shorn.

f. Meat output measured by tonnage slaughtered (carcass weight).

g. Grains output measured by intended acreage.

h. Output of dairy products measured by numbers of dairy cows.

For a number of reasons, some of the cross supply relations were constrained to zero.[13] Whilst the estimates depend, in no small measure, on our 'hunches' and prior beliefs about the underlying structure of the supply relationships—and cannot, therefore, be treated as final 'objective' evidence—they do, we believe, represent a consistent rationalization of the observed changes in output in terms of the constructs of economic theory.

All the own price elasticities in Table 7-4 are relatively small, showing that the scope for short run (i.e. one-year) changes in planned output in response to changes in expected prices is not very great. This is what one would expect; any group of farmers will normally change gradually from one type of enterprise to another and sudden movements in planned output are relatively rare, though weather fluctuations will quite often lead to substantial changes in *actual* production from one year to the next.

However, using the one-year supply reactions and a concept developed by Nerlove, it is possible to estimate the effect of price changes on supply over longer periods. Table 7-5 gives one-year and five-year own price elasticities for five of the six products discussed above. The five-year elasticities estimate the likely response of the planned supply for each product when expected price is raised by 1 per cent for a period of five years. Thus, to take the case of wheat again, whilst planned wheat acreages may be expected to rise by 1·8 per cent within one year, when the expected price is raised by 10 per

Table 7-5

Price Elasticities of Supply: One- and Five-Year Estimates[a]

Product	Own price elasticity of supply	
	Short run[b]	Intermediate run[c]
Wool	+0·051	+0·248
Lamb	+0·206	+0·935
Wheat	+0·181	+0·823
Coarse grains	+0·212	+0·805
Dairy products	+0·196	+0·429

a. See footnotes to Table 7-4.
b. One-year adjustment period.
c. Five-year adjustment period: Nerlovian estimate.

13. This was done partly because we expected certain cross supply elasticities (e.g. between wool and dairying) to be extremely low, and, given this prior belief, a method which estimates all transformation elasticities makes inefficient use of a strictly limited quantity of data. In other cases, elasticities were constrained to zero (e.g. between lamb and coarse grains) because some 'outputs' are in fact intermediate products within the system. However in some cases (e.g. between wool and beef) the short run supply elasticity was constrained to zero because we obtained incorrect signs (though statistically non-significant coefficients). Perverse signs have serious consequences for this particular model because homogeneity in prices is specified—this implies that cross plus own price elasticities must add identically to zero.

cent, maintenance of wheat prices at this higher level (whilst other prices are also held constant) can be expected to lead to an increase in planned wheat acreages of 8·2 per cent after five years.[14]

CONCLUSION

A distinction has been drawn between the growth in the aggregate level of farm output and the trends occurring within different sectors of the Australian agricultural economy. Australian farm output has grown at a fairly uniform rate of about 3 to 3·5 per cent per annum since the early 1950s. It is true that there have been occasional seasonal fluctuations but, until the onset of the serious 1965-66 drought, there was little evidence of slackening in the rate of growth of total farm output. If anything there was some suggestion of a faster rate of growth in the early 1960s than in the late 1950s.

The extent of the long run effect of the 1965-66 drought on total agricultural output cannot be fully assessed at this stage, but it seems certain that the losses of both sheep- and cattle-breeding stock will affect farm output for some years.

On the other hand, there have been very substantial changes in the rate of growth of output for individual products. The growth of wool production declined markedly after 1956-57; whilst wheat sowings started their steady upward climb at the same time. The output of some of the 'problem' industries such as dairying and dried vine fruits which rely heavily on protection and where incomes are relatively low, has increased less than total agricultural output. On the other hand, two of the most rapidly growing industries until 1965-66, namely cotton and tobacco, have been stimulated with heavy protective measures. In both cases, it seems likely that the *rate of growth* of output will decline substantially in the near future.

14. It is possible to estimate supply reactions for any number of years; however we have some reservations about the use of a very long run of years. In any case, the assumption of holding other prices constant becomes increasingly unrealistic.

CHAPTER 8

LAND POLICY

K. O. CAMPBELL

University of Sydney

Land policy loomed very large in public thinking and action in Australia in its early days. The colony of South Australia was in fact founded in 1836 as a practical test of Edward Gibbon Wakefield's particular theory of land settlement.[1] In the nineteenth century, revenue from land sales was for a long time a major source of public revenue. Parliamentary elections were won or lost on land policy issues.

Today, the administration of land is essentially concerned with carrying out settled policy. It is true that in some Australian States the platforms of the political parties still reflect the beliefs of 50 years ago that subdivision of pre-existing holdings (closer settlement) is the major means of promoting rural development. But as the public becomes more fully aware of the potentialities for agricultural expansion inherent in recent advances in agricultural technology, it is likely that this older emphasis on land redistribution as a means to development will be superseded.

The Australian Federal government as such has no land policy, except in so far as it is directly involved in the administration of the Northern Territory and the overseas territories of Papua and New Guinea. Upon the federation of the Australian States in 1901, the administration of land was one area of public responsibility which was left in the hands of the State governments. All of these States at that time had lands departments as constituent parts of their administrative machinery and this situation still prevails today.

Despite its lack of constitutional authority, the Commonwealth government can nevertheless exercise some indirect influence upon the direction of land policy. This arises mainly from the limited financial autonomy of the States in recent decades. The mark of the Commonwealth government upon land policy was most clearly seen with respect to the scheme for the settlement of ex-servicemen after World War II, which is discussed later. But the Federal government exercises a more continuous influence in a financial con-

1. Edward Gibbon Wakefield, *A Letter from Sydney*, London 1829, republished by J. M. Dent and Sons, London 1929. For an evaluation of the Wakefield doctrine see R. C. Mills, *The Colonisation of Australia, 1829-1842*, Sidgwick and Jackson, London 1915; and S. H. Roberts, *History of Australian Land Settlement*, Macmillan, Melbourne 1924.

text. Loan funds used by the States to finance closer settlement activities and for other purposes are reviewed annually on a federal basis at the meeting of the Loan Council, comprised of federal and State finance ministers. Major schemes for land development are also subject to federal review, if federal finance is required, as it usually is. Apart from its participation in land settlement activities, the Federal government levies land taxes and estate duties. These were originally conceived as a means of discouraging the aggregation of land into large holdings.[2]

LAND OWNERSHIP

Australia is probably unique among the western countries in that a high proportion of its land is still in public ownership. Table 8-1 shows in absolute and relative terms the areas alienated and unalienated in the various States in 1964. These figures now change very little from year to year. The

Table 8-1
Ownership of Land, 1964

State or Territory	Private lands		Public lands		Total area
	Alienated	In process of alienation	Leased or licensed	Other[a]	
	m. acres	m. acres	m. acres	m. acres	m. acres
N.S.W.	58·9	7·1	113·3	18·8	198·0
Vic.	31·8	2·4	6·1	16·0	56·2
Qld.	26·4	3·8	369·4	27·3	426·9
S.A.	16·0	0·4	146·4	80·5	243·2
W.A.	29·1	14·5	246·5	334·5	624·6
Tas.	6·6	0·2	1·5	8·6	16·9
N.T.	0·3	—[b]	191·4	141·2	333·0
A.C.T.	0·1	—[b]	0·3	0·2	0·6
Australia	169·1	28·5	1,074·8	627·0	1,899·5
	%	%	%	%	%
N.S.W.	29·7	3·6	57·2	9·5	100·0
Vic.	56·5	4·2	10·9	28·4	100·0
Qld.	6·2	0·9	86·5	6·4	100·0
S.A.	6·5	0·2	60·2	33·1	100·0
W.A.	4·7	2·3	39·5	53·5	100·0
Tas.	39·1	1·3	8·6	51·0	100·0
N.T.	0·1	—	57·5	42·4	100·0
A.C.T.	10·6	6·9	47·5	35·0	100·0
Australia	8·9	1·5	56·6	33·0	100·0

a. Land occupied by government agencies, reserved lands, and unoccupied lands.
b. Not significant.
Source: Year Book, No 52, 1966, Bureau of Census and Statistics.

2. J. M. Garland, Economic Aspects of Australian Land Taxation, Melbourne University Press, Melbourne 1934.

interesting point is that 175 years after the first settlement only 10·4 per cent of the total area of the country had been alienated or was in process of alienation.

The alienated lands, for the most part, are located in the older settled areas, Victoria being the only State with more than half of its lands in private ownership. The large acreages of land held under lease from the government are located predominantly in the more sparsely settled, more arid pastoral areas of Queensland, Western Australia, the Northern Territory, New South Wales and South Australia.

The various forms of land tenure in the various States are broadly similar, the similarity being strongest among the eastern States which originally formed part of New South Wales. Even so, the large number of types of tenure and variety of terms and conditions applying to particular tenures make it impossible to provide a succinct outline of the country's land legislation.[3]

FREEHOLD TENURES

There are two types of freehold tenure. The first, which applies to the greater part of the alienated lands, allows a high degree of freedom to the individual owner to use or to transfer the land as he wishes. The government does retain some control by virtue of the right of eminent domain, the right to tax, and the right to institute land-use regulations in the name of resource conservation.

However, in the case of some of the freehold land acquired in the past 50 years or so, governments have attached a caveat preventing their transfer to persons who already hold more than a specified area of land. This is true, for instance, of lands acquired under conditional purchase tenures and certain other tenures in New South Wales after 1909. In other words, some of the restrictions which apply to lands in process of alienation, described in the next section, apply equally to some freehold land.

THE TENURE OF LANDS IN PROCESS OF ALIENATION

The State governments typically place many conditions upon landholders who are in the process of purchasing their land. Usually there is a limit set on the area which can be acquired, the concept of 'the home maintenance area' or 'living area' being frequently employed as an administrative device in this connection. Sometimes, as with some tenures in New South Wales, there are, in addition, certain acreage maxima applicable to particular regions. In most cases also, it is incumbent on the owner to live on the

3. The most systematic attempt to provide an outline of Australian land legislation was made by the Surveyor-General of Western Australia, Mr W. V. Fyfe, in 1944. This report formed Annexure A of the *Ninth Report* of the Rural Reconstruction Commission, Government Printer, Canberra 1946, but the annexures were not published. A supplementary mimeographed report entitled 'Land Laws and Tenures' covering amendments up to 1948 was issued in 1949.

property for at least five years and to carry out within a prescribed time certain improvements such as clearing and fencing. These latter restraints sometimes impose substantial opportunity costs on the settler.[4]

The principle of the home maintenance area is a pivotal feature of much Australian thinking about land tenure. Various expressions of the concept are to be found in different Acts. A typical definition would be that used in the New South Wales Western Lands Act of 1949, viz. 'an area which when used for the purpose for which it is reasonably fitted would be sufficient for the maintenance in average seasons and circumstances of the average family'. This concept has been used as a criterion in a number of administrative decisions affecting land.[5] First, it has been used to set the maximum area which may be alienated to any one settler whether by allocation or as a result of transfers from others. By the same token, it serves to guide decisions on applications to transfer titles. In more recent times, the concept has been used in determining the area which may be retained by the original holder when land is resumed or surrendered for closer settlement. Third, it has been used in closer settlement programmes, particularly since World War II, to set the minimum areas to be allotted to settlers. As such it became a means of preventing excessive subdivision by over-enthusiastic State officials.

The language of the definition is extremely vague and its interpretation must necessarily be highly subjective. In practice, the ultimate interpretation has to be made by the local administrative units. Commonwealth government oversight of land settlement programmes after World War II did encourage greater objectivity by forcing State lands departments to resort to more precise budgets than they had been wont to use previously. However, whatever the degree of objectivity introduced, the criterion clearly sets a welfare objective in terms of a reasonable level of living and involves no consideration of efficiency. The 'home maintenance area' concept has also been criticized for its scant regard for questions of production variability.[6] The problem of the survival of pastoral businesses in areas of low and irregular rainfall is not amenable to solution in terms of average incomes and average seasons.

In addition to the various forms of freehold tenure, there are in most States several classes of leasehold where the tenant has some right of conversion to freehold tenures. This right is hedged about with a whole host of conditions not the least of which, usually, is the provision relating to home maintenance areas.

4. e.g. I. J. Moncrieff and R. G. Mauldon, 'The Effect of Land Clearing Regulations on the Rate of Farm Development, A Case Study', *Australian Journal of Agricultural Economics*, Vol 7, No 2, December 1963.
5. J. N. Lewis, 'Is the Concept of the Home Maintenance Area Outmoded?', *Australian Journal of Agricultural Economics*, Vol 7, No 2, December 1963, p 97.
6. K. O. Campbell, 'The Challenge of Production Instability in Australian Agriculture', *Australian Journal of Agricultural Economics*, Vol 2, No 1, July 1958, p 9.

LEASES FROM THE GOVERNMENT

There is a wide variety of government leases in operation in the various States. They range from annual leases to perpetual leases, the majority of them being for long periods. For most practical purposes, properties which are held under perpetual leases are virtually indistinguishable from alienated land. Usually the consent of the responsible minister is required before sales or transfers can be effected, but sales (and professional valuations) are made as if the properties in question were freehold. It should be emphasized that these leases relate solely to the land and not to the improvements upon it.

In some of the long-term leases, the rentals set are fixed over time. In other cases the rentals are re-appraised from time to time, e.g. at 10-year intervals. Except where land has been made available for closer settlement after resumption, the rentals charged are usually much lower than the rentals which would prevail on a free market. They can be as low as 1·25 per cent of the notified capital value, which may itself be fixed at a very conservative level. In some cases, as in the Western Division of New South Wales, rentals are fixed at so much per sheep carried, the actual amount payable being based on the assessed carrying capacity of the land.

As might be expected where the prevailing rentals are well below the economic level, the difference tends to be capitalized into the market value of the lease in question. Under certain circumstances, governments take steps to prevent existing tenants from benefiting, at the expense of their successors, from what are, in essence, concessional rentals.

Some of the leaseholds, particularly in Queensland and the Northern Territory, are for fixed periods, and have been criticized for their consequent failure to encourage the maintenance and improvement of the properties in question. The Queensland pastoral leases do however give the outgoing lessee the right to retain a portion of his lease equivalent to a living area. Some of the disabilities of the fixed lease may be offset by the incorporation of specific provisions in the lease. These may require the lessee to carry out, within a defined period, a specific programme of improvements such as construction of fences, or sinking artesian bores; or they may require him not to overstock the land, and to withhold stock from specific sections of the property. Until recently, Northern Territory leases have even specified a minimum rate of stocking. Most leases make provision for compensating the lessee for any improvements on the surrender or expiry of the lease, but others such as annual and forest leases do not.

PRIVATE LEASING

Though leasing of rural lands from the government is widespread in Australia, leasing from private individuals is rather rare, at least by overseas standards. In fact it is so inconsequential that agricultural statisticians do

N

not bother to collect information on this point. A figure of 2 per cent of rural lands has for many years been quoted as the extent of private leasing in New South Wales.

Share farming is practised to some extent, but is, by and large, confined to wheat and dairy industries. It is also found to a more limited extent in the potato and tobacco industries. In wheat areas, the landlord typically supplies the land and portion of the seed and fertilizer, the share farmer providing the remaining inputs. Half of the product usually goes to each, though in some cases the landlord reserves in addition some grazing rights. There is, however, great variation in the proportions of produce retained by the owner and also in the inputs he supplies. This applies particularly to share farming arrangements in the dairy industry. In some cases the share farmer merely provides his labour and his situation is hardly distinguishable from that of a paid employee.

Most of the States have attempted to afford some measure of legislative protection to agricultural tenants. By far the most ambitious of such legislation is the New South Wales Agricultural Holdings Act of 1941.[7] Originally modelled on the comparable United Kingdom legislation, the Act contains provisions covering (i) security of tenure (ii) payment of compensation for disturbance (iii) payment of compensation for unexhausted improvements (iv) measures for securing agreement between landlord and tenant on certain classes of improvements (v) payment of compensation to the landlord for deterioration in the value of his holding resulting from the failure of the tenant to follow the precepts of good husbandry and (vi) arbitration on the question of fair rents. For arbitration, the Act provides for the constitution of *ad hoc* committees to which both the landlord and the tenant nominate a representative and over which an officer of the Department of Agriculture presides. The committees may at any stage secure an opinion on any question of law from a judge of the district court.

Despite its wide-ranging provisions, the Act has fallen somewhat short of expectations and it is generally acknowledged to be in need of amendment. The chief defect of the legislation from a legal point of view is that both the provisions covering payment of compensation to tenants and those requiring adequate notice to quit have generally proved ineffective in the case of verbal agreements. This is because the Act conflicts with the seventeenth-century English Statute of Frauds which applies equally in Australian law and which provides that any agreement not performed within one year must be in writing if it is to be enforceable. Unfortunately verbal agreements are rather prevalent and landlords themselves are disposed to avoid written contracts in the present circumstances. There is also mounting agitation by land-

7. For details see A. W. S. Moodie and J. R. Butler, *Farm Tenancy in New South Wales*, New South Wales Department of Agriculture, Sydney 1952.

lords for amendment of the Act on the ground that the legislation as it now stands makes it excessively difficult to dismiss inefficient and incompetent tenants and share farmers.

CLOSER SETTLEMENT

Perhaps the most important feature of Australian land policy in the present century has been the policy of closer settlement pursued by the various State governments. The emergence of this pressure for the subdivision of large holdings cannot be fully appreciated except against the background of earlier Australian land policies.[8]

Historically the development of Australian land policy falls into several distinct periods. Initially in the years following on the establishment of the first settlement in New South Wales in 1788, free grants of land were made to induce settlers to come to and stay in the new country. Land was also granted to emancipated convicts on condition that a quit rent was paid after a specified period of occupation. By the 1830s, systems of land grants by purchase (or auction) had been introduced. With their introduction it proved impossible to confine the so-called 'squatters' to the official limits of settlement and occupation of the hinterland proceeded apace.

A rapid influx of population followed the discovery of gold in 1851. When many erstwhile miners began to look to farming as an alternative occupation after goldmining had lost its attractiveness for them, they found the best land already occupied by the squatters. Considerable agitation for land reform followed and this coincided with the establishment of self-government. In the early 1860s the new Victorian and New South Wales State parliaments passed legislation making land more accessible to would-be settlers and encouraging agricultural activities side by side with large pastoral leases. The New South Wales Acts of 1861 introduced the new principle of free selection before survey. This legislation led to various abuses such as dummying and within a quarter of a century further legislative enactments were necessary to remedy the situation. From that time forward the whole emphasis shifted to closer settlement.

By a series of legislative enactments all the States developed machinery for resuming large pastoral holdings, subdividing them, and making the smaller blocks available to other settlers usually by a system of simple balloting. Not all the closer settlement was promoted by compulsory acquisition. Provision was made for owners voluntarily to enter into agreements for the subdivision of their holdings. Pastoral companies having large holdings in favoured districts, particularly those companies with their headquarters overseas, have been particularly prone to resumption.

8. The classic work in this field is S. H. Roberts, *op. cit.* For New South Wales developments see C. J. King, 'An Outline of Closer Settlement in New South Wales', *Review of Marketing and Agricultural Economics*, Vol 25, Nos 3-4, September-December 1957.

The actual procedure of resumption has on occasions left much to be desired. The chief restraint, apart from the administrative one of limited staff, has been the availability of money to finance the purchase of the resumed estates and to finance the new settlers. (Traditionally credit for such settlers has been provided by the governments themselves, at concessional rates of interest.) This means that the pace of closer settlement has varied substantially over time, depending *inter alia* on the state of the economy, the rate at which capital has become available, the market prospects for rural products, the degree of success attending earlier settlements, and the rival claims of other public works programmes. To safeguard the government against paying higher values for estates resumed, the practice has grown up of 'proclaiming' estates destined for subdivision long before resumption was effected. This kept costs of resumption down, but it also discouraged further private investment on the properties concerned. The inequities of this system are apparently now being realized. In 1966, the New South Wales government announced the lifting of proclamations from a long list of estates the acquisition of which it could not finance for a considerable time to come.

Lands administrators have in recent decades been loath to subdivide properties where sheep studs are maintained. It is argued that these studs require large flocks (and consequently large areas) to work effectively and that the perpetuation of the studs is in the national interest.

Several attitudes and indeed myths have developed about closer settlement. It was long regarded as one of the chief means of developing the rural industries, and the beneficial effects of subdivision on the adjoining country towns were applauded. It was said to be a way of stemming the 'drift to the cities' and of providing opportunities for farmers' sons to remain on the land. It has also become identified in the public mind as a fitting method of rehabilitating ex-servicemen. After both world wars, emphasis has been put on the settlement of ex-servicemen to the exclusion of civilian settlers. In fact, in such periods, the activity becomes known as 'soldier settlement' rather than closer settlement.

Large numbers of ex-servicemen were in fact assisted to acquire properties after World War I. Even before the onset of the Great Depression many of these men were in severe economic difficulties. In some cases, they were inadequately trained in farming. In other cases the holdings on which they were placed were too small. In still other cases, soil and agronomic investigations before settlement had been inadequate. Several committees of enquiry were conducted, and a large amount of public funds was spent in reconstructing holdings and rehabilitating the settlers.[9]

9. See Commonwealth of Australia, *Report by Mr. Justice Pike on Losses due to Soldier Settlement*, Government Printer, Canberra 1929; and Rural Reconstruction Commission, *Settlement and Employment of Returned Men on the Land, Land Utilization and Farm Settlement, Financial and Economic Reconstruction of Farms (Second, Third and Fourth Reports)*, Government Printer, Canberra 1944.

THE WAR SERVICE LAND SETTLEMENT SCHEME

The prospect of further pressure for the settlement of ex-servicemen on the land after World War II led the Commonwealth government to prepare in advance for such an eventuality as part of its postwar reconstruction plans. In 1945 a series of agreements was drawn up between the Commonwealth government and the States covering their respective financial obligations for the acquisition of holdings, the development of these holdings and advances to settlers. In general, the States of Queensland, New South Wales and Victoria (the principal States) bore half the cost of most items, the remaining States (the agent States) bearing a smaller proportion.[10]

The most important feature of the so-called War Service Land Settlement Scheme was the set of principles enunciated in the course of concluding the agreements. It is fair to say that these set the stage for the closer settlement activities of the past 20 years. The principles were as follows:

(i) Settlement is to be undertaken only where economic prospects are reasonably sound; and the number of eligible persons to be settled is to be determined by the opportunities for settlement and not by the number of applicants;

(ii) Applicants are not to be selected as settlers unless satisfying a competent authority as to their eligibility, suitability and qualifications for settlement under the scheme and their experience of farm work;

(iii) Holdings are to be of a size sufficient to enable settlers to operate efficiently and to earn a reasonable labour income;

(iv) A suitable eligible person is not to be precluded by reason only of lack of capital, but a settler is expected to invest in the holding a reasonable proportion of his own financial and other resources; and

(v) Adequate guidance and technical advice is to be made available to settlers through agricultural extension services.[11]

Under this scheme, all subdivisions were examined by the Commonwealth government, before any Federal finance was authorized. Special training schemes for intending settlers were provided. In some States in accordance with custom, the blocks available were allocated by ballot among the persons who had applied and were approved for inclusion in the ballot. Though the Act authorizing it was declared constitutionally invalid in 1949, the scheme was continued. Judged on its objectives, the scheme was highly successful in marked contrast to the failures following World War I. Part of the success, no doubt, must be attributed to the improvement of commodity prices which

10. For fuller details of the scheme see 'War Service Land Settlement—Some Agricultural and Financial Aspects of Joint Commonwealth-State Legislation', mimeo., Bureau of Agricultural Economics, 1950; and *Year Book*, No 37, 1946-47, pp 113-119, Bureau of Census and Statistics.

11. Commonwealth of Australia, *War Service Land Settlement Agreement Act*, No 52 of 1945.

occurred in the early years of the scheme, and which resulted in many of the new settlers receiving incomes well in excess of those contemplated. Whether or not the community at large received benefits commensurate with the cost of the scheme is another question.

FARM CONSOLIDATION

Though the predominant theme of its land policy has been closer settlement, Australia has had some experience in the reconstruction of uneconomic holdings. This chiefly occurred as a result of the failure of some of the settlement schemes of the 1920s and was associated with the wheat industry in particular. The Commonwealth government assisted the States in a series of salvage operations, known as marginal wheat area schemes,[12] which were undertaken mainly in the 10 years following the Great Depression. In many cases, a writing-down of debts and restructuring of financial obligations were all that was involved. In other cases, bankrupt settlers were given a lump sum on the condition that they vacated their holdings, their properties were divided and the resultant portions were added to those of adjoining property owners in order to bring the reconstructed farms up to a size which was believed to be economically viable.

A similar system of reconstruction of farms was recommended in 1960 by the Dairy Industry Committee of Enquiry as a means of eliminating low-income farms from that industry, but the recommendations were not accepted by the government of the day.[13]

UNSETTLED ISSUES IN LAND POLICY

In recent years the emphasis in Australian lands administration has shifted primarily to problems associated with fostering the better use of the land already in use. In one sense this was true of the original policy of closer settlement, but even this policy has recently been questioned.

THE PLACE OF CLOSER SETTLEMENT

Several factors have been responsible for this re-examination. First, the development of Australian agriculture in the past 15 years has led to a realization that modern agricultural technology is likely to have a greater impact on the rate of economic growth than any policy of redistribution of rural holdings. It has also become apparent that the market outlook for products of intensive agricultural settlement is less favourable than is the outlook for products produced under more extensive pastoral systems, products in which Australia clearly has a comparative advantage. Third, the rising capital re-

12. See Rural Reconstruction Commission, *Financial and Economic Reconstruction of Farms, Fourth Report*, Government Printer, Canberra 1944, Appendix I.

13. Commonwealth of Australia, *Report of the Dairy Industry Committee of Enquiry*, Government Printer, Canberra 1961.

quirements of modern farming have increased the cost of government-sponsored settlement schemes. Finally, policy makers are coming to realize that in a competitive situation, there is a limit to the priority that can be given to equity objectives over efficiency objectives in any land programme.[14]

Those who favour the abandonment or at least the modification of traditional closer settlement policy point out that the important restraints to rising productivity today are not land and labour, as this policy implies, but capital and management.[15] To continue to attempt to put more people on smaller-sized farms is to fly in the face of historical tendencies for the rural work force to decline and the size of farms to increase.

It **is** argued that the social reasons advanced in favour of closer settlement frequently do not bear critical examination and that the policy is a very crude and unsatisfactory way of trying to achieve a more equitable distribution of rural income. Such an objective, it is claimed, could be achieved more effectively through such measures as progressive income taxation, land taxes and death duties. The allocation of landholdings by lottery, a procedure by which it is possible for large gains to accrue to a few fortunate people, is also criticized. However, financial pressures are forcing land settlement authorities increasingly to take into account the capital which the intending settler has or to which he can get access privately, in determining the eligibility of applicants for blocks of land. This has been true of the recent Colleambally Settlement Scheme in New South Wales, the Esperance Scheme in Western Australia and the Brigalow Scheme in Queensland.

The main economic arguments centre on the question of economies of scale. A size of farm determined on the criterion of the 'home maintenance area' is not necessarily the most efficient size under current conditions and it is likely to be less so with the passage of time. Unfortunately unequivocal evidence on the scale question is not available.[16] However, it is evident that family farms considered big enough for wheat farming in the days of horse traction are inadequate to achieve realizable economies of scale under mod-

14. Cf. Vernon W. Ruttan, 'Equity and Productivity Issues in Modern Agrarian Reform Legislation', paper presented to the Conference organized by the International Economic Association on Economic Problems of Agriculture in Industrial Societies and Repercussions in Developing Countries, Rome 1965.

15. For a useful summary of the issues involved in the reappraisal of closer settlement policy see D. E. Maccallum *et al.*, 'Closer Settlement in the 1960s', *Journal of the Australian Institute of Agricultural Science*, Vol 28, No 3, September 1962. For an advocacy of the continuation of closer settlement see T. H. Strong, 'Land Tenure in Australia in Relation to Technical Advances and Closer Settlement', *Journal of Farm Economics*, Vol 38, No 2, May 1956.

16. Production function analysis has revealed evidence of increasing returns to scale in the inland pastoral areas and constant returns to scale in the higher rainfall areas. See J. H. Duloy, 'The Allocation of Resources in the Woolgrowing Industry', *Australian Journal of Agricultural Economics*, Vol 5, No 2, December 1961. See also J. N. Lewis, *op. cit.*, pp 100-101; and A. G. Lloyd, 'The Economic Size of Farms', *Journal of the Australian Institute of Agricultural Science*, Vol 27, No 3, September 1961.

ern tractor technology. The pressing need is to find a means of preserving sufficient flexibility in the settlement pattern and the associated land legislation so as not to inhibit the nation from reaping the fruits of continuing technological advance. The establishment of a cotton industry in northern New South Wales a few years ago was originally threatened by anachronistic legislative provisions governing the size of farms.

In recent years closer settlement has gradually assumed less prominence as an instrument of government policy. This trend is likely to continue, if only because of the rising cost of settlement schemes and the realization that they tend to benefit the few rather than the many. It may also become clearer to governments that investment in other directions, whether within agriculture (for example, in education and research) or elsewhere in the economy, would be likely to contribute more to the economic growth of the nation than the investment of an equivalent amount of government funds in closer settlement activities.

LEASEHOLD VERSUS ALIENATION

There has been recurring argument whether additional land should be alienated. Political beliefs obviously colour attitudes to this question. But in an economic context a balance has to be struck between, on the one hand, the savings in private capital investment and the greater public control of land use which leasing arrangements permit and, on the other hand, the disincentive to investment and encouragement of land exploitation which often seems to be associated with such arrangements. The disadvantages of leasehold tenure tend to be more exaggerated the shorter the lease. The situation of landholders operating under perpetual leases, we have seen, differs little from landholders who own their own land.

The Rural Reconstruction Commission was asked by the Commonwealth government in 1943 to recommend the form of tenure which should apply in the settlement of ex-servicemen after World War II. The Commission reported in favour of private ownership,[17] but ultimately the Commonwealth government insisted that land be made available under leasehold tenures in the 'agent' States and subsequently the 'principal' States with the exception of Victoria followed suit.

Today, controversy largely revolves around the leases operating in the pastoral areas of Queensland and the Northern Territory. These leases usually run from 25 to 40 years. They do, it should be noted, give the government the opportunity to reassess property sizes periodically in the light of technological and economic developments. However, as has been pointed out earlier, the lessees claim that the limited term of the leases is not conducive to their developing their properties. There would seem to be substance in the view that the achievement of a satisfactory rate of development

17. See Rural Reconstruction Commission, *Rural Land Tenure and Valuation, Ninth Report*, Government Printer, Canberra 1946.

of the Northern Australian beef industry will be dependent on the institu-
tion of a more progressive land tenure policy.[18]

SOIL AND RANGE CONSERVATION

Between 1938 when the New South Wales Soil Conservation Service was
established and the end of World War II, most of the Australian States established agencies concerned with the promotion of soil conservation.[19] From
the beginning, particular attention was paid to the deterioration of the
vegetation in the more arid areas and to soil erosion on the catchments of
major dams. Legislation to enable the government to require corrective
action on freehold as well as leasehold land in such areas has gradually been
introduced, but in few cases have these powers been used. More recently the
question of the incorporation of more stringent controls in leases to prevent
pasture deterioration has arisen. One case involved the short-term snow
leases in the Australian Alps. Another concerned the pastoral leases in Central Australia.[20] In neither case did it appear that the administering authority
had sufficient knowledge of the behaviour and management of the native
vegetation to be in a position to institute rational controls over grazing.[21]

BALANCING DEVELOPMENT ON NEW AND OLD LANDS

Since the turn of the century, a proportion of public investment in land
development has gone into irrigation development. More lately the discovery
of minor element deficiencies in some areas and the development of chemical
and mechanical methods of land clearing have opened up new opportunities
for both corporate and government investment. Perhaps the really burning
question in Australian land policy today concerns the relative advantages of
public investment in different forms of land development—irrigation versus
dry-land development, the opening-up of new lands in Northern Australia
versus intensification of development in the already developed areas of the

18. For discussion of some of the issues with respect to the Northern pastoral leases see
Commonwealth of Australia, *Report of the Board of Inquiry into the Land and Land
Industries of the Northern Territory of Australia*, Government Printer, Canberra 1937;
Queensland Government, *Report of the Royal Commission on Pastoral Lands Settlement*,
Government Printer, Brisbane 1951; Queensland Government, *Report on Progressive Land
Settlement in Queensland by the Land Settlement Advisory Commission*, Government
Printer, Brisbane 1959; and H. Barclay, 'Land Tenure in Relation to Agricultural and
Pastoral Development', in *Proceedings of the Northern Territory Scientific Liaison Con-
ference*, Darwin 1961.

19. For a review of these developments see K. O. Campbell, 'The Development of Soil
Conservation Programmes in Australia', *Land Economics*, Vol 24, No 1, February 1948.

20. See Department of Territories, Northern Territory Land Board, *Report on the Cen-
tralian Pastoral Industry under Drought Conditions*, Darwin 1964. It is of interest to note
that this committee reported that the minimum size of an economic holding in Central Australia was in excess of 600 square miles.

21. K. O. Campbell, 'Problems of Adaptation of Pastoral Businesses in the Arid Zone',
Australian Journal of Agricultural Economics, Vol 10, No 1, June 1966, pp 15-16.

south and so on.[22] Details of some of the specific development schemes are outlined elsewhere in this book.

Clearly in a country where the man-land ratio is so low, questions of land policy will continue to exercise the public mind. But unless Australians come to appreciate better than they do now that other resources are to a considerable extent effective substitutes for land and water, they will fail to achieve the full agricultural potentiality of their country.

22. See K. O. Campbell, 'The Rural Development of Northern Australia', *Australian Journal of Agricultural Economics*, Vol 6, No 1, September 1962; B. R. Davidson, *The Northern Myth*, Melbourne University Press, Melbourne 1965; B. R. Davidson and J. S. Nalson, 'Investment Opportunities in Western Australian Agriculture', *Farm Policy*, Vol 3, No 4, March 1964; R. W. Prunster, 'Alternatives in Land Development', *Farm Policy*, Vol 4, No 3, December 1964, and K. O. Campbell, 'An Assessment of the Case for Irrigation Development in Australia', in Australian Academy of Science, *Water Resources, Use and Management*, Melbourne University Press, Melbourne 1964.

CHAPTER 9

RURAL LABOUR

H. P. SCHAPPER

University of Western Australia

Rural labour is the least studied of the major inputs of Australian agriculture. Official statistics are meagre, and economic, sociological and demographic studies of farm families, of permanent hired labour and of casual, seasonal and contract workers are virtually non-existent. Nor has the subject of farm labour yet attracted the attention of rural sociologists and economists, so that even for specific regions little is known.[1]

Indeed, the term, 'rural labour', has not yet been defined clearly either by scholars or common usage. Literally it includes all labour in employment beyond urban centres, but this definition is inadequate; even if it should be restricted to on-farm labour, such questions arise as, should it include the farmer himself, the owner-operator, and should it include the services of contractors, with their equipment such as bulldozers and bulk fertilizer spreaders?

In this chapter, rural labour includes owners, operators, lessees, share farmers, seasonal employees, permanent employees, paid and unpaid, and on-farm contract workers employed with or without their own equipment. However, to view these categories of personnel merely as labour involves restricting their input to their manual contribution to farming. To pursue this would require separating the manual input of the owner-operator from his managerial input. Such arbitrary separation is not likely to be meaningful, and the present discussion includes managerial skills as an element in the labour force, a shift in emphasis that broadens the subject beyond rural labour to farming manpower.

THE FARM WORK FORCE

SOURCES OF DATA

Official statistics about the farm work force are included in reports of the

1. Notable exceptions are: T. M. Burley, *Some Aspects of Agricultural Activities in the Hunter Valley*, Hunter Valley Research Foundation, Monograph No 14, 1963; J. S. Nalson, *The Farm Labour Force in Western Australia*, University of Western Australia Press, Perth (in press); and A. W. Hogstrum and J. S. Nalson, *Farm Population and Land Development in Western Australia*, University of Western Australia Press, Perth (in press).

Australian census, taken at periodic intervals, and in the annual agricultural and pastoral statistics.

Nevertheless, official demographic data on the nation's farming manpower are limited mostly to data about its size and its classification by sex, age, birthplace, and several major categories of occupational status. Data are not collected to distinguish between farm-family and non-farm-family labour, number of days of farm and non-farm work per year, place of residence of non-farm-family labour, or migratory habit, or type of farm work performed by various categories of farm-family and hired workers.

According to the Census of 1961, the number of males engaged in Australian farming was then 397,000. This is 134,000 fewer than that recorded by the 1933 Census, representing a decline in farm manpower of 25 per cent over these 28 years. As a proportion of all males in the total Australian work force, farm manpower fell from 25 per cent in 1933 to 13 per cent in 1961. (Table 9-1.)

By contrast, the so-called occupational status of farmers has remained constant. There are nearly 25 per cent of employer farmers and 75 per cent self-employed farmers. (Table 9-1.) In 1933 when unemployed urban labour sought employment on farms, and when the rate of the rural-urban labour drift slowed down, the employer farmers rose to 40 per cent of the total farmers. Also, the number of male wage and salary earners per farm employer has gone down slightly since the 1947 Census. The validity of these figures largely depends upon whether farmers at each census have correctly and consistently classified themselves as employers or as self-employed. That they have is open to doubt. Farmers regard themselves primarily as self-employed rather than as employers, and it is probably only the larger employer-farmers who think of themselves as employers.

Nevertheless, a significant change in occupational status has occurred within the total farm manpower force. It is reflected in the ratio of total employees to farmers, which distinguishes the non-managerial and the managerial components of the farm work force. From 1933 to 1961 the non-managerial, male farm labour force per farmer, dropped from $0 \cdot 91$ to $0 \cdot 56$. Conversely, farmers, that is, the managerial component, as a proportion of the total farming manpower, increased from 49 per cent in 1933 to 62 per cent in 1961 though they remained fairly constant in absolute numbers at about 250,000. This is the long-term picture recorded in the censuses.

More recent data suggest stability. The annual agricultural and pastoral returns, excluding the State of Victoria, show that for the 10 years from 1955 to 1965 the male owner, lessee and share farmer component is a constant proportion of the total farm manpower. In other words, the managerial and non-managerial labour components in the farm work force seem recently to have been constant.

Another classification of employees on farms in the annual agricultural

Table 9-1

Farm Manpower, 1933-1961

	1933	As at census, 30 June 1947	1954	1961
Number of males in work force, including those not at work at census date (000s)				
Agriculture, Grazing and Dairying	531·0	440·1	440·0	396·5
Total work force (all occupations)	2,140·3	2,479·3	2,856·6	3,165·9
Agriculture, Grazing and Dairying as per cent of total work force	24·8	17·7	15·4	12·6
Males engaged in Agriculture, Grazing and Dairying (000s)				
1 Employer	102·9	56·9	62·6	55·6
2 Self-employed	155·5	200·7	201·0	191·4
3 Total farmers (*1+2*)	258·4	257·6	263·6	247·0
4 On wages or salary	200·1	148·3	154·2	126·3
5 Helper not receiving wages or salary	35·1	21·2	15·6	11·1
6 Total employees (*4+5*)	235·2	169·5	169·8	137·4
7 Not at work	37·4	13·0	6·6	12·1
8 Total (*3+6+7*)	531·0	440·1	440·0	396·5
9 Employer farmers as per cent of total farmers (*1* as per cent of *3*)	39·8	22·1	23·7	22·5
10 Wage and salary earners per employer (*4÷1*)	1·94	2·61	2·46	2·27
11 Total farmers as per cent of total engaged (*3* as per cent of *8*)	48·7	58·5	59·9	62·3
12 Total employees per farmer (*6÷3*)	0·91	0·66	0·64	0·56
Number of rural holdings (from agricultural and pastoral statistics) (000s)	264·0	246·9	247·0	252·0[a]
Average number of males engaged per rural holding	2·0	1·8	1·8	1·6
Index of quantum of farm production (1933 = 100)	100	89	120	149
Index of total males engaged in Agriculture, Grazing and Dairying (1933 = 100)	100	83	83	75

a. After 1956 nearly 5,000 additional holdings were included for New South Wales and Northern Territory.

Sources: Census Reports; and *Rural Industries Bulletin No 1*, 1962-63, Bureau of Census and Statistics.
Census figures are from tables in which the category 'not stated' for occupational status has been distributed on a pro-rata basis. For 1933 the category 'not applicable' was excluded because this included 'pensioners, persons of private means not in business, engaged in home duties, scholars and other dependants'.

and pastoral statistics distinguishes persons who are permanently engaged from those who are temporarily engaged. Data for 1956 to 1965, from all States other than Victoria show that temporary employees declined by 21 per cent whereas persons, other than farmers, permanently engaged, declined by 12 per cent. These figures are for persons in employment on one day, namely 31st March each year, and from the official records indication cannot be obtained of the time worked on farms by those temporarily engaged. However, the total wages and salaries paid to each category of worker is recorded and each year permanent and temporary employees received on average almost equal amounts. This does not necessarily indicate equal times worked, because payments made to temporary employees include amounts paid to contractors. Normally they receive higher rates of pay, per day worked, than do permanent employees, and the payments probably include, in numerous cases, unspecified amounts for the contractors' own machinery services. The close agreement between the 440,000 males engaged in agriculture, grazing and dairying shown in the 1954 Census (Table 9-1) and the figure of 444,000 from the agricultural and pastoral statistics for that year (they are not available for other census years), suggests that many persons who are temporarily engaged by farmers are also permanent farm workers, working from farm to farm.

Contracting services constitute another important element of farming manpower. They are often highly organized, requiring skilled labour with specialized skills, capital equipment and a large clientele of farmers. Services for routine seasonal operations include seed grading and pickling; top dressing; spraying and dusting pastures, crops and orchards; cultivation; harvesting; cartage to and from the farms; pest destruction; and, in the sheep industry, tailing, docking, mulesing, mouthing, drenching, dipping, crutching, shearing and wool classing. There are a number of other labour contracting services which constitute capital improvements, such as clearing, fencing, dam sinking and pasture establishment. Most of these and other services, once part of the normal work of farm labour, have been developed by non-farm personnel. A spectacular example is aerial contracting services which top dressed, seeded, sprayed or dusted some $1 \cdot 5$ million acres in 1957 and $12 \cdot 7$ million acres in 1964. For the same years the area treated with artificial fertilizers from aircraft was $2 \cdot 6$ and $18 \cdot 4$ per cent respectively of the total area fertilized.

There is no doubt that the growth of these contracting services is partly responsible for the decline of the on-farm non-managerial labour force. Moreover, the efficiency of their performance (which they are able to develop by specialization) and the economies they permit in the capital equipment required for farming, are undoubtedly one source of improvement in farming efficiency.

Some of the labour component of these contracting services—for example,

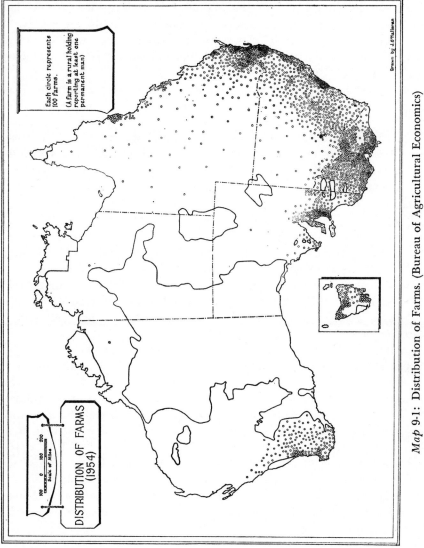

Map 9-1: Distribution of Farms. (Bureau of Agricultural Economics)

labour engaged in transport—is not shown as persons engaged in agriculture. It is the problem of incorporating this component into farm labour which makes it so difficult to measure accurately the real changes in the productivity of farming manpower. Moreover, it is not possible from official statistics to distinguish the numbers of persons temporarily engaged on farms from those providing contracting services. Doubtless there is considerable overlap. This, and the decline already observed in temporary employees, relative to the decline in permanent full-time employees, suggest that contracting services are contributing to the increased physical output of the manpower force remaining on farms.

Another nation-wide view of the farm manpower force is obtained from the national accounts of income and expenditure. For the 15 years from 1948-49 to 1962-63, wages and salaries paid by farmers declined steadily from 16 per cent of the total farm costs to 14 per cent. Some portion of these payments were paid to sons, both as family labour and in partnership with the farmer parents. However, they exclude adjustments for unpaid helpers and for the manual labour input of owner-operators.

FARM MANPOWER AND PHYSICAL OUTPUT

The number of rural holdings has been roughly constant since 1933 and approximately equal to the total number of farmers. (Table 9-1.) However, not all holdings are farms and the classification of rural holdings made for the year 1959-60 suggests that only about 84 per cent of them are commercial full-time farms.[2] With the fall in the number of non-managerial farm workers, the average number of males including the farmer, per rural holding has fallen from 2·0 in 1933 to 1·6 in 1961.

For 1961, the index of quantum of farm production was 49 per cent higher than in 1933. (Table 9-1.) This increase was associated with a decline of 25 per cent in the male farm work force. It is tempting to see this as *the* increase in productivity of farm labour. However, some of the increase in this estimate arises from the census classification of labour. As has already been pointed out, substantial growth in contracting services has occurred so that many farm labour services, formerly provided by persons included in census figures as being engaged in farming, are now substituted for by contract services provided by some persons classified as engaged in other industries.

Changes in the farm manpower force have been accompanied by changes in the volume of production and inputs. For recent years some of these major changes are shown below:

In the 10 years from 1956 to 1965:

• The on-farm male labour force declined by 11 per cent.

2. *Classification of Rural Holdings by Size and Type of Activity, 1959-60, No 7, Australia,* Bureau of Census and Statistics, Canberra.

- The land area of rural holdings increased by 66 million acres or 6 per cent.
- The area of rural holdings under crop, in fallow and under sown grasses and clovers, increased by 32 million acres, or 57 per cent. The balance of land in holdings (i.e. unimproved and undeveloped land) was 95 per cent in 1956 and 92·6 per cent in 1965.
- Total sheep one year and over increased by 25 million or 23 per cent.
- Total dairy cattle increased by 17,000 (to 1963) or 0·3 per cent.
- Total beef cattle increased by 2 million (to 1963) or 18 per cent.
- Tons of artificial fertilizer used increased by 1·5 million tons or 78 per cent.
- Total tractors on holdings increased by 94,000 or 46 per cent.
- Total milking stands increased by 27,000 or 13 per cent.
- Total shearing stands increased by 30,000 or 19 per cent.
- The index of quantum of farm production (base: average 1936-37 to 1938-39 = 100) increased from 131 to 181 or 38 per cent.

These changes are for the whole of Australia and the way they are shown masks tremendous differences between regions and types of farming. For instance, in Table 9-2 details are given for three different farming areas in Western Australia.

Table 9-2

Western Australia: Changes in Farm Structure and Productivity per Man, 1953-54 and 1963-64

District	1953-54 per male working permanently on holdings as at 31 March	1963-64
Merredin—Narembeen (cereals and sheep—12 inch rainfall)		
Crop —acres	332·0	495·6
Sheep—no.	450·9	529·4
Kojonup—West Arthur (intensive grazing—20 inch rainfall)		
Crop —acres	87·5	127·2
Sheep—no.	672·2	1,366·6
Cattle—no.	9·5	21·8
Manjimup (dairying, fat stock and fruit—35 inch rainfall)		
Crop —acres	6·3	13·6
Sheep—no.	13·3	68·2
Cattle—no.	24·6	48·9

Source: J. Carlin, 'Trends in Western Australian Agriculture', *Farm Policy*, Vol 5, No 3, December 1965.

The foregoing data for both Australia and Western Australia illustrate the nature, the magnitude and rapidity of the changes in the composition of

o

the inputs in Australian farming. Moreover, during this time, there are no signs that great structural maladjustments have emerged in Australian rural industries. This is evidenced, in part at least, by the relative size of farm and non-farm incomes, and by the low level of unemployment. In so many other countries structural maladjustment between agricultural and non-agricultural activities is evidenced by high rural unemployment and average farm incomes being much lower than average non-farm incomes.

FARM-FAMILY AND NON-FARM-FAMILY LABOUR

FARM-FAMILY LABOUR

Unlike that in many other countries, farming in Australia is organized on separate holdings with the farm family resident on the farm.

The farm-family and non-farm-family labour situation for Australia has not yet been assessed. One aspect which bears on the efficiency of farm man-power lies in the mode of recruitment to managerial responsibilities in farming. Traditionally this is by the bequest of farm property from father to son. The rights to ownership include the rights to manage. Thus, recruitment to management in farming is highly nepotic in character. It is not entirely so, because ownership and managerial rights are also obtained by persons otherwise occupied in business, commerce and the professions. These new entrants into farming displace or take over from existing farming families and also establish new farms. However, although there are no Australia-wide statistics on this point it is a matter of common observation that a large majority of farmers inherited their managerial responsibilities. In Western Australia an estimate has been made that 82 per cent of the farmers in the agricultural areas are the sons of farmers.[3]

Data are limited so that it is not possible to know how many of the permanently and temporarily engaged in farming are farmers' sons; whether they are on full wages or in partnership; and what degree of managerial responsibility they may have, if any. For Western Australia, however, a recent survey was made of all farms of more than 1,000 acres in the agricultural areas (as distinct from the unimproved pastoral) and of all farms between 200 and 1,000 acres in the higher rainfall areas of the south-west region.[4] It was estimated that the 14,000 full-time male farmers and share farmers (that is, managerial manpower) were supported by 11,000 non-managerial permanent full-time male workers. Of these 11,000, about half were farm-family and half were non-farm-family workers. Thus the total farming manpower consisted of 56 per cent with managerial responsibility and 44 per cent without. Seventy-five per cent were farmers and sons, that is, farm-family labour, and 25 per cent non-farm-family labour.

There is a degree of balance in these figures which may be more than

3. A. W. Hogstrum and J. S. Nalson, *op. cit.*
4. J. S. Nalson, *op. cit.*

fortuitous. It may be noted that for an assumed life of managerial responsibility of 25 to 30 years (from 25-30 years of age to 50-60) 14,000 farmers on average would require an annual intake of 500 new managers. There are 5,500 non-managerial farm-family workers from whom recruitment is normal. This number is of the order required, on the assumption that sons usually leave school between 15 and 18 years of age and work for up to 10-12 years followed by a period of several years of shared managerial responsibility with their fathers, and assume full responsibility from the age of 30-35 years, by which time some of *their* sons are preparing to join the family work force, and the cycle is repeated.

The non-managerial family work force should be seen differently from the non-farm-family work force. The former is both a source of manual labour and of trainees in farm management who will assume managerial responsibilities in due course. The latter will remain as part of the non-managerial farm manpower force for as long as it remains in farming and does not acquire farming property. For non-farm-family labour there is normally no progression from farm labourer to owner-operator farmer. In Australia this is a comparatively recent phenomenon. Since World War II, one to two-man family farming has become a large capital-hungry enterprise. There are now no civilian land settlement schemes involving special assistance for persons with insufficient capital to attract commercial loans. Thus farm-family labour has a much stronger incentive than non-farm-family labour to acquire farming skills and to remain in farming. This incentive is the high probability of inheritance of the farm business and this difference in incentives is, no doubt, at the root of so much that is unsatisfactory in the farm labour situation so far as employees are concerned.

NON-FARM-FAMILY LABOUR

Permanent farm work for non-farm-family labour is, generally speaking, not an attractive occupation, particularly now that it is no longer a means of acquiring a farm. Much of its unattractiveness arises from its general nature rather than from specific employer-employee relationships. Many full-time so-called permanent positions are really temporary in the sense that the employee is hired to fill in the manual labour gap on a two-man farm between the time of the waning of the farmer's strength, or of his retirement, and when his grandson completes his schooling. Depending on relative ages this gap may be several years, but however long, the employee, in this sense, is temporary. He is in competition for the job with the son and he is bound to lose. Where there is a non-managerial son or a son sharing managerial responsibilities with his father, and permanent non-farm-family labour, frictions inevitably arise from differences in status, both on the job and off it, in the local community. Generally, non-farm-family labour has low personal status on the farm and obviously low social status in the local community. On the farm there is always 'the boss'; off it there are strong social distinc-

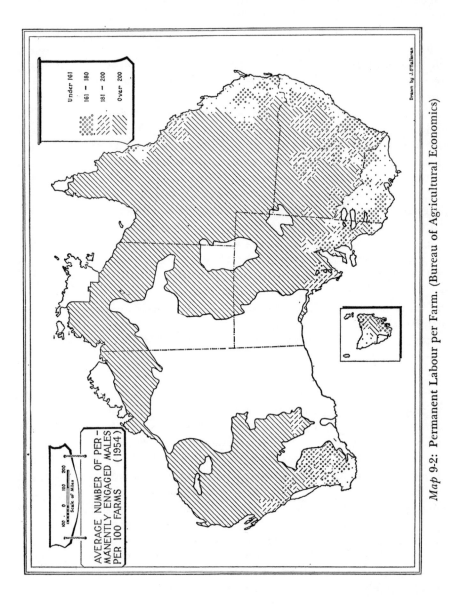

Map 9-2: Permanent Labour per Farm. (Bureau of Agricultural Economics)

AVERAGE NUMBER OF PER-
MANENTLY ENGAGED MALES
PER 100 FARMS (1954)

Scale of Miles

Under 161

161 — 180

181 — 200

Over 200

Drawn by J. O'Halloran

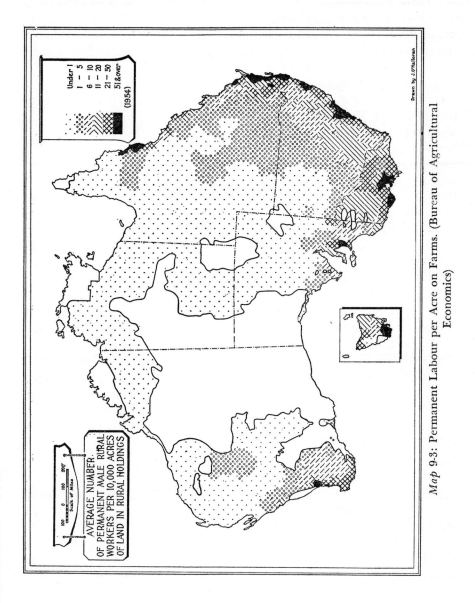

Map 9.3: Permanent Labour per Acre on Farms. (Bureau of Agricultural Economics)

tions, and in a close and small community there is no escape from the smallest difference in status.

There is also the propinquity of labourer and employer which is a feature of farming rather than of the factory. Factory supervision is close but it is formalized and not as personal as in farming. In farming the personal weaknesses of management—and its strengths—can be seen by employees more readily than in industry. Living on the job is another feature for both farmer and employee with the employee either living in the same house as the family or in his employer-provided house.

For these and other reasons, farm labouring tends to be a residual occupation. Often it is a last resort job and for persons who have no alternative employment opportunities. The quality of farm labour tends to be low and there are no strong incentives for farmers to improve it. In fact nothing is done to break what appears to be a self-reinforcing causal chain: farm labour is poor, it is treated accordingly, there are no incentives to improve it and there are none for it to improve. Because labour is poor, conditions too tend to be poor, sometimes poorer than those of public works construction camps. Farm labouring does not lead to farm management and there are no formal educational or apprenticeship requirements. For workers to improve their status and to advance occupationally, it is generally necessary to leave this form of work and become a contractor or share farmer.

There are, however, notable individual exceptions to the foregoing general picture, where farmers have bonus and superannuation schemes, house their permanent labour in a nearby country town, and obtain good non-farm-family workers and maintain them in employment on a lifetime basis.

Unionism is weak or virtually a non-existent force among permanent employees although it is active and powerful in respect to some seasonal employment, for example shearing. Permanent employees are protected by awards of the State arbitration courts. These set out minimal conditions and in Western Australia the award is the basic wage plus a margin of 60 cents for a six-day week.

TRAINING OF FARM MANPOWER

For the most part, manual labour skills in farming and farm management are self-taught. Farmers' children tend to leave city schools earlier than children at the same schools with non-farm parents.[5] In Western Australia the technical agricultural training facilities are used to teach elementary farm husbandries and farm work skills to farmers' sons aged 14-16 years and similar subjects at a higher level to 17-18 year-olds. Whereas there are about 130 in the first category, and 45-50 in the second, completing their training

5. Confirmed by information obtained for the study by J. S. Nalson and H. P. Schapper, *Manpower Training for Agriculture in Western Australia,* University of Western Australia Press, Perth 1966.

each year, the annual intake into farming in Western Australia is at least 1,000 persons. Institutional training facilities as used at present, cater for a mere fraction of the farm manpower needs, and training in farm management as distinct from the technical and manual aspects of farming, is virtually non-existent. This refers to formal training. Farmers are well served by the technical extension service of the State departments of agriculture and increasingly by private managerial consultancy services. (See Chapter 4.) The provision of more technical services for farmers appears to be considered appropriate by both farmers and government and financing of managerial services by farmers for themselves also appears to be more widely accepted. Both farmers and government might well be more interested in formal training for the development and improvement in future farmers' managerial skills. In fact governmental educational facilities for this purpose seem increasingly to be used for the training of technologists, technicians and commercial assistants for servicing farmers, and this trend is supported by the Report of the Committee on the Future of Tertiary Education in Australia to the Australian Universities Commission on Tertiary Education in Australia.

Another aspect of training farm manpower is that associated with the mode of recruitment to managerial responsibility. It has already been mentioned that this is typically by inheritance rather than by personal achievement, which probably constitutes a strong disincentive for farmers to encourage their sons to continue with their schooling beyond the compulsory minimum school-leaving age, and an equally strong incentive for sons to leave school at this time. No doubt this is reinforced by the generally low quality of non-farm-family labour. Understandably farmers still seem anxious to have their sons return from school as early as is permitted. Further reasons may be influential; the son may be cheaper, less likely to leave, and he may be more amenable, though less skilled, than the hired labour.

There is a tremendous potential for improvement in manpower efficiency through farm management training. That farmers and farm workers have considerably increased their output has already been shown. But there is a difference between an increase in output per man and improvement in managerial skill. It is possible for output per man to improve without any parallel improvement in managerial skill. In fact, it is likely that most of the observed improvement in managerial performances is the result of developments in farm implement and machinery engineering, in contracting services to farmers and in farm technology, rather than in the acquisition of managerial skills. This distinction between performance and skills may not be capable of being tested empirically. Conceptually, however, it stands as a challenge to farmers, to educationists and others who are concerned with improving the managerial skills component of manpower efficiency in Australia's farming.

CHAPTER 10

FARM INVESTMENT

A. W. HOOKE

University of Queensland

ESTIMATES OF FARM INVESTMENT

Estimates of the aggregate level of rural investment are available for the period 1861-1900, and of its aggregate level and composition for the period 1921-60. There are virtually no data on the distribution of investment among rural industries, and only scant information on its composition within industries.

LEVEL OF INVESTMENT

Estimates of the annual level of new and gross capital formation during the period 1861-1900 have been made by Butlin.[1] His figures probably understate the actual levels achieved as no allowance was made for the clearing of land which was an important component of investment during this period. Even so, Butlin estimates that for the period as a whole farm investment exceeded all other private investment activities with the sole exception of residential construction.

Butlin's estimates show both short and long period fluctuations in the levels of net and gross investment. The longer term movements include three periods in which the level of investment was quite low—the 1860s and early 1870s, the early 1880s, and the 1890s; and two periods in which it was very high—the later 1870s and 1880s. More than half the investment of the forty years from 1861-1900 was undertaken during these latter two periods.

Estimates of the level of net farm investment are also available for the period 1921-60. These estimates have been derived from several sources. Undoubtedly the major contribution came from Gutman, whose estimates cover the period 1921-47.[2] With the exception of irrigation, Gutman's

1. N. G. Butlin, *Australian Domestic Product, Investment and Foreign Borrowing, 1861-1938/39*, Cambridge University Press, Cambridge 1962.
2. G. O. Gutman, 'Investment and Production in Australian Agriculture', *Review of Marketing and Agricultural Economics*, Vol 23, No 4, December 1955.

estimates were carried forward to 1955 by Gruen[3] and O'Hagan,[4] and to 1960 by the Bureau of Agricultural Economics.

The estimates grouped in five-year totals are shown in Table 10-1. They indicate instability in the level of investment throughout the first three decades. The broad temporal pattern for this period shows a very high level of investment during the late 1920s, followed by a sharp decline during the depression years of the early 1930s. There was a partial recovery during the late 1930s, although investment in this period still reached only half the 1926-30 level. During the war years, investment was cut back sharply, and considerable disinvestment occurred. The level rose again during the late 1940s, although it still failed to reach the pre-depression figure.

Table 10-1
Net Farm Investment, 1921-60
(1962-63 prices: $A million)

Period	Land improvements[a]	Machinery and implements	Livestock	Irrigation	Total[b]
1921-25	432	100	90	125	747
1926-30	1,854	127	− 34	114	2,061
1931-35	144	− 27	56	42	215
1936-40	702	161	34	62	959
1941-45	− 549	60	140	31	− 318
1946-50	882	281	67	—	1,230[c]
1951-55	1,656	1,233	78	—	2,967[c]
1956-60	(1,575)	636	(84)	—	2,295[c]

a. Includes farm buildings, fencing, clearing, pasture improvement etc.
b. Totals rounded.
c. Excluding irrigation.
SOURCE: Estimates for 1956-1960 by the Bureau of Agricultural Economics, after earlier work by Gutman, O'Hagan and Gruen.

Investment was maintained at a high level during the 1950s. The volume of investment during these ten years was almost half as great again as that undertaken during the previous thirty years. Available indicators suggest that net farm investment has continued to increase during the 1960s. (See Table 10-2.)

COMPOSITION OF INVESTMENT

Estimates of the composition of net farm investment are available for the period 1921-60. The classification for these, and the estimates for years 1921-47, were made by Gutman.

3. F. H. Gruen, 'Capital Formation in Australian Agriculture', *Australian Journal of Agricultural Economics*, Vol 1, No 1, June 1957.
4. J. P. O'Hagan, 'Agricultural Investment in Australia', *FAO Monthly Bulletin of Agricultural Economics and Statistics*, Vol 7, No 6, June 1958.

Gutman divided investment into four components: land improvements (including buildings), machinery and implements, livestock, and irrigation.

The estimates are shown in Table 10-1. They illustrate clearly the dominating importance of land improvements in farm investment. For the period as a whole land improvements represented some two-thirds of total investment; machinery and implements accounted for roughly one-quarter; and livestock and irrigation each about 5 per cent.

Table 10-2

Gross Fixed Capital Expenditure on Farms, 1948-49 to 1962-63
($A million)

Year	Expenditure
1948-49	126
1949-50	182
1950-51	255
1951-52	301
1952-53	257
1953-54	299
1954-55	304
1955-56	303
1956-57	317
1957-58	322
1958-59	316
1959-60	338
1960-61	358
1961-62	331
1962-63	374

SOURCE: *Australian National Accounts*, 1948-49 to 1964-65, Bureau of Census and Statistics.

There were two major changes in the composition of investment during this period. The more notable of these was the increase in importance of machinery and implements. The share of this component rose from just over 10 per cent of total investment in the 1920s to more than 30 per cent in the 1950s.

The second major change occurred in the form of the land improvements. In the 1920s, a large share of this component represented investment in new land, clearing, fencing etc. Later the emphasis shifted from the development of new farming land to the improvement of existing land. This resulted in a rapid increase in the area sown to improved pastures, especially during the latter part of the period.

During the last decade there has been a renewal of the upward trend in the development of new farming lands. In Western Australia, in particular, there has been a marked increase in the clearing and development of new land for agriculture.

DETERMINANTS OF FARM INVESTMENT

LEVEL OF REAL FARM PRICES

The level of real farm prices has been one of the most important determinants of the level of farm investment. It has influenced both the ability and the willingness of farmers to invest. It has influenced their ability through its impact on the supply of investible funds and their willingness through its impact on the expected profitability of investment.

Investible funds may be derived from internal or external sources. While both have been important, funds from internal sources have financed by far the greater part of the investment purchases of Australian farmers. Campbell estimates that about 90 per cent of new capital formation between June 1950 and June 1957 was financed internally.[5]

Farmers' internal investible funds consist of their idle money balances and non-money liquid asset holdings. The volume available to them during any period of time is the sum of their holdings at the beginning of the period and their cash savings during the period.

Campbell suggests that farm investment expenditure may be primarily a function of the savings component of internal liquidity. He writes:

> These [empirical studies] seem to point unequivocally to the prime importance of internal liquidity in capital formulation. The most plausible formulation would treat investment outlay as a residual, defined as the net income realised from current operations *less* tax commitments and some conventional allowance for farm family living expenses.[6]

Available evidence suggests that level of real farm prices has been an important determinant of farm savings and liquidity. If Campbell's hypothesis is correct, it must also have been an important determinant of the level of farm investment.

Real farm prices have also influenced the ability of farmers to finance investment purchases out of funds derived from external sources. The volume of farmers' external investible funds during any given period is the sum of their unused borrowing power at the beginning of the period, plus any increase—or minus any decrease—in their gross borrowing power during the period. Gross borrowing power depends to an important extent on the liquidity of the rural lending institutions (which influences the ability of these institutions to lend to farmers), and on the equities and investment opportunities of farmers (which influence the willingness of financial institutions to lend to farmers). Real farm prices have influenced the liquidity of the rural lending institutions, the equities of farmers and their investment opportunities through their impact on incomes, savings and expected future

5. K. O. Campbell, 'Some Reflections on Agricultural Investment', *Australian Journal of Agricultural Economics*, Vol 2, No 2, December 1958.

6. *Ibid.*

prices respectively. They have thus influenced the supply of external, as well as the supply of internal investible funds.

Given the supply of investible funds, the level of investment depends mainly on the willingness of farmers to use these funds for investment purposes. This depends largely on the expected profitability of investment, a major determinant of which has been expected future prices. While farmers have clearly taken other factors into account, their best guide to future prices, in the absence of important and obvious special influences, has been current prices, and immediate past trends in prices. Through their impact on expected prices, actual prices have thus influenced significantly the expected profitability of farm investment.

The above analysis suggests that the level of real farm prices has been an important determinant of the level of farm investment. Gutman's study supports this conclusion, at least for the period before World War II. His farm investment index for this period is broadly parallel—with a one- or two-year lag—to an index of real farm product prices.

The relationship between the two has been less marked in the postwar period. During the 1960s in particular, real gross expenditure on fixed assets has remained at a relatively high level, in spite of a decline in real farm product prices.

OTHER FACTORS

While the level of real farm prices has been one of the major determinants of the level of farm investment, other factors have also played important roles. The ability of farmers to invest depends not only on the availability of investible funds, but also on the availability of inputs which do not require additional cash outlays. The most important of these inputs is the farmer's own labour. However, because of indivisibilities associated with the use of other productive factors (e.g. tractors), farmers may also have considerable access to these other resources for investment projects.

This was a particularly important element in the pioneering days, when most of the capital improvements were made by the farm labour force. Its relative importance has, however, diminished considerably, especially since World War II. Today, most physical capital is bought ready made from other sectors of the economy. Only on some of the marginal properties do farmers still rely heavily on the use of on-farm inputs for investment in real capital.[7]

The ability to invest has also been influenced by the physical availability of suitable capital items. This was an important factor during, and for some years after, World War II. In fact, it was not until the 1950s that shortages

7. E. A. Saxon, 'Changes in Volume and Composition of Rural Capital', *Quarterly Review of Agricultural Economics*, Vol 15, No 4, October 1962.

of capital items ceased to be a restraining factor on the level of farm investment.

The supply of investible funds is influenced by factors other than the level of real farm prices. The main immediate determinants of the supply of investible funds are the level and distribution of real farm income, and the liquidity positions of the major rural lending institutions. In Australia, climatic and technical factors have been important determinants of the volume of farm output and thus also of farm income. During the late 1950s, for example, above average seasons and the application of improved productive techniques offset, to a considerable extent, the effect of falling farm prices on the level of farm income. Increased depreciation deductions also helped maintain after-tax farm income during this period.

The Reserve Bank and the government have done much, especially in the postwar period, to offset the effects of fluctuating export prices on the liquid assets of the trading banks, and thus on the supply of external investible funds available to farmers.

Among other factors influencing the willingness of individual farmers to invest are the expected non-financial returns from investment, the expected returns from holding non-farm assets, farmers' existing debt positions, and their general attitudes towards debt. Among other factors influencing the willingness of the sector as a whole to invest are the distributions among farmers of investment opportunities and attitudes towards debt, in relation to the distribution of the various forms of investible funds and inputs.

In general, Australian farmers have been reluctant to incur debt. In part, this has been a rational response to the price and output fluctuations associated with their industry, and to the terms and conditions on which debt has been available to them. It has been also due to feelings of moral uneasiness about being in debt, and to inadequate appreciation of the contribution debt can make to farm income. It is probable that debt aversion has been declining during the postwar years as greater stability has been brought to the industry, more attractive forms of debt have become available and increased education has led farmers to a greater awareness of the advantages of borrowing to finance capital accumulation.

Finally, the expected profitability of investment is significantly influenced by factors other than current levels of real farm prices. Two other important factors operating in Australia have been the increasing cost of labour, and the extension of technical knowledge. The number of rural workers has remained more or less constant during the postwar period despite the considerable increase in rural activity. This has increased the expected profitability of machines which are close substitutes for labour, by creating additional opportunities for their use.

Technical progress has also been important. Many new techniques have required heavy capital outlays for their introduction. Others, especially the use of myxomatosis to control rabbits, have not directly involved farmers in additional outlays, but have encouraged this indirectly by their impact on the marginal physical productivity of existing capital items.

POSTWAR GOVERNMENT POLICY

FARM INVESTMENT AND ECONOMIC OBJECTIVES

Economic policy is designed to promote a variety of objectives. Among the more important of these are internal balance (full employment and a stable general price level), external balance (equilibrium in the balance of payments) and a high rate of economic growth.

The attainment of these objectives depends to an important extent on the behaviour of farm investment. The level of farm investment, for example, is an important determinant of the level and composition of Gross National Expenditure, and thus of the level of employment. It also influences the rate of change of the general price level and the level of imports. The level and composition of farm investment are also important determinants of the long run state of the balance of payments, and the rate of growth of final output, through their effects on the composition and rate of growth of the economy's productive capital stock.

In the early postwar years, the Commonwealth government continued its long-standing policy of priority towards the manufacturing sector. There were two main reasons for this: the experience of the 1930s, and doubts about the future availability of markets for agricultural products. On the first point, it was written in 1950, 'The experience of the depression years gave rise to the notion that the agricultural industries were to be regarded as the main source of economic instability in the Australian economy, rather than as the most important source of national wealth.'[8] This attitude, together with the fear expressed by the Rural Reconstruction Committee that suitable markets for agricultural products may be difficult to find,[9] discouraged the government from actively promoting a high level of farm investment. Such agricultural policies as did emerge in the early postwar years were concerned mainly with stabilizing various industries, rather than expanding them.

Developments of the late 1940s and early 1950s caused the government to reappraise its existing agricultural policy. Primary production was increasing at only 1 per cent per annum compared with a population increase of about 3 per cent per annum. These trends gave rise to fears that within a short period of time exports of certain commodities including wheat, meat and dairy products could be greatly reduced and even eliminated by rising

---

8. Editorial, *Review of Marketing and Agricultural Economics*, Vol 18, No 4, December 1950.

9. Rural Reconstruction Commission, *Commercial Policy in Relation to Agriculture*, *Tenth Report*, Government Printer, Canberra 1946.

domestic demand for these commodities.[10] At the same time the prospects for marketing primary products overseas were improving, and Australia's need for export income was increasing.

In February 1952, the Minister for Commerce and Agriculture announced the government's intention to promote actively the development of the rural sector:

> The Commonwealth Government has, therefore, decided to adopt as its policy objective a Commonwealth-wide programme of agricultural expansion, not only to meet direct defence requirements, but also to provide food for the growing population, to maintain our capacity to import, and to make our proper contribution to relieving the dollar problem.
>
> Out of consideration of all these circumstances, the Commonwealth Government has decided that activities directly concerned with the production of essential items of food and agricultural products in this country shall be classified in importance with defence and coal production.[11]

The general policy of encouraging rural development has since been maintained.

Australian governments have adopted a variety of measures to increase the level of farm investment. The most important have been in the budgetary and monetary fields. However, price stabilization and other measures may also have played significant roles.

BUDGETARY MEASURES

Postwar governments have granted both tax allowances and subsidies to promote a high level of farm investment. Taxation allowances have been especially popular. Since 1947, farmers have been allowed to deduct from income assessed for tax purposes the full costs of certain investments, including land clearing, pasture improvement and the provision of water facilities. Since 1951, they have been able to claim depreciation on plant, equipment and structures used exclusively for farm production, at the rate of 20 per cent per annum.

The effectiveness of these allowances has been disputed. Gruen believes that their impact on farm investment may have been quite small.[12] He estimates that in 1954-55 farm incomes as assessed for income tax purposes would have been 20 per cent higher in the absence of the special depreciation allowances. Assuming that a large part of capital expenditure is made

10. D. H. McKay, 'Stabilization in Australian Agriculture, A Review of Objectives', *Australian Journal of Agricultural Economics*, Vol 9, No 1, June 1965.

11. Rt. Hon. J. McEwen, Address to Australian Agricultural Council, 1952. Reprinted in *Report of the Committee of Economic Enquiry*, Commonwealth of Australia, May 1965, Vol I, ch 8, para 21.

12. F. H. Gruen, *op. cit.*

by farmers in the higher income brackets, and that 25 per cent of the tax saving is invested, he argues that the additional investment would have accounted for only about 3 per cent of gross agricultural investment in that year.

Lewis, on the other hand, believes these allowances may have had quite a substantial effect on farm investment. He argues that the effect of accelerated depreciation is similar to that of a price reduction for capital goods, since he 'suspect(s) a good many farmers tend to work out the "effective" cost of capital improvements by deducting the tax saving from the purchase price and either to ignore or to discount heavily the effects on their subsequent tax liabilities.'[13] The virtual price reduction is greater, Lewis points out, the higher is the marginal tax rate and the greater is the difference between the normal and the special depreciation rate. It is substantial in the case of those investments which can be written off fully in the first year, and is significant for those investments subject to the special 20 per cent depreciation rate. Further, accelerated depreciation reduces risk premiums by permitting assets to be written off more quickly.

In 1963 a further concession was granted to farmers in the form of an investment allowance of 20 per cent on new plant and equipment, other than road vehicles. This allowance is additional to the 20 per cent special depreciation allowance. Consequently farmers are able to deduct from income for tax purposes a total of 40 per cent of the cost of eligible new assets in the year in which these assets are bought, and 120 per cent of their cost over the first five years of the life of these assets.

There are several criticisms which can be made of the Australian system of depreciation and investment allowances. First, it is defective on distributional grounds. Since the deductions are made from taxable income they benefit the high-income much more than the low-income farmers. In fact, many low-income farmers may fail to benefit at all from the concessions. Secondly, it distorts the allocation of resources by encouraging investments among farmers according to the distribution of income rather than the distribution of investment opportunities. Investments by younger farmers may even be reduced by the allowances. Since wealthy farmers can reduce the incidence of tax on them by buying, developing and selling properties, the prices of the less developed properties have increased considerably. As a result, new farmers who are forced to compete with wealthier ones for properties have to use more of their own funds, and/or more borrowed funds, in order to acquire properties. They are thus less able to develop these properties than they would have been had the special depreciation and investment allowances never been granted. Against this, however, is the fact that the properties acquired by the wealthier farmers are probably developed

13. J. M. Lewis, Discussion on Gruen's Paper, *Australian Journal of Agricultural Economics*, Vol 1, No 1, June 1957.

much more quickly and extensively than if they had remained with their former owners, or been sold to relatively poor farmers at lower prices.

Bounties have also been used to influence farm investment. In 1963, the government granted a $6 per ton bounty on superphosphate 'to stimulate increased use of superphosphate as a means of improving still further the productivity of farm lands and pastures.'[14] The figures in Table 10-3 suggest that the bounty has been quite effective, at least with respect to the use of superphosphate.

In the 1966-67 Budget, it was announced by the Treasurer, Mr McMahon, that the superphosphate bounty scheme would be continued at least until 1969.[15] In the same Budget, a bounty on nitrogenous fertilizers was introduced, the rate of bounty being $80 per ton of the determined nitrogen content of naturally occurring sodium nitrates and products manufactured from inorganic chemical nitrogen.

Table 10-3

Superphosphate Sales and Area Sown to Grasses and Clovers,
1954-55 to 1964-65

Year	Sales of superphosphate m. tons	Change in area under sown grasses and clovers m. acres
1954-55	2·0	—
1955-56	2·0	1·7
1956-57	2·1	4·2
1957-58	2·2	1·0
1958-59	2·1	0·5
1959-60	2·4	−0·3
1960-61	2·5	2·3
1961-62	2·7	3·5
1962-63	2·8	1·9
1963-64	3·4	3·2
1964-65	3·7	3·2

SOURCE: *Rural Land Use and Crop Production Bulletins*, Nos 12-22, 1954-55 to 1964-65. Bureau of Census and Statistics.

MONETARY MEASURES

Measures affecting interest rates and the availability of external finance have also been introduced with the intention of promoting a high level of farm investment. Since 1956 the trading banks have made advances to certain categories of borrowers, including farmers, at rates below those applying to other borrowers. These preferential rates have probably increased the willingness of some farmers to borrow for investment purposes. It is not certain

14. Rt. Hon. H. Holt, Budget Speech, 1963-64.

15. Rt. Hon. W. McMahon, Budget Speech, 1966-67.

however, that they have increased the level of farm investment. By making rural loans less profitable than other loans the preferential rate system reduces the willingness of banks to lend to farmers, especially during periods when the demand for bank loans is high. The net effect, therefore, may have been to reduce rather than increase the amount of rural development lending by banks.

One of the most important steps taken to increase the supply of rural investible funds was the establishment of the Commonwealth Development Bank in 1959. Unlike other lending institutions, which are concerned primarily with the security loan applicants can offer, the Development Bank places emphasis mainly on the prospects for success of the projects for which finance is sought. It thus ensures a more adequate flow of funds to those farmers who have sound investment opportunities, but insufficient equity to obtain finance on reasonable terms and conditions from other sources.

The Development Bank has geared its rural lending operations fairly closely to the needs of primary producers. It makes finance available in the form of both hire-purchase and term loans. The hire-purchase rate of interest on items designed specifically for agricultural purposes is about 4·5 per cent flat, considerably below the rates charged by private finance companies. Repayments are generally made monthly, but farmers may choose to make them seasonally. For example, a farmer buying a harvester can wait for the proceeds of his crop to arrive before making any repayment to the Bank.

The Development Bank's term loans also go some way towards meeting the special requirements of farmers. Capital repayment may not be required for a few years in cases where the investments do not yield a cash return in the first few years, and provision is also made for deferment of payments in abnormally low-income years.

Further steps to improve the credit facilities of farmers led to the establishment in April 1962 of revolving term loan funds by the major trading banks. These funds are insulated from the liquidity controls which influence the provision of overdraft finance, and can be made available to borrowers on terms and conditions which are more suited to their development needs.

The term loans of the trading banks cater specifically to borrowers requiring medium term credit facilities. Loans are generally made for periods of three to about eight years. Repayments are made at regular intervals, although initial repayment holidays may be granted in some cases where the investments financed are not initially income producing.[16]

In July 1965 trading bank term loans drawn by rural producers amounted to $60·6 million. Not all of this, however, represents additional bank lending to farmers, as many borrowers would have secured overdraft loans from the trading banks, or loans from the Development Bank, if term loans from the trading banks had not been available.

16. Banks and Rural Finance, Australian Bankers' Association, October 1965.

On 8 March 1966 the Prime Minister, Mr Holt, foreshadowed new measures to improve the credit facilities of farmers.[17] In a parliamentary statement on government policy, he reported that the government was considering establishing a separate Rural Division within the Development Bank. This Division would concern itself exclusively with the credit needs of farmers, thereby—the government believed—better serving the special problems of farmers.

In the same speech the Prime Minister indicated the government's desire to provide farmers with greater access to development finance from their own private banks. To do this the government intended to discuss with the trading banks the possibility of these banks establishing farm loan funds separate from the existing term loan arrangements.

These discussions took place in March, 1966. The main proposals put forward by the government were:

(i) That a new system of Farm Loan Funds should be established for the financing of farm development. There would be an initial transfer of $50 million to these Funds, part from Statutory Reserve Deposits of the trading banks with the Reserve Bank and part from the resources of the trading banks as under the existing Term Loan Scheme. The purposes of the Farm Loan Funds would be to provide loans on longer terms than are now available under the Term Loan Scheme for development of both new and existing rural properties, and loans for drought rehabilitation and mitigation measures and the general enhancement of farm productivity;

(ii) That the existing Term Loan Funds would be increased by a transfer of $20 million part from the Statutory Reserve Deposits and part from trading bank funds. It was envisaged that rural loans would continue to be made from these Funds on the same basis as previously, i.e., for periods generally of three to eight years and that, over a period, much the same proportion of the Term Loan Funds would be used for rural purposes as hitherto;

(iii) That trading banks lending on overdraft to rural borrowers would not be diminished on account of the new arrangements which would thus represent a net addition to the finance available for rural purposes;

(iv) That releases from the Statutory Reserve Deposits of the trading banks for the above purposes should be without prejudice to the normal administration of the S.R.D. system from time to time for liquidity purposes.[18]

In a press statement made after the meeting, Mr Holt stated that the trading banks were generally in full agreement with the government's proposals.

PRICE STABILIZATION MEASURES

Stabilization schemes have been provided for a number of rural industries

17. Commonwealth *Parliamentary Debates*, 8 March 1966.
18. Press Statement, 18 March 1966.

in the postwar period. These may also have had an appreciable influence on the level of farm investment. The direction of such influence is, however, uncertain.

Campbell believes that price stabilization measures have probably reduced the level of farm investment.[19] He argues that people who have fluctuating incomes have higher marginal propensities to save than those with more stable incomes. By reducing fluctuations in farm incomes, price stabilization measures reduce farm savings, and probably also the level of farm investment.

It could be argued, however, that even if these measures do reduce average savings, they may still increase investment. Greater stability of incomes presumably reduces the need to hold liquid assets, and to exercise caution in incurring debt. Further, greater stability reduces the riskiness of investment. Thus the existence of the price stabilization measures may have caused farmers to invest a greater proportion of their savings in real farm capital, and to make greater use of external finance to purchase such capital. They may, therefore, have increased, rather than reduced, the level of farm investment.

19. K. O. Campbell, *op. cit.*

CHAPTER 11

CREDIT AND AGRICULTURE

F. G. JARRETT

University of Adelaide

The purpose of this chapter is to consider the role of credit in Australian agriculture; to describe the changes in the sources of farm credit and to discuss changes and modifications of credit policy as it relates to agriculture.

Two facets of rural credit can be distinguished. The first is the allocation aspect of credit, i.e., the role of credit in facilitating changes in the pattern of resource allocation within agriculture and between agriculture and the rest of the economy. The second is the distributive aspect of credit, i.e., where public policy endeavours, through the provision of credit, to improve the relative income position of particular groups in the community.

THE STATUS OF THE FARM SECTOR

In evaluating credit policy for agriculture, two general propositions are often made. The first is that the farm sector contributes to the economy in some 'special' way, and the second is that the agricultural firm has 'special' problems.

'SPECIAL' CONTRIBUTIONS OF AGRICULTURE

Just what is 'special' about agriculture is not often clearly stated.

One notion is that the family type farm contributes to stability in a broad social sense, and that the family farm produces citizens with certain socially desirable characteristics in terms of initiative, independence, and other traits.

The second notion is that agriculture makes a 'special' contribution to the Australian economy by virtue of its role in earning overseas exchange. In recent years farm income has contributed about 10 per cent of national income, although the contribution was as high as 25 per cent in the wool boom year of 1950-51. Since then, agriculture's contribution to national income has declined, although it has fluctuated as farm output and prices have changed. The rural work force has also fallen.[1] (See Chapter 9.) On these

1. P. H. Karmel and M. Brunt, *The Structure of Australian Industry*, Cheshire, Melbourne 1963.

two criteria—income and employment—Australia is now an industrialized nation and there is little that is 'special' about Australian agriculture.

It is only when we turn to Australian agriculture and the balance of payments that one 'special' feature of agriculture—the importance of rural exports—is revealed. Despite the industrialization of the Australian economy which has occurred since 1940, that is during and after World War II, approximately 75 per cent of Australia's overseas earnings still come from the export of farm products. Although exports of manufactured origin are growing rapidly, they are still only about 15 per cent of export earnings.

'SPECIAL' PROBLEMS IN AGRICULTURE

The second general proposition in evaluating credit policy for agriculture is that the agricultural firm has 'special' problems, because of the relatively small scale of its operations and because of the instability which characterizes these operations.

Because most agricultural firms are small, they have limited access to the national capital market, and availability of credit becomes a problem. However, small agricultural firms can obtain credit from banks, insurance companies, pastoral companies and other financial intermediaries which have more ready access to the national money market. In addition farmers can obtain credit from merchants, private individuals, dealers or large firms which supply them with many of their farm inputs. The use of what is principally debt capital from these sources poses particular problems for agriculture. It is sometimes suggested that the impact of monetary restraint falls more heavily on the small agricultural firm using bank credit, for example, than on a larger industrial firm also using bank credit. While it may be difficult for the bank to refuse credit to any client, it is even more difficult to refuse a large client who is actually or potentially a large depositor with the bank.

Another special problem area in farm credit arises from the instability of farm income. In Australia, rainfall variability is particularly important although price instability probably contributes as much, if not more, than production instability.[2] Income instability affects both the attitudes of lenders who make credit available and the attitudes of borrowers who use credit. Whether capital rationing be external or internal to the farm firm, it may inhibit the efficiency of resource allocation in agriculture and consequently the contribution the farm sector can make to overall economic growth. A further difficulty arises if the institutional arrangements for extending credit to agriculture do not recognize the process of so much of the capital formation in this sector. For example, more ready access to short-term credit will inhibit the adoption of new technology which requires intermediate to long-term credit if these are not so readily available.

2. Alan Powell, 'Production and Income Uncertainty in the Wool Industry: An Aggregative Approach', *Australian Journal of Agricultural Economics*, Vol 4, No 1, July 1960.

SOURCES OF RURAL CREDIT

INTERNAL AND EXTERNAL FINANCING

Not many Australian farmers are able to supply the whole of their capital requirements from sources internal to the farm itself. Most must rely on external sources to supply at least part of the finance needed to purchase and operate their farms. Information on all the sources of funds used by farmers is not complete, so that the relative importance of internal and external financing is difficult to measure. One position which seems fairly widely accepted is that 'a large part of agricultural capital formation is normally financed out of farm income'[3] while Chislett[4] states 'it is accepted that only a small proportion of the industry's development is financed through borrowing'. However, Tostlebe[5] points out that in the United States in the post-war period, capital formation financed from external sources has risen in importance, reversing the pre-war trend of a rising proportion of new capital financed from internal sources. For specific forms of capital, such as the purchase of farm machinery, external financing may be most important.

If retained earnings in the farm firm in the form of savings and depreciation charges are high, then gross investment in Australian agriculture might be financed predominantly from internal sources. On the other hand, farm savings may fall, either because farm income falls or because the propensity of the farm community to save falls, as it increasingly adopts urban consumption patterns. When savings fall, greater reliance will be placed on depreciation charges and external funds to finance the growth in capital formation.

Australian agriculture has for many years enjoyed tax concessions aimed at stimulating investment in agriculture. Most types of capital formation can be written off at accelerated rates. For example, most plant and equipment can be written off at 20 per cent per annum while expenditure on other types of capital formation is completely deductible for tax purposes in the year in which it occurs, that is a 100 per cent rate. The accelerated depreciation allowances for a single act of investment result in a postponement in tax payments. The allowances result in an interest-free loan which must eventually be repaid. In the case of a continuous stream of investment the loan need never be repaid unless the investment stream declines. On top of these accelerated depreciation allowances, initial investment allowances are also used in some cases as a further stimulus to investment.

Only empirical investigation will answer the questions associated with the sources of funds used for capital formation and indicate whether Australian farmers are placing greater reliance on external debt. But so far few investi-

---

3. F. H. Gruen, 'Capital Formation in Australian Agriculture', *Australian Journal of Agricultural Economics*, Vol 1, No 1, June 1957.

4. G. D'A. Chislett, *A Review of Factors Influencing Production in the Sheep and Wool Industry*, Graziers' Federal Council, Sydney 1960.

5. A. S. Tostlebe, *Capital in Agriculture: Its Formation and Financing Since 1870*, Princeton University Press, Princeton, New Jersey 1957.

gations have been directed at these questions. External debt has grown in absolute amount, but the evidence on debt reliance is extremely meagre. For agriculture as a whole, we do not know whether the ratio of debt to net worth of farmers is rising or falling. Saxon[6] considers that borrowed funds have declined in importance in total capital formation in the sheep industry in the eight years ended 1959-60. However, he states that his data do 'not enable a direct comparison to be made between borrowed funds and total capital over the whole period.' An approximate measure of debt reliance is presented later by using the published information on indebtedness of farmers and the gross value of rural production, to determine whether the ratio of indebtedness to output is rising or falling. Before presenting this information, however, it will be necessary to look at the information we have on farm indebtedness.

EXTERNAL SOURCES OF CREDIT

INSTITUTIONAL LENDING

Of the external sources of credit, the main institutional lending agencies for agriculture are:

(i) The trading banks Seven private banks and the Commonwealth Trading Bank are important in this field. Australian banking is characterized by the branch banking system so that banks have branch offices operating in various geographical regions.

(ii) The pastoral finance companies These have grown up around the wool and livestock industries, and are involved in providing credit to agriculture through their wool broking and livestock selling activities.

These wool broking firms receive wool in storage, arrange for its display for sampling by potential buyers and conduct the auctions at which the wool is sold. There are four major wool brokers in Australia although there are about twenty brokers in total. Two firms dominate the wool broking business as they handle between them about one-half of the wool sold at auction in Australia. Some 70 per cent of Australian wool is received into the wool brokers' stores in September-October-November but sales of wool do not show the same marked seasonality.

The pastoral companies provide 'carry on' advances to farmers before the wool clips are sold; provide credit and insurance facilities for wool growers; employ a field staff who give technical and managerial advice; provide farmers with credit to purchase livestock and sometimes provide finance for farm purchases.

(iii) Federal and State government agencies Direct involvement of government with lending to agriculture has been mainly associated with the estab-

6. E. A. Saxon, 'Changes in Volume and Composition of Rural Capital', *Quarterly Review of Agricultural Economics*, Vol 15, No 4, October 1962.

lishment of ex-servicemen on farms following both world wars. Settlers obtained short-term working capital, intermediate capital for purposes such as livestock purchase and long-term capital for farm development at low rates of interest. Often these low interest rates were accompanied by relatively small or no repayment obligation in the first few years of farm operation.

Indirect government involvement with rural lending may occur through State banks and State savings banks. At the State level, such banks may often more directly reflect government policy with respect to their lending activities than either the private trading banks or the Commonwealth Trading Bank.

(iv) The life assurance societies These societies constitute an important source of investment funds in Australia and they are substantial holders of both government securities and shares in corporate business.

(v) The Commonwealth Development Bank This bank, with capital provided initially by the Federal government, completed its first full year of operation in June 1961. Advances from the Development Bank have grown rapidly, although in terms of total lending, it ranks well behind the trading banks and the pastoral companies. Its particular importance rests on its policy of lending for farm development with an emphasis on the profitability of the investment contemplated. This criterion contrasts with the emphasis given by the trading banks to the security of the loan. Farmers who are unable to obtain funds from the trading banks may be accommodated by the Development Bank.

Estimates of Debts The estimated rural debt to specified lenders in terms of gross indebtedness is shown in Table 11-1. If one were concerned with the liquidity of the farm sector and the potential for financing capital formation, a measure of net indebtedness would be more relevant. The deposits of the farm sector with the lending institutions, and other liquid assets held by farmers, would need to be deducted from advances. However, many of these deposits are probably held for precautionary reasons and are not available for current capital formation.

Published information on deposits by farmers with both the banks and the pastoral companies has been available since 1960. Total farm deposits with these two agencies amounted to $A 836 million at 30 June 1965. The farm sector also holds substantial assets in the form of savings bank deposits, shares and debentures but the extent of these assets is unknown. Nevertheless, the gross indebtedness figures do measure the extent to which farmers rely on external financing from particular lenders.

NON-INSTITUTIONAL LENDING

In addition to the institutional agencies given in Table 11-1, the rural sector also obtains funds from other sources. For example, private lenders (often operating through lawyers in country towns), merchants and store-

Table 11-1

Rural Debt to Specified Lenders, as at 30 June 1950-1965
($A million)

	1950	1951	1952	1953	1954	1955	1956	1957	1958	1959	1960	1961	1962	1963	1964	1965
Major trading banks	236	250	288	296	384	442	426	400	462	460	474	450	480	494	514	584
Pastoral finance companies	66	102	98	94	110	132	148	160	186	182	204	212	208	214	228	258
Commonwealth Development Bank	8	8	8	8	10	10	10	10	12	12	14	22	34	46	56	72
Ex-service settlement[a]	32	44	52	60	64	70	82	92	100	106	110	114	118	114	108	104
Other government[b]	98	88	94	92	96	104	108	114	122	126	128	138	150	170	190	216
Assurance societies	14	16	16	16	14	18	20	24	32	34	42	48	50	52	56	66
TOTAL	454	508	556	566	678	776	794	800	914	920	972	984	1,040	1,090	1,152	1,300

a. Following both World Wars I and II, governments undertook to establish qualified ex-servicemen in farming.
b. Including State banks and State savings banks.

SOURCES: H. C. Coombs, 'Rural Credit Developments in Australia', *Australian Journal of Agricultural Economics*, Vol 3, No 1, July 1959, p 101. *Statistical Bulletin*, February 1961, Reserve Bank of Australia. *Personal communication*, Rural Liaison Service, Reserve Bank of Australia.

keepers, farmers' cooperatives and hire purchase companies all provide credit to agriculture. Intra-family lending may also be important sources of funds, particularly in financing the transfer of farm property. The extent of credit from these sources is unknown but in particular types of agriculture 'outstanding balances due to non-institutional sources (plus hire purchase) have been as much as 50 per cent of those due to the main institutional sources.'[7] The distribution of non-institutional lending to agriculture is not known, but private lending probably dominates, with trade credit and hire purchase sources being relatively small. In contrast to many other countries, farmer cooperatives in Australia are not major sources of funds and the total credit extended through cooperatives is probably small.

Apart from the sources of credit already mentioned, Australian farmers obtain substantial short-term credit through the operations of some marketing authorities. For wheat, the Australian Wheat Board acquires almost the whole of the annual wheat crop and is the sole selling agent. The Board makes advances on wheat awaiting sale, with the first and largest advance occurring just after the end of the harvest. To finance these payments, the Board borrows from the Rural Credits Department of the Reserve Bank.

CHARACTERISTICS OF DIFFERENT FORMS OF CREDIT

TRADING BANK LOANS

In terms of absolute indebtedness, the major trading banks are the largest single institutional source of funds. However, between 30 June 1950 and 30 June 1965, advances by the pastoral finance companies have increased by almost 300 per cent as compared with an increase of 147 per cent for the trading banks. The pastoral company advances were mainly for sheep raising with smaller amounts going to cattle raising. Trading bank advances for sheep raising over the same period have increased by 225 per cent, with much smaller percentage increases for other types of farming.

In the three years 1955-56, 1956-57, and 1960-61, the pastoral companies actually increased advances despite declining trading bank advances. (Table 11-1.) In these three years, the pastoral firms were more important sources of net lending than were the banks. Farmers offset the reduced availability of funds from the trading banks by increased borrowing from the pastoral companies. However, part of the increased lending by the pastoral companies was financed by their own increased use of bank overdraft.

Trading bank loans are made by way of overdraft up to an approved maximum limit. The overdraft is essentially an open line of credit and, in principle, is repayable on demand. The credit thus appears to be short term. In practice, however, overdrafts are extended for long periods although the banks may require periodic reductions in overdraft levels. Lending from the

7. *Australian Rural Credit Facilities*, Reserve Bank of Australia, 1964.

trading banks to the rural sector normally requires formal security, most often in the form of a first mortgage over land or buildings. Interest on the overdraft is paid on the daily balance owing to the bank. At one stage, the Reserve Bank set a maximum rate of interest on overdrafts; although an individual bank could charge less than the maximum on any particular advance, it was expected to maintain a given average rate over all overdrafts. While this interest rate policy existed, the banks were expected to grant preferential interest rates below the maximum to exporters. This policy of fixed maximum and average rates has now been discontinued, but the Reserve Bank does request the trading banks to grant lower rates to exporters. This has meant that the rural sector has been treated preferentially.

Term Lending Fund In April 1962, the major trading banks began experimenting with an alternative form of loan to the bank overdraft, and some $A 110 million was set up as a term lending fund. From this fund loans could be made for specified periods, usually on an amortized basis over three to eight years. The original $A 110 million was rapidly committed with about one-third going to the rural sector. In March 1966, the Federal government proposed to increase the term lending fund by $A 20 million. This increase in funds was to be achieved partly by releasing funds from the Statutory Reserve Deposits held by the trading banks with the Reserve Bank and partly from trading bank funds. The term lending fund was not exclusively for rural lending and the amortization period might be regarded as too short for some types of farm investment.

Farm Development Loan Fund In March 1966, the Federal government also proposed a farm development loan fund of $A 50 million which could provide a longer amortization period of up to 15 years or more. The $A 50 million was established partly by releasing Statutory Reserve Deposits of the trading banks with the Reserve Bank, and partly from trading bank funds.

It should be emphasized that both the term lending fund and the farm development loan fund are being financed and the loans executed by the trading banks. The Federal government's action has been to permit the release of some of the Statutory Reserve Deposits of the trading banks for rural lending.

PASTORAL FINANCE

The pastoral finance companies act as short-term lenders of 'carry on' finance.[8] Their preferred type of loan is an advance against wool already in store and awaiting sale. The advance may take the form of an overdraft with the pastoral company against which the farmer client can draw. Alternatively, the pastoral company may transfer an amount of the advance to the farmer's own bank account. The pastoral companies may also make short-

8. F. G. Jarrett, 'Agricultural Credit—Pastoral Finance Houses', in R. R. Hirst and R. H. Wallace, *Studies in the Australian Capital Market*, Cheshire, Melbourne 1964.

term advances on the basis of a lien on wool on the sheep's back. In any case, the pastoral company expects that the loan will be repaid in 'the year of income', that is, as soon as the wool has been sold.

The pastoral companies also finance short-term loans for livestock sales and property transfers, particularly where there is a substantial livestock component in the transfer. Relatively few of the advances are tied up with long-term mortgages although estimates of 5 to 15 per cent have been suggested by some pastoral company executives.

The granting of advances constitutes a major form of non-price competition for the pastoral companies. There is no price competition between them as the rates for wool broking services are, with minor variations, set by the National Council of Wool Selling Brokers. The companies compete to attract clients to market their wool and livestock through them, and consequently they are often able to exercise some control over a wool grower's income by insisting that if an advance is made, the wool and livestock transactions be handled by them. As a consequence the pastoral houses may have been less 'security' conscious than the trading banks. The interest rates charged on pastoral company advances are usually slightly in excess of those charged by the trading banks. One-half per cent above the bank overdraft rate seems typical.

FEDERAL AND STATE GOVERNMENT LOANS

The interest rates charged on farm loans by the different government agencies are often below those prevailing on overdrafts from the trading banks. There is, however, a somewhat more restricted limit to the size of any one loan than would obtain with respect to trading bank loans. Another difference is that some loans from the State banks have a term element in them rather than being an open line of credit. That is, the loan may be granted, particularly for the purchase of farm property, for a stated period over which the loan is to be amortized. Both State banks and State savings banks, although they may be important sources of funds in particular States, show a decline in their importance as rural lenders relative to other lending agencies.

LIFE ASSURANCE SOCIETY LOANS

The life assurance societies are relatively insignificant lenders to the farm sector. Detailed information is not available, but these societies do finance farm purchases and what lending they do is probably mainly for this purpose. The interest rates charged on their loans seems to be somewhat higher than those charged on trading bank overdrafts. The relative unimportance of the assurance societies in rural lending in Australia contrasts with experience in the United States where in some areas the insurance companies are the predominant holders of farm real estate mortgages.

NON-INSTITUTIONAL LOANS

Hire Purchase For specific types of capital such as plant and equipment, hire purchase agencies are particularly important. Farmers may be willing to use hire purchase as the hire purchase contract does not entail formal security even though the effective rates of interest are often double those charged on trading bank overdrafts. Indeed, the ease with which equipment purchases can be financed could result in the neglect of more profitable investment opportunities which are more difficult to finance. The hire purchase contracts require periodic repayment over a stated period, with the length of the period varying on the size of the contract.

DEBT RELIANCE IN AGRICULTURE

Changing technology has led to an increase in the total capital requirements per farm, so that farmers using credit now require larger loans than was previously the case. Although there is no information on the average total indebtedness of farms, some idea of the adjustment of the lending agencies to this increasing need is obtained by estimating real institutional indebtedness per rural holding. This average measure will understate indebtedness per farm because some farms are debt free and should be excluded; and also because some single farms which consist of several separate areas of land, farmed together as a single farm unit, may be classified in official statistics as more than one 'rural holding'.

The growth in real institutional indebtedness per rural holding is shown in Table 11-2. Apart from the growth in real indebtedness per farm, which reflects the lending agencies' awareness of the increasing capital intensity of agriculture, two years in particular are worthy of comment. The first is the fall in institutional indebtedness between 1949-50 and 1950-51, which was largely due to the boom wool prices of 1950-51. The second is the increase in indebtedness between 1956-57 and 1957-58, which reflected both an increased demand for credit associated with falling prices, and the effects of drought over many parts of Australia. In Australia's semi-arid to arid environment, drought can cause substantial losses of livestock, which result in considerable pressures on external funds to finance new capital and highlights any external credit rationing which may exist.

As was mentioned earlier in this chapter, one measure of debt reliance is the ratio of indebtedness to the gross value of rural production. Debt reliance ratios, for all farming, agricultural crops, pastoral products and for farmyard and dairy production are shown in Table 11-3. The Bureau of Census and Statistics' classification of agricultural crops includes annual cereal crops, fruit production, and vegetable production. Pastoral production includes sales of sheep, wool, and beef cattle. Farmyard and dairy production includes sales of milk, pigs and poultry. This classification corresponds approximately with the Reserve Bank's classification of trading bank advances which are 'mainly sheep raising', 'mainly wheat growing', 'mainly dairying and pig raising'. However, since the gross value of agricultural production includes both wheat and fruit and vegetables, the 'other' advances classification of the Reserve Bank is included in wheat growing advances. Moreover, since the pastoral companies are predominantly engaged in financing pastoral production their advances are added to the trading bank advances for sheep raising. It should be remembered that the debt reliance ratios for particular types of farming reflect only the reliance on trading banks and pastoral companies as sources of credit.

Table 11-2

Institutional Indebtedness per Rural Holding, 1949-50 to 1963-64
(1949-50 = 100)

Year	Index of debt per holding[a]
1949-50	100
1950-51	73
1951-52	91
1952-53	116
1953-54	105
1954-55	130
1955-56	130
1956-57	124
1957-58	151
1958-59	160
1959-60	158
1960-61	159
1961-62	179
1962-63	181
1963-64	204

a. The institutional debt per rural holding has been deflated by the Bureau of Agricultural Economics' index of prices received by farmers and expressed in index form.

SOURCES: Data on total institutional indebtedness from Table 11-1.
Rural holdings data from *Primary Industries Part 1—Rural Industries Bulletin*, Bureau of Census and Statistics.

The results in Table 11-3 suggest that for the rural sector as a whole ('all farming'), the debt reliance ratio has increased over the period considered. For the agricultural sector, the debt reliance ratio has fluctuated over time but with no clear trend. For the pastoral sector, the ratio shows the increasing reliance on advances from the trading banks and the pastoral companies. The ratio fell to a low of 12 per cent in the wool boom year of 1950-51, reached a high of 38 per cent in 1957, and fluctuated a little around this level in the following years. In contrast, the reliance of the farmyard and dairying sectors on advances from the trading banks has fallen over time. This fall presumably reflects a change in credit availability from this particular source, and a switch to other sources, rather than a decline in the credit requirements of this type of farming.

Table 11-3

Debt Reliance Ratios, 1949-50 to 1963-64
(indebtedness as a percentage of gross value of production)

Year	All farming[a]	Agricultural[b]	Pastoral[c]	Farmyard and dairying[d]
	%	%	%	%
1949-50	29	16	20	23
1950-51	22	17	12	24
1951-52	29	16	22	21
1952-53	24	14	18	17
1953-54	29	19	23	22
1954-55	35	22	30	22
1955-56	34	18	33	18
1956-57	31	18	25	19
1957-58	41	20	38	20
1958-59	37	15	38	17
1959-60	37	18	34	17
1960-61	36	14	38	15
1961-62	38	16	37	16
1962-63	36	15	33	16
1963-64	34	16	29	15

a. Ratio based on total indebtedness from Table 11-1.
b. Ratio based on trading bank advances for 'wheat growing' and 'other' types of farming.
c. Ratio based on trading bank advances for 'sheep raising' and pastoral company advances.
d. Ratio based on trading bank advances 'mainly for dairying and pig raising'.

SOURCES: *Statistical Bulletins*, Reserve Bank of Australia; and *Primary Industries Part 1— Rural Industries Bulletins*, Bureau of Census and Statistics.

MONETARY POLICY AND AGRICULTURAL CREDIT

The proposition was advanced earlier in this chapter that if agriculture was to be regarded as making a 'special' contribution to the Australian economy, then this 'special' contribution was through the balance of payments. However, balance of payments equilibrium is only one of Australia's general economic policy objectives.

Other objectives are full employment, internal price stability, and the rate of economic growth. These objectives are not mutually exclusive; they are interdependent and to a certain extent may be inconsistent. At times, relatively more emphasis will be given to one of these objectives than to others, and the particular policy objectives being emphasized may have implications for credit policy with respect to agriculture. For example, in periods of rapidly rising prices, price stability may overshadow all other objectives; if fiscal and monetary measures are used to control inflation then agriculture will have to feel the brunt of restraint just as any other sector of the economy; but the incidence should not fall differentially on the farm sector. There may be times when fiscal and monetary measures themselves are inconsistent so far as their effect within the same sector is concerned. Within agriculture, monetary restraint operating through the banking system may be offset substantially if special depreciation and investment allowances permit farmers to reduce the impact of taxation, even if only temporarily.

If new loans increase and repayments decrease aggregate spending in the economy, then the difference between the two—the change in outstanding advances—provides a measure of the primary stimulating or depressing effect of credit on total spending in any given time period. There may be differences in the secondary effects operating through the multiplier or the accelerator if different sectors have different characteristics with respect to the importance of multiplier and accelerator effects. For the sake of simplicity it is assumed that an increase in outstanding advances to the farm sector has the same effect on aggregate spending as an increase in advances to other sectors. From the point of view of economic stability, if monetary restraint were being urged, one would expect a decline in outstanding advances to all sectors, or at least, that the rate of increase would decline.

Two qualifications to the step from increases in outstanding bank advances to increases in aggregate expenditure must be made. The first is that the credit data subsequently used refer to advances by the trading banks and not to all credit in the economy. The expenditure-generating effects of increases in bank advances may be modified if there is credit contraction from other sources. However, if outstanding advances fall because repayments exceed new lending, and borrowers repay their bank loans by liquidating assets, the primary deflationary effect of repayment will not be as great as if repayment were made by cutting back consumption and/or investment. The second qualification is that some increases in bank advances may not immediately be expenditure generating. This would be the case if the bank advances were to finance the transfer of existing assets. For example, if a farmer uses the bank advance to buy a piece of equipment out of a farm equipment dealer's inventory, then in the first round, the effect of the advance is to add to the dealer's working capital. It will only generate further expenditure when the depleted inventory is replaced and the lag in such replacement might be considerable. Much the same argument would apply to bank advances used to finance transfers of farms and of land.

223

Q

Despite these qualifications one can ask, and attempt to answer, the question of whether bank advances to the various sectors have behaved consistently with monetary policy. Consistency in the behaviour of bank advances and monetary policy would require that bank advances fall when monetary restraint is being urged and that advances increase when an easier monetary policy obtained. To get a number measure of monetary policy is difficult but Jarrett and Dillon[9] have classified periods between 1949 and 1962 as periods of monetary ease or monetary restraint on the basis of statements on monetary policy appearing in the Reserve Bank's *Annual Reports*. The change in outstanding advances by both the trading banks and the pastoral companies as at 30 June and 31 December was tabulated and compared with monetary policy. The results are shown in the table below.

Table 11-4

Consistency of Monetary Policy and Advances to Different Sectors,
1949-1962

| | Trading banks | | | | | Pastoral firms |
	Agriculture	Manu-facturing	Persons	Commerce and transport	Finance	
Consistent with tight money policy	7	6	6	3	5	3
Inconsistent with tight money policy	9	10	10	13	11	13
Consistent with an easier money policy	8	5	8	4	4	6
Inconsistent with an easier money policy	3	6	3	7	7	5
Overall consistency	15	11	14	7	9	9
Overall inconsistency	12	16	13	20	18	18

SOURCE: Data on advances outstanding on 30 June and 31 December are from *Statistical Bulletins*, Reserve Bank of Australia. Monetary policy is inferred from statements about monetary policy in *Annual Reports*, Reserve Bank of Australia.

9. F. G. Jarrett and J. L. Dillon, 'Some Aspects of the Rural Credit Market', *Australian Journal of Agricultural Economics*, Vol 9, No 2, December 1965.

Of the 27 comparisons made, the behaviour of bank advances to the farm sector was most consistent with monetary policy when compared with other sectors, but even agriculture's score was only 55 per cent. Of the other sectors, the behaviour of advances to persons was, after agriculture, best in accord with monetary policy. Since, for both these sectors, the average size of loan and of deposit is small, the evidence supports the argument that in periods of monetary restraint it is easier for the banks to refuse a loan application from these sectors, and that in periods of monetary ease funds are more readily available and more readily used by these sectors. The particular problem, for agriculture in Australia, is that if an attempt to use monetary policy to achieve price stability falls with undue incidence on the farm sector, then capital formation in agriculture may decline. The balance of payments which is probably already under stress with a rising price level may worsen further as productivity in agriculture falls. However, fiscal measures aimed at furthering internal capital formation may more than offset the impact of monetary policy.

On the inconsistency side, the major reason for all sectors to score badly is the failure of bank advances to decline when monetary policy is one of restraint. It is interesting to note the inconsistency of pastoral company advances and monetary policy, again arising principally from the failure of advances to decline in periods of tight monetary policy. However, the pastoral companies have been able to increase their advances by running down their holdings of cash and government securities, by recourse to the capital market for additional funds, and by increasing reliance on bank overdraft.[10] This latter phenomenon makes them more susceptible to monetary restraint than was previously the case. This in turn will make it even more difficult for farmers to switch their credit demands from the banks to the pastoral companies in periods of tight credit.

CONCLUSION

Apart from any 'special' contribution argument, the point has been made that agriculture may have 'special' problems in external financing of capital formation. These 'special' problems arise essentially because of the limited access that agricultural firms have to the capital market. In this chapter, it is not possible to give any detailed analysis of the effect of monetary policy on capital formation in agriculture. The relative importance of internal and external funds and the attitudes of farmers to the use of external funds would need to be considered. Also, are leftward shifts in the supply of external funds through monetary policy positively or negatively correlated with shifts in the demand for external funds?

Agriculture's basic credit difficulties seem to arise from its limited access

10. F. G. Jarrett, *op. cit.*

to the capital market. The possibilities of encouraging equity participation by individuals in farm operations is probably restricted to a regional basis where individuals have particular knowledge of farmers and farming conditions in the area. Despite the limited possibilities that may exist, it seems worthwhile to investigate the scope for further incorporation of farms with a number of individuals providing savings for farming.

The bulk of institutional credit provided to agriculture comes from the trading banks and to a less extent, the pastoral firms. The overdraft form of lending has undoubtedly served agriculture well but it is questionable whether it is the most appropriate credit instrument for present-day agriculture. Since many of the new technologies in agriculture require relatively longer periods than in secondary industry to 'pay off', farmers need to be assured of a continuity in credit availability which is not always assured under the overdraft form. Yet it is probably the technologies most needing intermediate credit which will make the greatest contribution to agricultural productivity and through it to economic development. A beginning was made with term lending in 1962, and the speed with which these resources were committed suggests farmers' needs for intermediate length loans for stated periods were not being met by the then existing credit arrangements. The increase in March 1966 in the term lending fund and the establishment of a farm development loan fund will provide useful additions to the supply of intermediate and long-term lending funds available to agriculture.

Of the major institutional lenders, the assurance societies lend relatively little to the farm sector and one might ask what are the legal and institutional rigidities which prevent a greater flow of credit to agriculture from one of the most important sources of funds for investment in the Australian economy. A beginning has already been made in Australia with housing loans insurance in an attempt to increase the flow of funds into private housing. In March 1966, the Federal government indicated that it was exploring an insurance scheme to cover loans from the farm development loan fund. If such a scheme is to be implemented it might possibly be expanded to cover lending from the assurance societies. In either case, such lending should be channelled into capital formation which will increase productivity in the farm sector rather than into increased land prices.

The credit requirements of the small farmers may not be adequately met by existing institutions particularly where such farms are characterized by relatively high debts to assets ratios but which have the potential to grow to economic sized units. The Commonwealth Development Bank has made a beginning by not necessarily following a lending policy based on value of collateral but looking rather at whether the proposed use of funds will permit the debt to be serviced and still make an addition to net revenue. This type of lending has, of course, to be done extremely carefully with the need for detailed farm planning and supervision. The present resources of the Commonwealth Development Bank may limit the rate at which the growth to economic sized units can occur but in particular types of farming in Australia there is undoubtedly scope for increases in farm size. The reorganization of small farms in these areas into larger commercial units which are more heavily capitalized would often produce added returns in excess of the capital costs but the availability of credit may well prevent such aggregation and consolidation of farms.

In the context of low-income agriculture, the distributive aspect of credit would suggest the provision of credit with some element of subsidy. The identification of the low-income farmers presents a puzzle but presumably they could be identified if sufficient effort were put into the task of finding just who or where the low-income farmers are. Recent work by Hoffman and Hume[11] suggests that the income disparity between farm and non-farm incomes in Australia is nowhere near as large as exists in countries such as the United States, for example.

Even so, there may be pockets of poverty in Australian agriculture. It may be doubted whether subsidized credit is the most effective way of tackling any low-income problem, generally associated with inadequate farm sizes. Indeed, the provision of such credit may delay the consolidation of farms into economic units and perpetuate the resource misallocations which already exist.

11. E. S. Hoffman and J. R. Hume, 'Farm and Non-Farm Income in Australia', *Quarterly Review of Agricultural Economics*, Vol 18, No 3, July 1965.

CHAPTER 12

AGRICULTURAL DEVELOPMENT PROJECTS

E. S. HOFFMAN

Department of Primary Industry

Since 1946, there has been a great increase in the number and scope of public and private land development projects. This increase can be attributed largely to more favourable prices for rural products, new knowledge of development and production techniques, and increasing participation and financial contributions by the Commonwealth government.[1]

In this review the net is cast slightly wider than 'projects'. With few exceptions though, the developments all involve public sector finance. However source of finance in not necessarily the best way of classifying projects, despite the fact that most controversy centres around public policy decisions.

DRY LAND DEVELOPMENT

Two forms of land development have occurred in non-irrigated areas:

(i) intensification of existing land use, the significance of which has been outlined in Chapter 3; and

(ii) development by land clearing and cultivation or pasture establishment of areas that previously made little or no contribution to rural production.

Although attention in this chapter is concentrated on the second of these two forms of development, it should be emphasized that much of the increase in production and in productivity over the last two decades has been on existing farms, rather than on new farms established under the development projects described here.

LAND CLEARING AND DEVELOPMENT

The dry land development projects have certain common characteristics.

1. In this chapter, attention will be directed largely to events in the 20 years since the end of World War II. For a resumé of earlier events in Australian land development, see Rural Reconstruction Commission, *A General Rural Survey, First Report*, Government Printer, Canberra 1944, ch 3. Also see S. M. Wadham, R. Kent Wilson and Joyce Wood, *Land Utilization in Australia*, 4th ed, Melbourne University Press, Melbourne 1964, ch 2.

These include: *rapid* clearing of natural vegetation; upgrading of the phosphate level of the soils; sowing of leguminous pastures; heavy stocking at certain periods of the year as an essential for pasture management; considerable use of contract activities in development; and, above all, access to greater capital resources than is common in older established areas. In most cases some organization, public or private, has undertaken a significant part of the development in the early years.

WAR SERVICE LAND SETTLEMENT

By far the largest of the postwar land settlement projects is the Commonwealth War Service Land Settlement Scheme, which provides for the settlement of eligible ex-servicemen from World War II and the Korea-Malaya operations. Since the Scheme began in 1945, total gross expenditure by governments on acquisition and development of land and on the provision of credit facilities to settlers has exceeded $420 million. (Table 12-1.)

Table 12-1

War Service Land Settlement: Expenditure, 1945 to 30 June 1966

	$A million
Capital expenditure	
in 'Agent' States*a* from Commonwealth advances	196·4
in 'Principal' States from Commonwealth advances	27·9
in 'Principal' States*b* from own funds (estimated)	199·0
Gross expenditure on acquisition, development and credit facilities	423·3
Other expenditure*c* (excluding administration)	10·8
Total expenditure	434·1

a. In the 'Agent' States (South Australia, Western Australia and Tasmania) the Commonwealth has provided all monies required for the Scheme.
b. In the 'Principal' States (New South Wales, Victoria and Queensland), the State undertook to provide the capital required for acquisition and development of land and to provide credit facilities for the settlers.
c. Includes living allowances granted to settlers, operation and maintenance of headworks in some irrigation projects in Agent States, and Commonwealth contributions to Principal States for remissions of rent and interest. Costs associated with providing and operating irrigation headworks in Principal States is unknown and therefore not included in total expenditure.

SOURCE: War Service Land Settlement Division, Department of Primary Industry.

The *War Service Land Settlement Agreements Act* 1945 laid down the basic principles that guided operations under the accompanying Commonwealth-State agreements. These principles are listed in Chapter 8. Following a successful High Court challenge against the 1945 Act, the Commonwealth continued to provide money under the *State Grants (W.S.L.S.) Act* 1952-1953.

Under the *War Service Land Settlement Agreements Act* areas of land considered suitable were selected by the State authorities either on private

Table 12-2
War Service Land Settlement: Major Projects

State and project	Number of farms	Total area acres	Land use	Notes
NEW SOUTH WALES				
Edgeroi	65	115,300	Sheep and wheat	Intensification of land use.
Ghoolendadi	36	41,200	Sheep and wheat	Intensification of land use.
Coomealla	97	3,315	Horticulture	Virgin land brought under irrigation—chiefly vines for dried fruit and citrus.
VICTORIA				
Murray Valley	526	63,000	Dairying and horticulture	Cleared land brought under irrigation includes 458 dairy farms and 65 producing stone fruits for drying and canning.
Robinvale	246	43,000	Horticulture	Cleared and virgin land brought under irrigation for citrus, wine grapes and dried fruit production.
Marida—Yallock	44	6,930	Dairying	Intensification of land use.
SOUTH AUSTRALIA				
Kangaroo Island	174	258,000	Wool and prime lambs	Farms developed from virgin scrub.
Eight Mile Creek	32	7,100	Dairying	Drained virgin peaty swamp land.
Loxton	253	7,740	Horticulture	Mallee soils originally wheat farms, now irrigated for citrus, stone fruit, wine grapes and dried fruit production.
TASMANIA				
King Island	154	47,000	Dairying and prime lambs	Predominantly virgin scrub land developed.
Togari	45	6,040	Dairying	Virgin swamp drained and cleared.
WESTERN AUSTRALIA				
Gairdner River area	132	480,000	Sheep and cereals	Virgin heath and scrub developed to pasture.
Rocky Gully area	122	130,000	Wool, prime lambs and cattle	Virgin forest land developed to pasture.

SOURCE: War Service Land Settlement Division, Department of Primary Industry.

properties or on Crown lands. Land on private properties was acquired or purchased for the Scheme by the State. After the Commonwealth had given approval to a proposed plan of settlement, the State authorities proceeded to subdivide into 'home maintenance areas',[2] and to develop and improve the land to a stage where it could be brought into production by a settler within a reasonable time. Rates of interest for advances made to settlers varied from 2 per cent to 3·75 per cent per annum in different States. A year's grace was given before repayment of principal and interest began; during that year also a living allowance was granted.

The Scheme provided for intensification of existing land use and development of new farms. In Western Australia both types of settlement occurred; in New South Wales and Victoria, action has largely been intensification and closer settlement; while in South Australia and Tasmania settlement was predominantly developmental.[3] Table 12-2 contains examples of major W.S.L.S. projects in the different States.

During the 20 years of W.S.L.S. operation, 9,150 holdings have been allotted, totalling over 13·5 million acres. Data are not available of the extent of new land brought into production as a result of the Scheme, but it would appear to exceed 3 million acres. A summary of the land acquired and allotted in each State is given in Table 12-3.

Queensland withdrew from the Scheme in 1954. By 1959, demand for opportunities to settle had been largely satisfied in the 'Agent' States of South Australia, Western Australia and Tasmania, and the Commonwealth indicated to these States that no further acquisition of land should take place; allocations would continue from land already acquired. After 1960 the Commonwealth terminated its offer of loans to New South Wales and Victoria, and acquisition ceased in those States also. In 1966 virtually all W.S.L.S. development had been completed; the Scheme will continue indefinitely as a credit arrangement for development, working expenses and purchase of stock and plant. Redemption payments since 1963-64 have been returned to Consolidated Revenue and are not available for reinvestment in the Scheme.

STATE SETTLEMENT SCHEMES

All States have long-standing policies for closer settlement. The State of Victoria also engaged in soldier settlement on its own account. Settlements were established at Yanakie, where 12,000 acres of Crown land on the north-

2. For the origins and use of this concept, see C. J. King, 'An Outline of Closer Settlement in New South Wales', *Review of Marketing and Agricultural Economics*, Vol 25, Nos 3-4, September-December 1957; W. L. Payne, *Report on Progressive Land Settlement in Queensland*, Land Settlement Advisory Commission, Government Printer, Brisbane 1959; and J. N. Lewis, 'Is the Concept of the Home Maintenance Area Outmoded?', *Australian Journal of Agricultural Economics*, Vol 7, No 2, December 1963.

3. A. R. Callaghan, 'Progress in Land Development (Non-irrigation) 1949: Statement prepared for Commonwealth Grants Commission', *Journal of the South Australian Department of Agriculture*, Vol 53, No 5, December 1949.

ern neck of Wilson's Promontory were developed from 1954 onwards to provide 46 farms; and in the East Goulburn irrigation system, where between 1957 and 1965 over 170 orchard and dairy farms came into operation. However, in 1959-60, with the cessation of active acquisition under the Commonwealth W.S.L.S. Scheme and following the passing by the Victorian parliament of the *Land Settlement Act* 1959, the unallotted balance of the Yanakie

Table 12-3

War Service Land Settlement: Land Acquired and Holdings Provided, 1945 to 30 June 1966

State	Land acquired	Land allotted	
	000 acres	*Number of holdings*	*000 acres*
New South Wales[a]			
Western lands	6,060	212	6,060
Subdivision[b]			
Irrigation	198	356	198
Dry	1,277	1,102	1,277
Promotions[b]			
Irrigation	127	230	127
Dry	1,432	1,147	1,432
Total	9,094	3,047	9,094
Victoria			
Irrigation	95	989	95
Dry	1,087	2,059	1,087
Total	1,182	3,048	1,182
Queensland[c]	399	470	219
South Australia			
Irrigation	16	340	16
Dry	740	682	672
Total	756	1,022	688
Western Australia	1,905	1,010	1,905
Tasmania[d]	450	551	431
TOTAL AUSTRALIA	13,785	9,148	13,519

a. In New South Wales, properties are regarded by the State as being allotted at the date of acquisition.
b. Two methods of settlement were provided in New South Wales:
    (i) Acquisition and subdivision, under which the Crown through the machinery of the State Closer Settlement Act, acquired suitable properties by purchase or resumption, subdivided the land and after advertisement, allotted the farms to qualified servicemen by ballot.
    (ii) Promotions, whereby one (or several) qualified servicemen may, with the consent of the owner, apply for land to be acquired at an agreed price. The Crown then purchases the property, subdivides if necessary, and vests title of the farm(s) in the applicant(s).
c. War Service Land Settlement was discontinued in 1954 and unallotted lands (180,000 acres) were made available for general settlement.
d. As at 30 June 1966, there were 17 farms totalling approximately 8,000 acres still under development.
SOURCE: War Service Land Settlement Division, Department of Primary Industry.

area, together with the Heytesbury and East Goulburn lands, were transferred to civilian settlement.

In the Heytesbury forest area, following nine years of experiments, the Victorian Soldier Settlement Commission[4] commenced large-scale development of some 72,000 acres of virgin Crown land in 1956. By mid-1965 over 70,000 acres had been cleared. The timber was knocked, using two 150 h.p. crawler tractors, linked by a nine-ton anchor chain through an eight-foot diameter steel ball. The debris was pushed into windrows by bulldozers and burnt. The land was broken using 'Majestic' heavy-disc stump-jump ploughs, then fertilized with superphosphate, lime and copper and sown to pasture.

In New South Wales a civilian closer settlement scheme was introduced under the *Closer Settlement (Amendment) Act* 1960, with provisions similar to the W.S.L.S. Scheme in respect of methods of acquisition, subdivision and allocation of land. However, advances are not made to incoming settlers, and the annual lease rental (5 per cent of valuation) and interest on improvement debts (4 per cent) are higher than under W.S.L.S. By 30 June 1966, 74 estates comprising 236,000 acres had been acquired for over $6 million. From these areas 172 farms had been made available by ballot (some with preference for ex-servicemen) and 61 by promotion.[5]

Apart from the large-scale development that originated under war service land settlement, four dry land projects deserve special mention: the short-lived Queensland-British Food Corporation; development of the Coonalpyn Downs (on the border of South Australia and Victoria); of the Esperance plain (Western Australia); and of Brigalow land (Queensland).

QUEENSLAND-BRITISH FOOD CORPORATION

From 1948, the Q.B.F.C. made an effort to grow sorghum and fatten cattle and pigs in the Central Highlands region of Queensland. The Corporation was established jointly by the U.K. Government Overseas Food Corporation and the Government of Queensland. By 1952, it had acquired 13 properties, totalling over 720,000 acres, with headquarters at Peak Downs. However, agricultural techniques were poor, management was cumbersome, remote, inflexible and excessively expensive with undue emphasis on rapid expansion, and livestock turn-off was disappointing.[6] Ironically, when it was decided to terminate the project, the postwar rise in land values enabled the

---

4. This Commission was originally set up to carry out Victoria's activities under W.S.L.S. In 1959 the Commission was made responsible for civilian land settlement in Victoria, and in 1962 its name was changed to the Rural Finance and Settlement Commission when it assumed responsibilities for credit provided by the Rural Finance Corporation.

5. New South Wales Department of Lands, *Annual Report, 1965-66*, Government Printer, Sydney 1965, p 8.

6. *The Future of the Queensland-British Food Corporation*, Cmnd 8760, H.M.S.O., London 1953.

Corporation to recoup much of its heavy operating losses. The experience gained served to indicate that supplementary cropping does have a role as part of the farming system in the areas concerned.

NINETY MILE PLAIN (COONALPYN DOWNS)

In the first of the successful projects, the developer was a major insurance company, the Australian Mutual Provident Society. Following legislation by the South Australian government, the *Land Settlement (Development Leases) Act* 1949, the Society was granted leases of areas totalling approximately 500,000 acres at Coonalpyn Downs in the Ninety Mile Plain. Later some 330,000 acres adjoining the South Australian leases were obtained across the border in the Big Desert of Victoria, under the Victorian *Land (Development Leases) Act* 1951. About 60 per cent of the acreage was considered capable of development. In its natural state the region carried approximately one sheep to 40 acres.

Research by CSIRO into trace element deficiencies provided the technological basis for development. The Society 'logged'[7] or 'chained' the scrub, fired the debris, deep-disced, 'levelled', and sowed to improve pastures, using top dressings of superphosphate and lime, enriched with zinc and copper sulphates. Settlers were chosen from those who worked for wages for the Society for the five years needed to bring blocks to full development. About 80 settlers obtained holdings in this way in South Australia. A typical block of 1,000 acres carries about 750 ewes and 300 wethers, or better. In recent years a number of the older established properties have also grown some wheat.

Blocks were fully developed before settlers took over, including house, fencing, watering points, sheds, machinery and stock. This represented a combined value of about $60,000-$70,000, secured by mortgage over the block together with collateral life insurance policy. A further 120 blocks were sold to other purchasers. These blocks were larger, averaging about 3,000 acres. All of the land under the Society's leases in South Australia has passed to private lease holders.

Development is proceeding in Victoria on a slightly different basis. Previously the Society undertook development itself; now work is carried out on a contract basis and blocks of varying sizes to suit the buyer's financial resources are sold, in the main, in a partially developed state. This enables the settler to obtain the benefit of tax allowances for developmental expenditure.

The A.M.P. scheme has stimulated others to develop land in the region. Private owners have found that it costs approximately $45-$50 per acre, excluding house, to bring a property to full development.

7. 'Logging' is pulling two linked 40 ft logs behind a tractor. 'Chaining' is dragging 800-900 ft of inch and a half steel anchor chain between two 135 h.p. drawbar capacity caterpillar-tread tractors. 'Levelling' is dragging a welded structure of railway line rails across the ploughed land to level it roughly, consolidate it and bring to the surface roots that have not been completely extracted by the 'Majestic' disc ploughs.

As the Ninety Mile Plain project neared an end, the A.M.P. Society turned elsewhere in Australia to continue investment in rural development. In 1967, their subsidiary, Stanbroke Pastoral Co., is operating 15 cattle stations in Queensland, covering approximately 7,500 square miles.

ESPERANCE DOWNS

In Western Australia, Dunn[8] estimates that there are 38 million acres of light land country throughout the agricultural region of the south-west of the State, with 12-13 million acres of this yet to be developed.

Esperance Downs lies in the south-east of the agricultural region. It contains about 3 million acres of heath plain. To the north the Downs merge into about 3 million acres of Mallee country capable of cereal production. Esperance land is somewhat similar to that at Coonalpyn Downs, relatively easier to improve, with higher stocking capacity when fully developed. Clearing and pasture establishment costs, including fertilizing, average $15-$20 per acre. (See Table 12-4.)

The main enterprise is Merino wool and lamb production with beef cattle an important subsidiary form of production. Cereal cropping on clover ley is increasing in extent and economic importance. At present oats appear to be the best cash crop on the Esperance plain. Sheep carrying rates exceeding 3 per acre are obtained on established pasture, resulting in a good return on capital invested. However, transport expenses are heavy and lambs cost approximately $1.00 per head to market at Perth.

Large-scale land holdings have been a feature of the Esperance area since the earliest settlement in 1863. In 1956 an American group, Esperance Plains (Australia) Ltd., entered into an agreement to develop 1·5 million acres in the area. Because of poor planting techniques (and in 1957 an unfavourable season), plantings failed and the company did not continue development. However, the syndicate's efforts gave much publicity to the development possibilities around Esperance.

In 1960 the agreement was taken over by another group, the Esperance Land and Development Company, again with American capital. Somewhat more stringent conditions were imposed by the Western Australian government. Under the new agreement, approximately 1 million acres of land were made available to the company at a cost of 40 cents per acre plus survey fee, to be developed at approximately 100,000 acres per annum. The land is being subdivided into holdings of about 2,000 acres. Development means the erection of fencing, provision of water supplies and the establishment of pastures on not less than one-third of each area with a minimum of 700 acres.

8. W. P. Dunn, 'Development of Light Land in Western Australia', *CSIRO Rural Development No 19*, October 1964, p 2. See also F. L. Shier, T. C. Dunne and E. N. Fitzpatrick, *Agriculture on the Esperance Downs*, Bulletin 3080, Western Australian Department of Agriculture, Perth 1966; and *Esperance Hinterland*, Government of Western Australia, Perth 1966.

For each block developed and sold, the company is entitled to select another block for its own retention. The State of Western Australia has obligations under the *Esperance Lands Agreement Act* 1960 to provide for surveys, roads, subsidiary works and general civic and industrial development in the Esperance area. Port development has included a new wharf and bulk grain facilities and the Esperance fertilizer works began manufacture of superphosphate in 1964.

Table 12-4

Esperance Downs, W.A.: Clearing and Establishment Costs, 1966

	$A per acre
FIRST YEAR	
Rolling or chaining (September-November)	1·00
Burning and fire breaks (February-March)	0·50
SECOND YEAR	
First ploughing (July-August)	2·50
Second ploughing (March-April)	2·00
Root picking[a] (April)	2·50
Sowing pasture (May-June)	1·50
Seed (,, ,,)	2·00
Superphosphate[b] (,, ,,)	3·10
THIRD YEAR	
Superphosphate (22 per cent)	1·80
Spreading	0·50
Total cost	$17·40

a. Finger wheel rake.
b. Enriched with trace elements.

SOURCE: Western Australian Department of Agriculture.

Quite separately, the State surveys and throws open for ballot other lands on the plain and country to the north, and light lands elsewhere in the State. The land is made available as conditional purchase under Section 47 of the *Land Act Amendment Act* 1922-1965. Since World War II, 17·1 million acres of land have been cleared in Western Australia (to March 1966). Of this approximately 660,000 acres were cleared under the War Service Land Settlement Scheme and approximately 175,000 acres by the Esperance Land and Development Company. The remainder (approximately 3 million acres in the Esperance region and 13 million acres elsewhere in Western Australia) have been developed by private individuals without direct government intervention.

BRIGALOW LANDS[9]

Brigalow (*Acacia harpophylla*) occurs over areas of some 23 million acres in northern New South Wales and south-eastern Queensland between Collinsville (Qld.) and Narrabri (N.S.W.), a distance of about 700 miles. About 50 per cent of the area is Brigalow dominant, with associated eucalypt forest. Prior to the introduction of *Cactoblastis*, discussed in Chapter 3, much of the area was overrun with prickly pear (*Opuntia* spp.). Older forms of clearing such as ring-barking failed because of the rapid suckering habit of the tree; consequently, although soils are fertile, the productivity of the virgin Brigalow land was low. In favoured areas, the Brigalow belt had been developed for grain growing, dairying, wool growing, cattle fattening and other pursuits.

After World War II crawler tractors and 'Majestic' ploughs made rapid and successful clearing possible. Using ball and chain, about 30 acres per hour can be pulled at a cost of from $3 to $4 per acre. This is usually done in the autumn and if dry enough, the felled timber is burnt about the following December. The success of the burn is most important to minimize regrowth. Rhodes grass (*Chloris gayana*) and green panic (*P. maximum* var. *trichoglume*) are sown on the ashes of the burn. The new pastures are grazed lightly until the second season in order to assist establishment. In some cases, Brigalow land is cleared of stumps and roots for immediate grain production or forage crops.

Following preliminary investigations by the Queensland Department of Primary Industries and a benefit-cost analysis by the Commonwealth Bureau of Agricultural Economics, the Commonwealth agreed to provide financial assistance to Queensland for the development of approximately 10 million acres in the Fitzroy basin west of Rockhampton. Some 600 blocks will result, to be used for fattening store cattle or cattle bred on the eucalypt forest. Each block will carry about 1,000 head of cattle. At a later stage winter fodder cropping is envisaged.

AREAS WITH POTENTIAL FOR DEVELOPMENT

There are throughout Australia a series of areas which appear to possess possibilities for large-scale dry land improvement. In the south, the main

9. See *The Economics of Brigalow Land Development in the Fitzroy Basin, Queensland*, Bureau of Agricultural Economics, Canberra 1963; *The CSIRO Cunningham and Townsville Laboratories*, CSIRO, 1965; J. W. van Holst Pellekaan, 'The Application of Benefit/Cost Analysis to the Evaluation of Brigalow Land Development', *Quarterly Review of Agricultural Economics*, Vol 17, No 1, January 1964; J. W. van Holst Pellekaan and V. J. Robinson, 'Property Development in the Brigalow Areas of the Fitzroy Basin, Queensland', *Quarterly Review of Agricultural Economics*, Vol 17, No 4, October 1964; and J. H. Johnston and D. Wesney, 'Cropping as an Aid to Development on Brigalow Properties in the Fitzroy Basin', *Quarterly Review of Agricultural Economics*, Vol 17, No 4, October 1964.

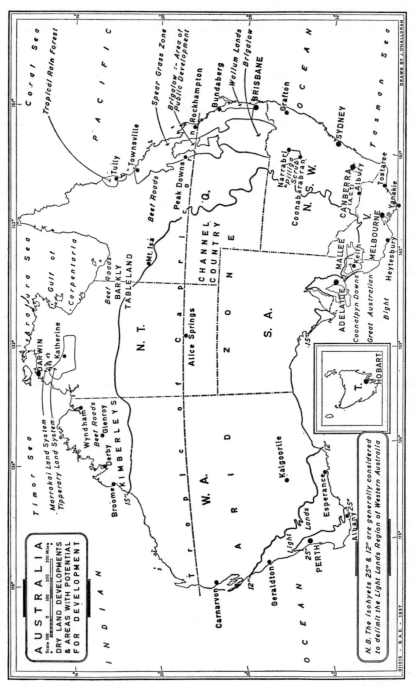

Map 12-1: Agricultural Development Projects: Non-Irrigated

increase in production will come from intensification.[10] However, some regions have been suggested for clearing and pasture establishment.

East Gippsland (Victoria) Forest land analogous to that at Heytesbury exists in East Gippsland. The Victorian Department of Crown Lands and Survey established a pilot farm at Tostaree in 1961-62 for the investigation of potential settlement opportunities.[11]

Pilliga Scrub (New South Wales) Between Narrabri and Coonabarabran lies 1·75 million acres of scrub country which could possibly respond to clearing, soil improvement and pasture development. Only limited research has yet been published as a guide to its potentiality. However, clearing costs are likely to be high.[12]

In the north, while the overall pattern of dry land development is the same—pull, burn, fertilize and sow—the key factor is the advent of legumes and grasses suited to tropical and subtropical conditions, notably Townsville lucerne *(Stylosanthes humilis)*.[13] There is evidence of potentiality for development in several areas.

Spear Grass Area (Queensland) Over 40 million acres of coastal and subcoastal land in Queensland from Brisbane to north of Townsville carry spear grass *(Heteropogon contortus)*. It also carries about 1·5 million head of stock, approximately one-quarter of Queensland's beef cattle population. Some 20 million acres appear suitable for improvement. Experiments suggest that in the Townsville area, the present carrying capacity of 1 beast to 14 acres may be raised to 1 beast to 7 acres (or better) by Townsville lucerne alone, and to 1 beast to 3 acres (or better) if fertilizer is also applied. Sown pastures offer scope for still higher production but the legumes tried so far do not always persist under grazing.[14]

Wallum Land (Queensland) The Wallum lands extend along the coastal fringe from the southern border of Queensland northward to Bundaberg. They cover about 3 million acres. Chippendale[15] has listed the steps to be

10. See for example Wollongbar Agricultural Research Station, *Annual Report, 1964-65*, New South Wales Department of Agriculture, regarding possible rejuvenation of the North Coast region of New South Wales. Should the promising 'feed year' system become widely adopted with concomitant increase in herd size, butterfat production could double over an area of 2-3 million acres.

11. Department of Crown Lands and Survey, *Report for the Financial Year ended 30 June 1964*, Government Printer, Melbourne 1964, p 14.

12. J. M. Vincent and F. C. Crofts, *Pasture Improvement in the Pilliga*, Report No 3, University of Sydney, Department of Agriculture, December 1958.

13. W. W. Bryan, 'Progress in Pasture Improvement in Northern Australia and Future Prospects', *Journal of the Australian Institute of Agricultural Science*, Vol 31, No 2, June 1965.

14. R. G. Moyle and N. F. Haug, 'Some Economic Aspects of Increasing Beef Cattle Production in the Spear Grass Zone Using Improved Pastures', *Quarterly Review of Agricultural Economics*, Vol 18, No 1, January 1965.

15. F. Chippendale, 'The Development of Wallum land—heath', *Journal of the Australian Institute of Agricultural Science*, Vol 30, No 4, December 1964.

R

taken to convert the low heath country to reasonably productive pasture in about 12 months: rotary slashing; burning; rotary hoeing; liming; fertilizing; discing or rotary hoeing; planting of seed of *Lotononis bainesii* and runners of pangola grass (*Digitaria* spp.). Potash and copper may be necessary as well as superphosphate. He estimates that a farmer who already owns the land and a small amount of cultivation equipment can develop a pasture on this type of country for $30 per acre. However, the profitability of development of the Wallum area is still in doubt.

Belyando-Suttor Area (Queensland) In the basin of the Belyando and Suttor rivers of central Queensland there are approximately 5·5 million acres believed suitable for development, including large areas of Brigalow and gidgee (*Acacia cambagei*) scrubs. The Bureau of Agricultural Economics is currently (1967) making an economic evaluation of the area. If favourable, the pattern of development would probably be based on the experience in the Brigalow Lands Development Scheme.

Tropical Rain Forest (Queensland) Considerable progress is being made with an area of some 50,000 acres of rain forest land leased near Tully (North Queensland) to the U.S. financed King Ranch Syndicate as a development block for fattening beef cattle. This private project is testing the practicability of pasture establishment using modern clearing methods and pasture species such as para grass (*Brachiaria mutica*), guinea grass (*Panicum maximum*) and centro (*Centrosema pubescens*). If the operation proves economic and successful, opportunities will be opened up for development of possibly 4 million acres of the Queensland tropical coast.

Tipperary Land System (Northern Territory) The Tipperary Land System[16] covers an area of over 10,000 square miles (6·5 million acres) in the 'Top End' of the Northern Territory, north-west of Katherine. At present it carries about 3 beasts to the square mile. Experiments have shown that it is possible to establish Townsville lucerne, but unless the native species are heavily grazed or otherwise cleared at sowing and in the succeeding wet season, the lucerne is likely to be smothered out. The problem may be one of managing flexible stocking rates rather than any difficulty in introducing tropical legume species. So far the economics of development of the area have not been fully worked out.

Marrakai Land System (Northern Territory) The Marrakai Land System[17] and associated areas embrace some 3,500 square miles (2·25 million acres)

16. C. S. Christian and G. A. Stewart, *General Report on Survey of Katherine-Darwin Region 1946*, Land Research Series No 1, CSIRO, 1952, p 100. The authors state (p 9): 'A Land System has been defined as an area, or group of areas, throughout which can be recognized a recurring pattern of topography, soils and vegetation'. See also N. H. Speck et al., *General Report on Lands of the Tipperary Area, Northern Territory, 1961*, Land Research Series No 13, CSIRO, 1965.

17. C. S. Christian and G. A. Stewart, *op. cit.*, p 109.

to the north of the Tipperary Land System. Cattle numbers on native species average less than 4 to the square mile. In 1964 three pilot farms were established to test intensive cattle production and a combined rice-cattle enterprise. Detailed records are being maintained on these farms to provide the basis for economic analysis.

Table 12-5

Summary of Postwar Large-Scale Dry-Land Development
Projects and Current Possibilities

Locality	Area million acres	Main forms of land use
PROJECTS		
War Service Land Settlement	13·5[a]	Various
Heytesbury (Vic.)	0·1	Dairying
Coonalpyn Downs (S.A. and Vic.)	0·8+	Sheep and wheat
Esperance region (W.A.)	3·0	Sheep and oats
Other W.A. regions	12·0+	Sheep and wheat
Brigalow (Qld.)	10·0	Beef and grains
Total approx.	40	
POSSIBILITIES		
Light lands (W.A.)	10·0	Sheep and wheat
East Gippsland (Vic.)	0·1	Dairying
Pilliga scrub (N.S.W.)	1·7	Sheep
Spear Grass Zone (Qld.)	20·0	Beef
Wallum country (Qld.)	3·0[b]	Beef
Belyando-Suttor (Qld.)	5·5	Beef
Tropical rain forest (Qld.)	4·0	Beef
Tipperary Land System (N.T.)	6·5	Beef
Marrakai Land System (N.T.)	2·2	Beef
Other	?	
Total approx.	50	

a. Includes approximately 10 million acres of land transfers involving intensification (including irrigation blocks) and approximately 3 million acres of new land development.
b. Doubtful.

DRY LAND DEVELOPMENTS: SUMMARY

Davies and Eyles[18] have calculated that there are 430 million improvable acres of which over 80 per cent remain to be developed. In Table 12-5 a summary is given of the postwar expansion in dry land development. The table shows that the areas at present under large-scale development still represent less than 10 per cent of the area in Australia considered capable of development under current technology. The areas where future large-scale dry land development appears technically feasible might be another 12-15 per cent.

18. J. G. Davies and A. G. Eyles, 'Expansion of Australian Pastoral Production', *Journal of the Australian Institute of Agricultural Science*, Vol 31, No 2, June 1965.

In a few areas development could possibly occur without public intervention; for most of these areas, however, development depends on public investment, which involves political as well as economic decisions.

Beyond there lies the even more difficult challenge of the Arid Zone.

WATER RESOURCES AND CONSERVATION

WATER RESOURCES

Australia is the driest of continents, with highly variable rainfall, prone to drought and flood. The total average annual discharge of Australian rivers is 280 million acre feet, with some 62 per cent occurring in tropical areas.[19] Wide fluctuations are experienced both in the seasonal flow of surface water within any one year and in the flow from year to year. Consequently a large volume of storage is necessary for each acre irrigated, in order to be able to meet runs of dry years.

Clearly there is need for strict control over water use. Policies about water control were determined by two Victorian Acts, *The Irrigation Act* 1886 and the *Water Act* 1905.[20] Later legislation in other States has followed parallel lines. The States have remained in individual control of their water resources except in the case of Murray river waters and Snowy river waters (where Commonwealth-State agreements operate) and the waters of streams on the border of Queensland and New South Wales (where a joint agreement exists). The Commonwealth controls water resources in its Territories. In 1966 the Prime Minister indicated that the Commonwealth Government was willing to contribute up to $50 million over 5 years towards additional State works for water conservation.

Co-ordination between government agencies responsible for water was achieved by annual interstate Water Resources Conferences, but more recently (late 1962) an Australian Water Resources Council was established. Its prime functions are to provide for comprehensive assessment of Australia's water resources and for related research.

STOCK WATER SUPPLIES

Artesian Waters Artesian or sub-artesian water occurs in 12 basins, with areas totalling some 1·25 million square miles, nearly 40 per cent of the continent. (See Map 12-2.) Over 18,000 bores have been put down in the Great Artesian Basin and about two-thirds of these are still active.

Most States provide some financial concession towards putting down approved bores. Control is exercised over the drilling of bores in order that the

---

19. *Review of Australia's Water Resources (Stream Flow and Underground Resources) 1963*, published by the Department of National Development for the Australian Water Resources Council, 1965.

20. The latter Act 'declared that the bed and banks of all streams should become and remain the property of the Crown, thus completing finally the nationalization of streams and other natural sources of water supply . . .'. See A. L. Tisdall, 'Australian Water Policy', *Journal of the Australian Institute of Agricultural Science*, Vol 27, No 2, June 1961.

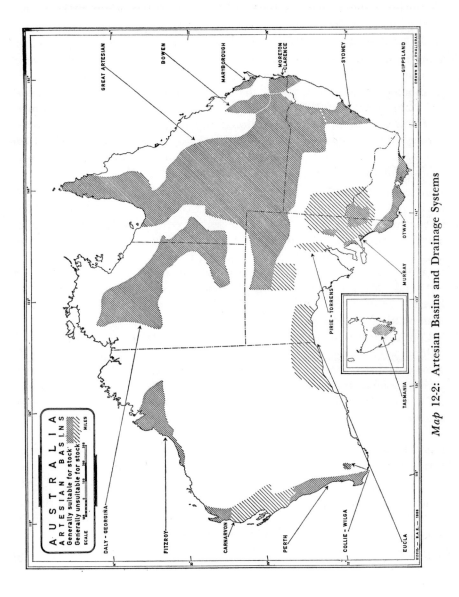

Map 12-2: Artesian Basins and Drainage Systems

basins may be brought to a steady state of balance between outflow and intake. The economic importance of the basins lies in the surety they provide for water supplies for stock watering purposes over significant areas of the continent; without them the uncertainty of the rainfall would make animal production even more difficult than it is.

Stock Routes All mainland States have programmes for the provision of watering facilities on main stock routes, which are public areas under government control to enable livestock to be driven from one part of the country to another, or to market. Under the *States Grants (Encouragement of Meat Production) Act* 1949-1954[21] the Commonwealth government agreed to meet half the cost of providing additional watering facilities on stock routes through the Channel Country and on the route from Camooweal to Mt Isa in Queensland. Funds were also granted to improve facilities on stock routes leading into Wyndham (Western Australia).

Western Australia Water Supply Scheme To provide the Kalgoorlie goldfields with water, a 30-inch steel main was completed in 1903 rising 1,200 feet from the Mundaring reservoir (close to Perth) to Kalgoorlie, 346 miles away. It was extended a further 100 miles in 1937 to Norseman. By 1946, over 3,000 miles of branch pipelines had been laid to mining and agricultural areas for human, industrial and stock use, but not for irrigation. Between 1947 and 1961, the area served by pipe was increased to over 4 million acres by the Comprehensive Water Supply Scheme, financed jointly by the Commonwealth and State governments.

Construction is in progress (1967) to reticulate water to a further 3·75 million acres. Under a Commonwealth Act, the *Western Australian (South-West Region) Water Supplies Agreement Act* 1965, the Commonwealth is providing financial assistance on a dollar for dollar basis, up to $10·5 million by way of repayable interest-bearing advances, to enable this work to be accelerated. Before the Commonwealth entered into the agreement, the economics of the agricultural aspects of the extension of the Scheme were tested by a benefit-cost analysis undertaken by the Bureau of Agricultural Economics.[22]

South Australian Pipelines South Australia has a series of similar smaller-scale developments, with a total of over 7,000 miles of pipes bringing water to country areas. The major schemes are in the Eyre Peninsula and the areas served from the Murray-Whyalla pipeline.

Mallee-Wimmera (Victoria) Supply Scheme An extensive domestic and

---

21. This Act was passed for the purpose of stimulating pastoral development in accordance with Australia's commitments under the 15 Year Meat Agreement (1952-1967) with the United Kingdom.

22. See *Extension of the Comprehensive Water Supply Scheme (Agricultural Areas of Western Australia): An Economic Evaluation,* Bureau of Agricultural Economics, Canberra 1965.

stock water supply scheme operates in north-western Victoria. The system serves a wheat-growing and sheep-grazing area of 7 million acres. The main source of supply is Rocklands reservoir in the Grampians, together with water drawn from the Goulburn, Loddon and Murray rivers. Supplies are distributed by gravitation in open channels through 6,500 miles of main channels and 3,000 miles of farm channels to 7,000 farms. As far as possible, water is moved in winter and spring to reduce evaporation losses. The farmers must provide storage capacity on their farms sufficient to hold their domestic and stock water requirements for the ensuing year.

IRRIGATION SCHEMES

Irrigation settlements were first established by the Chaffey brothers from California at Renmark (South Australia) and Mildura (Victoria) in 1887. Inadequate transport and difficulties with soil, water and finance rendered the economic existence of these settlements extremely hazardous for some 20 years before they were established on a sound basis. This experience was to be repeated time and again with irrigation settlements elsewhere in Australia.

Major expansion of irrigation took place following World War I, often on shaky technical and economic bases. Salting affected the Mildura and Murrumbidgee irrigation areas and those in the mid-Murray region. The complex relationship of soils, pattern of irrigation (such as optimum length of run of water) and crop types were mastered only slowly. Drainage provision was often inadequate. And, quite important, those going onto irrigated settlement blocks had frequently received little training in irrigation techniques.

On the economic side, the development of large irrigation projects has involved heavy public investment. It has been long-standing policy that the cost of headworks should be regarded as a national investment, thereby giving irrigation farmers a benefit not available to dry land farmers. Even so, considerable public assistance has been necessary to cover the time-lag before settlements reached full production; to rectify technical troubles; to reconstruct farms with inadequate size, as had to be done for example in the Murrumbidgee Irrigation Area[23] from 1926 on; and to counteract the depressing effects of the low prices that ruled for many farm and orchard products during the 1930s.

Further expansion occurred, although to a lesser extent, under the War Service Land Settlement Scheme. The doubtful outlook for vine fruits caused considerable controversy before decision was taken to expand the settlements in order to absorb ex-servicemen seeking land.

23. For an analysis of the history and difficulties of the Murrumbidgee Irrigation Area, see J. Rutherford and T. Langford Smith, *Water and Land: Two Case Studies in Australian Irrigation*, Australian National University Press, Canberra 1966. See also 'Murrumbidgee Irrigation—A Regional Study', *Current Affairs Bulletin*, Vol 31, No 10, April 1963; and 'A Reply', *Current Affairs Bulletin*, Vol 32, No 7, August 1963.

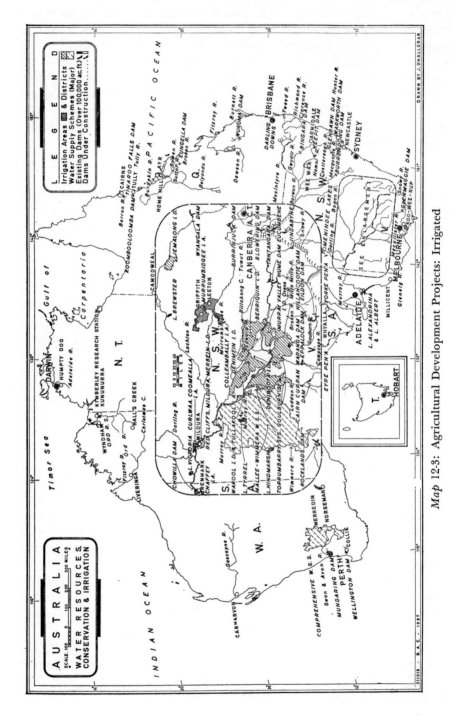

Map 12-3: Agricultural Development Projects: Irrigated

In Table 12-6 a list is given of the major irrigation storages. This table illustrates: the prevalence of postwar works; the paucity of storages in the tropics, e.g. the complete absence of any major works on the rivers emptying into the Gulf of Carpentaria; and the dominance of the Murray-Darling system in Australian irrigation.

The areas of irrigated land in Australia and the forms of production are shown in Table 2-9.

MURRAY-DARLING BASIN

Approximately 80 per cent of Australia's irrigation development has been in the Murray-Darling basin. The Murray river (1,600 miles), the Darling river (1,700 miles) and their tributaries drain an area of over 400,000 square miles, one-seventh of the continent. Today over 2 million acres are irrigated in the Murray-Darling basin, approximately 1 acre for each 2·5 acre feet of water diverted at river offtakes. The various irrigation regions in the basin together produce almost 100 per cent of Australia's rice, dried vine fruit, and canned deciduous fruit (peaches, pears and apricots); as well as considerable volumes of citrus, vegetables, fresh fruit, butter, lamb and cotton. The basin will in the near future reach maximum development of its water resources, including those diverted from the Snowy river (see below), although not of its land resources.

The *River Murray Waters Act* 1915 was passed by the Commonwealth parliament and the parliaments of New South Wales, Victoria and South Australia. The Act established the River Murray Commission, and provides for the construction of dams, weirs, locks and storages for the control and regulation of the Murray waters, such works to be carried out by State authorities under the general direction of the Commission. Equal capital contributions are made by the four governments to meet the cost of these works. The Act also laid down the way in which the water was to be shared between States.

Water Storage and Distribution   Existing storages on the Murray itself are the Hume reservoir, situated just below the junction of the Murray and the Mitta Mitta rivers and 10 miles upstream from Albury; and Lake Victoria, adjacent to the river, 35 miles below the Murray-Darling junction. Water released from Lake Victoria supplies South Australia. Between the Hume reservoir and the confluence of the Murrumbidgee, the Murray receives the waters of a series of Victorian tributaries (Kiewa, Ovens, Broken, Goulburn, Campaspe and Loddon rivers), most of which are now also controlled. (See Table 12-6.) The Murrumbidgee-Lachlan system is regulated by the Burrin-juck and Wyangala reservoirs which were constructed before the war and have since been enlarged.

On the Darling the major storage is provided at Menindee by an inter-connected series of lakes created by improvement of natural depressions and

Table 12-6

Major Irrigation and Stock Water Storages, 1966
(storages in excess of 5,000 acre feet, other than weirs)

Drainage division and stream	Storage	State or authority	Active capacity 000 acre feet	Height of wall feet	Crest feet	Hydro electricity	Date completed[a]	Cost $A million	Notes
MURRAY-DARLING DIVISION									
Upper Murray									
Swampy Plain	Khancoban	S.M.A.	21	65	3,320	–	1966	2	[d]
Upper Murray	Hume	R.M.C.	2,500	142	5,300	+	1936-61	17	Cost of enlargement
Murray tributaries									
Ovens	Buffalo	Vic.	20	80	2,090	–	1965	6	Eventually 800,000 acre feet
Broken	Winton	Vic.	300	35	4 miles	–	[c]		
	Lake Nillahcootie	Vic.	35	115	2,730	–	[b]	(4)	
Goulburn	Waranga basin	Vic.	333	40	4·2 miles	–	1910		
	Lake Eildon	Vic.	2,750	260	3,225	+	1955	25	
Campaspe	Eppalock	Vic.	252	160	2,200	–	1964	11	
	Coliban storages	Vic.	56						
Loddon	Cairn Curran	Vic.	121	44	2,800	–	1956	8	
	Tullaroop	Vic.	60	95	1,400	–	1959	4	
	Laanecoorie	Vic.	6	55	1,300	–	1891		
Murrumbidgee-Lachlan									
Murrumbidgee	Burrinjuck	N.S.W.	837	264	500	+	1927-57	11	Cost of enlargement (future development)
			(1,000)	(270)	(5,200)				
Tumut	Blowering	N.S.W.	1,300	370	2,700	+	[b]	(42)	
Lachlan	Wyangala	N.S.W.	245	200	1,100	+	[b]	(37)	Being enlarged to 1 million acre feet
	Lake Cargelligo	N.S.W.	29	..		–			
	Lake Brewster	N.S.W.	124	..		–	1951		

System	Reservoir	State							Notes
Darling system									
Darling	Menindee Lakes	N.S.W.	2,000	⋮	3,660	—	1960	8	Includes 397,000 acre feet for flood control
Macquarie	Burrendong	N.S.W.	1,361	250		—	b	(37)	
Namoi	Keepit	N.S.W.	345	177	1,750	+	1960	25	
McIntyre brook	Coolmunda	B.S.	61	61	7,800	—	b	(6)	
Condamine	Leslie	Qld.	38	95	1,250	—	1966	5	Eventually 87,000 acre feet
Lower Murray									
Lower Murray	Kow Swamp	Vic.	41	..	4 miles	—	1885		
	Kerang Lakes	Vic.	58						
	Lake Boga	Vic.	29						
	Lake Victoria	R.M.C.	550	..		—			To be inundated by Chowilla
	Chowilla	R.M.C.	5,000	41	3·3 miles	—	b	(43)	
	Lake Alexandrina	S.A.		..	15·0 miles	—			
SOUTH-EAST COAST DIVISION									
Snowy									
Eucumbene	Eucumbene	S.M.A.	3,540	381	1,900	+	1958	34	Transfers water to Murrumbidgee (and Murray)
Snowy	Jindabyne	S.M.A.	560	225		+	b		Transfers water to Murray (and Murrumbidgee)
Wimmera system									
Glenelg	Rocklands	Vic.	272	84	1,560	—	1953		⎫ For stock water
	Toolondo	Vic.	86			—			⎪
Fyans creek	Fyans lake	Vic.	17			—			⎪
	Lake Bellfield	Vic.	60	130	2,600	—	1966	6	⎬
	Lake Lonsdale	Vic.	53			—			⎪
Mt. William	Wartook	Vic.	23	36	4,646	—	1887		⎪
McKenzie	Taylors lake	Vic.	30			—			⎪
	Pine lake	Vic.	52			—			⎭

Table 12-6—Continued

Drainage division and stream	Storage	State or authority	Active capacity 000 acre feet	Height of wall feet	Crest feet	Hydro electricity	Date completed[a]	Cost $A million	Notes
Maffra-Sale system									
Macalister	Lake Glenmaggie	Vic.	154	122	969	–	1927-58		
Werribee system									
Pykes creek	Pykes creek	Vic.	19	128	1,452	–	1911-30		
Werribee	Melton	Vic.	15	116	939	–	1916		
Hunter system									
Hunter	Glenbawn	N.S.W.	293	251	2,700	–	1958	28	Includes 108,000 acre feet for flood mitigation
	Warkworth	N.S.W.	406	130		–	[c]		
NORTH-EAST COAST DIVISION									
Barron	Tinaroo falls	Qld.	330	136	1,750	+	1958	13	
Tully	Koomboolomba	Qld.	146	123	1,310	+	1961		
Burdekin	Gorge	Qld.	7	20	1,284	+	1953		
Broken	Eungella	Qld.	104	150			[b]		
Callide creek	Callide	Qld.	37	83	6,950	–	1965	7	
Nogoa	Maraboon	Qld.	1,170	148		–	[c]		
Yabba creek	Borumba	Qld.	34	102	1,125	–	1964	5	Mary valley
Nogo	Wuruma	Qld.	150	142	1,050	–	[b]	(5)	Burnett valley
Reynolds creek	Moogerah	Qld.	75	105	715	–	1961		Brisbane valley

TIMOR SEA
DIVISION

Ord	Bandicoot Bar	W.A.	80	66	1,500	(−)	1964	10	
	Carlton Gorge	W.A.	(10,000)	(180)	(1,000)	(+)	c	(30)	
Fitzroy	Liveringa	W.A.	6			(−)	1962	2	
SOUTH-WEST COAST DIVISION									
Harvey	Logue brook	W.A.	20	150	1,200	−	1963	2	
	Stirling	W.A.	46	152	900	−	1948		
	Harvey	W.A.	8	68	1,094	−	1916-31		
Collie	Wellington	W.A.	150	112	1,205	+	1933-60	3	
Samsons brook	Samsons brook	W.A.	7	103	797	−	1941		
Swan	Mundaring	W.A.	62	136	1,010	−	1902-61		For stock water

a. Where two dates are shown, the first date refers to completion of main storage, the second refers to the completion of any significant structural additions.

b. Under construction.

c. Under appraisal.

d. For Snowy Mountains scheme, only terminal dams and main dams transferring water between river systems have been listed.

ABBREVIATIONS: S.M.A.—Snowy Mountains Authority; R.M.C.—River Murray Commission; B.S.—Queensland–New South Wales Border Streams.

SOURCES: Department of National Development, *Major Development Projects, Australia*, June 1966 and earlier issues. Department of National Development, *Australia: Review of Water Resources Development 1964-66*. September 1966. *Year Book*, No 52, 1966, Bureau of Census and Statistics. Reports of State authorities responsible for water conservation, water supply and irrigation.

together capable at full supply level of retaining 2 million acre feet. Although intended partly for flood mitigation they are designed also to provide water for irrigation purposes and their operation has become linked with the Snowy-Murray scheme pending construction of the Chowilla dam. (See below.)

Storages on tributaries of the Darling have been a more recent development. A number of these are still under construction, including works on the border rivers between New South Wales and Queensland.

SNOWY MOUNTAINS SCHEME

The most important project in the Murray basin is the construction of the Snowy Mountains Scheme.[24] The Scheme diverts the waters of the upper Snowy inland through the Australian Alps, by means of a complex of 17 major dams, 100 miles of large-diameter tunnels, 7 power stations and 1 pumping station. Considerable falls are obtained for power generation and the water is then available for irrigation purposes on the Murray and Murrumbidgee.

There are two main series of works involved:

(i) from a dam on the Eucumbene (a tributary of the Snowy) to the Upper Tumut river which empties into the Murrumbidgee, *below* Burrinjuck;

(ii) from the Snowy river itself by dams at Island Bend and Jindabyne to fall into the Swampy Plains river and thence into the Murray *above* the Hume reservoir.

On completion, the estimated net gains of water to the Murrumbidgee and Murray will be respectively $1 \cdot 1$ million acre feet and $0 \cdot 8$ million acre feet per annum, sufficient to irrigate an additional 1,000 square miles. The Scheme is being built under an agreement between the Commonwealth, New South Wales, Victoria and South Australia, embodied in a Commonwealth Act, the *Snowy Mountains Hydro-electric Power Act* 1949 and in complementary State legislation. The Scheme is primarily one for the generation of electricity and it is planned that the power supplied will cover the full costs involved ($750-$800 million). Part of the finance is provided by a loan of $100 million from the International Bank for Reconstruction and Development.

Under the terms of the Snowy Mountains Agreement, New South Wales was required as soon as practicable to construct a storage at Blowering on the Tumut river. Without this dam, the additional water released through the Tumut power stations during the winter months could not be fully utilized. The cost was estimated at $44 million. Work was delayed by financial stringency on the part of New South Wales. In 1963 agreement was reached

24. Progress of the Scheme is recorded in the Annual Reports of the Snowy Mountains Hydro-Electric Authority. For a discussion of agricultural problems and uses of irrigation waters, see R. W. Prunster, 'Agricultural Uses of the Snowy Waters: III Agricultural Aspects', *Australian Journal of Agricultural Economics*, Vol 4, No 1, July 1960.

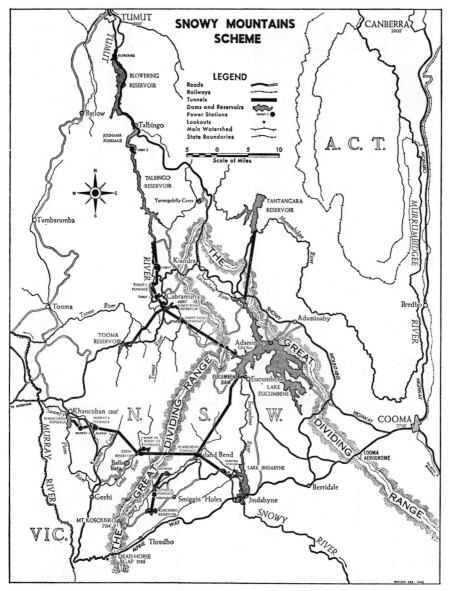

Map 12-4: Snowy Mountains Scheme: Surface Plan. (*Year Book*, No 52, 1966, Bureau of Census and Statistics)

whereby the Commonwealth undertook to pay half the cost and to advance the other half as an interest-bearing loan to the State. The loan was conditional on the State proceeding with the Coleambally Irrigation Area. (See below.)

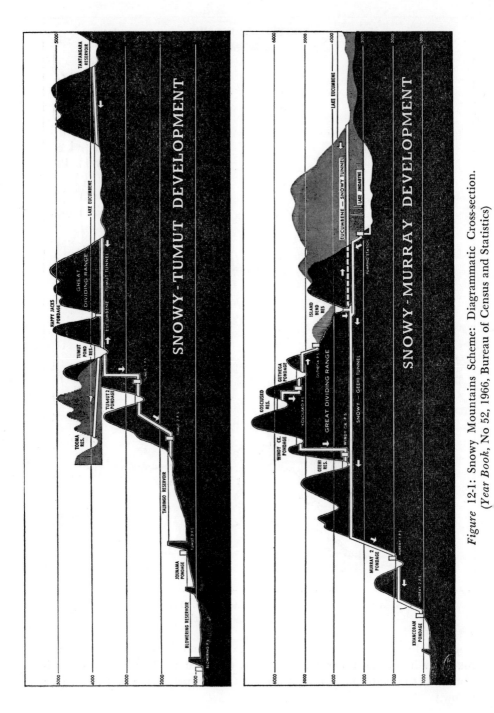

Figure 12-1: Snowy Mountains Scheme: Diagrammatic Cross-section.
(*Year Book*, No 52, 1966, Bureau of Census and Statistics)

OTHER MURRAY-DARLING SCHEMES

To complete control over the Murray-Darling waters, to reduce the drain on up-stream storages in adverse years and to assure South Australian supplies, a dam will be constructed at Chowilla somewhat downstream from where the Murray crosses into that State. The dam wall will be 3·25 miles long and will impound 4·75 million acre feet (including 0·55 million acre feet in the present Lake Victoria which will be absorbed into the new scheme). This will be the largest water storage in Australia. It is expected to require $43 million, this cost to be shared equally among the Commonwealth and the three State governments. Again the Commonwealth has agreed to provide temporary finance to New South Wales to cover its share of the cost.

One other works on the Murray may be noted. The Murray empties into the sea through Lake Alexandrina (South Australia). Five barrages were built across channels near the mouth of the river, to deny ingress of sea water into Lake Alexandrina and Lake Albert, and to back-up the level of the river for 50 miles. This enables reclaimed river flats to be watered by gravitation. The total distance across the barrages and intervening islands is 15 miles.

Coleambally Irrigation Area The additional waters available to New South Wales from the diversion inland of the Snowy river are being used predominantly to develop a new irrigation area, Coleambally, adjacent to the Murrumbidgee Irrigation Area. (Victoria is using its share of Snowy water to make possible expansion and intensification of existing areas, notably the Goulburn, Campaspe and Torrumbarry irrigation systems.[25])

Coleambally Irrigation Area will cover approximately 450,000 acres. Water is diverted from the Murrumbidgee by the Gogeldrie weir, near Leeton. The current phase of development, while Blowering dam is being built, envisages about 200 farms. When the dam is complete, there will be about 750 mixed farms and 125 horticultural farms supplied with irrigation water. The latter will contain a minimum of 40 acres of first-class land (with a water right of 1 acre foot per annum per acre) plus varying acreages of less favourable land. After some debate on the question of appropriate farm size, the mixed farms are being allocated 500 acres per block with a minimum of 400 acres commanded by water. These farms will be devoted mainly to prime lamb and beef production. In designing the large-area farms, no provision has been made for rice growing on a permanent basis, but with a view to achieving quick returns, settlers are being supplied with sufficient water for the irrigation of 60 acres of rice each year on each farm for the first six years of occupation. This concession has already been extended by two more years for the first 200 settlers. Demand for mixed blocks has been strong.

England[26] states that the cost of land and of irrigation and incidental works

25. Victorian State Rivers and Water Supply Commission, *Sixtieth Annual Report 1964-65*, Government Printer, Melbourne, p vii.

26. H. N. England, 'The Agricultural Use of the Snowy Waters: II Irrigation Plans and Policy', *Australian Journal of Agricultural Economics*, Vol 4, No 1, July 1960, p 66.

S

for the Coleambally scheme will be about $24 million. Private investment, on the basis of $50,000 per farm will be of the order of $54 million. It follows that the use of all the additional water turned into the Murrumbidgee (including allowance for the cost of Blowering dam and part of the cost of enlarging Burrinjuck dam) will require an investment estimated at over $140 million.

Namoi Valley (Wee Waa and Narrabri)   There has been a remarkably rapid development of cotton growing on the deep black soil flats near Wee Waa. The area depends on water from the Keepit dam which regulates the Namoi river. Encouraged by the results of cotton trials at the Narrabri Experiment Station, two Californian growers planted the first commercial cotton in 1961. A strong inflow of American capital and expertise followed and the area under cotton increased by 1965-66 to 28,000 acres, producing approximately 68,700 bales, worth approximately $8·7 million in gross returns to growers (exclusive of payment of Commonwealth bounty). Soil and climate are well suited for highly mechanized cotton production and the area is relatively close to Australian markets. Future expansion may, however, be limited by availability of water, unless further storages are constructed.

The rapid development of cotton culture on the Namoi has an added significance: it presents governments with the necessity for a direct and fairly immediate choice between alternative areas for further expansion of irrigated cotton—between public investment there or on the Ord.

ORD RIVER

The Ord river in northern Western Australia drains an area of 18,000 square miles of rugged country overlapping the Northern Territory border. It empties into Cambridge Gulf, near the deep-water port of Wyndham. About 120 miles upstream the river breaks through the Carr-Boyd ranges at Carlton Gorge (500-800 feet deep). It then passes through extensive heavy black clay (Kunnunurra) grassland flats, approximately 200,000 acres of which would be commandable for irrigation.

These geographic features make the Ord project most attractive from an engineering point of view. The river has a mean annual flow of about 2 million acre feet. A dam only 1,000 feet long and 180 feet high could impound 10 million acre feet (6·5 million acre feet for flood mitigation and 3·5 million acre feet for irrigation and hydro-electric generation) at a cost of less than $6 per acre foot of stored water.[27] This would render it both the largest and cheapest of Australia's major reservoirs, per unit of *stored* water.

The project is, however, not merely an engineering problem, but an agronomic and economic one. Sugar, rice, peanuts, cotton, linseed, safflower, grain and pasture have been grown successfully under irrigation at the Kimberley Research Station. Domestic demand for the first three named was already fully satisfied, so the West Australian government decided on cotton

27. R. A. Patterson, *The Economic Justification of the Ord River Project*, ANZAAS 38th Congress, Hobart 1965, p 40.

growing. At the time, in the late 1950s, only 3 per cent of Australia's cotton needs were being supplied by Australian production, and cotton growing on the Namoi had not yet come into prominence.

The State government obtained $5 million (later increased to $13·5 million) finance from the Commonwealth under the *W.A. Grant (Northern Development) Act* 1958-1959 to supplement State funds in order to commence development.

This first stage comprised the construction of a diversion weir at Bandicoot Bar at the head of the flood plain and the irrigation of approximately 30,000 acres. The township of Kunnunurra was established nearby. Farm size was set at 600-750 acres, with 300 acres annually under cotton. Selected applicants hold their farms on leasehold, with option to purchase at $2·5 per acre after five years provided stipulated conditions have been observed, including adherance to the advice of State agricultural officers on crops and cultural practices. Since 1962, some 36 farms have been established, the limit of first stage development. One pilot farm (2,200 acres) operated by a private company, Northern Developments Limited, has also been established. The State government has repeatedly sought funds (approximately $65 million) from the Commonwealth to enable it to begin the second stage, the construction of the Carlton Gorge dam. So far, the Commonwealth has regarded the economics of the scheme as not proven.

Meanwhile, controversy has flourished in the press, in parliament and among agricultural economists.[28] Debate has tended to focus around the yield question, although the 'break-even' yield is merely a shorthand way of expressing the outcome of the multitude of assumptions necessary for budgeting.

The controversy has had a major impact on public policy concerning investment in large-scale development projects in Australia. In Lloyd's words: 'Nowadays, properly calculated benefit-cost ratios and returns on invested capital are at least considered and are sometimes decisive. Non-economic goals will properly continue to play a role, but at least the cost of pursuing them will be estimated.'[29]

28. See House of Representatives, *Parliamentary Debates*, Hansard, 10 May 1966, pp 1612-25. Proponents of the Ord Scheme include C. W. Court, 'Northern Australian Development', *Public Administration*, Vol 24, No 1, March 1965. See also R. A. Patterson, *op. cit.* The fullest published statement of those advocating caution appears in B. R. Davidson, *The Northern Myth*, 2nd ed, Melbourne University Press, Melbourne 1966. For a balanced view of the controversy, see A. G. Lloyd, 'The Controversy on Northern Development', *Review of Marketing and Agricultural Economics*, Vol 33, No 3, September 1965. On secondary benefits, for and against, see the exchange involving C. A. Cannegeiter, I. Bowen, N. F. Laing, K. O. Campbell, W. F. Musgrave and J. N. Lewis in the *Economic Record*, Vol 40, No 91, September 1964, and in the succeeding two issues.

29. A. G. Lloyd, *op. cit.*, p 124. This point is pursued further in *Investment Analysis*, Supplement to Treasury Information Bulletin, Commonwealth Treasury, Canberra, July 1966.

OTHER IRRIGATION AND WATER CONTROL SCHEMES

Other Irrigation Areas   Community irrigation schemes of any consequence do not exist in New South Wales and South Australia other than those in the Murray-Darling. No public irrigation scheme has so far been found necessary in Tasmania.

In Western Australia, Northern Developments Ltd is also conducting irrigated land development on the Fitzroy at Liveringa, under an agreement with the West Australian government. Further south, at Carnarvon over 3,000 acre feet of water is pumped annually from shallow aquifers mostly in the sandy bed of the Gascoyne river, which is dry for the larger part of the year.

In Queensland it has been estimated that about two-thirds of the total area irrigated is supplied from underground water, principally in the Burdekin delta (Ayr-Home Hill area), the Pioneer valley, Callide valley, Lower Burnett (Bundaberg area), Lockyer valley, Redland Bay (near Brisbane) and on parts of the Darling Downs. Seasonal conditions make year-round irrigation necessary in Queensland.

Northern Territory (Humpty Doo)   In the Northern Territory a large-scale attempt in the 1950s to develop land at Humpty Doo on the Adelaide river failed. The project was privately financed by Territory Rice Ltd, a company backed by American and Australian capital. An agreement was entered into in December 1955 between the Commonwealth government and the company, under which Territory Rice was granted agricultural leases in the sub-coastal plains conditional upon their development for rice production and subsequent allocation to individual settlers. The company's difficulties can be attributed to inadequate agronomic knowledge, ineffective water control (in 1958-59, 1,200 acres failed from *lack* of water), and to the inability of the management to handle the many and unusual problems arising from the large-scale operations.[30] Areas of up to 5,000 acres were sown to rice in some years.

Despite the failure of the Territory Rice Ltd project, research is continuing on rice culture and cattle investigations at the Coastal Plains (CSIRO) and Beatrice Hills (Northern Territory Administration) Research Stations on the sub-coastal plains, and at the Upper Adelaide River Research Station (N.T.A.) on the Marrakai land system. It is near the latter station that pilot farms are testing different farming systems.

Flood Control   The coastal rivers of New South Wales are subject to serious floods, particularly the Hunter and the northern rivers. Considerable flood mitigation is in progress on these rivers financed by local authorities, State government and Commonwealth government, on the basis of 1:3:3 on the Hunter and 1:2:2 on the northern rivers.

30. H. C. Forster, C. R. Kelly and D. B. Williams, *Prospects of Agriculture in the Northern Territory*, Department of Territories, Canberra 1960, p 202.

In Victoria, at Koo-wee-rup near Westernport, 80,000 acres have been reclaimed from flooding and put to primary production.

South-Eastern Drainage Systems (South Australia) In the south-east of South Australia, large areas of land have been reclaimed by drainage channels which cut through the ancient consolidated low sand dune 'ranges' that run parallel to the coast. The first of these drainage systems (around Millicent), completed in 1885, reclaimed 100,000 acres. Over 1 million acres have been or are being regained by more than 750 miles of drains built partly at government expense, partly in cooperation with landholders.

GENERAL

Over much of the continent the availability of water is the limiting factor to land development. But within that limit there are ample development opportunities. The choice lies continually between devoting resources to pushing back the water constraint or applying them to dry land technology. 'The difficulty is that while irrigation developments are more predictable, the scope and potentialities of technical advance are much greater. Even so, . . . irrigation development would still assume an important supplementary role in providing insurance against production uncertainty.'[31]

TRANSPORT DEVELOPMENTS

In the postwar period there has been major improvement to rural roads, expansion of air services, contraction of rail mileage, port development and an increase in bulk handling.

ROADS

Improvement has occurred mainly through the upgrading of roads, as a result of additional finance being provided by the Commonwealth to States under the *Commonwealth Aid Roads Acts*, and for beef cattle roads.

Grants in aid have been made by the Commonwealth to the States for expenditure on roads since 1923-24. After World War II, the sums granted have increased greatly. Over the period 1947-48 to 1966-67, the Commonwealth has made available $1,362 million under Aid Road Acts and comparable legislation, and is now providing approximately one-third of the public authority net expenditure on roads and bridges throughout Australia.[32] Since 1947 it has been a condition of these grants that portion (cur-

31. K. O. Campbell, 'The Challenge of Production Instability in Australian Agriculture', *Australian Journal of Agricultural Economics*, Vol 2, No 1, July 1958.

32. 'Commonwealth Payments to or for the States 1966-67', *Budget papers 1966-67*, Table 51. This figure is apart from monies spent on road and bridge construction in the Northern Territory and Australian Capital Territory, and special assistance e.g. beef roads. For 1966-67, the grant under the Act is $A150 million. See also *Pattern and Trends of Transport of Goods and Passengers in Australia and Demands which the Traffic is Creating for Transport Development Generally*, Department of Shipping and Transport, Melbourne 1966.

rently not less than 40 per cent) shall be spent on roads in rural areas. Expenditure on roads now comprises approximately one-quarter of all public works expenditure in Australia.

As a separate measure, to increase the turn-off and quality of beef cattle for export, and to provide better access to breeding and fattening areas, the Commonwealth has, since 1961, made specific grants and loans to Queensland ($16·6 million) and Western Australia ($7·9 million) for construction and improvement of certain designated roads, and has provided funds ($12·5 million) in the Northern Territory for similar purposes.[33] The total length of beef roads in Queensland being financed under the Commonwealth-State agreement is 934 miles of which 596 miles had been sealed by June 1966. In Western Australia the total length of roads financed under the Acts is 1,084 miles, with 90 miles sealed and the remainder gravel and earth formed. For Northern Territory, by the same date, 890 miles had been or were being upgraded. An interim arrangement operated for 1966-67, with expenditure on a scale similar to recent years (Queensland $3·9 million; Western Australia $1·5 million); this enabled construction work to continue pending consideration of a review that has been made by the Commonwealth of the entire road programme throughout the beef cattle areas of Northern Australia. The review resulted in a decision by the Commonwealth Government to grant a further $49 million over seven years to supplement State expenditures in Queensland and Western Australia on beef road development. In addition, $11·3 million will be provided over 5-6 years to upgrade certain beef roads in the Northern Territory and $1 million to improve the Birdsville Track leading down through north-eastern South Australia.

The improvement in rural roads has enabled the use on an increasing scale of road trains—a series of up to four large transport units each capable of carrying about 20 beasts, linked together and drawn by a prime-mover. Studies in the economics of the use of these vehicles and an analysis of comparative costs of road transport and droving have been conducted by the Bureau of Agricultural Economics.[34] Increased use of road haulage appears likely.

From October 1965, a system of petroleum products subsidies has operated in Australia. Under the *States Grants (Petroleum Products) Act* 1965, federal grants are made to the States to enable them to subsidize sales of petroleum

33. The relevant Acts are the *Queensland Grant (Beef Cattle Roads) Act* 1961, which was superseded by the *Queensland Beef Cattle Roads Agreement Act* 1962, and the *Western Australia (Beef Cattle Roads) Acts* 1961 and 1962. The Agreements attached to these Acts specify the roads concerned. Investigations leading to the decision to invest in beef roads are reported in *The Economics of Road Transport of Beef Cattle: Western Australian Pastoral Areas*, Bureau of Agricultural Economics, Canberra 1958; *The Economics of Road Transport of Beef Cattle: Northern Territory and Queensland Channel Country*, Bureau of Agricultural Economics, Canberra 1959.

34. *Road Transport of Beef Cattle in Queensland*, Beef Research Report No 1, Bureau of Agricultural Economics, Canberra, August 1965.

products in country areas, so that the wholesale prices of these products will be not more than $3 \cdot 3$ cents a gallon above the relevant capital city prices. The scheme aims to assist decentralization by reducing transport costs for country people and country industry. The Commonwealth government provided $9 \cdot 9$ million in 1965-66 and \$14 million in 1966-67 for this purpose.

RAILWAYS

The main features of the Australian railway system in the postwar period have been the moves to rail standardization and diesel traction; closure of uneconomic lines; and problems of road-rail co-ordination.

Following the war, the State and Commonwealth railway systems engaged in a programme of rehabilitation and modernization. Lines joining major capitals have been or are being converted to standard 4' 8½" gauge. Standard gauge was extended from Grafton (New South Wales) to Brisbane in 1930; from Albury (New South Wales) to Melbourne in 1962; and the extension from Kalgoorlie (Western Australia) to Perth is expected to be completed in 1968. These essential and costly works have probably had little influence on rural development. More important has been the shift to diesel traction. This switch has conferred substantial economies in railway operation, particularly in long-distance haulage.

About 1941, route-mileage open in Australia reached a maximum of some 27,000 miles. Since 1945-46 nearly 10 per cent of this has been closed, mainly in Western Australia, Queensland and Victoria. Webb[35] attributes the contraction to poor location of some lines in relation to later development; working-out of resources served by branch lines; abandonment of certain lines that were built to a low standard of construction; decline of ports away from the capital cities; and loss of rail traffic to road transport.

Most States have legislation which tends to lessen the competition from road transport, through the imposition of charges on road vehicles. The application of such charges to *interstate* transport has been the subject of much legal argument.

Railway freight schedules in most States are favourably oriented as far as the carriage of rural commodities or of goods essential to rural production are concerned. In areas declared drought-stricken, substantial freight concessions are provided on the movement of livestock and fodder.

AVIATION

In Australia, the use of aircraft for agricultural purposes began in 1948. During recent years an increasing use has been made of aircraft for top dressing and seeding, for spraying and dusting of crops and pastures, and for pest and vermin extermination. For 1956-57, the first year for which data are available, the total area treated was $1 \cdot 5$ million acres; in 1963-64 the total

35. G. R. Webb, 'The Closure of Uneconomic Rail Lines in Australia', *Economic Record*, Vol 39, No 88, December 1963.

area treated was 12·8 million acres—eight times as great. In the latter year 10 million cwt of superphosphate was distributed aerially on as many acres.

In the early postwar years an endeavour was made to develop inland killing works at Glenroy Station in the Kimberleys with the transport of beef by air 180 miles to Wyndham and later to Derby, for export. After some years of operation, assisted by Commonwealth subsidy, the project was terminated, having been found to be uneconomic.

SHIPPING

One postwar trend in transport development has brought considerable cost-savings to rural industries: the shift to bulk handling of rural commodities, both inland and at the seaboard. The major export ports in Australia have been provided with bulk handling equipment for sugar and wheat, while both railways and road transport have been geared to bulk handling of wheat, fertilizers, etc. At the same time attention has been given to reduction in the volume of wool for shipment. The change to the export of boneless meat has meant similar economies in freight charges.

An extensive programme of port improvement has taken place. However, considerable economies are possible at major ports in the handling of rural products. Studies have also been made in the possibilities of moving cattle from northern producing areas to Queensland coastal meat works by sea but this method has not so far appeared profitable.[36] The shift towards use of larger vessels and tankers for the movement of bulk commodities will require still deeper channels and longer berthing facilities. Recently there has been increasing emphasis on 'containerization'.

POLICY FOR DEVELOPMENT PROJECTS

PRINCIPLES OF LAND SETTLEMENT

From a study of some of the development projects outlined above, the Committee to Enquire into the Prospects of Agriculture in the Northern Territory (Forster Committee) enunciated principles for successful land settlement under Australian conditions. The Committee saw six facets as essential for success.[37] These are summarized below.

1. New knowledge. Land development is dependent on new knowledge capable of providing a stimulus for more intensive settlement on an economic basis. The system of land management must render it possible to make use of the constant flow of new knowledge and to follow up new needs and new problems which this knowledge creates.

2. Command of land. Arrangements have to be made to acquire control or ownership of land intended for settlement. Many legal problems and prob-

36. *Development of Water Transport for Beef Cattle: Gulf of Carpentaria and Cape York Peninsula*, Bureau of Agricultural Economics, Canberra 1961.
37. H. C. Forster, C. R. Kelly and D. B. Williams, *op. cit.*, ch 19.

lems of equity are involved, as between the settlement authority, the original owners and the future settlers.

3. Selection of settlers. Selection of settlers is now accepted as a vital feature of successful land settlement; potential settlers may not have enough finance to enable them to develop their farms and low-equity financing in government settlement schemes is being increasingly accepted, together with control of allocation of farms by the government authority.

4. Farming systems. Three distinct phases need to be recognized: (i) development of the land prior to allocation to the settler, usually involving large-scale land clearing; (ii) the initial years of establishment by individual settlers; and (iii) stable operation of an efficient farm unit once the settler is established. Settlement schemes which have failed have done so largely because of reasons associated with the internal structure of the development organization; this led the settlement agency to become caught up in an unrealistic enthusiasm which ignored the need to take time.

5. Finance. Finance needs to be provided for each of the three successive stages in land development and settlement. Main points to be considered are liquidity or access to cash in the early years of establishment, pointing to the desirability of deferred interest and capital payments; the need for financial authorities (as distinct from settlement authorities) to appreciate the three phases of establishment and the importance of sufficient time for development; and the problem of land valuation, which involves not only the land acquisition price, but how the benefits of development are spread among the different groups involved (State, developers, settlers).

6. Research and advisory services. Access to technical services is essential, to provide information about the results of research and advice about farming methods.

The above principles pre-suppose the decision to proceed with the development of a particular project.

CRITERIA FOR DEVELOPMENT

In view of the very considerable resources required for any large-scale development scheme, a more crucial question for government policy is the determination of suitable projects from among the spectrum of investment opportunities clamouring for support. Criteria are required. Four main groups of criteria may be distinguished:

   (i) Economic, such as potential net contribution to national income or to balance of payments; type of product in relation to longer-term market outlook; relationship of direct benefits to direct cost over the reasonable life of the project; indirect transmitted multiplier effects (positive and negative) on the region concerned, on related industries, on the rural or other sectors.

   (ii) Social, such as regional development; decentralization; generation of hospitals, schools and other amenities in non-metropolitan locations.

   (iii) Defence.

   (iv) Political.

On the economic side, this decade has seen the application in Australia of the technique of benefit-cost analysis. Projects so far subjected to analysis exceed $400 million in terms of public capital cost.[38]

However as the Committee of Economic Enquiry remarked:

> Economic analysis, and cost-benefit analysis in particular, cannot be the sole determinant of public investment decisions. The role of analysis is to point out clearly, in financial terms, the costs and benefits involved and to bring these into public discussion *before* major development decisions are taken.[39]

As presently applied, benefit-cost analysis acts as a sieve, to assist in selecting projects which qualify for further consideration. While helpful, this is only part of the problem; for it does not enable orders of priority to be established among the variety of projects that come forward. In theory, the technique is amenable for use to such purpose. In practice, this is rendered impracticable for want of the requisite basic data or by lack of comparability in the assumptions which have to be made for the purpose of evaluation.

Satisfying economic criteria for inter-project comparison are still lacking. Yet such criteria are greatly needed in Australia where labour and capital are both scarce. Although possibilities for land development exist in plenty, development itself is most demanding of resources, and, as always, choices must be made. The search for suitable criteria to guide these choices remains one of the important tasks facing agricultural economists.

---

38. *Investment Analysis*, Supplement to Treasury Information Bulletin, Commonwealth Treasury, Canberra, July 1966.

39. *Report of the Committee of Economic Enquiry*, Government Printer, Canberra, May 1965, Vol I, paras 3 and 10.

CHAPTER 13

CHANGES IN FOOD CONSUMPTION

F. H. GRUEN AND G. C. McLAREN

Monash University

SOURCES OF DATA

The Commonwealth Bureau of Census and Statistics publishes annually a 'Report on Food Production and the Apparent Consumption of Foodstuffs and Nutrients in Australia'. This is the basic source for most food consumption statistics. Apparent consumption is normally estimated as a residual from production plus imports minus exports, non-food usage, wastage, etc. For most products changes in stocks of marketing authorities and of factories are also allowed for. Little information is available regarding changes in retailers' stocks.

Australia is one of the few western, high-income countries where no full-scale sample surveys of food consumption patterns have been undertaken since World War II; hence one can only discuss trends in *average* consumption per head. Little information is available about the food consumption patterns of different occupational or income groups in Australia.

SOME INTERNATIONAL COMPARISONS

Table 13-1 provides some recent comparisons of average food consumption per head in Australia and in five other western, high-income societies—United States, Canada, the United Kingdom, Western Germany and France. The figures are presented in a comparative form, with Australian consumption figures being taken as a base of 100. Thus a figure of 80 for U.S. beef and veal consumption means that U.S. consumption of beef and veal was 80 per cent of the Australian level during the particular period.

While international income comparisons are notoriously difficult and subject to numerous statistical problems, it can be taken that real incomes per head in the U.S.A. and Canada were approximately 75 and 40 per cent above Australian incomes during the period of comparison, whilst incomes in the three European countries were probably 10 to 20 per cent below the Australian level.

Table 13-1

Selected Foods: International Comparisons of Average Consumption per head,
1959-60 to 1961-62
(Australia = 100)

| Products | | Countries | | | |
	U.S.A.	Canada	United Kingdom	West Germany	France
Total meat	78	72	63	53	79
Beef and veal	80	81	53	46	75
Pork and bacon[a]	347	282	275	351	301
Mutton and lamb	4	3	25	1	6
Poultry	373	318	143	102	189
Fish	96	157	188	133	206
Whole milk	96	141	111	79	79
Cheese	135	121	155	235	335
Eggs	165	140	134	115	97
Butter	25	68	62	60	58
Total fats and oils[b]	141	135	158	175	118
Total cereals	77	80	95	95	115
Wheat	70	85	96	71	124
Potatoes	105	156	213	290	234
Sugar	73	87	93	55	55
Fruit	108	88	78	127	79

a. United States and United Kingdom figures obtained from 'The World Meat Economy',
Commodity Bulletin Series 40, FAO, Rome 1965.
b. Figures relate to the three-year period 1960-61 to 1962-63, obtained from 'The State
of Food and Agriculture 1965', FAO, Rome 1965, Annex Table 9A.

SOURCES: For U.S.: 'Food Consumption in the O.E.C.D. Countries', Organization for
Economic Co-operation and Development, Paris, November 1963. (U.S. figures are
averages of calendar years 1960 and 1961.)
For Canada: 'Food Balances for 24 Countries of the Western Hemisphere, 1959-61',
E.R.S. Foreign 86, United States Department of Agriculture, U.S. Government
Printing Office, Washington, April 1964.
For U.K., West Germany and France: 'Food Balances for 16 Countries of Western
Europe, 1959-61', *E.R.S. Foreign 87*, United States Department of Agriculture, U.S.
Government Printing Office, Washington, August 1964.
For Australia: 'Report on Food Consumption and the Apparent Consumption of
Foodstuffs and Nutrients in Australia', No 19, 1963-64, Bureau of Census and
Statistics.

The major differences disclosed between the Australian pattern of food
consumption and that of North America and Western Europe are:

(i) Meat consumption is about 25 per cent higher in Australia than in
the U.S. and France. In addition the composition of the meat diet in Australia is very different. As might be expected in overseas countries, mutton
and lamb consumption is only a small fraction of that in Australia; on the
other hand pigmeats are a relative luxury here and consumption is about

one-third of the levels reached in the U.S., Canada, France and West Germany. Australian beef consumption was about 25 per cent higher than in North America in this period, but poultry consumption (where the Australian estimates are not very reliable) was less than one-third of the North American level. These differences are partly the result of the relative prices for the different meats. Because of our particular resource endowment, lamb, mutton and beef have long been relatively cheap in Australia whilst pigmeats and poultry are more expensive.

(ii) Probably partly as a result of the high level of Australian meat intake, consumption of fish, cheese and eggs are comparatively low.

(iii) Although Australian butter consumption has been declining in the postwar period, it is still very much higher than in the other five countries. On the other hand, total fat consumption in Australia is relatively low. Restrictions on the use of table margarine probably account for at least part of the higher butter consumption in Australia, whilst the generally warmer climate may explain the lower level of total fat intake.

(iv) Cereal consumption has tended to decline in most countries as real incomes rise beyond a certain level, which has long been reached in the countries we are examining. It is therefore not surprising that consumption of wheat and other cereals in North America is below the Australian level, or that French consumption is higher. Since real incomes in Australia exceeded those of the U.K. and West Germany it might also be expected that Australian consumption would be lower. In fact, it is slightly higher, but the differences are relatively small. Potato consumption might be expected to follow the same pattern; however except for the U.S., consumption of potatoes in the overseas countries listed was very much higher than in Australia. (To a minor extent this is the result of two poor crops in Australia during the period of comparison.)

(v) No clear pattern is discernible for fruit or sugar. Australian total fruit consumption is 10 to 20 per cent above the levels recorded in Canada, the U.K. and France but somewhat below the U.S. and West German figures. On the other hand, sugar consumption in Australia is comparatively high.

TRENDS IN AUSTRALIAN FOOD CONSUMPTION
MEAT

Postwar trends in the consumption of meats and dairy products are given in Table 13-2. It also contains a comparison with the pre-war situation. As pointed out earlier, Australian meat consumption per head is very high, though it has tended to decline since the 1930s. Meat was rationed during the later war years and until June 1948. In the immediate postwar period of meat rationing, carcass meat consumption (i.e. beef and veal, sheep meats and pork) was about one-fifth below the pre-war level of 224 lbs per head.

Table 13-2

Consumption per head of Meat and Dairy Products, 1936-37 to 1964-65

Commodity	Unit of quantity	Average 1936-37 to 1938-39	Average 1946-47 to 1947-48 [a]	Average 1948-49 to 1949-50 [a]	Average 1950-51 to 1952-53	Average 1953-54 to 1955-56	Average 1956-57 to 1958-59	Average 1959-60 to 1961-62	1962-63	1963-64	1964-65
Carcass meat—											
Beef and veal	lb.	140·3	102·7	122·8	123·4	116·7	123·7	92·0	100·4	104·6	99·3
Mutton	,,	60·0	45·2	45·3	42·9	50·9	50·9	61·1	51·6	48·3	46·3
Lamb	,,	15·0	23·7	27·8	25·8	26·4	29·3	40·0	42·1	41·7	39·3
Pigmeat	,,	8·5	7·0	7·3	6·7	9·2	10·1	11·8	12·0	11·5	12·0
Total carcass meat	,,	223·8	178·6	203·2	198·8	203·2	214·0	204·9	206·1	206·1	196·9
Offal	,,	8·4	9·2	9·0	9·4	10·5	11·4	11·4	12·4	12·9	12·3
Canned meat (canned wt)	,,	2·1	2·7	3·0	2·6	2·8	4·2	4·0	4·3	4·3	4·6
Bacon and ham (cured carcass wt)	,,	10·1	12·4	10·0	7·6	7·5	7·0	7·1	7·4	7·3	7·4
Fluid whole milk	gals	23·4	30·3 _(1946-47 to 1949-50)_		28·1	28·4	28·3	28·6	27·8	28·2	29·1
Butter	lb.	32·9	24·9		30·5	29·9	27·3	25·1	23·8	23·4	22·6
Margarine—table	,,	0·9	0·9		1·1	2·5	3·6	3·4	3·3	3·2	4·5
Margarine—other	,,	4·0	4·7		6·1	5·2	4·9	5·8	6·3	6·6	6·1
Cheese[b]	,,	4·4	5·8		6·0	5·9	5·9	6·4	6·8	7·0	7·2
Total processed milk products[c]	,,	4·0	6·1		6·2	6·8	7·9	9·9	9·6	10·9	10·8

a.   Postwar rationing period for butter 1946-47 to 1949-50. For meats 1946-47 to 1947-48.
b.   Estimates from 1950-51 onwards provided by M. Singh of the Australian Dairy Produce Board.
c.   In terms of milk solids.

SOURCE: *Statistical Bulletin, Report on Food Production and the Apparent Consumption of Foodstuffs and Nutrients in Australia*, No 20, 1964-65 (and earlier volumes), Bureau of Census and Statistics.

After the abolition of rationing in 1948, carcass meat consumption rose, but it remained about 5 to 10 per cent below pre-war levels. In addition the composition of the meat diet changed. A growth in the popularity of lamb was more than offset by a reduction in beef and mutton consumption. However, until 1958-59, beef and veal accounted for about 55 to 60 per cent of carcass meat consumption, mutton for about one-fifth and lamb for 10 to 15 per cent.

For three years from 1958-59 the consumption of beef and veal fell sharply and by 1960-61 consumption per head had dropped by more than 30 per cent. The decline was associated with the development of the U.S. as an export market for Australian beef and with relative increases in retail prices of about 25 per cent. There was some substitution of sheep meats (particularly lamb) for beef, but total carcass meat consumption also fell.

Between 1960-61 and 1963-64, beef and veal consumption recovered somewhat; lamb consumption remained fairly steady; and mutton consumption tended to decline. Under the influence of higher prices, 1964-65 saw a renewed decline of beef consumption with marginal declines in the consumption of the two sheep meats.

Consumption of the various meats in Australia has been relatively sensitive to changes in retail prices. The relationship between meat consumption and retail prices has been investigated by a number of research workers and some quantitative estimates of the response of consumption to changes in prices and incomes have been obtained.[1]

Table 13-3 presents some of the estimates of income and price elasticities obtained for beef, mutton and lamb by Taylor, McLaren and Marceau. None of the estimates obtained is entirely satisfactory. Those of McLaren and Marceau are single equation estimates. McLaren uses annual data for Australia, 1949-50 to 1963-64; Marceau uses quarterly data for New South Wales, March 1951 to June 1963. On theoretical grounds these equations suffer because they ignore identification problems; i.e. they do not distinguish clearly between demand and supply influences. They are, however, of use for purposes of prediction and can give us some quantitative estimates of the percentage changes in consumption of the various meats which have been associated with given percentage changes in prices and incomes. Taylor's estimates do not suffer from this particular defect, but his specification of the

---

1. A. Fletcher, 'The Australian Market for Lamb', *Quarterly Review of Agricultural Economics*, Vol 13, No 4, October 1960. G. W. Taylor, 'Beef Consumption in Australia', *Quarterly Review of Agricultural Economics*, Vol 14, No 3, July 1961. G. W. Taylor, 'Meat Consumption in Australia', *Economic Record*, Vol 39, No 85, March 1963. J. H. Duloy and J. Van der Meulen, 'Meat Consumption in Australia—A Comment', *Economic Record*, Vol 39, No 87, September 1963. G. W. Taylor, 'A Reply', *Economic Record*, Vol 40, No 89, March 1964, p 127. I. W. Marceau, 'Factors Affecting the Demand and Price Structure in the New South Wales Meat Market', unpublished M.Sc.Agr. thesis, University of Sydney, August 1965. In addition we have drawn on G. C. McLaren's examination of the relationships which will be published by Monash University in 1967.

relationships between consumption and price has also been subjected to some criticism.[2]

The results obtained by Taylor, McLaren and Marceau suggest that a 1 per cent rise in the retail price of beef, relative to other prices, has been associated with a decline in *beef* consumption of 1 per cent to 1·3 per cent. Changes in the retail prices of mutton and lamb and in incomes have relatively smaller effects on beef consumption. *Mutton* consumption appears slightly more sensitive to changes in mutton retail prices, with a 1 per cent increase in the mutton retail prices being associated with a decline in the consumption of 1·1 per cent to 1·4 per cent. The results of all three workers suggest that mutton consumption is also responsive to changes in beef prices.[3] According to McLaren's single equation estimate quoted above, the income elasticity of demand for mutton is —1·7, so that a 1 per cent increase in income has been associated with a 1·7 (±0·5) per cent decline in mutton consumption.[4]

All three research workers obtained relatively large price elasticities for *lamb* consumption (ranging from —1·5 [±0·2] to —2·1 [±0·4]). McLaren's income elasticity for lamb (0·8 [±0·3]) is substantially larger than that

Table 13-3

Price and Income Elasticities for Beef, Mutton and Lamb

	Taylor	*McLaren* Single equation		*Marceau* Single equation	
	Own price	*Own price*	*Income*[a]	*Own price*	*Income*
Beef and veal	—1·0 (n.a.)	—1·0 (±0·3)	+0·6 (±0·5)	—1·3 (±0·2)	—0·0 (±0·2)
Mutton	—1·2 (±0·2)	—1·4 (±0·3)	—1·7 (±0·5)	—1·1 (±0·1)	not included as variable
Lamb	—2·0 (±0·2)	—1·5 (±0·2)	+0·8 (±0·3)	—2·1 (±0·4)	+0·1 (±0·5)

a. Total consumption expenditure per head was used as the income variable.

SOURCE: See footnote 1, p 269.

2. J. H. Duloy and J. Van der Meulen, *op. cit.* An attempt by McLaren to construct a model of the meat market using a set of four simultaneous equations has also encountered some difficulties.

3. McLaren obtained a cross elasticity between mutton and beef prices of +1·2 [±0·3]; the corresponding estimate of Marceau is also +1·2 [±0·2].

4. This seems somewhat more negative than one would expect; in other formulations of the equation a less negative income elasticity was obtained. It seems likely that, with increasing incomes, mutton consumption tends to decline though perhaps less than suggested by McLaren's equation.

obtained by Marceau (0·1 [±0·5]);[5] but in both cases the prices of other meats are relatively less important in influencing lamb consumption.[6]

Because of its high price, Australian consumption of *pork* is relatively low, though it has increased by about 50 per cent since the 1930s. Because it is a luxury item in the Australian diet, we would expect consumption to be sensitive to both price and income changes. We obtained an own price elasticity of —2·2 (±0·6) and an income elasticity of 2·8 (±0·5) from a single equation estimate.[7] This income elasticity seems somewhat high: it may ascribe to secular income growth part of the consumption response which should rightly be attributed to other factors, such as the growing migrant population which is likely to be more accustomed to pork than to mutton and lamb. On the other hand *bacon* consumption has remained relatively static (7-8 lbs per head per annum) over the last 15 years, though it was somewhat higher both before the war and especially in the period of meat rationing.

Little official information is available about the consumption of *poultry* in Australia. Unofficial estimates suggest that consumption of broilers amounted to 3·6 and 4·3 lbs per head for 1960 and 1961 respectively. Since then there has been a sharp increase in the production of broilers, and 1964-65 consumption has probably risen to about 10 lbs. A large part of this increase is attributable to the decline in the price of poultry relative to the prices of red meat.

DAIRY PRODUCTS

Liquid Milk   The available data on the consumption of liquid milk include the consumption of cream and milk used in the production of ice cream and confectionery. In fact the data represent a residual after the total whole milk production has been allocated to the other forms of utilization.

As shown in Table 13-2, liquid milk consumption rose by almost one-third between the pre-war level of 23·4 gallons per head per annum and the postwar period of butter rationing. After butter rationing was lifted in June 1950, milk consumption declined slightly. Since 1950-51, consumption per head has remained fairly constant at about 28·0 to 28·5 gallons.

In considering factors influencing the demand for liquid milk it is very difficult, in the face of a steady consumption per head, to assign quantitative

5. However, Marceau uses a different measure of real income.
6. McLaren obtained a cross elasticity between lamb and beef prices of +0·5 [±0·2].
7. $\log C_P = -2.182 + 2.182 \log C - 2.191 \log P_P + 0.186 \log P_{OM}$
   $(0.489)(0.553)(0.457)$
   $(R^2 = 0.895)$

   where C_P is per capita consumption of pork, in pounds,
   P_P real price of pork (1952-53 = 100),
   P_{OM} real price of other meat (1952-53 = 100),
   and C   per capita personal consumption expenditure at constant 1953-54 prices.

T

importance to specific factors. There is evidence of a slight response of milk consumption to changes in real incomes, real prices, and the birth rate (used as a measure of the proportion of the population under one year of age).[8] But on the whole the Australian situation seems to be similar to that in other developed countries where, according to FAO, 'increases in disposable income and relatively small price changes have but little effect upon liquid milk consumption. On the basis of the information available, such factors as food habits, availability and quality of milk seem to have a greater impact upon milk consumption levels.'[9]

Butter and Margarine During the postwar period of butter rationing, consumption averaged 25 lbs per head per annum, i.e. about three-quarters the pre-war level. When rationing was lifted, consumption quickly rose to 31 lbs (or 1·5 lbs below the pre-war level). Since then butter consumption has shown a fairly steady decline and by 1964-65 it had fallen to 22·5 lbs per head—well below the level reached during the period of rationing. While it is not possible to arrive at quantitative estimates of the various factors which have been responsible for this decline, the following have contributed to it:

(i) The increase in margarine consumption—as shown in Table 13-2 there has been a marked increase in the consumption of both table and 'other' margarine. Table margarine has been restricted by all State governments which have placed a quota on table margarine manufacture. However the rise in table margarine consumption cannot be held to be solely responsible for the decline in the use of butter since the consumption per head of butter and table margarine combined has fallen steadily since 1953-54. In addition Ross, using consumption figures for individual States, has shown that the decline in butter consumption cannot be attributed solely to the increase of table margarine consumption.[10] The fall in the consumption of butter and table margarine combined is partially offset by the rise in the consumption of 'other' margarine. Its production is not subject to quotas. It is used mostly in bakeries and by large-scale pastrycooks and has, in the main, replaced lard, dripping and copha, but there may have been some small replacement of butter.

(ii) The increase in real income per head has probably led to some decline

8. $\log Q_m = 1\cdot768 + 0\cdot118 \log C - 0\cdot0566 P_1 + 0\cdot375 \log B$
$\qquad\qquad\quad (0\cdot147) \qquad\quad (0\cdot143) \qquad\quad (0\cdot411)$
$$(R^2 = 0\cdot253)$$
where Q_m is per capita consumption of liquid milk, in pounds,
$\quad$ C $\quad$ per capita consumption expenditure at constant prices,
$\quad$ P_1 $\quad$ real price of liquid milk (1952-53 base),
$\quad$ B $\quad$ crude birth rate.

9. 'Means of Adjustment of Dairy Supply and Demand', *Commodity Bulletin Series 37*, FAO, Rome 1963, p 47.

10. A. D. Ross, 'The Problem of Australian Butter Consumption', *Quarterly Review of Agricultural Economics*, Vol 15, No 3, July 1962, p 21.

in total fat consumption. Rutherford reports a small survey conducted in Sydney showing evidence of a decline in butter consumption per head as incomes increase.[11] This is partly the result of the decline in consumption of bread as incomes rise.

(iii) The change in the structure of the Australian population may also have affected butter consumption. Rutherford's survey suggests that 'migrant' households tend to have a somewhat lower consumption of butter than Australian households. Migrants have become an increasing proportion of the Australian population in the postwar period.

(iv) Lastly, and perhaps most importantly, changes in tastes and preferences have contributed to the decline of butter consumption. In particular the connection between saturated fats and heart disease has been given wide publicity and this is likely to be an important factor in discouraging consumption of butter.

Cheese The Commonwealth Statistician's estimate for cheese consumption in Australia shows erratic movements from year to year between 1950-51 and 1958-59. These are believed to be due not to changes in consumption but resulting from substantial changes in the stocks of retailers in anticipation of price changes. These price changes have usually been announced at the beginning of each financial year. Singh has provided an adjusted series which is reproduced in Table 13-2. His figures show that from 1950-51 to 1958-59 consumption per head remained steady at $5 \cdot 9$ to $6 \cdot 0$ lbs per annum, an increase of almost 50 per cent on the pre-war level. More recently there has been a further increase, largely as a result of a rise in the sales of imported cheeses which have become more available in greater variety, in better condition, and at more competitive prices than before. But there has also been some increase in consumption of Australian cheese both of the Cheddar and non-Cheddar variety. An attempt to explain changes in cheese consumption in terms of changes in income per head, price of cheese, and the retail price of meat (which is often regarded as a possible substitute for cheese), suggests that cheese consumption is mainly responsive to changes in income—with a 1 per cent increase in income leading to a $0 \cdot 75$ per cent change in cheese consumption.[12]

Processed Milk Products Included in this category are condensed, concen-

11. R. S. G. Rutherford in 'The Australian Dairy Industry—An Economic Study', edited by N. T. Drane and H. R. Edwards, Cheshire, Melbourne 1960, pp 71-81.

12. The relevant equation derived by us is as follows:
$$\log Q_c = -1 \cdot 461 + 0 \cdot 747 \log C - 0 \cdot 0693 \log P_c + 0 \cdot 244 \log P_v$$
$$(0 \cdot 193) \qquad (0 \cdot 126) \qquad (0 \cdot 204)$$
$$(R^2 = 0 \cdot 786)$$

where Q_c is per capita consumption, in pounds,
P_c real price of cheese (1952-53 base),
P_v real price of meat (1952-53 base),
C   per capita personal consumption expenditure at constant 1953-54 prices.

trated and evaporated full cream milk; powdered full cream milk; infants' and invalids' foods, including malted milk; powdered skim milk; and other manufactured milk by-products. In calculating the consumption of the combined products, consolidation was made on the basis of the milk solids content of the different products. Although consumption per head of these products changed little from 1946-47 to 1954-55, there has been a steady increase of about 50 per cent in consumption since that time. This increase seems to have occurred mainly with unsweetened condensed milk and powdered skim milk.

EGGS

Available statistics of egg consumption in Australia are summarized in Table 13-4. In estimating the consumption of eggs in Australia the Commonwealth Statistician draws on data supplied by the egg boards of the various States. However, a large part of annual consumption (probably about half) came from small backyard flocks or poultry farmers who wished to avoid the payment of the marketing levies imposed by the various boards. As a result, the Statistician's estimate of total egg consumption is subject to an abnormally wide margin of error. The official figures suggest that since 1950 Australian consumption per head has been lower than before.

SUGAR

The total quantity of sugar consumed per head in Australia has fluctuated between 105 and 120 lbs for many years, with a slight downward trend since 1950. However this conceals a long-term tendency for the consumption of sugar in manufactured products (e.g. canned fruit, confectionery) to increase and for the direct consumption of sugar to decrease. Thus the consumption of sugar in manufactured products has risen by approximately 20 lbs since the 1930s whilst the consumption of sugar as such has gone down by 17 lbs.

WHEAT

The consumption of wheat is recorded by the Statistician in terms of two products—flour and breakfast foods. Breakfast foods have comprised only about 4 per cent of the total in recent years. The most important use of flour is in the making of bread. Because of the nature of our factory statistics, data on bread consumption are of doubtful reliability. After rising slightly between the 1930s and the postwar period of rationing, flour consumption has been declining by approximately 1 per cent per annum since 1950. This trend is attributable to a number of factors including the increase in real incomes, increasing urbanization, and the reduction in the proportion of the population engaged in heavy manual work. All these factors tend to produce a declining consumption of cereals. A factor which would counteract this to some extent is the growth in the migrant population in Australia. As pointed out by Honan: 'many of the immigrants come from countries where the

Table 13-4

Selected Foods: Consumption per head, 1936-37 to 1964-65

Commodity	Unit of quantity	Average 1936-37 to 1938-39	Average 1946-47 to 1949-50	Average 1950-51 to 1952-53	Average 1953-54 to 1955-56	Average 1956-57 to 1958-59	Average 1959-60 to 1961-62	1962-63	1963-64	1964-65
Total eggs and egg products	lb.	26·6	27·4	23·4	22·5	22·5	25·3	26·2	26·7	26·9
(Equivalent number of eggs)	no.	(243)	(255)	(217)	(205)	(206)	(211)	(210)	(214)	(215)
Flour	lb.	187·1	201·1	196·9	185·9	181·5	171·8	166·6	172·5	168·3
Sugar and syrups—										
Refined sugar—as sugar	,,	70·6	68·4	65·7	63·6	60·5	54·1	52·3	53·3	51·7
—in manufactured products	,,	35·9	49·9	50·1	49·7	52·0	55·7	56·7	55·7	58·7
Vegetables—potatoes	,,	106·7	122·1	100·3	106·0	115·3	101·0	124·5	103·1	93·4
—tomatoes	,,	15·7	25·6	21·9	23·3	28·6	28·4	28·0	29·1	31·7
All other vegetables	,,	n.a.	134·9[a]	119·7	107·0	115·5	108·8	114·1	112·5	117·9
Citrus fruit	,,	31·9	37·2[a]	32·5	37·7	35·4	39·8	47·7	42·4	50·9
Fresh fruit (excl. citrus)	,,	94·0	68·5	72·1	81·5	78·4	86·4	83·2	88·4	78·2
Jams, conserves etc.	,,	11·4	12·3	9·9	9·3	8·6	8·4	8·2	7·8	7·3
Dried vine fruits	,,	5·2	6·3[a]	5·9	4·8	4·1	4·7	5·3	3·1	5·5
Canned fruits	,,	10·4	11·0[a]	12·8	13·3	13·6	16·4	20·6	18·6	17·3
Beverages										
Tea	,,	6·9	6·6	6·8	6·2	6·0	5·9	5·8	5·7	5·9
Coffee	,,	0·6	1·0	0·7	1·2	1·3	1·8	2·2	2·2	2·5
Beer[b]	gals	17·5	24·1	30·8	35·7	34·5	34·7	35·1	36·3	37·8
Wine[b]	,,	0·9	2·0	2·3	1·8	1·7	1·7	1·9	1·9	1·9

n.a. Not available.

a. Average 1946-47 to 1948-49.

b. Consumption per head of adult population (18 years and over).

SOURCE: *Statistical Bulletin, Report on Food Production and the Apparent Consumption of Foodstuffs and Nutrients in Australia,* No 20, 1964-65 (and earlier volumes), Bureau of Census and Statistics.

diet contains a large amount of starchy foods and relatively little of the high protein foods such as meat and dairy products.'[13] The increasing proportion of southern Europeans in Australia has contributed to an increase in the use of flour for macaroni, vermicelli and spaghetti. Production per head of these commodities has more than doubled between 1948-49 and 1961-62. However exports are negligible and consumption of vermicelli and spaghetti only accounts for approximately 2 per cent of total flour consumption.

FRUIT

Consumption of *citrus fruit* has increased by about 50 per cent since pre-war; most of this increase has been in the form of increased consumption of oranges; grapefruit and other citrus fruit consumption has remained relatively constant. *Fresh fruit* consumption (excluding citrus) declined between the 1930s and the immediate postwar period but has tended to rise since then.

The consumption of *jam* and *dried vine fruits* has tended to decline. In both cases this is probably related to the declining consumption of cereals, since jam would be eaten mainly with bread, whilst a large proportion of the consumption of raisins, sultanas and currants occurs as an ingredient in bread, cake and other baked goods.

Canned fruit consumption in Australia has risen substantially. In 1963-64 it was almost double the pre-war and immediate postwar levels. This increase has not been spread evenly over the postwar period; instead increases have been particularly marked since 1958-59. Since that time average retail prices of canned fruits have been falling. In addition a vigorous promotion campaign has been undertaken since 1960 by the Australian Canned Fruit Sales Promotion Committee which was established by the Commonwealth Government at the request of growers. Attempts to relate canned fruit consumption to income, price and expenditure on sales promotion suggest that these factors could explain between 80 and 90 per cent of the variation in canned fruit consumption; however the coefficients obtained have large standard errors and do not, as yet, give us reliable estimates of the separate effects of these individual factors.

CONCLUSION

Economists often discuss changes in consumption in terms of three possible factors: *incomes, relative prices,* and *'tastes'*; where the last is really a substitute for 'all other' and would include new technology, new products, changing knowledge about nutrition etc. The discussion above has produced examples of changes in food consumption resulting from all these factors. Thus, growing incomes have probably played an important part in

13. N. D. Honan, 'Wheat Consumption in Australia', *Quarterly Review of Agricultural Economics,* Vol 15, No 4, October 1962, p 158.

the changes of the consumption of cereals, mutton, lamb, canned fruit and cheese, whilst price changes have also affected the relative consumption of the different meats. However, changes in 'non-economic factors' such as tastes, preferences based on health or other grounds, and the emergence of new products have probably been of equal importance in changing the pattern of food consumption though they are obviously more difficult to measure. Thus the decline in the consumption of butter, the rise of margarine, of new varieties of cheese, the growth of the consumption of tomatoes and citrus and of canned fruits are at least partly the result of this large third group of factors which are likely to influence consumption—a miscellaneous group which economists have so far found difficult to analyse.

CHAPTER 14

MARKETING AGRICULTURAL PRODUCTS

R. M. PARISH

University of New England

Probably the most distinctive feature of marketing arrangements for Australia's agricultural products is the existence of a plethora of statutory boards which, to varying degrees, regulate or perform marketing functions. Ten marketing boards operate under Commonwealth government statutes, and more than fifty under State government legislation.

Commonwealth boards either engage in, or regulate export trade in wheat, dairy produce, meat, eggs, canned fruits, apples and pears, dried fruits, wine and honey. State marketing boards are usually established after a referendum of the producers concerned, and perform the trading and processing functions of producer cooperatives. However, producer participation in these 'cooperatives' is compelled by law, so far as intra-state trade is concerned: hence the quaint term, 'compulsory cooperatives', which is sometimes applied to them. There is much variation in the degree of control over marketing exercised by State marketing boards. Some, by virtue of the geographical concentration of production of the commodity concerned, enjoy effective Australia-wide monopoly power, while others face competition from boards and private traders in other States. The favourite device of marketing boards, and of orderly marketing arrangements in general, is the home consumption price scheme, whereby, through the diversion of supplies to the export market, a price greater than export parity is established in the domestic market.

In view of the Australian propensity for orderly marketing, it may seem surprising that probably about two-thirds (by value) of Australian agricultural produce is marketed under free market conditions. No statutory control is exercised over the marketing of wool, which accounts for 30 per cent of the gross value of rural production; of meats (in the home market); of livestock; of most fruits and vegetables; or of most fodder crops. It is also noteworthy that marketing boards seldom have any control over the volume of output marketed by farmers: only in the case of two crops, sugar and rice, is there control of the acreage planted. Access to the higher value fresh milk market is rationed among producers by means of marketing quota schemes, administered by State milk marketing boards. Production of margarine is restricted in each State, production quotas being allotted to manufacturers.

The fostering of orderly marketing arrangements or, more precisely, the creation of producer-controlled or producer-dominated marketing monopolies, is the one policy which Australian State and Federal governments have pursued consistently in the field of agricultural marketing. Some evaluation of this policy is made in the next section of this chapter. The remainder of the chapter is devoted to brief descriptions of the salient features of the marketing of each of the principal agricultural products.

ORDERLY MARKETING

Government encouragement of orderly marketing[1] has found expression, first and most directly, in the setting up of statutory marketing boards; second, in the passage of enabling legislation whereby a procedure is established for the formation of statutory marketing boards on the initiative of producers (i.e. 'orderly' arrangements for implementing 'orderly marketing'); third, in measures such as tariffs, import or production quotas, designed to protect marketing boards from overseas and domestic competition; fourth, in the passage of complementary Commonwealth and State legislation as a means of strengthening marketing arrangements against possible legal challenge on constitutional grounds;[2] and, fifth, in the provision of cheap finance for marketing boards.

That producers should press for orderly marketing arrangements is not surprising since frequently they have something (and sometimes have much) to gain from obtaining control over the marketing of their product. Nor is it altogether puzzling that governments, and the community should not only acquiesce in, but positively encourage, the development of marketing monopolies. The consumer interest is diffuse and lacks political effectiveness; there is widespread acceptance of a restrictionist economic philosophy and distrust of free markets; and measures to assist primary industry are frequently justified by analogy with the Australian policy of tariff protection for secondary industry, or by the need to foster power vis-à-vis industrial firms and trade unions.

Producers may benefit from orderly marketing in various ways. They may

1. For a general discussion of orderly marketing in Australia, see J. N. Lewis, 'Organized Marketing of Agricultural Products in Australia', *Australian Journal of Agricultural Economics*, Vol 5, No 1, September 1961. For a more detailed study, see John A. Morey, 'The Role of the Statutory Marketing Board in the Organized Marketing of Australia's Primary Products', M.Ec. thesis, University of Sydney, 1959. The functions of the major marketing boards are described succinctly in *Rural Industry in Australia*, rev ed, Bureau of Agricultural Economics, Canberra 1964, ch 12.

2. Constitutional limitations on government intervention in Australian agriculture are discussed in Chapter 15.

appropriate for themselves any abnormal profits obtainable from processing and distributing their products. A marketing board may pool sales receipts over a year or shorter period, and reduce the variability of prices received by farmers—who do not all share the theorist's delight in the random walk of free market prices. A marketing authority may also secure greater price stability and higher returns by evening out supply through storage operations to a greater extent than would occur under a regime of private storage. Any indeterminancy in market price may perhaps be exploited by a single seller having the power to set prices. However, the power of marketing monopolies to raise prices generally is severely limited by the fact that they usually lack control over production. This means that apart from the possibility of reducing supplies by destroying part of the crop, marketing monopolies can exploit their power only through the practice of price discrimination.

Price discrimination as practised by marketing boards in Australia generally takes the form of the diversion of supplies from the domestic to the export market, though in some cases, discrimination by end use is possible. A home consumption price higher than export parity can thus be obtained. Export demand is generally much more elastic than home demand, so that the higher home consumption price can be obtained at little or no cost in terms of a lower export price. If a marketing board were motivated solely to secure the maximum revenue obtainable from the sale of available supplies, it should attempt to raise the domestic price to the point where marginal revenue obtained on the home and export markets was the same. However, boards' pricing policies may be constrained by some regard for the consumer interest and fear of the political consequences of too blatant an exploitation of their monopoly powers. A full analysis of a marketing board's behaviour would also need to take account of administrative inertia and the fact that the interests of marketing authorities cannot simply be assumed to be identical with the interests of the producers of the products concerned.

Some products are more suited to orderly marketing arrangements than others, either because the potential gains to producers are greater, or the difficulties of implementing the arrangements are fewer. In order to secure the benefits of price discrimination, an export market for the product must be available. But the larger the home market relative to the export market, the greater is the effect on the average price received by producers of an increase in the home price. The less elastic the home demand relative to export demand, the greater the degree of discrimination possible, and the less elastic the supply of the product, the less will the benefits of a high home price be eroded by expansion of output and exports. The more unstable the price of a product, the larger are the potential benefits to producers in the form of greater price stability. A set of standard grades is necessary if pooling and price equalization are to be practised. When the home price substantially exceeds the average price received, producers have a strong incentive to sell their whole output on the home market, by-passing the marketing authority. Compliance with compulsory orderly marketing arrangements is more easily enforced, or voluntary adherence to them secured, if the product must be processed before sale to consumer, and if opportunities for interstate trade outside the constituted marketing authority or authorities are limited.

For these and other reasons, including the ideological attitudes of producers and constitutional difficulties, there is considerable diversity among agricultural commodities in the extent to which orderly marketing arrangements have been implemented, and in the economic effects, particularly the price effects, of these arrangements. At one extreme, wool marketing is in private hands and is largely free of regulation by government or statutory authority, while, at the other, all domestic and overseas trade in wheat is undertaken by a single statutory body, the Australian Wheat Board.

Among export products which benefit from home consumption price schemes, made possible by orderly marketing arrangements, there is considerable variation in the degree of protection obtained. If the protective effect is measured by the percentage by which the equalized price exceeds export parity, the principal commodities concerned receive protection as follows: wheat and barley, 7 per cent; rice, 14 per cent; dried vine fruits, 18 per cent; cheese, 34 per cent; sugar, 35 per cent; eggs, 53 per cent; butter, 59 per cent. (See Table 15-2.) The figures are based on average prices received in the three years ended 1962-63; those for wheat, butter and cheese include the effect of subsidies, as well as of home consumption price schemes.

It is possible to make a case for protection of Australian agriculture, on the grounds that such protection is desirable to correct the allocative distortions introduced by the existence of tariff protection for secondary industry.[3] (Acceptance of this argument is likely to involve rejection of the usual arguments used to support protection of local manufacturing industry.) Alternatively a case for protecting individual primary industries might be made on the basis of their specific characteristics. But neither of these arguments provides a satisfactory justification for a policy of giving to those industries which ask for it the privilege of monopolistically exploiting the home market to the best of their ability, tempered only by their judgement as to what is socially and politically acceptable. The first argument would favour the granting of a more or less uniform degree of protection to primary industries, whereas the degree of protection afforded by home consumption price schemes varies greatly from product to product. Furthermore the existing pattern of agricultural protection probably serves not so much to offset the

3. A. J. Little, 'Some Aspects of Government Policy Affecting the Rural Sector of the Australian Economy with Special Reference to the Period 1939/45-1953', *Economic Record*, Vol 38, No 83, September 1962.

effects of protection given to secondary industries as to divert resources from the unprotected rural sector, containing wool and meat, the two major export commodities, to the protected rural industries. The second argument implies a varied pattern of protection among primary industries, but there is little reason to believe that the optimum pattern would bear any resemblance to the pattern which has in fact evolved through the adoption of orderly marketing arrangements.

While the nature, if not the magnitudes, of the effects of home consumption price schemes on resource allocation and consumer welfare is reasonably clear,[4] the effects of orderly marketing arrangements on the efficiency of marketing operations are far from obvious. Research on this topic is generally lacking, probably because comparisons of the actual performance of marketing boards with efficiency norms, or with the hypothetical performance of a free market, are likely to be inconclusive. The author's view—based on impressions rather than systematic analysis—is that marketing boards may be able to carry out routine marketing functions somewhat more efficiently than they would be performed by competing private organizations; that boards are slow to innovate, particularly in product and market development; that economic efficiency is often sacrificed for administrative convenience; and that, in general, board managements are 'satisficers' rather than 'maximizers'.

WOOL

The marketing of Australian wool[5] has two outstanding features: the great bulk of the clip is sold at auction, and each individual lot (or a sample from it) is inspected and appraised by buyers before it is sold. The practice of visual inspection by buyers is a costly one, involving the provision of display facilities in brokers' warehouses, the movement of sample bales from store to display floor and back to store, and the services of skilled appraisers. It is made necessary by the fact that wool is a heterogeneous product. A system of classification and grading which would enable it to be sold by description has not yet been devised.

The only significant government intervention in wool marketing is the levying of a tax on wool sold, for the purpose of financing wool promotion and research. Proceeds of the tax, together with a proportional contribution from the Federal government, are remitted to the Australian Wool Board, a Commonwealth statutory body. Expenditure of the bulk of these funds is entrusted to the International Wool Secretariat, a body which is

4. For a discussion and estimation of the welfare costs of protection, see R. M. Parish, 'The Costs of Protecting the Dairying Industry', *Economic Record*, Vol 38, No 82, June 1962; also see E. L. Banks and R. G. Mauldon, 'Effects of Pricing Decisions of a Statutory Marketing Board', *Australian Journal of Agricultural Economics*, Vol 10, No 1, June 1966.

5. Much useful information on wool marketing is given in *Report of the Wool Marketing Committee of Enquiry*, Government Printer, Canberra 1962.

controlled by the Australian, New Zealand and South African Wool Boards. The I.W.S. has embarked on an ambitious promotion campaign in major wool-consuming countries. The campaign is aimed at building a 'quality-image' for wool, differentiating wool from synthetic fibres, and involves cooperative advertising with manufacturers and the certification of garments and fabrics as being of pure virgin wool manufacture, through the use of a distinguishing symbol, the 'woolmark'.

Other major activities of the Australian Wool Board include the collection and publication of wool statistical data, the operation of a wool testing service for buyers and manufacturers, and the ownership of wool stores which it leases to private firms. The Board also has power to investigate and make recommendations on wool marketing.

THE AUCTION SYSTEM

The existing system of wool marketing has been under heavy fire in recent years, principally on account of the instability of wool prices. It is not simply—not even mainly—the effects of price fluctuations on the welfare of growers and the efficiency of production, or on the stability of the economy as a whole, that causes concern, but rather their effect on wool's competitive position vis-à-vis synthetic fibres. The price risks involved in handling wool are a factor encouraging the use of synthetic fibres, the prices of which are subject to much less frequent alteration.

Fluctuations in demand, rather than in supply, are the major source of instability of wool prices.[6] Despite the existence of synthetic fibres which for some purposes are close substitutes for wool, the world demand for wool may be rather inelastic in the short run. Supply in any one year is very inelastic. However, since wool is a storable commodity, the combination of an unstable demand and inelastic supply is, in itself, insufficient explanation for fluctuating prices. Rather, any explanation must run in terms of the existence of insufficient stabilizing speculation, or excessive destabilizing speculation in wool stocks. It is not known whether either of these conditions prevails, or whether prices are about as stable as could be expected, or as could be achieved at reasonable cost, given the uncertainty which exists concerning future supply and demand conditions, and the relatively high costs of buying, storing and selling wool.

Despite the importance of these more fundamental factors, there is a tendency to blame the auction system itself for wool's price instability. It is true that the auction system gives rise to a certain amount of avoidable instability in the form of transaction to transaction and day to day variations in price. Also, the existence of a free market may encourage some destabilizing speculation. However it is generally recognized that for a worthwhile reduction in

6. Alan Powell, 'Production and Income Uncertainty in the Wool Industry: an Aggregative Approach', *Australian Journal of Agricultural Economics*, Vol 4, No 1, July 1960.

price variability to be achieved, a closer adjustment of supply to demand, through some type of buffer stock operation, would be required. In July 1964 the Australian Wool Board recommended the introduction of a reserve-price scheme, akin to those already operating in New Zealand and South Africa.[7] After an extensive debate, the proposal was put to a referendum of growers in December 1965. The proposal was defeated by a small majority.

The auction system is an effective and equitable method of distributing the clip among users, in that access to the market is open to all, and it is free of the taint of manipulation in the interests of growers or users of wool. It provides a sensitive barometer to supply and demand conditions, not only for wool as a whole, but also for the many different types of wool. (Translating the abstract concept of 'the' reserve price into a structure of many reserve prices would have been one of the more difficult theoretical and practical problems facing a reserve-price authority.) It can, perhaps, be given most of the credit for the high standard of preparation for market which is a feature of Australian wool.[8] In any case the obverse of unstable prices is a high degree of market clearance and a greater stability in the quantities of wool flowing into the processing pipeline.

PREPARATION OF WOOL FOR SALE

After it is shorn, wool is classed, that is, sorted into reasonably homogeneous 'lines'. This operation is usually performed in the shearing shed; however, a significant fraction of the clip is 'bulk classed' in stores in selling centres, having received only a cursory sorting, or no sorting at all, in the shed. Wool is classed according to several characteristics, the most important being staple length, 'quality' or 'count' (which is mainly determined by the number of crimps per inch and is an indicator of the spinning potential of the wool), and the extent to which it is contaminated by vegetable matter. Other less important characteristics that are taken into account are soundness, handle, density, freedom of growth, character, colour, definition of crimp, regularity of crimp, and lustre.

Although wool is classed by the grower or his agent, and despite the existence of a standard classification which recognizes about 3,000 types of wool—this is the classification used by the Australian Wool Board for the purpose of statistical description of the clip and of prices realized at auction—buyers find it necessary to inspect lots of wool prior to bidding for them at auction. Buyers appraise wool not only in terms of the characteristics mentioned above, but also in order to assess the likely 'yield' of each lot, that is, the

7. Australian Wool Board, *Report and Recommendations on Wool Marketing*, Canberra 1964.

8. F. H. Gruen, 'The Case for the Present Marketing System', in Alan Barnard (ed), *The Simple Fleece*, Melbourne University Press, Melbourne 1962, ch 32, pp 496-7.

quantity of clean wool obtainable per 100 lbs of greasy wool.[9] Nor does the appraisal of wool cease at this point. Wool is again assessed by the processor, and may be 'mill-sorted', that is, reclassed to the processors' satisfaction.

Yield of wool can be determined objectively by means of laboratory testing of sample cores of wool taken from the bale: but in fact it is assessed subjectively by buyers before auction. However, some use of laboratory testing for yield is made after auction by buyers, merchants and processors. Staple length and fault are assessed reasonably well by visual inspection, but the determination of 'quality' by this means is less satisfactory. This is because mill performance is affected mainly by fibre diameter, whereas 'quality' is determined mainly by the number of crimps per inch. There is a correlation between crimps per inch and fibre diameter but it is not a particularly strong one, so that visual assessment of quality is not very accurate. However, errors made in the appraisal of individual lots tend to cancel when a number of lots are amalgamated to meet a processor's order, so that mill lots can be assembled which, on the average, spin to the counts which are specified.

The major criticism that is made of existing methods of appraising Australian wool is the failure to use objective methods of measurement of the characteristics of lots before their sale. The use of objective measurements of yield and fibre diameter would presumably enhance the value of wool to manufacturers, and strengthen its competitive position. It would also result in some marketing costs being reduced: for example, buyers' appraisals of lots could be more cursory than at present. On the other hand laboratory testing involves costs which are by no means negligible.[10] Whether the benefits of pre-sale testing would exceed the costs is thus an open question. If, through objective testing or by other means it became possible to sell wool on description, a very worthwhile saving in marketing costs could be effected. However, this does not seem to be a practical proposition at the present time.

As well as the possibility of making radical changes in the marketing of wool, there is scope for improvement within the framework of existing practices. Two methods for improvement which have received some attention are a raising of standards of wool classing and a reduction in the proportion

9. Two studies, giving virtually identical results, have been made of the relationship between the physical characteristics of wool and the prices received at auction. Between 80 and 90 per cent of the variation in wool price can be explained by three variables: crimps per inch (or quality number), staple length and colour. See A. A. Dunlop and S. S. Y. Young, 'Selection of Merino Sheep: An Analysis of the Relative Economic Weights Applicable to Some Wool Traits', *Empire Journal of Experimental Agriculture*, Vol 28, No 111, 1960; J. N. Skinner, 'Some Factors Affecting the Clean Price of Greasy Wool', *Australian Journal of Agricultural Economics*, Vol 9, No 2, December 1965.

10. According to B. H. Mackay and H. G. David, 'Some Problems of Sampling the Australian Wool Clip for Objective Appraisal', *Wool Technology and Sheep Breeding*, Vol 12, No 1, July 1965, p 59, the cost of yield testing would, on the basis of current commercial charges, be of the same order of magnitude as the broker's commission.

of very small lots offered at auction. The two desiderata are somewhat conflicting, since, for a given size of clip, the finer the classing the smaller the size of lots.

In an attempt to raise classing standards, a scheme of voluntary registration of wool classers has been introduced. The clips classed by provisionally registered classers are inspected by technical officers of the Wool Board, who also note the standard of classing of registered classers, and, where appropriate, make suggestions for improvement.

A reduction in the number of small lots—or star lots, as they are known in the trade—submitted for auction will involve an increase in the use of store classing and interlotting. That is, wool from a number of growers is intermingled and sold under the brand of the classing store, or bales of wool of similar type but of differing ownership are offered as a single lot. In 1964 the Australian Wool Board recommended that all one-bale lots, except of speciality wools, be eliminated by means of bulk classing, interlotting, or in some other way.

In general there is a small price differential in favour of big lots as compared to star lots, and the variability of price is greater for star lots.[11] The price differential is greater in Victoria than in other States, and, since the proportion of star lots sold at auction is much higher in Victoria, it would appear that the marginal disutility of star lots to buyers increases as their proportion increases. Except for Victoria, the price difference in favour of big lots is insufficient to warrant the use of bulk classing—or even, in most cases, the cheaper procedure of interlotting—solely in order to increase lot size.[12] Hence the Wool Board's recommendation that one-bale lots be eliminated is hardly justifiable in terms of its likely price-raising effect. The proposal might be defended on the grounds that small lots are responsible for a disproportionate share of selling brokers' costs, but if this is the case, a more appropriate solution is for brokers to revise their selling charges so as to offer growers greater encouragement to sell their clips in large lots.

MARKETING COSTS

The major items of cost in the marketing of wool, and recent estimates of their magnitude, are shown in Table 14-1. At approximately 10 cents per lb, marketing costs represent about 20 per cent of the average market price of 48 cents received for wool in recent years.

---

11. The relationship between lot size and price is discussed in the following: *Economics of Bulk Classing of Wool*, Wool Economic Research Report No 2, Bureau of Agricultural Economics, August 1960; F. H. Gruen and J. O. White, 'Shed Classing Versus Store Classing', *Australian Journal of Agricultural Economics*, Vol 4, No 2, December 1960; R. B. Whan, 'The Effect of District of Origin on Wool Prices', *Australian Journal of Agricultural Economics*, Vol 9, No 1, June 1965.

12. R. B. Whan and R. A. Bowman, 'The Cost of Classing Wool in the Shearing Shed and Wool Store', *Wool Technology and Sheep Breeding*, Vol 12, No 2, December 1965.

Table 14-1

Wool Marketing Costs, 1963-1964

Item	Estimated average cost in 1963-1964
	Cents per lb. (greasy) [a]
Clip preparation	
Classing	1·38
Wool packs	0·51
Transport to selling centre	
Freight	1·10
Insurance	0·03
Storage awaiting auction	
Warehousing	0·64
Insurance	0·05
Transfer of ownership	
Selling commission	0·86
Promotion and research levy	0·96
Total costs incurred by seller	5·53
Buying commission	0·78
Transport to processor's plant	
Delivery charge	0·44
Wharfage	0·06
Sea freight	3·30
Marine insurance	0·09
Total costs incurred by buyer	4·67
Total marketing cost	10·20

a. The figure for classing is a 'guesstimate', based on data given by Whan and Bowman, *op. cit.* The other figures are taken from P. H. May, 'Costs of Marketing Australian Greasy Wool, 1960-61 and 1963-64', *Quarterly Review of Agricultural Economics*, Vol 18, No 3, July 1965. The costs of commissions, insurance and the promotion and research levy have been adjusted to conform to an assumed average selling price of 48 cents per lb.

The major component of marketing costs is internal and overseas freight, which represents 44 per cent of the total costs. Wool growers have reason to be grateful for Section 92 of the Federal Constitution, which limits the powers of the State governments to tax interstate road hauliers. Several State railway systems have lowered their freight rates for wool in border areas where such competition is most intense. It has been estimated that if these border concessions were removed, total internal transport costs would be increased by about $A25 million per annum, or by 22 per cent.[13]

Commissions amount to about 20 per cent of marketing costs. Both selling

13. W. T. Dent, 'Optimal Wool Flows for Minimisation of Transport Costs', *Australian Journal of Agricultural Economics*, Vol 10, No 2, December 1966.

U

and buying commissions are assessed as a percentage of the value of the transaction and hence vary directly with the price of wool. Percentage selling commissions may be regarded as a form of incentive payment whereby the broker is motivated to secure the highest possible price for his client, as an arrangement whereby the broker shares with the producer a small part of the risk associated with price fluctuations, or as a discriminatory pricing device for exploiting producers of high value wools and, possibly, for subsidizing producers of cheaper wools.

Uniform selling charges are set collusively by the brokers operating in each State. There is less uniformity in buying commissions, however; also, probably at least 30 per cent of wool bought at auction is not bought on commission, but by a buyer acting as merchant or speculator.[14]

Wool selling is a highly concentrated industry, about half of the broking business being in the hands of the two largest firms.[15] Furthermore, not all selling brokers operate in all selling centres. Wool broking companies are also substantial suppliers of finance to the pastoral industry, so that many of their clients are tied to them through indebtedness. In these circumstances it would be surprising if wool selling charges did not contain a component attributable to the brokers' monopoly power.

Most growers leave to their broker the decision as to what reserve price to place on their wool. As Lloyd has pointed out, 'the brokers' incentive to set a reasonable reserve price is blunted by the fact that the broker must resubmit 'passed-in' lots at no charge—an apparent pricing inefficiency'.[16]

Combinations among wool buyers to restrict competition at auction are known to occur, and have been subject to a judicial investigation.[17] At wool auctions such combinations are known as 'pies'. From the limited evidence that is available on the incidence and operation of pies, it has been estimated that their existence might exert a depressive influence on the average price received for the whole Australian clip of from 0·13 to 0·25 cents per lb.[18]

PRIVATE SELLING OF WOOL

A small but growing proportion of the clip is handled by dealers, who buy directly from the grower and resell at auction, to wool buyers, or directly to processors. Selling to a dealer is called 'private selling' in Australia. About

14. See *Report of the Wool Marketing Committee of Enquiry*, Government Printer, Canberra 1962, Appendix 11.
15. This statement is based on data given in *Report of the Wool Marketing Committee of Enquiry*, Government Printer, Canberra 1962, Appendices 12 and 16, account being taken of mergers which have occurred since 1961.
16. A. G. Lloyd, 'The Reserve Price Scheme for Wool—A Defence', *Economic Record*, Vol 41, No 96, December 1965, p 506.
17. *Report by the Honourable Mr. Justice Cook under Section 8 of the Monopolies Act, 1923, concerning the Trade in Wool*, Government Printer, New South Wales 1959.
18. F. H. Gruen, 'Goulburn, Forward Prices and Pies', *Review of Marketing and Agricultural Economics*, Vol 28, No 2, June 1960.

3 per cent of the clip was sold privately in 1952-53, but by 1963-64 the proportion had risen to 10 per cent. Private selling is particularly favoured in Western Australia where over one-third of the clip is handled by dealers. There is no evidence that growers who sell privately receive lower prices than those who sell at auction; there may, indeed, be some price advantage in private selling.[19] In addition, private selling brings immediate payment, whereas with auction selling payment may be deferred for two and three months or more, and the grower runs the risk that price may change while his clip is waiting to be sold. Some dealers will buy forward from growers and sell forward to users, thus further reducing price uncertainty.

The growth of private selling is viewed by some with alarm, as constituting a threat to the auction system. This viewpoint was espoused by the Australian Wool Board in 1964, when it recommended that private selling of wool for export be prohibited. However, one can argue that the growth of private selling should be encouraged rather than discouraged. Dealers are providing a service which evidently appeals to many growers and users of wool, and by amalgamating and bulk classing small clips, are easing the strain on the auction system caused by the submission of small lots. Dealers also provide a much needed element of competition with selling brokers. The growth of private selling in New South Wales and Queensland is hampered by the refusal by members of the wool buyers' association to trade in wool that has not first been submitted to public auction.

WOOL FUTURES MARKET

The Sydney Greasy Wool Futures Exchange is now the world's leading wool futures market, although it was established as recently as 1960. The structure of futures prices on the Sydney market is usually characterized by backwardation, but a contango structure has prevailed at times. The degree of backwardation appears to be positively associated with the level of the spot price.[20] On the London wool tops market it has been shown that a high degree of backwardation occurs at times when stocks are low in relation to the rate of consumption, while contango is associated with the opposite situation.[21] This is consistent with Working's theory that spot-futures price differences represent the costs of carrying commodity stocks.[22]

According to a study by Weisser, the Sydney market leaves something to be desired as a vehicle for routine short hedging of wool. In the 1960-62

19. G. M. Scobie, 'The Private Selling of Wool in Australia', *Quarterly Review of Agricultural Economics*, Vol 17, No 3, July 1964.

20. G. W. Edwards, *Futures Prices and the Risk Premium*, unpublished undergraduate thesis, University of New England, 1964, p 15.

21. G. F. Rainnie (ed), *The Woollen and Worsted Industry, An Economic Analysis*, Oxford University Press, London 1964, Appendix A.

22. Holbrook Working, 'The Theory of the Inverse Carrying Charge in Futures Markets', *Journal of Farm Economics*, Vol 30, No 1, February 1948.

period, hedging would have been much more effective in reducing gains from price rises than in reducing losses from price falls.[23] Nor can the financial outcome of selective hedging be predicted accurately by reference to the basis (i.e. spot-future price differential) existing at the time a hedge is opened.[24] However, the increasing use of the futures market by the wool trade suggests that the market is providing a useful service, despite its imperfection as a medium for hedging. And, as has been emphasized by Working and Gray, the economic role of a futures market may be that of facilitating rational stock-holding decisions, and price-formation, rather than simply facilitating risk transference through hedging.[25]

MEAT

Overseas marketing of beef, mutton and lamb is regulated by the Australian Meat Board, a Commonwealth statutory body. By means of a licensing system the Board has power to control the kinds of meat which may be exported and the destinations to which it may be shipped.[26] The Board may buy and sell meat for the purpose of administering any international agreements to which Australia may be a party, and also as part of export promotion and market development activities. It has acted as principal in negotiations regarding minimum guaranteed prices under the 15 Year Meat Agreement with the United Kingdom, and in negotiations with shipping companies about overseas freight rates. Approximately 45 per cent of total annual production of beef, 33 per cent of mutton, and 9 per cent of lamb is exported.

Livestock auction markets exist in all capital cities, and in country centres; direct (non-auction) transactions are also commonly made. Most livestock is sold after inspection on the hoof, and on a per head, rather than a per weight basis, but some is sold on the basis of carcass weight and grade. Some abattoirs are operated by State and local government authorities, others by private firms and cooperatives. Meat is still largely retailed through butchers' shops, but supermarket sales are increasing, albeit slowly: in 1961-62—the most recent year for which figures are available—96 per cent of meat was sold by butchers' shops, as compared with 99 per cent five years previously.

Marketing margins for meat tend to vary inversely with meat prices. For beef in the Sydney market, for example, it has been found that a 1 per cent rise in the wholesale price is associated, on average, with a 1 per cent fall in

23. *The Sydney Wool Futures Market*, Wool Economic Research Report No 4, Bureau of Agricultural Economics, June 1963.

24. G. W. Edwards, *op. cit.*, p 25.

25. See, for example, Holbrook Working, 'New Concepts Concerning Futures Markets and Prices', *American Economic Review*, Vol 52, No 3, June 1962, pp 452-4.

26. Exporters are licensed by the Minister of Primary Industry, on the recommendation of the Board.

the retail margin.[27] This relationship means, of course, that retail prices are more stable than wholesale, and wholesale prices are more stable than livestock prices. From the producers' point of view, the more interesting implication is that livestock prices will be less stable than they would if margins were not inversely related to price level. However, to the extent that livestock prices are determined by the demand for meat for export, they will be unaffected by the mark-up policies of wholesale and retail butchers.

Possible explanations of the behaviour of marketing margins are to be found in conditions of demand, of cost, and of market structure. The demand facing individual sellers may be more elastic at high prices than at low, in which case profit-maximizing behaviour on the part of sellers would result in the observed type of fluctuations in margins. Frequent changes in prices and in quantities sold may increase sellers' costs. Retailers may be reluctant to vary prices if price differentials between shops reflect quality differences in the meat sold, and, in the absence of official meat grading, are so identified in the eyes of consumers. Stable prices might also be a consequence of oligopolistic market structure in the wholesale and retail meat trade. Butchers' pricing policies might also be viewed as an attempt on their part to interpret price signals to consumers, whereby they ignore (i.e. do not pass on) price changes which they believe to be transitory, only adjusting retail and wholesale prices to changes in livestock prices which seem to be of a relatively permanent nature.

There are official export grades for meat, but apart from the branding of lamb carcasses, and a limited beef grading scheme in Queensland, there is no comparable system for meat sold domestically. There is, however, official inspection of meat at abattoirs to ensure compliance with health regulations. The lack of an official grading system is widely deplored and the system in use in the United States held up as an example to be emulated. On the other hand the American practice can be criticized for perpetuating distinctions without real differences—it has been found that consumers frequently cannot tell the difference between adjacent grades—and for serving the interests, not only of consumers, but of special groups among producers and distributors. Absence of a set of standard grades does not imply absence of grading. Butchers tend to specialize in the type of meat they sell, some selling 'good' meat at a relatively high price, while others cater for those seeking cheaper meat of poorer quality. Hence it is not certain that introduction of official meat grading would widen the range of choice open to consumers. The case for official grading must rest largely on its effects on the efficiency of marketing. A set of standard grades would enable meat to be bought with confidence on

27. Ian W. Marceau, 'Quarterly Estimates of the Demand and Price Structure for Meat in New South Wales', *Australian Journal of Agricultural Economics*, Vol 11, No 1, June 1967. A similar finding is reported by G. J. Butler, 'Marketing of Beef in Victoria', unpublished M.Agr.Sc. thesis, University of Melbourne, 1965.

description only, without the need for inspection by the buyer, thus reducing buying and selling costs and widening the market. Butchers could be expected to oppose official grading, since their incomes presumably include at present a quasi-rent deriving from their skill in selecting meat of the quality preferred by their customers. Also, the introduction of grading would probably hasten the growth of supermarket sales of meat.

WHEAT

The marketing of wheat within Australia, and of wheat and flour for export, is undertaken by a single statutory authority, the Australian Wheat Board. The Board's trading monopoly derives from complementary Commonwealth and State government legislation. State legislation empowers the Board to acquire wheat grown in each State, except for wheat committed to interstate trade, and also makes the Board responsible for intra-state marketing. Under Commonwealth legislation the Board is made responsible for handling exports of wheat and wheat products, and for interstate marketing of wheat. However, because of the constitutional guarantee (Section 92) that 'trade, commerce and intercourse among the States. . . . shall be absolutely free', the Board does not possess monopoly power with respect to interstate trade in wheat. While private interstate, and 'black-market' intra-state trading in wheat is known to occur, its volume has been insufficient to jeopardize the Board's position.

Storage and rail transport of grain is handled by grain elevator boards, or their equivalent, which act as agents for the Wheat Board in each State. Upon delivery of wheat to the railway siding, the grower receives a first advance from the Board: the first advance represents a substantial proportion of the estimated final price of the wheat, and is financed by means of a government-guaranteed loan from the Reserve Bank. Receipts from the sale of each season's crop are pooled, successive interim payments made to growers, and when the crop is disposed of, a final price is determined, and a final pool payment is made.

Overseas sales of wheat are made on the basis of its being of 'fair average quality' (F.A.Q.). The F.A.Q. standard is measured in terms of bushel weight and is determined, each season, by the weighing of a representative sample obtained by mixing samples from major wheat-growing districts. A farmer's wheat is accepted as being of F.A.Q. standard provided it meets certain minimum requirements. Sub-standard wheat is stored and marketed separately from F.A.Q. wheat. Wheat is segregated according to State of origin, and a separate F.A.Q. bushel weight determined for each State. However, in New South Wales two standards are fixed, one for the northern area, where predominantly semi-hard varieties are grown and from which wheat is shipped through the port of Newcastle, and one for the southern and western area, where the wheat is mainly soft and is shipped from Sydney. In South Australia wheat of a uniform vitreous appearance is segregated and marketed as semi-hard wheat. In addition to the F.A.Q. and semi-hard grades, high protein wheats from Queensland and northern New South Wales are stored separately and marketed as Premium Wheat on the basis of a guaranteed minimum protein content. This wheat is mainly used by local millers, but some is exported.

The system of segregating wheat by State of origin allows economical storage and results in a degree of product differentiation, in that, for example, Victorian F.A.Q. wheat consists predominantly of soft varieties, whereas northern New South Wales wheat is of a semi-hard character. However, the grading of Australian wheat is much less 'fine' than that practised in other major exporting countries. Whether the benefits of a more elaborate grading system would outweigh the additional cost remains, for the present, a matter for conjecture. Probably the main benefit would be a widening of the potential export market for Australian wheats. The pattern of world trade in wheat is subject to rapid changes, but, so far, Australia has experienced little difficulty in selling its exportable surplus. However, the advantage of having a product that is more accurately graded, and hence better matched to particular end uses, could be of importance in the future.

DAIRY PRODUCTS

Australia's principal dairy products are butter, which uses more than 60 per cent of total whole milk production; fresh milk, 20 per cent; cheese, 9 per cent; and preserved milk products, 6 per cent. About 40 per cent of butter production and 44 per cent of cheese production is exported, mainly to the United Kingdom. A Commonwealth statutory body, the Australian Dairy Produce Board, is the sole exporter of butter and cheese to the United Kingdom; it also regulates exports to other markets. The Board purchases butter from factories, paying them an interim advance from funds made available by the Reserve Bank under Commonwealth government guarantee.

Domestic prices are fixed by the Australian Dairy Industry Council, which comprises representatives of the Australian Dairy Farmers' Federation, the Commonwealth Dairy Produce Equalization Committee Ltd., and the Australian Dairy Produce Board. In recent years the home prices of butter and cheese have, on average, exceeded the f.o.b. export prices by over 60 and 40 per cent respectively. A voluntary price equalization scheme, whereby all factories receive the same price irrespective of whether their output is sold at home or overseas, is administered by an incorporated body, the Commonwealth Dairy Produce Equalization Committee Ltd.[28] The equalized price

28. Although participation by factories in the equalization scheme is voluntary, they have a strong incentive to do so, since otherwise they are ineligible for the subsidy mentioned in the next sentence.

is supplemented by payment of a Commonwealth government subsidy of $27 million annually: currently, subsidy payments amount to 5·4 cents per lb for butter and 2·1 cents per lb for cheese—or to 12 per cent and 11 per cent, respectively, of the price received by producers. Producer exploitation of the home market is assisted by tariffs and restrictions imposed by each State on margarine production. Exports of processed milk products are encouraged by payment of an export subsidy.

The marketing of fresh milk in metropolitan areas, and in many country centres, is controlled by milk marketing boards operating under State legislation. Milk boards have power—within proclaimed areas—to fix producer and consumer prices and to license suppliers, distributors and vendors. Their concern with the consumer interest seems largely to consist in ensuring continuity of supply and the policing of minimum health and quality standards for the product, prices being fixed at an artificially high level for the benefit of producers. The policies of one such board, the New South Wales Milk Board, have been subject to a detailed study.[29] The major criticisms that can be made of the Board's operations are as follows:

(i) The price paid to producers, which is more than double the price they receive for manufacturing milk, is unnecessarily high.

(ii) Rather than expanding and contracting its milk procurement area in accordance with the seasonal pattern of production, the Board has encouraged winter production, at high cost, within a restricted area.

(iii) Increased winter production has been accompanied by a large increase in the quantity of milk, surplus to its requirements, that is produced within the milk zone, particularly during the spring and summer months. This surplus milk, after conversion into dairy products, has to be exported at a low price.

(iv) Winter production of milk has been encouraged, and access to the lucrative fresh milk market rationed among producers by an individual marketing quota scheme. The non-transferability of quotas among producers fosters production inefficiencies.

(v) The Board incurs unnecessarily high transport costs by hauling milk from the periphery of the milk zone even though surplus milk is available closer to centres of consumption.

(vi) Until 1960, the Board set a price for sweet cream which was probably excessive even from the point of view of maximizing producer returns from this product. It was forced to abandon this policy by competition from suppliers of cream to which a small amount of gelatine had been added; not being pure cream, this product was not subject to the Board's control.

(vii) The Board could also be criticized for not encouraging marketing

29. Udom Kerdpibule, 'An Economic Evaluation of the Policies of the New South Wales Milk Board', unpublished M.Sc.Agr. thesis, University of Sydney, 1964.

innovations, such as the promotion of homogenized milk, the use of larger containers, increased sales through supermarkets, and a reduction in the frequency of home delivery.

OTHER PRODUCTS

SUGAR AND RICE

Marketing arrangements for these two commodities have several features in common. Production of each is limited to particular geographical areas; the Queensland and northern New South Wales coast in the case of sugar; the irrigation areas of south-western New South Wales in the case of rice. Each product is marketed through marketing boards operating under State legislation, but, because of the geographical concentration of production, each board enjoys effective monopoly power in the Australian market. (By an arrangement with millers, all of New South Wales production of sugar is purchased by the Queensland Sugar Board.) About two-thirds of total production of each crop is exported, at prices substantially below the home consumption price. The high domestic price of sugar is maintained through an embargo on sugar imports and by an import duty on saccharine. Rice is also protected by tariff, but imports, particularly of long grain rice, have increased in recent years. Finally, both products are distinctive in that they are subject to production control.

Sugar production is regulated by a system of marketing quotas ('mill peaks') for sugar mills and acreage allotments ('farm assignments') for individual farms. Mill peak production receives a pooled price which reflects the returns obtained from 'high price' markets,[30] while production in excess of the mill peak receives a lower price based on free export market prices. Rice production is limited by means of individual acreage allotments, which are determined by the irrigation authority in consultation with producer, processor and marketing interests. Not surprisingly, each industry is characterized by high and rising yields per acre.

POULTRY PRODUCTS

In each State except Tasmania, intra-state marketing of eggs is controlled by egg marketing boards. The Australian Egg Board, established by Commonwealth statute, handles the export trade, acting as agent for the State marketing boards. In recent years exports, mainly in the form of egg pulp, have amounted to about 14 per cent of total commercial production. Prices received for exports are substantially below prices charged on the domestic market. For the three years ended 1962-63, the pooled price received by growers exceeded export parity by 53 per cent, but if the pooled price is compared with the import parity price, the degree of protection was less than 20 per cent.

---

30. More precisely, the price is a weighted average of prices received for domestic sales, for exports under the British Commonwealth Sugar Agreement, for exports to the U.S.A., and for exports to Japan (at world prices).

There are several reasons why the monopoly power of State egg marketing boards is severely limited. First, small-scale and 'back-yard' producers, whose aggregate production is substantial, are exempt from board control. Second, commercial producers have a strong incentive to sell eggs illegally, within their own State, so avoiding the levies imposed by the boards to equalize returns between the home and overseas markets. Illegal sales are difficult to police since many small producers are involved. Third, commercial producers are free to sell eggs interstate on their own behalf under the protection of Section 92 of the Constitution. Data on non-commercial production, and illegal commercial sales are not available, but, according to official estimates of egg consumption—which must, of course, be accepted with some reserve—about half of total Australian consumption of shell eggs is not marketed through egg marketing boards. Interstate sales have been estimated at at least 30 million dozen in 1963-64, compared with total domestic sales through egg boards in that year of 85 million dozen.

In order to protect the boards from interstate and illegal competition, the Commonwealth government in 1965 introduced a scheme whereby a levy is imposed on hens kept for commercial purposes. The receipts from the levy are used to meet trading losses on exports, the rate of levy being varied as necessary for this purpose. An anticipated by-product of this legislation is a substantial rise in the productivity of Australian hens.

Production of broiler chickens has expanded rapidly in Australia in recent years. According to unofficial estimates, consumption per head of this type of poultry meat increased from 3·3 lbs to 9·5 lbs between 1959-60 and 1964-65. As is the case overseas, this industry has a vertically-integrated structure: probably in the vicinity of 90 per cent of broilers are produced under contract between the grower and a processor (who may be associated with a feed mill or hatchery).[31]

FRUITS AND VEGETABLES

Commonwealth marketing boards regulate the export of dried vine fruits, canned fruits, and apples and pears. Each board has power to license exports, to determine minimum prices and terms of sale, to negotiate freight rates, and to engage in promotional activities. In the case of the Australian Canned Fruits Board, these powers are exercised only in respect of exports to the United Kingdom.

Sales of dried vine fruits on the home market are regulated by an industry organization, the Australian Dried Fruits Association. This body also arranges for equalization of returns to growers from all markets. Participation in the home marketing scheme is voluntary, but it receives overwhelming support from packers, agents and distributors. The structure of orderly marketing for dried vine fruits thus closely resembles that for butter and

31. D. McConnell, 'Contract Farming and the Broiler Industry', *Australian Journal of Agricultural Economics*, Vol 10, No 2, December 1966.

cheese. A price stabilization scheme for dried vine fruits was introduced in 1964.

The Australian Canned Fruits Board's costs of administration and its promotional activities are financed by a levy on canned fruit exported and an excise tax on canned deciduous fruit consumed in Australia. Canners receive a rebate on sugar used, provided they buy fresh fruit at prices which are considered to be reasonable by the Fruit Industry Sugar Concession Committee. This is to compensate them for the high domestic price of sugar and enable them better to compete on overseas markets.

Fresh fruits and vegetables are sold in local markets but predominantly through central markets in capital cities. The physical facilities in these markets are usually owned by the city council and leased to market operators who include grower-sellers, commission agents, producer cooperative societies, and primary and secondary merchants. The principal buyers are retailers, but purchases are also made by wholesale merchants, agents for catering establishments, ships providors, processors, and by householders. Sellers tend to specialize in the type of produce they handle. The physical facilities are in general old and inadequate and located in areas of considerable traffic congestion.[32]

Prices of fresh fruits and vegetables fluctuate considerably due to their perishability and seasonal production pattern.[33] Demand for some—for example potatoes—is very inelastic, so that fluctuations in output result in very sharp price movements. Unstable prices, together with grower suspicion of middle-men has led to the establishment of State marketing boards for some horticultural products. However a number of these boards have not lived up to expectations and have been dissolved. The indifferent record of orderly domestic marketing of fruits and vegetables can probably be attributed to the difficulties of dealing with perishable products of variable quality, conflicts of interest among growers, limited opportunities for practising price discrimination, and managerial incompetence.

In Queensland, a statutory organization, the Committee of Direction of Fruit Marketing (C.O.D.), undertakes a variety of marketing activities. Some of these, such as the organization of rail transport of produce to market, operation as wholesale agent, as canner, and as retailer in competition with the private trade, are essentially the activities engaged in by a producer

---

32. Further information on fruit and vegetable marketing in Sydney and Melbourne is available in the following: *Official Year Book of New South Wales*, No 58, 1964, pp 935-6; J. Van der Meulen, 'The Organization of the Sydney Potato Trade', *Review of Marketing and Agricultural Economics*, Vol 28, No 4, December 1960; N. D. Honan, 'The Marketing of Fresh Fruit and Vegetables in Melbourne', *Quarterly Review of Agricultural Economics*, Vol 11, No 1, January 1958.

33. Seasonal price patterns for fruits and vegetables in New South Wales are described in 'Some Economic Aspects of Vegetable Marketing', *Review of Marketing and Agricultural Economics*, Vol 26, No 1, March 1958, and 'Some Economic Aspects of Fruit Marketing', *Review of Marketing and Agricultural Economics*, Vol 26, No 2, June 1958.

cooperative. However, the C.O.D. has power to issue directions regarding the disposal of produce. Directions have been used to exclude lower grade or small size produce from the market in times of glut, and to control the sale of fruit to processors.[34]

Specialist fruiterers' shops are the main retail outlet for fresh fruits and vegetables. Between 1956-57 and 1961-62 fruiterers' share of total retail sales declined very slightly, from 75 per cent to 73·7 per cent. Over the same period sales by grocers increased from 16·7 per cent to 18·2 per cent of the total. As has been the case with meat, growth of self-service retailing of fruits and vegetables has been slow.

CONCLUSION

The story of agricultural marketing policy in Australia is for the most part one of the efforts of primary producers to organize themselves and governments for the purpose of obtaining higher prices for their products. Improving marketing efficiency, in the sense of getting the operations making up the distribution process performed with the expenditure of less resources than previously, has not engaged the attention of organized agriculture or of governments to anything like the same extent. Pricing efficiency and the whole problem of integrating agricultural production and marketing more effectively, have likewise been subordinated.[35]

Unfortunately, these remarks apply to research in agricultural marketing, as well as to marketing policy. Hence while there is a relative abundance of descriptive and some analytical material on orderly marketing arrangements, little research has been done on such topics as price formation, transportation and storage problems, grading, promotion, the processing and retailing sectors, market structure, and marketing efficiency. However, in fairness it must be said that this situation is changing for the better. The Australian Wool Board is financing research into wool marketing, and the recent controversy concerning wool marketing also stimulated research in this area. However, other rural industry organizations have disbursed research funds mainly for production research, with the result that marketing research has received much less support than it surely deserves. Much of what has been spent by industry organization on market research has been devoted to projects undertaken by commercial research organizations and the results are not available to the public.

34. John M. Clark, 'The Direction of Fruit and Vegetable Marketing in Queensland', *Quarterly Review of Agricultural Economics*, Vol 10, No 1, January 1957.

35. J. N. Lewis, *op. cit.*, p 1.

CHAPTER 15

AGRICULTURAL PRICE POLICIES

J. N. LEWIS
University of New England

Unique features are not to be expected in Australian price policy for agriculture, as there is a limited number of basic methods for controlling or influencing commodity prices. Nevertheless, because of the way these methods are employed and combined, Australia's policy does have a number of characteristics which distinguish it from policies in other countries, and impart to it a certain antipodean flavour.

In order to identify these characteristics and to explain how and why they have developed, we need to take account of the objectives of price programmes; the institutional constraints and economic background; methods of price support, and the levels of protection afforded agricultural industries.

The varied and piecemeal nature of price programmes for Australian agriculture prompted Crawford to observe that perhaps the most tempting thing to say about Australian agricultural policy was that there isn't one.[1] However Crawford went on to reject this proposition, for there are consistent patterns running through Australian price policy for agriculture. Much of the diversity results from differing circumstances and needs.

SETTING AND OBJECTIVES OF AUSTRALIAN POLICY
OBJECTIVES

The usual difficulties of identifying the objectives of government agricultural policy apply in Australia where white papers or official manifestos expressing government policy about agriculture are rare.[2] Proceedings of the Australian Agricultural Council are not made available to the public. One must rely mainly on fragmentary indications of intentions such as press releases and public statements of government members, officials and industry leaders together with second-reading speeches of ministers introducing legislation into parliament.

1. J. G. Crawford, 'Australian Agricultural Policy', Joseph Fisher Memorial Lecture, University of Adelaide, 1952.
2. Two such statements issued since World War II are: A Rural Policy for Postwar Australia, Ministry of Postwar Reconstruction, Canberra 1946; and Agricultural Production Aims and Policy, Department of Commerce and Agriculture, Canberra 1952.

Moreover, objectives are not always frankly or fully stated, and rationalizations of policy tend to be based on appeals to abstract goals and to be expressed in emotive terms. Nearly all support measures introduced in Australia have been presented as being imperative for more efficient use of resources, for greater welfare of farmers, for the achievement of stable prices which are fair to producer and consumer alike, and for the avoidance of unfair, ruinous, cut-throat or destructive competition. Objectives are often more accurately expressed in actual decisions than in statements of intention.

THE EMPHASIS ON STABILIZATION

When the sacrifices tolerated to achieve a measure of price stability are considered, the conclusion is inescapable that either Australian price policy has been particularly inept or that very high values have been placed on stabilization as such. Price stabilization in the pure sense, as distinct from stabilization upwards, has been a major element, if not a costly obsession, in the objectives of Australian policy. Stabilization has usually been put forward on the grounds that it facilitates farm management planning, reduces capital rationing and supplements fiscal and monetary measures for general economic stability. The strong desire of governments and producers for price stabilization undoubtedly reflected the lingering attitudes left behind by the depressed conditions of the 1930s, and from certain aspects of wage policy discussed below.[3]

The preoccupation with price stabilization has been attacked by Campbell[4] on the grounds that under certain conditions it could accentuate income instability, discourage growth and mask the need to deal with the more serious problem of production instability in a most uncertain environment.

On several occasions in the last decade measures to provide greater price stability for wool have been advocated on somewhat different grounds. A buffer stock scheme has been advocated for wool as a means of safeguarding demand against competition of man-made fibres which, it is alleged, is intensified by their greater price stability. This campaign culminated in a referendum of wool growers in 1965, which resulted in the rejection of the plan. The issue was clouded by the industry's well founded distrust of the claims of some of the more extreme proponents of the plan, who were inclined to look on it either as the first step towards more ambitious organized market-

---

3. The wide range of considerations underlying the stabilization objective and their relationship to the Australian institutional setting have been reviewed in D. H. McKay, 'Stabilization in Australian Agriculture, A Review of Objectives', *Australian Journal of Agricultural Economics*, Vol 9, No 1, June 1965.

4. K. O. Campbell, 'National Commodity Stabilization Schemes: Some Reflections Based on Australian Experience', in R. N. Dixey (ed), *International Explorations of Agricultural Economics*, Iowa State University Press, Ames 1964, ch 6; and K. O. Campbell, 'Economic Aspects of Agricultural Stabilisation Schemes', *Journal of the Australian Institute of Agricultural Science*, Vol 16, No 4, December 1950.

ing programmes or as all that was necessary to achieve major increases in average prices.[5]

Stabilization in the limited sense of dampening fluctuations has been prominent amongst the objectives of price programmes. But it would be quite misleading to suggest that this motive has been consistently the dominant one. Many programmes have clearly, if not always explicitly, set out to put farmers in a position to exert the monopoly powers necessary to enable them to appropriate consumer surpluses or otherwise to achieve income transfers from other sectors of the economy. The initial justification advanced for such programmes, of course, often stresses the need to strengthen the position of weak sellers confronted by elements of monopsony in product markets.

Moreover price programmes have in a number of cases been used as a means of encouraging interregional resource shifts, including the stimulation of agricultural production in the 'empty' North. Price programmes for sugar in particular and possibly beef (the 15 Year Meat Agreement with the United Kingdom) have been influenced by this goal. Other instruments of policy, such as government expenditures on beef roads, water conservation and land development projects, have also been used extensively for this purpose.

INSTITUTIONAL FACTORS

Two major institutional factors influencing the shape of Australia's agricultural price policy are the marketing boards described in Chapter 14, and the limitations of marketing powers under the Federal Constitution.

The constitutional division of powers has been one of the most pervasive and powerful influences upon the development of Australian agricultural price policy.[6] Indeed it is hardly an exaggeration to say that the history of agricultural price policy in Australia is largely the story of frustrations suffered by primary producers in achieving the necessary conditions for successful price discrimination and of the devices resorted to in order to circumvent or overcome limitations upon group or government action towards this end.

The most troublesome provision in the Commonwealth Constitution is Section 92 which states that:

> on the imposition of uniform duties of customs, trade, commerce, and intercourse among the States, whether by means of internal carriage or ocean navigation, shall be absolutely free.

5. For a review of the discussion of this issue and a bibliography, see A. G. Lloyd, 'Reserve Price Scheme for Wool—A Defence', *Economic Record*, Vol 41, No 96, December 1965; and J. H. Duloy and R. M. Parish, 'An Appraisal of a Floor Price Scheme for Wool', *New England Marketing Studies No 1*, University of New England, Armidale, December 1964.

6. See A. G. Lloyd, 'The Marketing of Dairy Produce in Australia', *Review of Marketing and Agricultural Economics*, Vol 18, No 1, March 1950; and Rural Reconstruction Commission, *Commercial Policy in Relation to Agriculture, Tenth Report*, Government Printer, Canberra 1946, ch 1.

The drafters of the Constitution almost certainly had in mind nothing beyond the immediate abolition, upon federation, of tariffs and other protective measures affecting items entering interstate trade. However, as interpreted by the courts, Section 92 has hampered the efforts of Australian primary producers and of State and Commonwealth governments to organize price support programmes. It provides a convenient escape for persons unwilling to participate in programmes or seeking to appropriate for themselves a disproportionate share of the benefits. Thus producers, processors and distributors have been able to plead Section 92 as justifying non-compliance with measures to compel marketing through a board or to impose supply controls. Until recently egg producers in southern Queensland managed to evade marketing controls in their State by sending their produce on a short joyride across the New South Wales border on the way to market on the Queensland Gold Coast. The legal doors have now been closed against this practice.

However, some of the more important court judgments continue to impede and curtail the practicability of price programmes for agricultural products. The constitutional validity of two price schemes for dairy produce and dried vine fruits was tested in the *James* case of 1936. James, a dried vine fruit grower and packer, sought to evade the requirement imposed by regulations that fruit could not be sold interstate until prescribed export quotas had been filled by shipping his fruit interstate. His fruit was confiscated and he appealed to the Australian High Court citing Section 92. James emerged the ultimate victor in the prolonged litigation which followed and the legality of the price support schemes was overturned.

The use of a tax on local consumption, with the proceeds used to make up the return on exports to a guaranteed level or by a specified amount, has been one method employed from time to time to overcome the consequences of the *James* case. However, even to this day, the schemes for dairy products and dried vine fruits still rest, strictly speaking, on voluntary price equalization arrangements, backed by some persuasion in the form of licensing of packing houses. This necessity tends to make two-price schemes more practicable for commodities passing through a relatively limited number of processing points than for those sold largely unprocessed to consumers.

As a further consequence of this position, and because of the changing interpretations of the Constitution over the years, there has been uncertainty about just what is practicable. Section 92 has been a happy hunting ground for lawyers but a source of hesitance and occasionally a rationalization of inaction amongst producer organizations and governments. Moreover, many attempts to organize supply management programmes have been frustrated via this constitutional escape route.

Further difficulties are caused by the constitutional division of powers. Powers over production and price control are amongst the residual powers allocated, by non-specification in Commonwealth powers, to State governments. Consequently, many price support and stabilization schemes require complementary legislation by both State and Federal governments. This prolongs and complicates the passage of enabling legislation; it also restricts the application of certain methods, such as production controls. Consequently other approaches to price support and stabilization tend to be preferred.

This situation persists despite several attempts at constitutional amendment. Constitutional referenda in Australia have an almost unbroken record of negation of proposed change. Proposals to transfer powers of orderly marketing and price control to the Commonwealth government have invariably been rejected.

ECONOMIC BACKGROUND

A further important factor underlying the particular forms of Australian agricultural price policy is the relationship between agriculture and the general economy.

Industrial protection and the concept of the 'living wage' have given rise to pressures from primary producers for price supports to compensate them for the higher burden of costs resulting from the operation of the tariff. This was particularly so during the 1930s when many of the multiple-price programmes for agricultural products had their beginnings or were intensified. Most of the more intensive industries, e.g. dairying and irrigated crops, have sought a hair of the protection dog for themselves. In the pastoral industries, on the other hand, there has often been a strong disinclination towards government control over marketing, with consistent opposition to protection for secondary industries and to wage cost increases.

This difference in approach to protection between industries can possibly be explained, to some extent, by the fact that about 95 per cent of wool production is exported. A home price scheme would offer no substantial benefit. Moreover it is widely felt that wool is so important in the economy that subsidy payments of any kind could not be afforded. This attitude possibly reflects a lingering belief in the dictum that 'Australia rides on the sheep's back'. Although wool still accounts for about 35 to 40 per cent of export income, its share of the Gross National Product is now only about 4 per cent.

So far as welfare aspects of price policies are concerned, Australia does not have a serious farm problem in the sense of relatively depressed labour earnings in agriculture; but it does have a proportion of low-income farms and several depressed agricultural regions.[7] Price policies have been used as a means of dealing with these problems.

7. J. N. Lewis, 'Agricultural Science and Productivity in the Next Decade—Economics', *Journal of the Australian Institute of Agricultural Science*, Vol 28, No 2, June 1962; and see also *Report of the Committee of Economic Enquiry*, Commonwealth of Australia, Canberra 1965, Vol I, pp 155-83.

v

CLASSIFICATION OF PROGRAMMES

A classification[8] of the price support and stabilization measures for each of the major agricultural commodities is presented in Table 15-1.

The framework used for this classification is the usual division into: measures to control or influence supply; measures to influence demand and measures which directly augment or stabilize prices. In applying this division, there may be legitimate differences of opinion concerning the appropriate pigeonhole for particular devices or instruments of price support. For example, some writers choose to regard the various forms of price discrimination as measures to shift demand, presumably because, for a given quantity, total revenue is increased by separating markets and discriminating between them.[9] The aggregate demand schedule, it is contended, is thereby moved upwards and to the right.

Despite this viewpoint, the present tabulation of measures regards such multiple-price schemes as a form of supply management. Their purpose is to capture for agricultural producers some of the consumer surplus formerly existing in part of the market. The task is essentially to control the flow of supply to separate markets and to prevent intermarket substitution. The underlying demand relationships are not necessarily changed.

Export subsidies to reduce supplies on the home market have been included under the same general heading of supply management rather than regarded as direct price influences. On the other hand, public consumption measures such as school milk programmes have been included with the demand shifters on the somewhat arbitrary ground that the industry is not itself pursuing price discrimination; it is the government that distributes free milk after buying it from producers at the usual wholesale price. Furthermore, supply restrictions on substitute commodities have been treated as a measure to increase demand for the agricultural commodity concerned, although here it is simply a matter of how widely the commodity is defined (e.g. as butter or as edible oils and fats) which determines whether specific measures are properly supply controls or demand influences.

Product promotion campaigns, financed through levies on producers (with, in the case of wool, a matching contribution from the Commonwealth government), are not tabulated as price support measures. They are so imprecise in their effects that they have not here been regarded as part of agricultural price policy. If these were included in price policy measures, there would be a case for also including general economic measures such as taxation, social services programmes, and assisted immigration which often have incidental

8. This section is based largely on an earlier paper: J. N. Lewis, 'Methods of Agricultural Price Support and Stabilization', *Illinois Agricultural Economics*, Vol 4, No 2, July 1964.

9. Amongst those who classify some or all forms of price discrimination as measures to increase demand are D. G. Johnson, *Trade and Agriculture*, Wiley, New York 1950, p 35; D. E. Hathaway, *Government and Agriculture*, Macmillan, New York 1963, ch 11; and R. Schickele, *Agricultural Policy*, McGraw-Hill, New York 1954.

Table 15-1

A Classification of Agricultural Price Programmes, 1966[a]

	Wheat	Whole milk	Butter, cheese and processed milk	Beef	Sugar	Cotton	Tobacco	Rice	Raisins, sultanas, currants	Eggs	Peanuts
1. SUPPLY MANAGEMENT CONTROLLING											
(i) Supply level											
Restrictions of inputs (W = water, L = land).					L			L/W	W		
Import restrictions (T = tariff, Q = quantitative).	T		T		Q	T	T	T	T	T	T
Marketing quotas		X			X		X		T	T	T
(ii) Supply diversion											
Time (buffer stock)	X										
Place (home consumption price)			X		X			X	X	X	
Purpose (price discrimination by end use)		X			X					X	X
Class of consumer (price discrimination by income class or quantity purchased)		X[b]									
2. DEMAND INFLUENCES											
Mixing regulations or induced purchase by tariff arrangement		X			X	X	X				X
Restriction of substitutes		X	X		X						
Public consumption					X						
Export contracts—bilateral	X			X[c]	X						
3. DIRECT PRICE AUGMENTATION											
Buffer fund	X								X		
Deficiency payment subsidy	X					X			X		
Flat rate or fixed amount subsidy			X								

a. No price support or stabilization programmes currently operate for wool or for mutton and lamb.

b. Discounts on retail deliveries to consumers in excess of certain level.

c. The 15 Year Meat Agreement with United Kingdom until 1967.

effects on demand for agricultural products. Classification of measures by intent is admittedly unsatisfactory but a line must be drawn somewhere, and Table 15-1 helps to identify some of the features of Australian agricultural policy and to indicate the preferred methods and combinations of methods of price support and stabilization.

The classification in Table 15-1 shows that some measures, such as buffer stocks and price discrimination by income group (e.g. food stamp plan) are not used at present although some use of the buffer stock principle has been made from time to time, as in wool marketing during and after both world wars. However, Australia makes use of most of the other cards in the price policy pack, and some of them are particularly well thumbed.

As between commodities there are certain noteworthy tendencies. No price supports as such operate for products of the pastoral industry—wool, beef, lamb and mutton. A long-term contract for Australian meat survives, until 1967, the termination of bulk purchase by the United Kingdom Ministry of Food.

There is a strong predisposition in Australian price policy towards supply diversion programmes. The home consumption price scheme, involving price discrimination between domestic and export markets, is the most preferred means of price support. It is used, in conjunction with other methods, for wheat, dairy products, dried vine fruits, sugar, rice and eggs. Multiple-price schemes, involving price discrimination between end uses of products are used for milk, sugar, eggs and peanuts. Price discrimination in favour of wheat used for livestock feed was a part of the Wheat Industry Stabilization Plan during the war and immediate postwar years.

Except in the case of whole milk, where quota entitlements to higher priced outlets operate, pooling has been the usual method employed in Australia for sharing the benefits of multiple-price programmes equitably amongst producers. This involves the payment of an equalized price, the average net realization from all markets and end uses, to all producers. The use of price pooling of this kind has been criticized by agricultural economists.[10] The essential difficulty is that this device creates divergence between private and social marginal returns. Individual farmers plan their operations on the basis of receiving the equalized price for additional output, but only the export price or the return from a lower priced use accrues to the industry as a whole. As production responds to higher prices erosion of benefits of multiple-price schemes occurs, unless the home market grows as fast as production and export returns are not depressed by the additional quantities sold. Moreover the differences between the equalized price and the industry's marginal return tend to be capitalized into fixed asset values, especially land and livestock. The result is that alternative enterprises, such as forestry or

10. J. N. Lewis, 'Organized Marketing of Agricultural Products in Australia', *Australian Journal of Agricultural Economics*, Vol 5, No 1, September 1961.

beef production in dairy areas, often face inflated factor prices, which impede land-use adjustments and distort interregional competition in these
products. Incentives for marketing improvements and for aggressive competition also tend to be reduced.

This weakness in Australia's two-price programmes is compounded by the
lack of production control to offset inbuilt inducements to expand output.
Production controls operate in relatively few industries. For sugar, restrictions on land inputs operate side by side with marketing quotas both for
individual farms and for mills. Sugar is produced mainly in one State,
Queensland, and problems of imposing and enforcing production restrictions
are thereby simplified. For tobacco, individual grower quotas have operated
since 1965. For rice, the New South Wales Water Conservation and Irrigation
Commission limits the area which may be grown by individual producers as
well as the supply of irrigation water. For dried vine fruits some degree of
production control, in the form of restrictions on water diversion for irrigation also exists. In general, however, so far as supply control is concerned,
the constitutional allocation of powers over production to the State governments puts severe practical difficulties in the way of this form of price
support.

Considerable use is made, however, of supply controls which restrict imports or increase the price of imported supplies. Import duties and in a few
cases quantitative restrictions (for example, an embargo on sugar imports
and prohibition of margarine imports unless coloured pink by the admixture
of alkanet root) are often used in conjunction with home consumption price
programmes. These are a necessary adjunct, to keep domestic and export
markets separate by discouraging re-imports and to discourage or prevent
altogether imports which might otherwise be attracted by higher domestic
price levels. Import duties on some products are vestigial and not currently
needed to protect the Australian industry's home consumption price. Thus
the small import duty on wheat would appear unnecessary in the light of
present price relationships and ocean freight rates.

A characteristic feature of Australian price programmes is the partiality
towards measures to induce full purchase of the domestic crop without increasing the landed price of imports. For several products, waiver of import
duties or concessional rates have been granted to individual processors under
by-law, provided they have used prescribed minimum percentages of Australian products; or to processors generally if disposal of the Australian crop
has been completed.

A deficiency fund type subsidy on domestic cotton production is used with
the same objective of avoiding unnecessary increases in the prices of raw
materials obtained principally from overseas, flowing from price support
operations.

A further characteristic has been the extent of the use of the buffer fund or stabilization fund device, by which transfers of export receipts over time are made. Under such schemes, when export prices exceed the guaranteed price, proceeds of a tax or levy are paid into a stabilization fund, which is drawn upon later when necessary to augment prices received for exports. In all cases to date in Australia this device has been associated with a minimum price guarantee with an obligation on the part of the government to make up by deficiency payment any inadequacy in the fund. A stabilization fund of this kind is currently part of the price support programmes for wheat and dried vine fruits. It was also a feature of the first five-year dairy industry stabilization plan adopted in 1947 but was not continued in subsequent extensions of the plan.

LEVEL OF SUPPORTS

Since 1947 some use has been made in Australia of the criterion of unit costs of production or movements in production costs to determine levels of guaranteed prices (and price supports without specific guarantee). The 'principle' that prices received by producers should equal costs of production, was accepted in the government price programmes for wheat and dairy products introduced in 1947 and 1948. Naturally enough, pressures ensued for the extension of this criterion to other industries and costs of production surveys became one of the main preoccupations of the Commonwealth Bureau of Agricultural Economics. This preoccupation was unfortunate in that it prevented the Bureau from engaging in more analytically oriented and productive research. It used the name of agricultural economics to lend respectability and an air of objectivity to the annual haggle over cost assessments.

Australian policy makers soon retreated from the use of the costs of production criterion in price determination. This criterion is a particularly inappropriate one for a country whose agriculture is so dependent upon external markets and a particularly difficult one to apply meaningfully when more than one commodity is produced on the farms concerned. Nevertheless assessment of cost movements continues to form part of the industry stabilization schemes for wheat and dried vine fruits.

Levels of protection of Australia's agricultural commodities have been calculated by Harris on a number of alternative bases.[11] His measures include protection afforded by tariffs, other price support measures and government-enforced or government-facilitated marketing organization. His results are shown in Tables 15-2 and 15-3. Levels of price support are extremely variable between commodities. On the basis of the ratio of actual returns received to export parity prices, he found that amongst the highest levels of protection

11. S. F. Harris, 'Some Measures of Levels of Protection in Australia's Rural Industries', *Australian Journal of Agricultural Economics*, Vol 8, No 2, December 1964.

Table 15-2

Protection Levels for Agricultural Export Industries: Ratios

Commodity	Ratio I[a]			Ratio II[b]			Ratio III[c]		
	Averages for 3 years ended			Averages for 3 years ended			Averages for 3 years ended		
	1948-49	1955-56	1962-63	1948-49	1955-56	1962-63	1948-49	1955-56	1962-63
	%	%	%	%	%	%	%	%	%
Butter[d]	98	125	159	89	114	139	−22	23	73
Cheese[d]	102	122	134	87	105	111	−28	9	22
Wheat	79	101	107[g]	73	93	102[g]	−81	−22	11[g]
Sugar	89	114	135	78	104	126	−39	10	72
Eggs	102	125	153	85	108	119	−27	13	30
Currants									
Sultanas	103	113	118[h]	97	108	113[h]	−8	27	40[h]
Raisins									
Barley[e]	80	104	107[h]	77	97	100[h]	−72	−14	−2[h]
Rice[f]	97	109	114	94	104	109	−25	10	23

a. Total actual returns as percentage of total sales valued at export parity.
b. Total actual returns as percentage of sum of total domestic sales valued at import parity plus total actual export returns.
c. Actual returns from domestic sales (including direct support) less domestic sales valued at import parity, expressed as a percentage of domestic sales valued at export (f.o.b.) values.
d. Includes bounty.
e. Relates to barley produced in South Australia and Victoria only.
f. Relates to rice produced in New South Wales only.
g. Includes Commonwealth contribution to Wheat Stabilization Fund.
h. Estimates shown are for three years ended 1961-62.

SOURCE: S. F. Harris, 'Some Measures of Levels of Protection in Australia's Rural Industries', *Australian Journal of Agricultural Economics*, Vol 8, No 2, December 1964, p 134.

during the three-year period 1960-61 to 1962-63 were those for several import-competing or non-export products, notably cotton 86 per cent, tobacco 53 per cent and peanuts 39 per cent for 1963. Of export products, butter 59 per cent, cheese 34 per cent, sugar 35 per cent and eggs 53 per cent enjoyed the highest rates of protection. Returns on grains were somewhat above export parity during this period—wheat by 7 per cent, barley 7 per cent and rice 14 per cent. Average returns for dried vine fruits were 18 per cent above export parity. On the other hand wool sold at export parity and beef, lamb and mutton, although subject to an import duty of 1·5d (1·25 cents) per lb, were in effect unprotected because domestic sales were at export parity modified only by internal transport costs and seasonal price differentials.

The general trend, apparent from Harris' tabulations, is increasing relative protection for Australia's agricultural commodities during the 10 to 15 years ending 1962-63. As he points out, much of this increase is explainable in terms of declining world prices for agriculture commodities rather than rising absolute levels of price support in Australia.

A further important feature, revealed by Harris, is that Australia's price

Table 15-3

Protection Levels for Agricultural Export Industries: Values[a]

Commodity	Column I[b] Average for 3 years ended			Column II[c] Average for 3 years ended		
	1948-49	1955-56	1962-63	1948-49	1955-56	1962-63
	$m.	$m.	$m.	$m.	$m.	$m.
Butter[d]	1·4	35·4	66·6	−9·0	20·8	50·2
Cheese[d]	0·2	4·2	7·0	−1·6	1·2	2·8
Wheat	−54·0	4·4	25·2[g]	−71·8	−36·8	8·0[g]
Sugar	−4·4	12·4	35·2	−10·4	4·2	27·6
Eggs	1·0	9·4	37·0	−4·2	3·4	7·8
Currants Sultanas Raisins	0·2	1·4	2·6[h]	−0·2	1·0	2·0[h]
Barley[e]	−4·4	1·2	1·6[h]	−5·6	−1·0	−0·1[h]
Rice[f]	−0·1	0·8	1·4	−0·2	0·2	1·0

a. Converted to dollars.
b. Transfer cost (excess of actual returns over export parity).
c. Transfer cost (excess of actual returns over domestic sales at import parity plus total actual export returns).
d. Includes bounty.
e. Relates to barley produced in South Australia and Victoria only.
f. Relates to rice produced in New South Wales only.
g. Includes Commonwealth contribution to Wheat Stabilization Fund.
h. Estimates shown are for three years ended 1961-62.

Source: S. F. Harris, 'Some Measures of Levels of Protection in Australia's Rural Industries', *Australian Journal of Agricultural Economics*, Vol 8, No 2, December 1964, p 134.

policies have often resulted in negative protection for farm products, especially in the early postwar years. Total actual returns have at times been substantially less than export parity, and sometimes for considerable periods. Commodities affected include wheat, barley, sugar and, briefly in the early postwar period, linseed. Moreover actual export returns for several products were depressed by sales, at less than realizable prices, under bilateral contracts to the United Kingdom. Beef was the commodity principally affected. Until 1959 the entire exportable surplus of Australian beef was guaranteed to the United Kingdom under the 15 Year Meat Agreement. Average beef prices rose sharply following the release from the prohibition on exports to other destinations of beef of second quality or lower. Butter exports between 1948 and 1953 probably also suffered substantial price reductions as a result of bulk-sale contracts.

Considerable care is needed, of course, in comparing the ratios calculated by Harris with levels of protection in other countries or for secondary industries in Australia. His paper provides a detailed discussion of the conceptual and measurement problems involved and of potential pitfalls in interpretation.

CHANGES OVER THE YEARS

Superficially one might easily conclude that Australia's policies show a singular lack of responsiveness to changing conditions. Methods and levels of price supports often persist long after changed circumstances would indicate that some recasting of, or more radical changes in, programmes would have been appropriate. However, this conclusion would be expecting an orderliness that seems to be unattainable in agricultural policy. It would ignore both the complex pressures in which such affairs are so often conducted and the fact that policy formulation is a continuing process with its roots firmly in the past.

In this section, therefore, an attempt is made to outline some of the major turning points in agricultural price policy during the last 30 years and to enumerate the most important factors conditioning such changes.

Provision for the first home consumption price scheme was introduced for sugar in 1901 when federation began, although it did not operate as such until Australia became a net exporter of sugar in 1923-24.

A two-price scheme for butter was instituted in 1926. This programme, the Paterson Plan, provided for a levy of 1d (0·83 cents) per lb on factory butter production and payment, from the proceeds, of a subsidy of 3d (2·5 cents) per lb on exports. It was thus a means of diverting butter from the home market to enable domestic prices to be raised above export parity. The scheme had outlived its usefulness by 1934, its benefits to producers having been considerably eroded by expansion of output and consequently a rising proportion of exports, and to a more limited extent by the growth of farm butter production not subject to the levy.

The Paterson Plan was replaced with a different set of arrangements to implement a basically similar two-price plan. The diversion of supply to export was to be achieved by compelling adherence to export quotas, prescribed by export control boards. A similar scheme was extended to dried vine fruits. Although the legislation for these programmes was declared unconstitutional in 1936 the schemes still continue along much the same lines by voluntary equalization arrangements.

The 1930s saw a considerable stimulus to price support programmes. The collapse of world prices combined with increased tariffs sheltering secondary industries, produced pressures for home consumption price schemes. The failure of the use of stockpiling as a means of price support, as experienced by the Federal Farm Board in the United States and similar schemes elsewhere, undoubtedly contributed to the popularity of the two-price plan as a method of price support in Australia, which has persisted to the present day. It also has political appeal in that it is less open to recurring scrutiny than subsidies financed from taxation.

In 1938 the first stabilization programme introduced for the wheat industry also made use of the home consumption price principle. It was implemented through a tax on wheat used for flour milling, the proceeds of which were utilized to support returns from the export market.

During World War II, a new objective influenced agricultural price policy. Home price schemes and other price programmes were employed to contribute to internal wage and price stability. Australian wage policy contained provision for automatic wage adjustments in accordance with movements in the cost of living. Price controls were imposed under defence powers during the war and consumer subsidies were paid on milk, potatoes and tea, which were important components in the cost of living. Price pegging was applied to other items heavily weighted in the consumer price index. Moreover government tolerance for low prices under bilateral export contracts with the United Kingdom was heightened by the same considerations. This form of price control continued during the immediate postwar years. Home consumption prices for a considerable number of products, including leather, rice, wheat, barley, grain sorghum and tallow, were maintained below export price levels in order to prevent inflationary pressures from rising overseas prices for primary products. This use of home consumption price programmes as an anti-inflationary device gave an unusual symmetry to stabilization. As Little[12] put it, the principle of reciprocity was added to the principle of compensation.

Prices substantially below 'world levels' were willingly, even anxiously, accepted by farm organizations as the price of sometimes vaguely defined

12. A. J. Little, 'Some Aspects of Government Policy Affecting the Rural Sector of the Australian Economy with Special Reference to the Period 1939/45-1953', *Economic Record*, Vol 38, No 83, September 1962.

arrangements for future stabilization. The experiences of the Great Depression dominated thinking of farmers and policy makers alike. Between the years 1946-47 to 1952-53 stabilization programmes for wheat transferred no less than $331·8 million from Australian wheat growers to other sections of the community.

Previously, Australian price programmes had exercised perverse effects on production only when export prices were depressed. In the first five years following World War II perverse production effects of price programmes occurred during the period of world food shortage. The consequences of these price relationships, combined with the prolonged disinvestment on farms during the depression and war years and the postwar shortages of producer equipment and materials, caused Australia's rural production to stagnate. By 1951 the index of volume of rural production stood at only 103 per cent of the pre-war level (three years ended 1938-39). A recasting of Australia's agricultural policy at this stage led to higher price support levels for cotton and tobacco together with special steps to relieve shortages of machinery and materials and to encourage rural investment.

Wartime price controls, based largely on cost-plus formulae, also influenced primary producers to press for adoption of the costs of production criteria in the determination of price support levels.

The relative stagnation of international commercial trade in agricultural products during the 1950s and the spread of protectionism and illiberal trade policies for agriculture in other countries, has reinforced Australia's attitude of protection for part of its rural economy. Moreover Australia's approach to international commodity policy has been modified accordingly. Australian negotiators in international trade now seek less vigorously a code of behaviour for national price support policies, which would reduce the disruptive effects on international trade in agricultural products. They do not campaign so strongly for the dismantling of trade barriers. Instead they are often in the vanguard of those who propose international management of agricultural trade in the form of extensive commodity agreements and market access arrangements.

Within Australia price support and stabilization policies have consistently tended to transfer resources to industries in which Australia's competitive position is weakest. As will be apparent from Harris' price ratios, the highest levels of protection are provided for irrigated crops and for dairying, sugar, eggs and other labour intensive enterprises. Those industries in which Australia's generous land base makes it possible for commodities (wool, beef, mutton and lamb, wheat and other grains) to be produced most efficiently enjoy little or no protection.

Such perverse allocative effects represent probably the most serious defect of Australia's price programmes. Other adverse consequences are the discouragement of enterprise in marketing and of quality improvement by price equalization arrangements and the induced inflation of land and livestock values which makes protected industries dependent upon protection.

A further weakness of Australia's agricultural price policy is that many programmes are incomplete in that they fail to nullify the incentives contained in them which encourage expansion of output. If unchecked these supply responses must tend to undermine the effectiveness of the price support measures. Fortunately, Australia has not suffered the full consequences which its price programmes might have been expected to produce, given the probabilities existing when they were instituted. For example the accumulation of stocks might have been expected to follow the decision in 1963 to extend the wheat industry stabilization scheme for another five years along broadly similar lines to earlier programmes. Yet fortuitous marketing opportunities for wheat in mainland China and the U.S.S.R., together with drought conditions in Eastern Australia during 1965 have so far enabled us to dispose of all the wheat grown.

In dairy products the chickens released by the price support programme have come home to roost but they can always be attributed to external factors and not recognized as consequences of Australia's own action.

Agricultural price policy in Australia has always consisted of a series of expedients with the future left to cope with the consequences. In so far escaping most of the unpleasant consequences of these expedients, Australia has justified its designation as 'The Lucky Country'.[13] In any case, as such consequences are usually insidious and difficult to identify from among the complex of variables affecting productivity and welfare in agriculture, policy makers need seldom fear too glaring an exposure of their past ineptitude.

13. Donald Horne, *The Lucky Country*, Penguin, Melbourne 1966.

CHAPTER 16

AGRICULTURAL TRADE AND TRADE POLICY

S. F. HARRIS

Bureau of Agricultural Economics

Trade policy has been defined as 'the broad strategy behind a country's total export and import trade',[1] and commodity policy as 'the extension into the international sphere of national agricultural (or mineral) policy.'[2] This chapter gives less attention to the relationship between domestic agricultural policy and export trade than would be necessary in a discussion concentrating on commodity policy; and although it considers the broad policies designed to maintain and expand rural export markets, it falls short of a discussion of trade policy as defined above. Trade policies interact more and more with policies affecting capital flows, international liquidity and foreign aid; consequently, they need to be seen in the perspective, not only of Australia's agricultural production and marketing policies, but also of the whole range of her international economic relationships.

AGRICULTURAL TRADE

AGRICULTURAL IMPORTS

Australia's interest in agricultural trade is primarily as an exporter. Imports of agricultural commodities are relatively small. This can be seen from Table 16-1 which, following Saxon,[3] classifies imports according to whether they supplement or complement Australian production. Supplementary imports are those similar to agricultural commodities produced commercially in Australia (e.g. cheese), together with those in any significant way interchangeable in use (e.g. soya bean oil). Complementary agricultural imports are those which are not competitive with Australian production (e.g. rubber).

---

1. A. C. B. Maiden, 'Some Aspects of Commodity Policy', *Australian Journal of Agricultural Economics*, Vol 4, No 1, July 1960, pp 3-4.

2. Ibid., p 3. Maiden deals at length with the relationship between commodity policies and domestic stabilization and marketing arrangements.

3. E. A. Saxon, 'Australia as an Agricultural Importer', *Quarterly Review of Agricultural Economics*, Vol 16, No 3, July 1963.

Since 1938-39 total agricultural imports have increased in absolute terms, but have declined as a proportion of total imports. While there has been little difference in the rates of growth of supplementary and complementary imports, the tendency has been for supplementary imports to increase slightly more rapidly.

Table 16-1

Value of Imports of Agricultural Products, 1936-37 to 1965-66
($A million f.o.b.)

		Average for 3 years ended		
	1938-39	1948-49	1956-57	1965-66
Supplementary[a]				
Food	1·2	2·3	6·1	16·8
Non-food	9·0	23·0	54·9	55·4
Total	10·2	25·3	61·0	72·2
Complementary[a]				
Food	8·0	23·9	48·1	49·7
Non-food	7·7	19·9	46·0	47·2
Total	15·7	43·8	94·1	96·9
Total Agricultural Imports	25·9	69·1	155·1	169·1
Total merchandise Imports	251·9	640·3	1,584·0	2,734·5
Value of agricultural imports as per cent of all merchandise imports	10·3	10·8	9·8	6·2

a. These terms are explained in the text.
SOURCE: *Oversea Trade*, Bureau of Census and Statistics.

THE IMPORTANCE OF AGRICULTURAL EXPORTS

The importance of rural commodity exports to Australia explains the emphasis given to agricultural trade policy in Australia. At the same time, her importance as a world trader implies that Australia has a substantial interest in international trade discussions. In terms of the absolute value of total trade, Australia now ranks about thirteenth; as an exporter of agricultural products she ranks second, after the United States.

As explained in earlier chapters, Australia's earnings of foreign exchange depend heavily on agricultural exports. Data in Table 16-2 show that between 70 and 80 per cent of Australia's merchandise exports are of rural origin.[4] Four commodities—wool, wheat, meat, and sugar—have in recent years accounted for almost two-thirds of Australia's export income.

4. For commodity trade policy it is also relevant that mineral commodities form an important part of the remainder of Australia's exports; these commodities are subject to many of the same problems in international trade as are agricultural commodities.

Table 16-2

Value of Major Rural Export Items,[a] 1936-37 to 1965-66

| | 1938-39 | | Average for 3 years ended | | | | | |
| | | | 1948-49 | | 1956-57 | | 1965-66 | |
Commodity	$Am.	Per cent of merchandise Exports	$Am.	Per cent of merchandise Exports	$Am.	Per cent of merchandise Exports	$Am.	Per cent of merchandise Exports
Wool	107·6	39·9	352·1	42·6	816·4	49·7	916·3	34·9
Wheat and flour	43·0	16·0	141·1	17·0	142·3	8·7	342·5	13·1
Sugar	7·9	2·9	11·8	1·4	56·5	3·4	121·0	4·6
Beef and veal	9·3	3·5	11·1	1·3	45·7	2·8	190·8	7·3
Other meats	12·8	4·8	25·3	3·1	54·6	3·3	54·3	2·1
Fruits	11·0	4·1	13·1	1·6	56·4	3·4	84·1	3·2
Butter	21·7	8·0	38·5	4·7	53·8	3·3	60·7	2·3
Other dairy products	3·3	1·2	17·0	2·1	29·7	1·8	44·9	1·7
Eggs	1·6	0·6	10·4	1·3	10·6	0·6	4·3	0·2
All other rural exports	13·0	4·8	77·1	9·3	98·5	6·0	155·7	5·9
Total exports of rural origin	231·2	85·8	697·5	84·4	1,364·5	83·0	1,974·7[b]	75·3
Total merchandise exports	269·4	100·0	826·9	100·0	1,644·1	100·0	2,623·8	100·0

a. All figures in this table refer to Australian produce.
b. Estimate by Bureau of Agricultural Economics.

SOURCE: *Oversea Trade*, Bureau of Census and Statistics.

Australia is the world's largest exporter of wool, supplying over 40 per cent of world trade in this commodity. For some other commodities, such as dried vine fruits and meat, Australian exports represent an important percentage of world trade, as the following table shows.

Table 16-3

Major Agricultural Exports as a Percentage of
World Export Trade, 1935-1965

	Average for			
	4 Years	*3 Years*	*3 Years*	*3 Years*
	ended	*ended*	*ended*	*ended*
Commodity	*1938*	*1948*	*1956*	*1965*
Wool[a]	33·3	38·8	43·6	49·7
Wheat and flour	16·1	8·9	9·7	12·5
Beef and veal	14·7	14·7	19·3	17·1
Mutton and lamb[b]	25·9	11·6	12·4	16·2
Butter	16·2	22·5	14·0	13·2
Cheese	3·1	8·7	4·9	4·7
Sugar[c]	4·4	7·4	5·2	5·9
Eggs in shell	3·0	7·1	2·7	1·7
Eggs (liquid powder)[d]	0·3	19·3	27·7	12·8
Dried vine fruits[e]	17·2	22·4	16·7	16·8

a. Greasy.
b. 1962-1965 figures refer to meat of sheep and goats; mutton and lamb figures being unavailable.
c. Sugar figures up to 1954 were calculated by summing refined and raw sugar. From 1955 onwards, figures are on a raw sugar basis.
d. 1962-1965 figures were calculated on a value basis because of the incompatibility of quantitative data.
e. Dried grapes, raisins, currants and sultanas.
   See also Table 6-8.
SOURCE: *Trade Yearbooks*, FAO.

As a proportion of world trade, Australian exports have shown increases since pre-war days for wool, for sugar and for beef in particular. By contrast, for wheat,[5] butter and shell eggs there has been a decline. For cheese, egg products and dried vine fruits the trend has been variable.

THE PATTERN OF AGRICULTURAL EXPORTS

The geographical distribution of Australia's agricultural trade has changed quite significantly from the pre-war or early postwar periods. (See Table 16-4.) Western European imports of wheat and meats from Australia have tended to fall. Western European imports of wool and sugar have been fairly stable but have declined in relative importance as other export markets have developed.

5. The figure for Australian exports of wheat and flour would be substantially higher if the calculations were based on commercial trade: in recent years, some two-thirds of U.S. exports of wheat and flour have been on non-commercial terms.

As the U.S. market for Australian meat developed in the late 1950s the decline in North America's importance as a market for Australian exports was reversed. Subsequently, increased U.S. imports of Australian sugar, following the curtailment of U.S. imports from Cuba, helped to preserve the level of exports to the U.S.

The major change in Australian export trade in the postwar years has been a switch towards Asia. For wool, meats and sugar this is due primarily to the rapid growth of Japan as a market. For wheat the pattern is more complex. Mainland China in 1963-64 took almost one-third of Australia's wheat exports, whereas no wheat was exported to this market in the early postwar years; and Japan's imports of Australian wheat have increased, though less spectacularly. By contrast, wheat exports to other markets in Asia have declined.

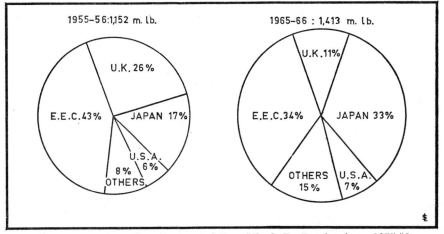

Figure 16-1: Australian Exports of Raw Wool: By Destinations, 1955-56 to 1965-66 (actual weight). (Bureau of Agricultural Economics)

The present trade situation reflects the development of important new markets for Australia's rural exports. Some markets, particularly Japan, are being accepted as permanent changes in the trade pattern. Others, notably the Russian and mainland Chinese markets for wheat, must be regarded as subject to more than normal uncertainties.

Nevertheless, Western Europe, particularly Britain, remains important for most commodities, some of which remain very dependent on these markets. This is particularly so for dairy products—over 80 per cent of butter exports go to Britain—and fruit. It is also true for commodities such as wine and egg products not included in Table 16-4. More generally, for all major commodities other than wheat, Australia still markets over half—and for most, well over half—of her exports in her traditional markets in the industrialized countries of Western Europe and North America.

W

Table 16-4

Destination of Agricultural Exports, 1946-47 and 1965-66

Percentage exported to

Commodity	U.K. 3 years ended		E.E.C. 3 years ended		North America 3 years ended		Japan 3 years ended		All other countries 3 years ended	
	1948-49 %	1965-66 %	1948-49 %	1965-66 %	1948-49 %	1965-66 %	1948-49 %	1965-66 %	1948-49 %	1965-66 %
Wool	31·38	13·46	18·23	28·12	1·07	7·46	36·38	30·74	12·94	20·22
Wheat and flour	25·46	9·88	—	1·22	0·67	—	3·47	6·80	70·40	82·10
Beef and veal	80·65	24·52	—	3·78	1·99	61·79	—	1·68	17·36	8·23
Other meats	73·47	36·16	1·48	1·72	—	27·61	—	10·63	25·05	23·88
Sugar	65·40	37·45	6·16	—	0·47	25·26	—	29·44	27·97	7·85
Butter	88·84	79·83	0·89	1·13	0·37	0·09	0·16	0·36	9·74	18·59
Other dairy	33·29	19·09	—	2·39	0·25	2·42	0·86	4·74	65·60	71·36
Fruits	57·32	55·19	11·42	13·60	—	10·70	—	0·39	31·26	20·12

SOURCE: *Oversea Trade*, Bureau of Census and Statistics.

INSTABILITY OF EXPORT PRICES

There is little need to demonstrate empirically the price instability characteristic of world commodity markets.[6] The reasons for such instability —notably the nature of agricultural production, the conditions of demand and the residual nature of trade for most temperate agricultural products— are well documented and need no elaboration.[7]

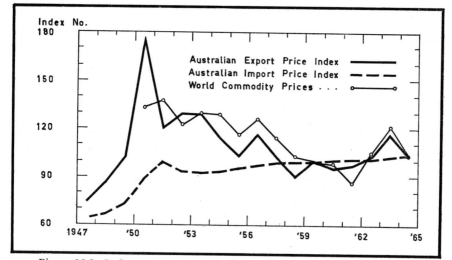

Figure 16-2: Indexes of Prices of Exports and Imports. Base year 1959-60 = 100. (Australian Export Prices: Bureau of Census and Statistics; Agricultural exports by other primary producers: *National Institute Economics Review*, No 1, January 1959 and No 34, November 1965, National Institute of Economic and Social Research, London and *Quarterly Review of Agricultural Economics*, January 1966; Australian Import Prices: Reserve Bank of Australia)

Australia's export income has suffered no less from the instability of world commodity markets than the income of other agricultural exporters. (See Figure 16-2.) The declining proportionate contribution of the rural sector to Australia's Gross National Product and improved methods of economic management have reduced the overall impact of such instability. Nevertheless fluctuations in Australia's export receipts still have considerable significance and the reduction of such instability has been, and remains, an important objective of Australian policy.

6. Some measures of the instability in the markets for 39 major traded commodities for the period 1950 to 1961 are given in 'International Commodity Problems', Department of Economic and Social Affairs, United Nations Secretariat, reprinted in *Proceedings of the United Nations Conference on Trade and Development*, Vol III (Commodity Trade), United Nations, New York 1964, Table 2-1, p 85.

7. A brief summary of the main factors is given in *Trends in International Trade: A Report by a Panel of Experts* (the Haberler Report), General Agreement on Tariffs and Trade, Geneva, October 1958, ch 3, esp. pp 37-39. See also A. C. B. Maiden, 'Stability and Progress in Australian Agriculture', Agricultural Bureau Oration, Adelaide, August 1964.

Because of the geographical concentration of a number of important export industries, income fluctuations in these industries have a more concentrated impact on the economies of the regions associated with them. Domestic marketing arrangements are designed to reduce the impact of price instability in some industries but these arrangements limit, rather than remove, price instability. Furthermore, they do not exist for all industries, the wool and meat industries being notable exceptions.

TRENDS IN EXPORT PRICES

Economists differ on whether there is any basis, theoretical or empirical, for expecting world commodity prices to trend downward in the long term.[8] Nevertheless, since the commodity boom in the early 1950s, prices of Australia's rural export commodities have moved downwards, particularly in relation to prices of imports. (See Figure 16-2.) However, in a world trading system characterized by governmental intervention, stock levels are often more valid indicators of disequilibria in world commodity markets than price levels. Australia has not experienced serious stock accumulation problems in the postwar period, although excess stocks of wheat were held in the mid-1950s. Generally, however, the response to potential surplus accumulation has been some dampening of production, as with wheat in the late 1950s.

AGRICULTURAL TRADE POLICIES

THE HISTORICAL BACKGROUND

In the pre-World War II period, the existing world trading system became completely disorganized. In the 1920s, rather special problems of trade in agricultural commodities had developed and 'agriculture had begun to claim a special place within international trade policy.'[9] Importing countries devised internal support systems which required heavy protection at the frontier. The problems which followed were accentuated and became more general with the commodity price slump and balance of payment problems of the depression years. The disintegration of the world trading system took the form of exchange controls, import quotas and other non-tariff barriers to trade, and the widespread development of bilateral trading arrangements.

Agreement was reached by Commonwealth countries at Ottawa in 1932 to formalize existing preferential arrangements and substantially to extend them. This agreement was important to Australia in providing a firm and continuing link between a number of Australian rural industries and the

8. See G. Haberler, 'An Assessment of the Current Relevance of the Theory of Comparative Advantage to Agricultural Production and Trade', in *Proceedings of the Twelfth International Conference of Agricultural Economists*, Oxford University Press, London 1966, pp 23-25.

9. J. H. Richter, 'The Place of Agriculture in International Trade Policy', *Canadian Journal of Agricultural Economics*, Vol 12, No 2, 1964, p 1.

British market.[10] It was designed to offset the effect of action taken individually by Commonwealth countries to protect their balance of payments in the face of falling commodity prices and the trade restrictions imposed by other countries, including the U.S. Smoot-Hawley tariff.

In the early postwar period, therefore, Australia feared a recurrence of low-commodity prices and was seeking greater security and stability in commodity trade. It was also seeking freer trade in agricultural commodities than existed before the war.

It is probably a fair assessment of the Australian position at this time that in the long term, at least, the international price mechanism was accepted as a satisfactory basis for the allocation of international resources—provided restrictive practices were minimized, particularly quantitative import quotas, dumping and heavy subsidization. Removal of such impediments would provide better marketing opportunities for the more efficient agricultural exporters, in which category for most products Australia had reason to classify herself.

Australian policies of tariff protection to secondary industry and the existence of home consumption price schemes for agricultural products were not necessarily inconsistent with this view. Tariffs for infant industries had a theoretical justification as a departure from free trade; for the most part they did not rule out the possibility of trade, and they were negotiable. Two-price schemes for agricultural products could be regarded either as stabilization schemes, meeting the special short-term problems of trade in agricultural products, while being consistent with the long-term operation of the international price mechanism; or as a defensive reaction to the imperfect operation of the international price mechanism.

THE MAIN AIMS OF AUSTRALIA'S POLICIES

Australia's early postwar agricultural trade policy consisted, and with some variation in emphasis still consists, of three major aims.[11]

First, there was the broad aim of reducing those restrictive practices which affected trade in general and in particular the non-tariff barriers affecting trade in agricultural commodities. This aim was pursued principally through General Agreement on Tariffs and Trade (GATT) but also to some extent through bilateral negotiations.

Second, there was the aim of improving Australia's own competitive position, by means of bilateral trade agreements and negotiations, including those carried out under GATT.

10. W. R. Carney, 'The Ottawa Agreement Now', *Economic Record*, Vol 32, No 52, May 1956.

11. Particular elements of these policies, such as trade promotion activities and export inspection services, while of considerable importance in determining the success of the general policies, will not be discussed here.

Third, a reduction in the instability and unpredictability of primary commodity trade was sought, basically through multilateral commodity agreements, though also through bilateral arrangements.

Each of these three aims will now be considered in the light of the evolution of trade policy over the postwar years.

REDUCING RESTRICTIVE PRACTICES

Clearly, the aim of removing artificial barriers to trade in agricultural commodities has not been achieved. No doubt, the situation would have been substantially worse without the GATT,[12] but during the 1950s it became clear that early hopes of a significant dismantling of agricultural protection would not be realized. For Australia this has had serious repercussions in the search for markets. Developments over the postwar years illustrate how Australia's position has been affected by changes in international trade policies over this period.

In the early postwar period the use of quantitative controls on agricultural trade was widespread. In many cases countries were unwilling, or unable, to remove these when the immediate balance of payments problem had passed; consequently, many tariff concessions, including those negotiated in the early postwar years under the terms of the GATT were rendered of limited value.

Non-tariff barriers and other measures of agricultural protection do not in general enable the efficient producer to sell at the expense of the less efficient producer; they tend to be subject to arbitrary variation and thus to be an insecure basis for trade; and they do not lend themselves to negotiation in a non-discriminatory manner, whereas they are internationally accepted bases for mutual negotiations of tariff reductions. Often their imposition frustrates tariff concessions achieved as the result of bargaining; yet non-tariff barriers have the appearance of not violating the non-discriminatory, most favoured nation, rule which is accepted as the general international principle for tariff protection.

One example of a tariff concession rendered practically valueless for Australia was that negotiated at Geneva in 1947 on dairy product imports into the U.S. These products subsequently became subject to import restrictions, which virtually prohibited imports into that country.[13] Swerling, an Ameri-

---

12. '. . . while in practice the sanctions that can be taken (in the GATT) are limited and can only further restrict international trade, the moral suasion of an international forum, so evidence suggests, has led to the diminishing application of quantitative restrictions,' Gerard Curzon, *Multilateral Commercial Diplomacy*, Michael Joseph, London 1965, p 165.

13. As a result of protests by a number of countries the GATT subsequently authorized the Netherlands, one of the countries affected, to take retaliatory action. The Australian government did not seek such an authority, '. . . which it did not regard as a satisfactory solution to the problem.' D. F. Nicholson, *Australia's Trade Relations*, Cheshire, Melbourne 1955, pp 206-7.

can writer, referring to the GATT waiver granted to the U.S. on its agricultural import restrictions, commented:

> In effect, the waiver was a unilateral privilege granted the United States, that violated the balance of rights and obligations negotiated under the GATT and jeopardised future efforts to free agricultural trade from governmental restrictions.[14]

Although some attempt was made in the 1954 Review of the GATT to strengthen the provisions of the Agreement relevant to agriculture, it was still possible for a Committee of the GATT to reach the broad conclusion in 1961 that:

> there has been extensive resort to the use of non-tariff devices, whether or not in conformity with the General Agreement, which, in many cases, has impaired or nullified tariff concessions or other benefits which agricultural exporting countries expect to receive from the General Agreement. Hence, the Committee concluded that the balance which countries consider they had a right to receive under the General Agreement has been disturbed.[15]

A development of significance for Australian trade was the establishment of the European Economic Community (EEC) in 1957. Australia's agricultural trade problems appeared likely to increase significantly when Britain sought to enter the EEC.[16] The U.K.'s accession to the EEC promised for many important export commodities a situation in which Australia's long-standing preferences would disappear and competing suppliers within the EEC would have a preference over Australia.

Customs Unions such as the EEC are an exception to the GATT principle of non-discrimination. The GATT rule regarding such arrangements is that the regional grouping's restrictions on trade with outside countries should not exceed the average of individual members before the regional grouping came into operation.[17] The agricultural policy of the EEC fell far short of this requirement and and promised to hasten rather than reduce progress towards agricultural self-sufficiency of the Community.[18]

14. Boris C. Swerling, 'Current Issues in Commodity Policy', *Essays in International Finance*, No 38, June 1962, Princeton University, Princeton, New Jersey, p 9. See also Royer's comments on the importance of the U.S. waiver as an influence on attitudes towards the GATT rules affecting agricultural commodities in J. Royer, 'Commercial Policies and Techniques', *Conference on International Trade and Canadian Agriculture*, Queen's Printer, Ottawa 1966, pp 236-7.

15. *Third Report of Committee II*, GATT, Document L/1461, Geneva, May 1961, p 25.

16. See R. J. Cornish and D. L. Carrington, 'The Common Agricultural Policy of the European Economic Community', *Quarterly Review of Agricultural Economics*, Vol 15, No 2, April 1962.

17. Though, as has been pointed out, this is impossible to define operationally. See Harry G. Johnson, *World Economy at the Cross Roads*, Canadian Trade Committee, Private Planning Association of Canada, Montreal 1965, p 27.

18. See R. J. Cornish and J. A. Hempel, 'The Agricultural Policy of the European Economic Community', *Quarterly Review of Agricultural Economics*, Vol 14, No 2, April 1961.

Australia had some basis, therefore, in believing that there was a severe imbalance in its rights and obligations under the GATT; and in questioning an approach based primarily upon attempts to achieve reductions in agricultural protection in Western Europe and the U.S.

IMPROVING AUSTRALIA'S COMPETITIVE POSITION

This second aim of Australia's commodity policy was based on bilateral agreements and negotiations. Many of the wartime bilateral agreements with Britain for Australian agricultural commodities were continued into the postwar period, although trade in wool was freed at the end of the war. The continuation of these contracts reflected in part the fear of substantial declines in commodity prices; it also reflected the beliefs of the parties in office in the two countries as to the methods appropriate for achieving stability and security in agricultural trade.

By the mid-1950s, practically all such bilateral commodity agreements had been discontinued at the initiative of the U.K. For two items, meat and sugar, they had, however, been replaced by long-term agreements. To offset Britain's concern at possible meat shortages and to encourage investment in the Australian beef industry a 15 Year Meat Agreement was negotiated in 1951. It was subsequently extended by one year to 1967. An agreement between the United Kingdom government and the sugar industries in a number of Commonwealth countries, including Australia, was also negotiated. This, the Commonwealth Sugar Agreement, runs until 1973.

Another bilateral agreement which is more widely applicable to Australian export commodities is the 1956 United Kingdom-Australia Trade Agreement. This largely embodies amendments to concessions negotiated or formalized in 1932 at Ottawa including preferences on a number of Australian export products, particularly dairy products, eggs, fruits, and sugar.[19] A major objective of this agreement was to rectify the imbalance in the Ottawa agreement which had developed to Australia's disadvantage over the 24 years of its existence. Reasonable success was also achieved in the objective of obtaining scope for the subsequent negotiation with other countries of improved conditions of access for Australian exports. A number of such trade agreements of significance to agricultural exports were ultimately negotiated, most notably those with Japan.

These trade agreements for the most part are not firm contractual arrangements, though there are some exceptions to this.[20] Where quantitative commitments are negotiated, they do not usually provide assurances of either stable or remunerative prices. Quantitative commitments are particularly

19. The preference on butter has been temporarily waived while the U.K. butter import quota arrangements are in operation.

20. For example, the flour import arrangements negotiated with Ceylon.

difficult to negotiate even where the importer operates quantitative controls on imports, unless the exporter also operates such controls and is prepared to negotiate to operate them in a discriminatory manner. Again, provisions of some agreements related not to import markets in the country concerned, but to the country's subsidized agricultural exports (such as French and German flour) in third markets of interest to Australia.

More recently, arrangements of a rather different kind have operated for particular commodities. In 1962 the United Kingdom introduced quotas on its imports of butter. In 1964 it negotiated, with its major suppliers, including Australia, bilateral agreements to operate minimum price arrangements on cereals.

In 1964, Australia negotiated voluntary quota arrangements with the U.S. for meat. This assured the U.S. that its domestic meat market would not be swamped by imports, while providing Australia with some assurance of access to the U.S. market. The U.S. Congress subsequently imposed a quota arrangement to apply if meat imports exceed a certain level. The quotas which would apply within this arrangement would still, however, provide some assurance of access to Australian exporters as do the sugar import quotas which the U.S. operates.

These various bilateral arrangements have, in a defensive sense perhaps, benefited Australia's agricultural exports; but while the effects of agricultural protection on world agricultural trade remain, the scope and role of these arrangements are limited. They are more likely to be effective in the context of a comprehensive and meaningful solution of overall commodity problems either through GATT action or by means of multilateral commodity arrangements.

REDUCTION OF INSTABILITY IN COMMODITY TRADE

This third aim of Australian agricultural trade policy has been pursued by multilateral commodity agreements and by bilateral arrangements. Commodity agreements, to some extent, could be regarded as one means for some countries to offset the effects of quantitative trade barriers and subsidized competition by other countries; but such agreements, designed to reduce instability in prices, complement rather than replace action limiting or removing restrictive practices. Provided satisfactory action could eventually be expected from GATT to make for the efficient working of the market mechanism in international trade, it was reasonable to view commodity agreements as, for the most part, a means of removing the short-term price instability resulting primarily from characteristics of production and trade in primary commodities. These characteristics such as the short run inelasticities of supply and demand would exist even were governmental barriers to trade removed. This was essentially the basis for Chapter VI of the Havana

Charter, which has at least until recently been the guide book to the negotiation and operation of commodity agreements.[21]

The attempt to achieve international commodity agreements has been an important part of Australia's commodity policy[22] although, as Maiden has pointed out, it is important not to exaggerate its importance:

> an examination of Australian attempts to secure commodity arrangements and other means of procuring some form of price stability for exports is coloured by the absence, since 1951 at any rate, of such direct efforts for wool.[23]

Australia was a member of all but one of the formal postwar commodity arrangements[24] including those for tin and coffee as an importer rather than as an exporter. Nevertheless, agreements have been successfully negotiated for only five commodities and only three,[25] those for wheat, tin and coffee, are at present of significance in world trade.[26] Attempts are being made to negotiate agreements on cocoa and sugar.

There has been disappointment at the limited success achieved in the field of commodity agreements even though, as late as 1958, the stated purpose of the commodity agreements being sought was the stabilization of prices around the long-term trend.[27]

21. Although the Havana Charter was not given formal acceptance, Chapter VI was adopted by the Economic and Social Council of the United Nations in 1947, Resolution 30 (iv). The wording of Chapter VI does envisage a wider role for international commodity agreements. As Gerda Blau has pointed out, however, the equality of voting power provided for producing and consuming countries has virtually limited attempts to negotiate to agreements of a price stabilizing nature where there is, at least in principle, a clear identity of interests. See G. Blau, 'International Commodity Arrangements and Policies', *FAO Monthly Bulletin of Agricultural Economics and Statistics*, Vol 12, No 9, September 1963, p 2.

22. e.g. 'Subject to the overriding importance of buoyant international trade, the most promising and suitable form of international collaboration is through commodity agreements. Rural Reconstruction Commission, *Commercial Policy in Relation to Agriculture, Tenth Report*, Government Printer, Canberra 1946, p 79. See also J. B. Chifley, 'A Rural Policy for Post-war Australia; A Statement of Current Commonwealth Policy in Relation to Australia's Primary Industries', 1947, para 18.

23. A. C. B. Maiden, 'Some Aspects of Commodity Policy', *loc. cit.*, p 7.

24. The only exception was the Olive Oil Arrangement, which was primarily an agreement among Mediterranean regional producers and consumers; it provides for a series of co-ordinated national measures and does not attempt to regulate international trade.

25. At the time of writing, only two, the Tin Agreement being effectively inoperative. The market price had exceeded the ceiling and there were no buffer stocks to release.

26. That is, under the United Nations auspices. The Commonwealth Sugar Agreement should really be regarded as a commodity agreement and a broader definition would include such agreements as the U.K.-Australian Meat Agreement, as well as industry arrangements such as that currently operating for dried vine fruits.

27. Commonwealth governments agree to 'participate in an examination of the situation on a commodity by commodity basis, with a view to arriving, wherever necessary, at understandings about how best, consistently with a recognition of long-term trends in supply and demand, short-term fluctuations could be moderated', *Report of the Commonwealth Trade and Economic Conference*, Montreal 1958, Government Printer, Canberra, p 6.

REASONS FOR LIMITED SUCCESS

The above discussion has indicated how the inadequacy of existing institutional arrangements to cope with the problems of international commodity trade limited the progress that Australia could make toward achieving each of its three main aims of its agricultural trade policy. These inadequacies might now be summarized as follows:

(i) High levels of agricultural protection suggested that long-term prospects were for continued reduction of commercial markets for temperate products and intensified competition from dumped and subsidized products in world markets.

(ii) Agricultural protection and its concomitant non-tariff trade barriers, subsidies, variable levies, etc. have not proved susceptible to action in GATT or elsewhere.

(iii) Tariff concessions negotiated earlier continued to be impaired by non-tariff barriers.

Australia made considerable use of the increased scope for negotiations with other countries obtained as a result of the 1956 review of the U.K. Trade Agreement and relaxations obtained in the conditions of the 15 Year Meat Agreement. While some provisions concerned with market access were negotiated for agricultural commodities in markets where quantitative controls of imports operated, these arrangements frequently remained an insecure and unpredictable basis for trade.

Finally, limited progress was made towards achieving effective multilateral commodity agreements. There appeared little reason to expect, under conditions operating in the 1950s, future negotiations to be significantly more successful than in the past. The failure of postwar commodity agreements was that they had attempted to deal only with the barriers to trade which operated at the frontier, and not with the policies which made those barriers necessary. With the failure to achieve reductions in agricultural protection and meaningful trade rules for agricultural commodities, the reduction of short-term market instability being sought in commodity agreements was insufficient for the development of trade in agricultural commodities.

THE NEED FOR A NEW APPROACH

THE WORLD CONTEXT

Clearly, agricultural trade policies must reflect trends in the world situation for these commodities; similarly they must take account of the development of policies or of policy thinking in the other major trading countries.

An influence of increasing relevance in international discussion of agricultural trade policies is the attitude of the developing countries to problems facing their agricultural exports; and the growing pressures from these countries for new measures to deal with these problems. Although the concern of these countries is frequently directed more immediately to the problems of tropical products, as a group they have a real interest in temperate agricultural commodities both as exporters and as importers.

The predominant feature of the world situation for temperate agricultural commodities in the postwar period has been the tendency for production to exceed effective demand. In the postwar period large surpluses were built up of commodities such as wheat and dairy products, particularly in the U.S., while in Western Europe and the U.S. direct subsidies to exports of surplus agricultural production became more widespread.

Many developing countries were unable to produce, or import commercially, adequate food supplies. This enabled substantial quantities of U.S. surplus food commodities to be disposed of on non-commercial terms. By the early 1960s, concessional sales by the U.S. under P.L. 480[28] became an important feature of trade in a number of commodities. These disposals contribute to meeting the food needs of developing countries; nevertheless they have important implications for countries dependent upon agricultural exports apart from their effects on prices and incomes, and eventually on supplies produced, in the recipient country. Of particular concern to Australia have been concessional sales of wheat: in recent years P.L. 480 disposals of wheat have averaged almost 25 per cent of world wheat exports. Although consultative arrangements were operating under FAO's code of guiding principles,[29] Australia's markets were particularly vulnerable to the effects of this development.

Increasing attention is being given to the means of meeting the gap between the food needs of the developing countries and the productive capacity of existing exporters. Although P.L. 480 was originally a means of making constructive use of surpluses, the U.S. has looked to other temperate food exporters to share this food aid burden. Australia has argued, however, that while it has itself made sizeable donations of wheat, and of other commodities not in surplus in Australia, to developing countries:

> the responsibility should not fall on the food exporting countries alone. The burden of meeting the legitimate food needs of these countries must be shared by all countries which have the ability to contribute.[30]

Increasingly, emphasis in international discussions has been placed on international commodity agreements as a means of resolving problems of

28. The Agricultural Trade Development and Assistance Act of 1954, Public Law 480. See D. L. Riley, 'Recent Developments in U.S. Surplus Disposals', *Quarterly Review of Agricultural Economics*, Vol 16, No 2, April 1963.

29. *FAO Principles of Surplus Disposal and Guiding Lines*, FAO Document C55/22, Rome, July 1955.

30. J. McEwen, Minister for Trade and Industry, *Parliamentary Debates*, House of Representatives, 28 April 1966, p 1288.

international trade in agricultural commodities, and in meeting the food and development needs of developing countries. Undoubtedly, at times, suggestions for international commodity agreements are made too blandly to avoid or defer facing up to the real problems of trade in a commodity. Nevertheless, to many countries, international agreements offer scope for meaningful solutions to problems of trade in agricultural commodities.

By the end of the 1950s, the U.S. found it necessary to reverse its long-standing reluctance to canvass the merits of commodity agreements. This was partly, though not entirely, due to its growing awareness of the problems of agricultural exports from Latin America; although it subsequently has taken a broader view of commodity agreements, in its initial thinking it had in mind only the short-term stabilization role of such agreements.[31] On the other hand, the United Kingdom tended to follow its traditional line of support for the free market mechanism in international trade and, consistently, to limit its support for commodity agreements largely to the short-term stabilizing concept. Some consideration of commodity agreements was, however, one avenue it offered to explore as a means of protecting Commonwealth interests during its 1962 negotiations for entry into the EEC. More recently, domestic considerations have also led the United Kingdom to seek minimum price arrangements with suppliers of several commodities.

France has taken a rather different approach in proposals she has put forward to deal with world commodity problems. These proposals were circulated originally as the 'French Plan'[32] and made public in November 1961.[33] They involve the organization of international commodity markets and are based, broadly, on the proposition that the international market mechanism has broken down completely. Instead, it is proposed to introduce some management or 'organization' of these markets, comparable to managed marketing arrangements which operate for agriculture within most developed economies. At the 1961 GATT Ministerial Meeting, France suggested that world trade in agricultural products might operate more satisfactorily under a system whereby industrialized countries would pay a standard price for imports related to the producer prices in those countries. This system would be combined with a 'concerted policy of food aid' with safe-

31. One of the first statements implying a revision of existing U.S. attitudes to commodity agreements was made in 1961 by President Kennedy: 'the United States is ready to co-operate in serious case-by-case examinations of commodity market problems. Frequent violent changes in commodity prices seriously injure the economies of many Latin American countries, drawing their own resources and stultifying their growth. Together we must find practical methods of bringing an end to this pattern'. Address to Latin American Ambassadors, Punta del Este, Uruguay, 13 March 1961.

32. See J. N. Lewis, 'The French Plan—Blueprint for World Trade Without Tears?', *Review of Marketing and Agricultural Economics*, Vol 30, No 3, September 1962.

33. M. Pisani, Ninth Plenary Meeting, FAO Conference, 11th Session, Rome 1961; M. Baumgartner, *GATT Press Release* 633, Geneva, November 1961.

guards against over-production.[34] The French proposals stimulated a favourable response in Australia. They represented an initiative, from an EEC country, which attempted to deal with the problems of prices and of surpluses.[35]

TESTING THE NEW APPROACHES

The Kennedy Round of trade negotiations in progress in 1966 reflects a change in policy direction in the GATT and provides a testing ground for the new approaches to agricultural trade problems. For the first time, a series of GATT negotiations have covered all classes of products, including agricultural products, and include non-tariff barriers to trade as well as tariffs. A GATT Group on cereals has been set up, with similar groups established subsequently for meat and dairy products, to negotiate comprehensive arrangements for these commodities.

In the establishment of the GATT Action Programme of which the Kennedy Round is part, the major agricultural exporters, with Australia to the forefront, insisted on the meaningful inclusion of agriculture in the negotiations;[36] the U.S. Trade Expansion Act of 1962, which led to the initiative for the Kennedy Round itself, departed significantly from U.S. tradition by providing for agricultural policy to be covered in the negotiations.

The solutions Australia is seeking to its agricultural trade problems are in many respects similar to those being sought by developing countries. The developing countries, however, consider that the developed countries should make concessions on commodity prices, on access, etc. without seeking from them the compensation which is normal to trading negotiations. This principle has been given qualified acceptance by the GATT in the Kennedy Round. Australia has stressed in the United Nations Conference on Trade and Development (UNCTAD) that, while it would expect concessions granted on commodity trade in the UNCTAD context to apply to Australia,

34. *Loc. cit.* For further discussion of the French proposals for the organization of markets, see M. J. 't Hooft-Welvaars, 'The Organisation of International Markets for Primary Commodities', paper submitted to the 1st UNCTAD Conference, reprinted in *Proceedings, op. cit.*; 'International Organisation of Commodity Trade', *FAO Monthly Bulletin of Agricultural Economics and Statistics*, Vol 15, No 2, February 1966.

35. 'The French Government, in the course of the last year or so, has given the lead internationally in putting forward solutions along lines which I myself have long proposed and advocated. The occasion when the French came forward was the first on which a leading industrial country had given the lead in sponsoring world-wide solutions for commodity problems.' J. McEwen, Minister for Trade and Industry, Second Reading Speech on the International Wheat Agreement Bill 1962, *Parliamentary Debates*, House of Representatives, 8 May 1962, p 2013.

36. For Australia, along with New Zealand and South Africa, a special category of country was established in the negotiations which recognized, in broad terms, that concessions given by these countries on industrial items could be paid for only in terms of concessions received by them on agricultural items.

unlike the developing countries Australia would expect to pay for these concessions as in normal trade negotiations.[37]

The GATT Kennedy Round takes on further importance because of other developments in GATT and of those in UNCTAD. In response to the pressures of the developing countries, the UNCTAD machinery is gradually expanding to cover the whole range of issues touching upon trade and economic development. Considerable emphasis is being placed, in UNCTAD and in GATT, on the role of commodity trade, and particularly of commodity agreements, in economic development. There has also been a significant movement in thinking away from the Havana Charter concept of commodity agreements.[38]

Compared with the Havana-type arrangements for commodity agreements, the GATT Cereals Group discussions in 1966 had four significant features:

(i) it was generally accepted that the outcome would not be a self-balancing arrangement; concessions obtained by exporters on cereals would not be balanced by obligations assumed by exporters, but would be paid for in terms of concessions on other, mainly industrial items;

(ii) the discussion on price was not based simply on the proposition that what was being discussed was the long-term free market price;

(iii) it was proposed that negotiations would encompass more than action taken by participating countries at the frontier—the whole range of domestic production and marketing policies should be in the ring for discussion;

(iv) it was proposed that the question of concessional sales be explicitly recognized as a necessary part of the agreement.

Proposals put forward by Australia in the GATT Cereals Group attempted to take account of these features and envisaged an agreement between major producers and consumers which would result in improved conditions of trade for exporters in commercial markets for wheat; at the same time a fund was proposed, to be financed by all member countries, to make grains available on concessional terms to countries which are unable to meet commercial terms.

Australia's attitude is that the circumstances of individual commodities differ so widely as to make a commodity by commodity approach essential. International solutions to trade problems for other commodities could

37. A point not brought out in a useful examination of Australia's position, in a world in which countries tend to be classified as either 'developed' or 'developing', by H. W. Arndt, 'Australia—Developed, Developing or Midway?', *Economic Record*, Vol 41, No 95, September 1965.

38. UNCTAD has also taken over the role of ICCICA in organizing negotiations for commodity arrangements such as those in 1965 and 1966 for cocoa and sugar.

therefore be expected to range from a full multilateral commodity agreement to a loose series of bilateral arrangements.

THE PRICE MECHANISM IN WORLD TRADE

It seems reasonable to infer from Australia's cereals proposals that Australia's commodity policy is based on the premise that the international pricing mechanism has broken down as a means of allocating resources in world agriculture, at least so far as temperate agricultural products are concerned, because of the artificial nature of domestic and international prices in the major commodity markets.[39] In Australia's cereals proposals, referred to above, Australia placed considerable emphasis on some improvement in the prices received for cereals traded on world markets.

The problem of prices is long-standing in international commodity discussions, discussions which are complicated by the fact that price significantly affects income distribution as well as resource allocation. For most temperate agricultural commodities, the price on world markets is a residual price, reflecting imbalances of supply and demand in the national markets of the major industrial countries. There is little economic foundation for this price, except that, subject to any operating constraints, it clears the market; the price does not reflect reliably world supply and demand, nor the costs of major producers. Rather, it reflects the effects of subsidized or dumped supplies produced under conditions insulated from world markets.

Nevertheless, for many products marketed in residual markets, existing prices do not appear to have been disincentive prices to the efficient low-cost producers, e.g. dairy products in New Zealand, wheat in Canada and Australia. An important consideration, therefore, is whether arrangements providing for increased prices could be maintained without some form of supply control. For both dairy products and wheat, however, other factors have operated. For dairy products, the British quota arrangements and short-term reductions in European supplies have helped to maintain prices; for wheat, U.S. action to limit the quantity of her wheat entering commercial markets, Canadian stockholding and the emergence of China and Russia as significant markets have had a similar effect.

The residual market, however, remains vulnerable to the effects of production policies in industrialized countries. Given the political and practical

39. This should be distinguished from the view taken by writers such as Prebisch, Myrdal and Singer that the international price mechanism had an inherent tendency to work against primary exporting countries. See *Towards a New Trade Policy for Economic Development*. Report by the Secretary-General of the United Nations Conference on Trade and Development, R. Prebisch, United Nations, New York 1964. For a more extreme version see R. Prebisch, *The Economic Development of Latin America and its Principal Problems*, Economic Commission for Latin America, New York 1950. While this approach takes into account the effects of agricultural protection in industrialized countries, it is also based on differences in the bargaining strength of factor groups in the two classes of country.

problems to be faced by industrialized countries in providing for increased quantitative access to their markets, it may be that significant improvement in trading conditions for these commodities would depend upon an increase in price.

ACCESS TO MARKETS

In recent years the U.S. has been rather more optimistic about the chances of successful negotiation of meaningful access commitments and concerned less with an increase in world prices.[40] These attitudes are partly matters of judgement about the effects of any increase in world prices, and about the willingness of the major importing countries, particularly the EEC, to restrain domestic support policies. For wheat these attitudes may also reflect the different marketing situations for the two countries. The U.S. is a major commercial exporter of soft wheat to a few markets—mainly to Europe and to its partly tied markets in Latin America. For its part, Australia depends on several major markets and a large number of small markets. Australia must be concerned therefore that concession of access by importing countries could simply mean that for some countries imports would increase, while they would export more dumped or subsidized wheat or flour onto third markets. This danger is potentially greater for Australia than for the U.S.[41] To Australia, access commitments are of little meaning unless they result from genuine increases in consumption or use in the country concerned, or unless effective measures are taken to dispose of any surpluses as food aid. For the longer term, at least, effective commitments on support policies in the industrial countries are essential to make access commitments effective.

Whether, in the long term, the demand for concessional sales of food-stuffs to developing countries will be large is of some importance. In the short term the need is likely to remain. The problem is one of resolving the inequity of leaving the food exporters to shoulder the main burden of providing food aid and the willingness of donor countries to contribute to food aid in addition to, or instead of, other forms of aid.

THE IMPORTANCE OF THE KENNEDY ROUND

Important to current discussions on world commodity policy is the increasingly accepted view that agricultural protection has reduced substantially the validity of arguments that the world price mechanism is operating efficiently. It is also accepted more widely, and this is an important development in Australia's own thinking, that it is unrealistic to expect indus-

40. See Irwin Hedges, 'The World Wheat Situation; Grains Negotiations in the Kennedy Round'. Address to Annual Convention of the U.S. National Association of Wheat Growers, 15 December 1965. A summarized version is given in USDA, *Foreign Agriculture*, 24 January 1966, pp 3-5.

41. A major limitation of the French approach was the lack of substantive proposals regarding access provisions for commercial exporters.

x

trialized countries, in the short run at least, to reduce substantially the protection they are providing to their own agricultural sector even though it would be economically beneficial for them to do so.

Agricultural trade policy, in so far as it relates to temperate products, has been complicated by a situation where there has been a persistent tendency to surplus accumulation in the world. At the same time, the need has been growing for staple food products in the developing countries, who cannot afford to satisfy them.

There is logic in seeking to embrace all these elements in comprehensive commodity arrangements. Nevertheless, the fundamental difficulty is that, even though one may accept that the market mechanism no longer provides an adequate indicator of the basis for trade, or even if one were to regard trade as not merely an economic matter,[42] the situation remains that the result will depend primarily on the relative bargaining strengths, direct and indirect, of the participants.

The Kennedy Round is important because it has provided a practical opportunity for entering into a non self-balancing type of negotiation on commodities. It has provided the opportunity to test both the effectiveness of this type of bargaining process as such, and its advantages for Australia. It also points to presently unanswered, but important, questions about the ability and willingness of Australia to provide growing markets for the products, particularly manufacturers, of countries which are or may be substantial purchasers of Australian exports.

---

42. One of the French delegates at a meeting of the Preparatory Committee for the 1st UNCTAD Conference in elaborating on the French Plan said, 'The French Plan as a whole was based, not on economic theory, but on political and social factors and was indeed a form of aid.' UNCTAD Document E/Conf. 46/PC/SC.1/SR.21.

INDEX

INDEX

Aborigines, 39, 68
Abattoirs, 41, 290
Administration, agricultural:
before federation, 88; Commonwealth, 89; Commonwealth-State, 91; State, 89
Aerial agriculture, 261
see also Contract services
Agricultural chemicals, 60, 79
Agricultural colleges, 58, 102
see also Education
Agricultural consultants, 97, 99, 197
Agricultural Bureaux, State, 98
Agriculture:
State departments of, 90; extension services, 197; founded, 58; research, 94
Amalgamated Shearers' Union, 106
Apples, 59, 296
Artesian waters, 14, 39, 175, 242
Australian Agricultural Company, 4
— Agricultural Council, 91, 299
— Agricultural Extension Conference 1962, 98
— Apple and Pear Growers' Association, 105
— Cane Growers' Council, 112
— Canned Fruit Sales Promotion Committee, 276
— Canned Fruits Board, 297
— Country Party, 124
— Dairy Farmers' Federation, 110, 293
— Dairy Industry Council, 111, 293
— Dairy Produce Board, 110, 293
— Dried Fruits Association, 296
— Egg Board, 295
— Farmers' Federation (proposed), 118
— High Court, 302
— Institute of Agricultural Science, 104
— Labour Federation, 106

— Labour Party, 126
— Meat Board, 290
— Mutual Provident Society, 234
— Oversea Transport Association, 109
— Primary Producers' Union, 105, 114, 116, 125
— Sugar Producers' Association, 113
— Tariff Council, 107
— Water Resources Council, 242
— Wheat Board, 281, 292
payments to growers, 160, 217, 292
— Wool and Meat Producers' Federation, 108, 114
— Wool Board, 108, 283, 289, 298
— Wool Industry Conference, 108, 117
— Wool Industry Tripartite Council, 108
— Woolgrowers' and Graziers' Council, 107, 114
— Wheat Growers' Federation, 109, 125
Australia-U.K. 15 Year Meat Agreement, 161, 290, 301, 306, 311, 326, 329

Bacon, 271
Balance of payments, 129, 133, 138, 204, 212, 222, 225
crisis 1952, 155; instability, 137, 141
Banks:
advances, 223; foundation, 4; State, 26, 215
agricultural, 90; interest rates, 219; loans, 219
State Savings, 215
trading, 214
advances, 217, 226; Farm Development Loan Fund, 218, 226; interest rates, 207, 218; loans, 208,

339